Reflections

Edwin Courtenay

Reflections

The Masters Remember

The Prince of the Stars

The Prince of the Stars
is in the world but not of it.
He is the visionary and builder of a better future.
Therefore he is bringing books telling of love,
healing and a higher consciousness.

Cover Design: Rosi Weiss based on an illustration by
Hans Georg Leiendecker, www.leiendecker.com.

Master portraits © 1999 by Swetlana Moa.
Reproduced by kind permision.

Editing and proofreading: Carole Humber.

Edition Sternenprinz
P.O. Box 228
79002 Freiburg, Germany

info@sternenprinz.de

ISBN 3-929345-20-X

TABLE OF CONTENTS

List of Illustrations

THIS BOOK IS DEDICATED TO

those people in my life who have filled it with love and joy: my mother and father Joyce and Ron Courtenay, my brother and sister Graham Courtenay and Jane Courtenay Moore, my oldest friends Michael Eley, Andrew Lidster, Polly Willmington, Carole Humber and Paul Harrison and my new friends Steve Breeson, Hannah the giggle-fairy, Rachael Kelly, Robert Burnett and Kieron Morgan (my little brother in spirit). A special mention goes to my god-children Charlie Eley and Joshua Alder as well as my nieces and nephews Amy, Liam, Dennis and the newest addition Tegan Courtenay Moore.

A final and special dedication goes to Chad Lyon my fellow walker on the way and dearest heart who helped me remember what was sacred in life and how best to honour it. Namaste! May the Great Goddess bless you all with memories to treasure and keep in this world and the next.

Introduction
by
Solomon

Sometimes it is difficult to imagine that we are anything other than ourselves in this small and present life. We are born and we live and grow. We mature, we age and die. This is the cycle that we have been taught, that has been our reality for many hundreds of years. And yet now, as we move more rapidly towards the fast-approaching Age of Aquarius, many people are beginning to reawaken to the truth that this is but one of many lives that we have lived.

Our resistance to this truth comes partly from the complacency that is achieved when we think that this one life lived will one day bring us to an eternal, restful peace that will find us in heaven or in hell. To contemplate and consider that we have had lifetimes before or lifetimes that yet wait for us in the fast approaching future, fills us with terror and dread – to think that life will go on and that life has been going on since the beginning of time and space.

To think that we are the sum of all these lives which we have lived and yet are still imperfect and fallible in so many ways, to harbour the responsibility of continuing a succession of incarnations that are designed to provide our higher soul selves with knowledge, wisdom, experience and ever-growing, ever-deepening spiritual truth, means that we must contemplate the fact that our lives have more meaning than simply existing, that we have more purpose than simply finding joy, that there is a spiritual significance and reason behind who we are and why we are, and where we are and what we do.

It would indeed be comforting to think that our lives were like small, bright explosions, visible one minute and gone the next and that after this point we were released to an eternal bliss. It would be wonderful to think that it did not truly matter how we chose to live our life — whether we wasted it or used it. Whether we idled through our incarnation or plotted our way meticulously, absorbing and embracing every experience, every opportunity for learning and spiritual growth. It would be a comfortable thing indeed to imagine that we had no destiny or fate, that we were here to do nothing other than to please ourselves and that we need not think of anyone else, that we need not be kind or loving, that we need not contemplate the truth that we are part of a great whole and that our actions affect the rest of mankind.

But these of course are not the truths. We have existed before and we will exist again in other bodies, in other genders and other roles in society. We have laboured and lived on. We have known the heights of decadence and riches. We have known the lowliness of poverty and starvation. We have killed and been killed. We have lived life with joy and toiled through life in misery and torture. We have seen great sights and we have lived closed lives. We have known great people and we have lived surrounded by those who will never be remembered by anyone on Earth again.

It is difficult for the average soul to believe that tales of previous incarnations are anything more than fiction and fantasy, spoken by the crazed or by those who seek to fool, those who seek to use this intricate charade to draw trust or money from those who are gullible enough to believe.

There are very few people upon the Earth who have at this time the capacity to re-live the experiences of the past, to see the memories that were once theirs, the lifetimes that they have lived through. And yet there are many on the Earth at this time who have experienced an intensity of emotion connected to a person or a place or an object that they cannot truly explain or understand.

Many people have met someone for the first time and yet felt instantly that they loved them, or they knew them, or they hated them, or they feared them. These emotions have been real, illogical, based upon no fact, with no viable reason for the intensity of their power. But they have been real and strong. Many people have journeyed to places throughout the world and there they have felt at last at home or there they have felt ill or fearful that they would be murdered or destroyed. These places are those realms that they have journeyed to before, that they have shared great experiences with or experiences of great terror and horror.

Some people are fortunate enough in this lifetime to be reunited with an object that was once theirs in a previous incarnation. And the object reawakens in them emotional stirrings and memories of that life, the feelings that they had towards this object in the past that makes it so special to their distant memory.

Emotions are powerful things, much more powerful than thoughts. They are stored within the very core of our being. Our emotional memories of the past, and people, places and objects can revitalise these feelings, overwhelming us with emotions that do not belong in the present, but belong in the past.

Many people who have become interested and fascinated with the concept of reincarnation have allowed themselves to be so infatuated with the possibilities of their previous lives, that they have become dangerously obsessed. Dislocated from their present life they live instead in an eternal and unending fantasy land of memories that cannot be verified and emotions that are no longer real. It is dangerous to allow this to be so and it is more important for people to live within the present moment of their existing incarnation and look upon their memories of the past or those memories that are passed on to them by others more sensitive to these energies and areas of life as examples that can teach them where they have come from, what they have learned, what mistakes they have made, what triumphs they have earned and succeeded in and by these markers and these points see why they are where they are today, what they are meant to achieve, what they are meant to do, where they are going. Judging, deciding and plotting the course of this life with the knowledge that their previous incarnations give them. For if we are truly to decide where we are to go then we must know where we have come from.

And so it is under these conditions that the Masters have chosen to step forward and recount stories of their previous incarnations to let the world know about who they were and what they have done. Not to satisfy the idle curiosity of those who seek to gather greater details about the Masters who they worship as saints or gods, but rather to guide the serious spiritual student who walks upon the path of light with examples of their own previous incarnations, in order that they may present spiritual lessons through their own lives led, that they may show us that once they were very human too, and prone to indecision and mistake, both small and large, to educate us to the fact that by looking upon the previous lives of others and ourselves we can glean great guidance that will help us see those areas of our own life that need to be amended and attended to.

Before then I open this door and let you browse inside this library where you will find the stored records of these Ascended Masters' past lives, let me detail briefly for those new to these subjects and these mysteries a brief concept concerning the Masters themselves and also the reasons for and the mechanics of reincarnation.

The Ascended Masters are those beings that have gone before — human souls like yourselves who have lived upon the Earth and through a succession of incarnations which were most enlightening on a spiritual level, have reached a point here on Earth where they have become ascended, God-realised, enlightened – capable of liberating themselves through the perception and expansion of their consciousness from the limitations of the physical laws of your reality, capable of altering themselves and the world around them, performing miracles and magic, if you will.

These beings, no longer needing to return to this place in order to continue to grow, have journeyed to a spiritual realm free from the limitations of form, sound, time, space, colour or light, a dimension of consciousness known as Shambhala or the ascended realms. These Masters, as they are called, are not masters of us but masters of themselves. They are Ascended Masters, who reside now as a collective consciousness, their light combined and joined together, having cast off their characters and personalities in order to become pure thought and light. They are surrounded by a multifaceted constructed diamond, each window representing one of those lives that they have led, that they draw experience and knowledge from, and at times reanimate when they send their collective light down to Earth in order that it may speak through channels and mediums alike to those here on Earth to guide them and help them with their continued evolution, too.

Reincarnation is a simple process. The soul, the higher self, born from God, detaches a part of its own light and sends it down upon the Earth in order to incarnate into physical form. The soul has chosen the parents and the time lines in which it will live, knowing a little about the circumstances in which that part of itself that journeys down to the Earth will grow, knowing that it has chosen these things in order that the spirit may learn examples and lessons that will complement the higher self's absent knowledge, that will provide it with a greater opportunity to be complete through the emotional and mental experiences, through the physical and spiritual experiences that it will have. The spirit journeys down and roots itself into the growing body of the unborn child and soon is born. The child lives, grows, guided always by the will of the higher self which is guided by the will of the Divine, in order that it may experience those things that are needed to be seen and done. The spirit has free will of course and often exercises this to deny the higher self its need for experience and growth. But the more spiritual the incarnated soul or spirit becomes, the more it will align itself with the higher self's will and allow itself to be drawn to those people, places and opportunities that will benefit it the most. Even if these opportunities and situations are harsh, painful or difficult, it will know that these offer teachings and growth, and that the greatest teachers are often the most painful situations to be seen or experienced.

The soul continues on its journey and eventually ages and dies or is returned all too quickly to the spiritual realms by accidents or matters of a darker nature. Of course these occur in accordance with the higher self's and the Divine's will. Nothing is left to chance but all to a certain extent is planned. Through a process of continued reincarnation the higher self grows and expands until it has completed all those areas of knowledge that it was created to discover and learn, upon which it rises to a higher dimension and continues its spiritual evolution in these realms of light. It is not the quantity of incarnations upon the Earth that provides one with great knowledge or spiritual power, but the lessons learned within, the quality of experience, the quality of knowledge achieved. An old soul therefore is not accounted as such because of the amount of lives lived, but by the intensity of experiences had.

So now journey with me, take my hand and let me guide you to this large and beautiful old wood door that opens wide before we touch it with our hands. Inside you see a large and ancient library, with oak panelled walls and winding spiral wrought iron staircases. With walls that are lined with book upon book upon book – leather bound, brown, black and red, embossed with golden writing and golden spines.

You see people moving silently from shelf to shelf, inspecting the books and from time to time plucking them from the shelves and reading them intently. And you see attendants too, who guide these seekers to the right records and aid them in the reading process. These assistants are angels, beautiful beings composed of light that bear upon their shoulders tall and magnificent wings. And you realise that this is no ordinary library, but in truth the Akashic library, the Akashic planes where all knowledge of all lives once lived, lived now, and to be lived in the future, are stored. It is a place beyond time, beyond space. A place that carries all thoughts, all feelings, all physical experiences, all spiritual experiences ever lived by anyone or anything on Earth. A place that hums and breathes with knowledge. Guided by my hand we walk to a special section of the library, where very few people wander. This section carries the Akashic records of the lives of those beings who have now become the Ascended Masters and it is here where we hover and stay.

Pick a book, I say, pick any book and slide it from the shelf. Open the ancient leather cover and look inside and you will find that the book will speak to you, will tell you a tale and a story of a life long since lived, will speak with slow and crackling words of the lifetimes of the Masters. Pick a book, pick a book and read and allow the knowledge and the lessons contained therein to change your life.

I am your humble servant, your friend, your guide, your teacher.

I am Solomon, Cosmic Ascended Master of wisdom and truth.

Jesus

My Life in Atlantis

Though the concept of reincarnation is commonplace to many now, and the acceptance of life after death a quite easily acceptable belief in the minds of many, the concept of famous characters in history having more than one lifetime, is often for some challenging. The most famous lifetime that I have lived upon the Earth, that as Jesus, is one which in many people's minds is a definitive of existence, one that defines the beginning and the end of my character and personality, of who and what I am, what I represent, what I have come to be. And yet of course that lifetime was my last. And so before it there must have been, and indeed there were, many others.

Some of these lifetimes are too insignificant to mention, preparatory existences that did nothing for mankind but were educational experiences for me, teaching me basic truths as well as complex spiritual and universal ones. But there is one other lifetime that I would care to mention, apart from that most famous lifetime that I have led, a lifetime that carries with it many valuable lessons and much interesting information, a lifetime that took place not too long after the beginning of the world.

Suspend then your disbelief about those things that you are about to read. Suspend your scepticism and your doubt. Try not to be offended by the concept that I have lived before but see within those words that describe the history of my past life, the essence of my nature that shines through the life that I lived then. Look, read, listen and feel the underlying thread, the light, the theme, the strand that is the quintessential part of my soul, that can be felt beneath the camouflage of any form or any duty, that part of me that is recognised on a soul level as the essence of my being.

The lifetime of which I speak was in Atlantis. But before I can speak of it I must set the scene and so, like all good storytellers, I will begin at the beginning.

The Universe was created. A limited space with limited time inside it. Forged through the powers of illusion, from energy that crystallised into matter. A place full of stars and planets and suns, full of moons and satellites. A place that held within it one tiny planet that would later be known as the Earth. In the beginning there existed only one large continent, one large mass of land, and this island was called Mu, or Lemuria. And it was here that life first came to be; the life of trees and flowers, of grasses and of stones, the life of crystals and of animals, of birds and of fish, and in time the life of man.

You would not recognise the shape and form of early man now, very different from your forms so solid and so defined. Humanity in the beginning was a genderless creation, an ectoplasmic manifestation, not solid in any defined manner, but light and energetic. Humanity was neither male nor female but genderless, a balanced form of polarity, of energy. Man was androgynous in nature and through its androgyny it was perfect. Mankind in the beginning did not live off vegetables or animals but off the prana of the air. Mankind existed through grace, through manna, and mankind lived to experience the world that the Divine had created for it to live inside. But very quickly mankind evolved and grew and needed to be taught directly how to live in such a physical place, at times harsh, cold and unforgiving, at times warm, beautiful and loving.

And so God created five angels to watch over man. They represented the five elements and those energetic qualities that were attributed to them. The Archangel Uriel, who taught mankind about matter and the animal and vegetable kingdoms as well as the kingdoms of the stones, the mineral children of God. And Raphael, who taught mankind how to communicate with each other and with the other living beings in their world as well as teaching man how to invent, how to recognise inspiration and how to heal. The Divine created Michael who taught mankind about passion and in time sexuality, who taught mankind about protection from the elements and protection from the psychic forces that existed wild and primal on the Earth at that time. The Divine created Gabriel who taught mankind about dreams and love, purification and forgiveness, the unconditional nature of beauty.

But the form was becoming more solid day by day as the vibrations, once high in the creation of the Earth, were now beginning to fall. Mankind was not ready to live upon the Earth in such a structure, such a shape. And so it was decided that the Divine would reconstruct the blueprint of mankind in order that they might live a more limited existence, through the embodiment of polarity, of gender and of heavier flesh, that they might create themselves in a more dense way and have the power to recreate themselves and thus perpetuate the Earth.

And so the fifth angel created from God's grace was Azrael, the angel of spirit, of transformation, rebirth and death. And the Lemurians were liberated from their physical forms in order that their spirits might rise once again into the heavens, so that in time they would be reborn. Whilst they rested in the celestial starry heavens, the Earth was changed. The great land mass was split asunder and the continents in their earliest shapes and sizes were formed.

And one of these was called Atlantis, and this island was favoured by God. Whilst mankind evolved all over the Earth, here on fair Atlantis human beings were made manifest, who would — God decided — lead the rest of the world to harmony and peace and spiritual attainment through the example of their life and living.

In the beginning, seven Atlanteans were formed who would, through perpetuation, create the continent's populace. They were given special instruction and understanding by God and special power that was maintained by the high vibration of the land upon which they lived. They were given crystals, shaped like skulls, lenses through which God's light would pass in order to make manifest a home as wondrous as these beings themselves. And so, focussing God's light, they drew from the earth crystals which grew rapidly and were more powerful than any others on the Earth under the shimmering radiance of God's grace.

These crystals erupted from the earth and formed themselves into the cities and towns of the Atlantean continent. And in the central tower the first High Council of Atlantis sat and planned the structure of their future and the nature of their being, their rules, their laws, the way in which the generations who would follow them would carry out the Divine's will, passed through these original elders and bring about that which God sought for his children upon the Earth: peace, harmony and love. And in the beginning indeed Atlantis was a fair and beautiful place. And in the third dynasty I was born on Earth, incarnated for the first time, into this wondrous world of matter and limitation, of light and nature, of need and beauty and awe.

Atlantis by this time had become a thriving civilisation. Five royal families had been created, each representing and embodying one of the five spiritual elements of earth, air, fire, water and spirit. These royal families were given sacred symbols or hallows to hold and guard and protect, and through these symbolic representations of the elements' power they stabilized and maintained the vibration, the spiritual qualities of these elements on Earth. These royal families as well as the high priests of Atlantis communicated openly and freely with the angels who were their teachers, guardians and friends, and who carried the words of God to their ears and hearts. The Atlanteans were a highly spiritual race, steeped in meditation and contemplation, who were divided through an act of the High Council into sociological orders of priests and priestesses who would develop and devote their time to pondering the mysteries of the universe and understanding the beauty and awe of the Divine.

There were those priests who were trained to separate their spiritual bodies from their physical forms and who, in sleeping chambers of crystalline light, would rise out of flesh into the universe and into the spiritual dimensions that interpenetrated our physical world in order to search for other forms of life, in order to contact the realms of the devas and elementals, in order to communicate with the animal collective consciousness and the collective consciousness of the rest of mankind. These were spiritual astronauts, explorers, who had no fear in their hearts and their minds, but trusted that the Divine would care for them always and that those priests and priestesses who monitored over their physical forms, would maintain their health whilst they left their body far, far behind.

There were prophets and seers who lived within a tower which was know as the *Tower of the Eye*, a tower formed from a mineral akin to sugilite which now exists on Earth. These prophets and seers were people of vision who had the gift of sight and could see in the finer world which interpenetrated our own, could see all forms of devas and elemental beings, all forms of invisible intelligences and would communicate openly to the unincarnated souls who sought entrance onto the Earth plane or had just departed from the physical realms. In those early days the Atlanteans' perception of the cycle of life was quite different from your own at this time. They acknowledged that the ending of a physical incarnation was a natural cycle and not something that should be pitied or grieved over, but something that was simply acknowledged as a part of existence. Souls that desired to be born would communicate to one of the prophets or seers who would then on their behalf look for a suitable mating couple that would be enabled to produce for them a physical body that would suit the soul's requirement. When the coupling had been made and the woman had fallen pregnant, the father would have no further need for communication with the mother or the child and would go about his business in the Atlantean society. Once the child was born it would be taken away from the mother and reared in the Temple of the Divine Mother, and the physical, the gene-mother of the child would go about her business and no longer have any need or requirement to visit the child that she had birthed. There was no attachment to the baby because all the Atlanteans understood that the soul that incarnated through them, through their act of physical creation, was individual, was not connected to them in any other way than honouring them by choosing them to form a physical shell through which it would eventually grow and live. The Temple of the Divine Mother was a temple exclusively inhabited by women who had dedicated their lives to attuning themselves to the feminine aspect to the Divine, to the cosmic nurturer, Sophia, and they would care for the babies, rear them until they were ready to be taken into one of the many temples that existed within the Atlantean society. They were responsible for maintaining the feminine vibration on the Earth and making sure that the balance between the masculine and feminine energies in Atlantis was always finely maintained.

There were those priests and priestesses who lived and operated in the Temple of Peace, which was dedicated to the healing arts. Here efforts were made constantly to find new methods and ways of restoring harmony to those who had fallen out of balance in any way, mentally, emotionally, physically or spiritually. Healing was performed here with the aid of the mineral kingdom, with colours, with liquids, with herbs, with sounds, vibrations, angels and eventually, in Atlantis' future history, with the assistance of extraterrestrial entities, too. There were those temples of meditation, temples of contemplation, temples of manifestation that maintained the city's existence and created new structures for new temples or new living accommodation to be made and formed. There were temples of creation, temples of record where crystals were kept that stored inside them on a vibrational level the historical records of Atlantis. There was the Hall of Resonance, where the vibrational pitch of the entire Atlantean continent was maintained through large halls, which contained within them vibrational fields of energy which sent out harmonic frequencies, allowing the mineral kingdom to stay in constant contact with each other and the Atlanteans telepathically at the same time. Atlantis was a wonderful, mystical, magical place and indeed had its secret orders and temples too, where the elders passed on to those that they had chosen from one of the many other temples in the Atlantean citadel, those who would in time replace them as the leaders of Atlantis and the High Council. The decisions of the Council were never opposed because the Atlanteans knew their place within society and if they had not chosen to reincarnate into a form or body, into a life or character that would be chosen to become an Atlantean leader, then they acknowledged that they were not ready yet to harbour the responsibility of this role.

In the council there was one member from each of the five royal families that also contributed their views and opinions on the evolution of not only

Atlantis but the world. And often trips were taken from Atlantis to the other areas of the geographical world in order to supervise the evolution of the other races, of the other states of being. Atlantis had been chosen to be the pinnacle, the focus of God's love and light, to be the examples, the leaders, the guides for the rest of humanity of how the Earth should evolve, of how the Earth should become. And indeed in the beginning the Atlanteans had many beautiful plans for the rest of the world and how they would teach their brothers and sisters who had incarnated in other places, in primitive cultures and civilisations, how to embrace the divinity that existed inside themselves, acknowledging these races and these cultures' valuable experiences and planning and plotting the right time and the right way in which to guide them gently towards the greater truths.

Atlantis may sound to many a cold place and indeed, because of the Atlanteans' ascended nature and their miraculous powers, it was. The Atlanteans died when they desired to. Accidents hardly ever occurred. They were telepathic and empathic, telekinetic and some, with the aid of the Divine and those tools that it provided them, had the power to manifest thought into reality. They were divinely realised beings, gods on Earth. In the future the Earth will — to a certain extent — return to this type of society and civilisation. When mankind has become more enlightened in their nature, they will abandon certain emotions and reactions and ways of being. Grief will become a thing of the past, as will fear, as will emotions such as paranoia, envy, jealousy, rage. Once mankind recognises that their singular exis-tence is one in many, is a continuing process of evo-lution, once mankind begins to see the overall pic-ture once again, they will acknowledge that there is no need for all these petty emotions, that all they have to do is acknowledge their part within the uni-versal plan, fulfil it to their greatest extent, continue to live until they decide to die and then be born again, for ever growing, for ever embracing new experiences, new emotions, new responsibilities and duties, finding that in time they will experience all the wonders of their world.

Atlantis however was not destined for a continued evolution in this way. And I was one of those who was the first to see how Atlantis would fall. Even in my first lifetime in Atlantis I was unusual in nature. I was born possessing both the abilities of healer and prophet and so found home in neither one of these temples. I was taken and taught by the elders to replace them when their time had come to an end in Atlantis. I was trained to become one of the Council that would eventually decide and rule. I witnessed this perfect society, I saw it, I felt it, I understood it. It was sublimely beautiful: the prayers, the medita-tions, the bliss. And yet I sensed too an unsettling undercurrent of change. Not the smooth evolution-ary curve that I had grown to recognise, but some-thing else. Something that was bubbling beneath the conscious mind of the Atlanteans. Something that was beginning to itch from the very core of their beings. It was only in my later life, when I had indeed risen to the dizzy heights of Council member, that through a series of visions my fears became revealed and realised. And I recognised that these images that I was being shown and that were indeed at a later date shown to many, many others, were a warning. A warning about Atlantis' possible destruction at its own hands.

As occurs in society, people were being born who were searching for something more. People who found it difficult to content themselves with bliss, people who found the slow process of evolution irritating, tedious, boring, people who desired movement, people who desired speed. These people began to try to contemplate exactly who and what and why God was. In the past we had never done this. We had never questioned the Divine. We had simply accepted and believed and had faith and given thanks.

At first the questioning was looked upon with great excitement and enthusiasm. A new riddle to ponder, a new paradox to solve, something daring and innovative, something that no one had ever thought of before, yet something blindingly obvious, beautifully clear. In the beginning no harm came from it. Much poetry was written, many songs, many beautiful visions were seen and this all added to the glamour and the wonder of Atlantis.

But through the visions that I was shown, it became clear to me that through the Atlanteans' desire to understand simplicity, they would create complexity. And the complexity that they would create would be purely illusion. And the illusion that they would create would perpetuate itself, because complexity would lead to complexity as the Atlanteans sought to understand more and more. True understanding could not be achieved because the Atlanteans, although being perfected beings, were not perfect and their minds were finite, not infinite like God's. And so they would create an illusion to fool themselves that they had reached the answer when in all truth they could find none. The visions told me that the complexity would create other things, ways and means of manipulating power and force that did not need to be manipulated but which could be petitioned, evoked, cajoled and that this invention, this creation, would in turn bring about the destruction of the respect for the structure of society, of the acknowledgement of those who were less gifted than others, of the belief in the eternal and infinite wisdom of the Divine. And these prophecies were written and recorded and discussed. But they seemed so far removed from the present perfection that we lived in, that they were not acted upon.

After my seven hundredth year on Earth in Atlantis I decided to return to spirit. I felt that everything that I had come to the Earth to achieve had been done, and so in a beautiful and yet severely cold ritual I left my physical form to the Earth in the care of those priests who would recycle it in the appropriate way and rose to the spiritual heavens to rejoin my higher self. I did not return to Atlantis but stayed for some time in the spiritual realms and then returned to another land. It was only after this incarnation upon my return to the spiritual planes, upon my reunification with the higher self, that my awareness fell upon where Atlantis once was, and I recognised and saw that the prophecies of my past life had come to fruition and that Atlantis had destroyed itself. Something that was once perfect had become so rotten, so defiled in such – on a cosmic level – a short space of time. The Atlanteans had indeed continued to question the existence of God and then in time had questioned the Divine's decisions, the Divine's rulings, the Divine's laws and had sought to break them. They had utilised scientific knowledge of a false reality, illusionary methods created to control an illusion, and with the aid and assistance of extraterrestrial beings who sought, at first, to aid (and then some sought instead to destroy), had created a tower that would house an energy that would be powerful enough to challenge the authority of God. Once this tower was under construction it was simply a matter of time before the Divine destroyed this continent, that would in all truth never have threatened the Divine's power but which insulted the Divine's grace; which would have turned its manipulative forces to the rest of the world and corrupted the plan that God has set in motion for his children here.

The reflective nature of the life that I led in Atlantis, and the lesson of my story, is the mirror of your society now. Mankind has lost its way. It has tried to understand and explain away a mystery that should have always remained a mystery, the mystery of God. It has given God a name, many names, many faces and many religions. And yet, although the answer is obvious and true, mankind has refused to see the interconnecting link that joins all these things together as one, the one light from which all these facets and faces take their power and are born. Mankind has utilised science to control harshly the world, to enslave the elements, to manipulate the very building blocks of your reality, the atoms and the molecules of your world, and against the natural flow of God and of all God's creations, mankind has forged from the earth a civilisation, born from power and overthrowing and manipulation of the assets and beauty, of the ingredients of the globe. Mankind has even begun to follow in their Atlantean forefathers' footsteps with the manipulation of genetic material and the creation of flying machines, with the abhorrence of cloning and the destructive forces of lasers and nuclear weaponry.

Mankind is not without hope. But if the Earth indeed is to be saved, is to be healed before it is too late, and if humanity too is to find the divinity inside themselves which will save them from a fate far worse than death, the fate of eternal repetition of evolution, then they must recognise the sins of their greed and need for explanation, understanding and truth, for in truth the only explanation that is ever needed is that we and God are one and if we trust ourselves then we must trust God. For our divine parent, who took such effort and made such detail to create us perfect as we are in a perfect world, would only have our best intentions at heart.

If we surrendered ourselves to the Divine and to the divinity of his world, if we aligned ourselves to our brothers and sisters that exist within the earth, within the sky, within the sea, within the fire, within the spiritual nature of our being, then we would live in peace as we once did, and be closer to the mysteries of the Divine through simple grace than we ever were through our strivings to understand the un-understandable.

And so, through my experiences in Atlantis I learned of man's curiosity, of man's insatiable desire to know why and who and where and when, and how these desires, pointless and unrewarding, were often the cause of mankind's downfall and destruction. We must not make these mistakes again, but instead we must replace them with faith and trust and belief in the Divine's plan.

My Birth and Childhood as Jesus

Beginnings are as important as endings, in their own way. And it is the beginning of my life as Jesus that I would now like to detail for you.

All births, all incarnations, begin when the soul, the higher self of that being that is wishing to journey to the Earth, looks down and peruses through the life strains of those that exist at that time, choosing for itself a period in history in which to live, a place, parents, a social climate and a potential path that will lead the soul forward and provide it with opportunities to meet with those that they are destined and ordained to meet, in order that they can complete their spiritual destiny, bring forward their potential or release karmic situations which hang heavy between those people who they are meant to meet.

It is a complex decision to make, made easy only by the multidimensional perception of the higher self, which sees all things simultaneously on many different levels interconnecting and interlacing as one. Potentials of the future like ghostly fore-patterns waiting to be realised and manifested.

Once the process is completed and the parents chosen, they must be guided gently to the time and place where conception can be achieved and allowed, in order that the higher self may begin the process of incarnation by binding a fragment of itself to the mother's womb, by beginning to draw closer and closer from the point of conception onwards and impregnate the growing mortal shell with spiritual life.

The bible speaks of my beginning in a holy context. It talks of a blessed virgin who becomes heavy with her child through the impregnation of the Holy Spirit. This in essence is not completely true. In truth, Joseph and Mary had been together for some time and they had attempted to have children many times before. Their attempts had never met success and it was decided between them that this was not meant to be their destiny, not meant to be their spiritual path. But of course, in time it was. Mary was virgin in her heart and in her mind, in her spirit and in her soul — in all the places where it truly counted and was meant to be.

The physical form is as illusionary as the world in which we live. And its purity is important only in the sense that it is not contaminated by drugs, alcohol or viruses. The purity that is afforded the physical form by men who have perceived a change in the energy of the being prior to and after sex is a purity that is important for some procedures and some spiritual paths and adepts of evolution. But for others it is not essential, it is not a need. Sex, procreation and lovemaking are beautiful things, a marrying-together of energies and forms, a uniting of hearts and minds. Mankind must transcend the social stigma of this act being anything other than divine, for it is part of the divine process to procreate, to bring forth manifestation through form, linking and likening mankind to God through this divinely creative act. The Divine saw fit to alter the physiological makeup of Mary in order that she would be prepared to create a body that would be powerful enough to receive my soul and the energy that would flow through it from the very beginning of my life, the power of the Christ.

Attempts to create a child had fallen foul before, because of Mary's inability to hold the power of man, to hold the conception of a child. When the time was right and Mary and Joseph were ready and I was ready to return to Earth and complete my lives, the change was made and Mary fell pregnant with Joseph's child.

Indeed Mary was told by the Archangel Gabriel, who is the Archangel of birth. She was visited by him and part of the future that was to be was explained and made clear: how she had become impregnated with the child that would grow to be a great spiritual teacher and leader, who would in time revolutionise the way that mankind would perceive themselves and the world; that through this teacher the great divine light would shine, that was connected to him but not of him. And that she would have to nurture and love this child but also surrender the child to the will of God, and in time to my uncle Joseph of Arimathea, who would become my teacher and my guide.

She was told that she had been chosen because of the preparations that had been made in previous lives where through her devotion to the Divine she had proven herself to be a loyal and willing servant of the light. She was told that she was chosen because of her purity of mind, heart and soul and because of her destiny, which would be enriched and strengthened through the combination with my own. She was prepared for what would occur. She was not given the entire details of my life, but she was told some of the ups and downs that she would experience through her love for me. And in essence her sadness, her suffering, the pain that can be felt beyond the tranquil face that people see portrayed in churches and in books, began with this message. With her realisation that this child that would in one way be for her the most special child that she would ever have, would be a child that she in one sense would never have, but would have to share always with the world.

She told Joseph what had occurred and he was outraged. Of course, in those days of ignorance, understanding of the process of birth was unknown. Joseph had assumed that their inability to have a child was his fault. And when he heard that Mary had fallen heavy with a child, his only conclusion was that the child could not be his. That is why the angel Gabriel visited him too, to strengthen Mary's story and to provide him too with understanding of what would occur.

You see, Joseph was not of mortal birth. He did not come from the mind of God. He was not a human being, but he was an angel, incarnate in human flesh. Born from the heart of God, brought to the Earth through God's grace and through the angelic collective's desire to carry out God's wishes and guide and teach mankind on Earth through these invisible agents which would continue to be God's thoughts, God's will, God's conscious action, shaped and formed in flesh, unknown to man for what they truly were and indeed at times unknown to themselves, too.

Gabriel told Joseph that he had been placed upon the Earth to guide and teach mankind indeed as he had done in lifetimes long since passed, but also to aid in the creation of this vehicle that I would incarnate into and live inside, and also in the energy that was required in order for my soul to be anchored and brought to this place, in order for the Christ light to flow through me. Joseph was told by Gabriel that he would never be truly acknowledged by history, that he would never truly be seen, that his part would be invisible, unnoticed, camouflaged by the wonder of Mary's life and mine, as would my uncle Joseph, too, whose life is only known by those who walk the spiritual path, and truly not acknowledged by others who would profess to be knowing in the religious context.

Joseph was my father as much as Mary was my mother. And although Joseph too had to surrender me to the world, he contributed in my upbringing as Mary did and taught me strength, respect, authority, power — what I needed to know in order to be a man.

A pregnant Mary indeed was taken and indeed gave birth to me in humble surroundings. They were guided by a star and the light of this celestial convergence did indeed settle upon the place where I first breathed and knew life. Here in this humble place I was indeed visited by those who it is recorded came to the light emanating from this celestial wonder and myself.

And indeed I was honoured and worshipped and I was given gifts and presents that marked my appearance, that marked the prophecies of my life, that marked my return. I was given gold and frankincense and myrrh, prophetic symbols and indications of my divine sovereignty and eventual tragic death, and I was also given a grail, fashioned from a star that had fallen to the Earth, a meteorite. I was given a grail fashioned from moldavite, a meteoritic glass, green, that came to a final rest in Glastonbury, after it had been used in the last supper and taken by my uncle to England where its powers were used to merge with the heart centre of the world.

Indeed we were hunted down and were protected by the divine powers of God. The darkness was drawn to the light of my birth almost instantaneously. My young life which hangs in mystery because of the lack of information that is available concerning it, was not recorded because of its normality. As a child I grew in modest, humble surroundings, the prophecies of my life kept beneath the silent lips of my mother and my father who continued their lives much as they always had done. My mother continued to bear children for Joseph, the gift of my birth healing the imbalance that had prevented them from having children in the past. And I grew as children grow, curious, intuitive, interested, creative, tired, happy, sad. Indeed from time to time my light could be seen through the words that I would speak or the memories that I would speak of from lifetimes long since lived in other places. Indeed at times I would see things that others could not see, or know things that others did not know. And in time too my healing power blossomed and shone and I removed illness from other children, animals and even adults who sometimes visited my mother and father at home.

For hours I would sit in my father's workroom and watch him busily working away with his wood and his carpentry. For hours I would sit and watch my mother bake and wash and clean and talk to the other women. She had been profoundly affected by my birth and although she did not speak of my destiny, as was the Archangel Gabriel's instruction, she began to develop spiritual understandings of her own. It was as if my birth had awakened the awareness of spiritual truth inside her and with her women friends she would talk about the things she felt or knew or saw in dreams. She would encourage them to recognise the power of their womanhood and by aligning themselves to the seasons and cycles of nature and the moon grow strong, and this would become a central part of her work, a part of her work that she in turn will describe.

As I grew, my brothers and sisters followed me and soon, very soon, it was time for me to leave. I left behind a normal, simple world; my father a carpenter, my sweet, loving mother, a mother to her children and to many others. I left my brothers and my sisters who I loved dearly.

Waving goodbye to my mother as she carried another child inside her womb, and hand in hand with my uncle, whom I had always been besotted with and drawn to, who always to me had been a magical man, I walked away from the normality of my life and did not return for many, many years.

Although my mother was not pleased to see me go, she remembered the words of the angel and knew that it was time and tried not to cry as she waved me goodbye. My father was not present. His anger and his rage did not allow him to demonstrate his sadness and his tears. Over the years that had led to the point where I would be taken, he had grown ever fearful of what the angel had told him of my destiny. He had grown ever more connected to the sweetness of my youth and did not want to see me leave.

He had pleaded with God, and ranted and raved, shaking his fist at the sky and asking why his son, who was so light, so bright and joyful, so good should be chosen to carry the burden of the world upon his shoulders. For some time God had not answered him and then one night in a dream Joseph was shown more, in the hope that this would ease his questioning and his pain. His rage was silenced but his sadness deepened. And from that point on, whenever he looked at me, I could see that there were tears in his eyes. Joseph had found something precious in me. He had found understanding for who he was. He had found love and innocence and purity that on a subconscious level reminded him of his angelic home. To see that walk away towards a destiny that in its own way was full of pain and sadness, was too much for him. And to a certain extent I think it broke his heart.

My adventures however had just begun and in my uncle's care I sailed and journeyed to many places and learned many things. My life was beginning, a wonder of spiritual education and understanding, a blossoming of my soul and the gifts of light that I had come to offer the world.

And as for the Christ light, the Maitreya energy that flowed through me, when I was in my prime, this power I had seen and known since the earliest days of cognitive memory, a shimmering column of the palest, most translucent rose pink light, a genie, a spirit, a shower of the Divine, that was sometimes outside of me, that sometimes spoke without words sweet messages in my mind and sometimes a shower of light that was within me, that filled my body, my hands, my form, that made my head tingle and spin, that helped me sleep or made me feel strong, that gave me the power to see and to heal things that before that were blurred or unsure. I had never questioned the presence, always thinking that it was natural, that it was normal, that everybody saw it or had one. It was only much, much later that I recognised it for what it was and embraced it as part of my reason for being.

I journeyed back to see my parents after I had achieved the majority of my learning. My mother was much the same as she had always been; her children, who had grown and left her, had now been replaced by other people's children whom she cared for. And her small mothers' meeting of women had grown too into a collection of disciples of her own, her eyes had truly been opened, and she had begun to see strange and wondrous things and been able to contact the deep powers of the feminine energy of the Earth and the feminine energy of her own heart and soul.

My father too was much the same as he had always been, still working with his wood, still plodding slowly on, supporting my mother and loving her, caring for his children. He had aided and helped people in his own way with words of wisdom that had fallen easily from his tongue when he had hardly thought about them, by providing people with gentleness and love and care, by healing them through the work he did for them, by showing them a kindness that they could not see in any other man. He had continued to guide invisibly as all angels do, even to the point where he could not see the divinity of the work that he did for himself.

I was welcomed home and stayed there for a little time before I journeyed away again with my uncle to complete my learning and my study. It was nice to be back and my parents were a little more at ease this time than in the beginning when I left. Even my father smiled and laughed, but we did not talk about what the future held for any of us. The times that I would see them again would be as dim and distant faces in the crowd. Sometimes we would spend brief moments together at the end of long days as we ate before we slept. But we would never know moments of intimacy and peace like that one again. In my lifetime as Jesus I had my parents for a very short time, a very short moment. They were very special to me. They taught me a great deal.

It is important in life to acknowledge our beginnings. To look back and see the sacrifices that our parents make for us. No matter how harshly we feel we have been treated by them, there is always somewhere – even if it is only at the very beginning of our lives – evidence of a powerful love, much deeper than the love that is held for a friend or a partner. Because this love is for a thing that you have helped create and that you now begin to shape and form. It is a love indescribable, indefinable, incomparable with any other.

The lesson of my early life then is this: Honour your beginnings however humble, however simple, however bare. Look at the things that have shaped you and made you who you are, that have given you your light, your goodness, your strengths, as well as your imbalances and your pains.

Look at your parents and acknowledge the sacrifices that they have made for you and thank them whether they be living or dead. Try to remember them with love. Try to forgive them their misdemeanours and indiscretions. Try to give thanks for all that they have done and hope that you too, whether you have children of your own or whether you will care for others who will become like children to you, can find the strength and power in your heart to do as well if not better than they did.

Remember, love is the key. And as God's love for his children is strong, our parents' love for us, their children, is as strong also.

My Life as Jesus

Time moves on. Fast for some and laboriously slow for others. Memories of lifetimes long since lived ebb and flow, disappearing and bowing down to experiences that are far more lasting, far more permanent than details.

I have lived many lifetimes upon the Earth. I have known many places. I have known many people. I have lived inside many different cultures and religions. I have known tragedy and beauty. I have known sorrow and sadness, triumph and joy.

The most remembered lifetime that I have led, the lifetime most remembered by others, is the lifetime from which I carry my present name: the lifetime when I was Jesus. And it is this lifetime that I wish to discuss today.

Thinking back upon it now I can relive each memory as if it were happening. I can feel the warmth of the sun upon my skin, I can smell the strange perfume of the air. I can taste people's tears. I can hear their cries of pain and sadness and of joy and wonder. I can see the landscape and their faces with crystal clarity. I can feel their skin as it brushes against my own.

When you have transcended life and live as I do with a consciousness that is merged and blurred into a thousand others, reinvestigating your memories is a strange experience — knowing that these experiences were once yours, feeling them so vividly and yet remaining detached and aloof from them like a casual observer reading a fictitious book.

There are so many things that are said about this lifetime that are not true. The bible, which has become the only written historical text that details my life, is unfortunately heavily influenced by the editors and writers of its time. It has changed shape and form in many ways dependent upon those who have reproduced and copied it, those who have looked through its philosophies and spiritual teachings and decided to omit this line and remove this chapter — for the good of all of course! It has become a means through which mankind has suppressed and controlled their kindred. It has become an instrument of war and a means of threatening. It has become an aberration, compared to its original form. Still, truth remains hidden there, encoded, described in symbolic manner and sense, and for those with an astute eye the bible can be read and can provide them with a great deal of spiritual truth. But for those who at this moment in time lack the penetrative depth of consciousness to look between the words and phrases and see the truth that is hidden and buried, the bible can mislead, the bible can beguile with its untruths, can enslave and prevent people from following the path that will lead them back to God. And so I have come to eradicate some of these misdemeanours, to purge this ill-fitting story and to provide some truths of my own that I feel will more strongly support the reason for my life then.

Trivial details are important – sometimes. But in this case details of where and when are not relevant.

I begin by focussing upon a time that is of greatest importance and I will shift backwards in time to speak of those other moments of my life, less important now, which I will speak of for the curious of heart. I begin then my story at the beginning of my learning and move quickly forwards towards the instigation of my education. My uncle Joseph of Arimathea, was an unusual man. As much as I was prepared for my spiritual path, so too was my uncle Joseph. Throughout his life he was born with a clear and defined understanding that his purpose in life would be one day to teach and guide another who would be enabled to do more than he. His life was a life of service and selflessness. Although he had the knowledge and the power to go forward and spread the word of God, he had to content himself at an early age with knowing that this was not his path and that instead he was to give all of his understanding and the benefits of his life to another. He was a man who I admired greatly and to whom in a sense I am still indebted to this day. For without his valiant teaching, patience and guidance, I would not have become the person that I became.

Joseph was to many a man of mystery. He had travelled a great deal throughout his life, experienced many things. He was blessed with a memory that reached before the lifetime in which he lived and he knew of places and of cultures and religions that he had lived in many lifetimes before. He also occasionally recognised people who he had shared previous incarnational relationships with, and even some who still lived, who he knew from lifetimes that he had led. Throughout his early life he journeyed throughout the world reconnecting himself to these places of ancient wisdom and power and to these people, his presence fulfilling small prophecies which have long since been destroyed from record which talked of a man who would bring with him in time a child who would need to be taught spiritual truth, understanding and given power. His initial journeys were preparatory in nature, making connections, making sure that these connections and the routes that took him there were safe, and establishing in his own consciousness the order of education that he would begin to unfold when the child came into his care. He was a member of many different organisations and fellowships. His wisdom, his knowledge, his light was obvious to see. And his ever willingness to help and heal and guide and give, often assured himself recognition and belonging in these places that he journeyed to.

In time of course he was presented with me and slowly and gently it dawned upon him that I was the reason that he lived, that I was the child that he would teach, not his own children, but me. And so our life together began.

His consciousness was vast in the beginning in comparison to my own, granted even from the very earliest ages of my youth I had known that I was different, that my destiny was great. The knowledge that he possessed, the way that he controlled his emotions, the belief and faith and trust that he had in this tenuous destiny that had been unveiled to him in dreams and visions was so strong, so inspiring. He reared me with his confidence, the power of his belief and his love not only for the Divine, not only for himself, but also for me. The confidence he entrusted into the work that I would one day do, richer than any mother's milk, was enough to strengthen the foundation that I needed for the future. At great expense and pain we journeyed together to places of great beauty and great spirituality and there he watched and endured as I grew faster and faster, more and more hungry for spiritual truth. He stepped back, aware that my consciousness would in a twinkling of an eye dwarf his own, would surpass his wildest expectations and all the time he fed me, all the time he gave me life and light and encouragement and love. All the time he told me that I had the power, that I could do all the things that were beginning to be revealed to me. And in those youthful days, when I was focussed only upon the light of the soul, and those days that would come when I would teach and heal and guide, when I would do God's work on Earth, I did not see this man's humility, this man's piety, but only the necessity for his presence, the necessity of his role. It was later that I sensed the insecurities that had existed within him, that he had tucked deep within his heart and mind. Feelings of fear of what would become of him when he had outlived his usefulness to me.

Feelings of jealousy, feelings of envy and rage that he had suppressed, internalised, transformed, for the sake of the greater good.

We journeyed to many, many beautiful places, and I spent time in monasteries and brotherhoods, learning and growing, and finally – finally I was ready to return. He receded into the background of my life and sometimes I noticed that he was not there at all. My concerns did not follow his absence, for I knew that he was more than capable of dealing with any difficulties that the universe would present him with. I was busy with other things. I sometimes fear that maybe I did not even pause to say: "I love you", or "I thank you", or "I appreciate all that you have done". I was so consumed by my own fate. Little did he suspect that his work would continue for many years after mine had stopped. Towards the latter part of my existence upon the Earth I knew this truth. And I knew that he would receive all the rewards that he had not received when he was my teacher, that he would be a great leader and guide to men, and that they would praise him as mankind now praised me. Of course praise is not the issue here. But praise is a form of acknowledgement and acknowledgment is something that most mortals need and will continue to need for some time. It is a good way of recognising that the universe is providing you with something that you require, a form of energy that is needed in order to continue to do your work.

My life then and the destiny within it had now truly begun and very soon I was drawn to those who would form a close circle of disciples, of apostles, of friends. In the beginning I was filled with great love and enthusiasm for my work. It was wondrous to be enabled to speak divine truths out loud to these people that I had for such a long time carried inside myself, knowing that it was the right time, that these were the right people, that the messages were most poignant now. It was marvellous to see their faces change as the pieces fell into place, as their jigsaw puzzles became apparent, as they recognised the wisdom that I spoke within the context of their individual lives, as they saw the truth for the first time and recognised that it had the potential to answer all their questions, to change their lives and give them purpose and meaning. But I was quick also to see the loneliness of my life. How I had always been alone but had never truly recognised or seen it amongst the camouflage of education and remembrance and learning.

Now with no wise men to visit, save for the wisdom that I would find sometimes in the words that my disciples spoke to me, with no uncle to turn to, with no father or mother apart from the Divine with whom of course I communed, I was alone on Earth, surrounded by people whose consciousness could not begin to match my own. And there was a sadness inside me and a sorrow and an emptiness, a void that could not be filled, and there was a space between myself and these my dearest friends that could not be bridged. And I was alone. I knew that I would be alone for quite some time, that no matter how much I spoke or taught, there would always be things that these others would not see, would not understand, would not be able to do because I was different from them. I was closer to God, not because I was God's son, but because I was close to the point of ascension. I was close to the point of personal mastery. I was close to the point of breaking free from limitations of the Earth and becoming a limitless human being. And because of the Christ, because of the Maitreya, because of the cosmic ascended being that poured through my mind and heart, my spirit and every cell of my body and physical form, because of this glorious entity that had allied itself with me since the beginning of my birth, that had attuned itself, so that when we spoke we spoke as one, that when we sang our voices merged in perfect harmony and union, and when we laid our hands upon those who were sick or in need they could be corrected through the grace of the Christ that flowed through me. Because of this energy I was different, augmented, altered, expanded, sharing in this great cosmic being's perception of all reality, of God, and that this was something that could not at that time be shared with others, not in any other way than through words spoken or deeds done. Because there was no-one else close to me who could be filled with such radiance. There was no-one else who was ready, no-one save myself.

My destiny unfolded before me like a carpet. With each step I took along its path, more could be seen. I knew what words I was to speak, what demonstrations I was to do. Which people to heal, which people to bless, which people to invite to join me and my merry band and which to leave to their own destinies and fates. I knew exactly what repercussions my words would have on each and every person that I spoke to. It was like living a story that I had already read – in places marvellous, in places so sad. For I knew there were things that I could not alter, that I could not change for all my understanding and my power, for all the angels that I could speak to. I knew that there were things that were meant to be, that could not be altered, that could not be changed. I knew which people were meant to die and which people were meant to run away, brokenspirited, confused and unsure. I looked at the faces of my disciples and knew which ones would take their own lives when my life had come to an end. And although there was a part of me that transcended sadness, that knew that this was all part of the greater scheme, that these lives were twinkling existences in a night sky full of a thousand lifetimes led and waiting to be led, there was a part of me that still wept. There was a part of me that was still so sad, a part of me I suppose that was still very human, still very mortal, still very unascended.

Very quickly the rest of the storybook was read into my mind and I knew what had to be done.

The Divine had hoped for so much more, as had I. But mankind was not ready. In part, the message had been successful and my words would go on long after my death. And from them an extension of the existing religion through which I focussed a great deal of my teachings and my truths would be recorded, would spread out, would convert many and guide them closer to the truth that they were so sorely looking for and so sorely lacking at this time.

But I also knew that fundamental core issues that I had spoken of many, many times before had been lost upon even my closest friends, even my most wise and ascended students. I realised that they could not believe that they, too, had the power to perform the miracles that I performed, that they could not understand that their reality was illusionary, was a limitation that could be discarded, transcended. I realised that they could not begin to understand the concept of life after death, of what that truly meant, of how it extended life, opened life up, gave us the ability to begin to conceive a thousand other worlds and dimensions. I realised that no matter how many stories I spoke of concerning the glories of heaven, my students could not truly envision it, could not truly believe that it was real. And so I chose to end my existence.

Although my end was presented to me by the Divine, there was still an element of choice involved: the how, the where, the when, the who. And with an eloquence and gracefulness that had been a central theme of what my life was, of what I had become, I orchestrated a spectacular finale. I chose individuals who would play key roles because of their archetypical characteristics, because of their karma, because of the lessons that they needed in order to complete major issues within their life, within their souls.

And, seemingly coldly and carelessly, I engineered these pieces on the game board into position in order to fulfil a pattern that I had been creating that would liberate me from life and enable me to move into the realm of light in which I now stand. You see, I was no longer acting from the perspective of a human being. I was divine. I had recognised my divinity, and with the aid of the Christ I had attuned the resonance of my soul completely to the resonance of God. God's will was my will. We were one. And so this manipulation was divinely approved. And however cold and harsh it may have appeared to be, or still appears to be on Earth, it was most definitely what was meant to be.

There was sadness on my departure. I knew that I would never perceive these people through human eyes again, or with the same consciousness. There is always sadness with endings and there is always also joy. And it would be wrong to say that I did not have my doubts, because they did exist. And although I acknowledged the transient nature of time, the pain and hardship, the suffering that I knew I would have to endure concerned me — more for those who would endure more, than for my own sake. And I contemplated, shifting and changing the plan, but I recognised that it would accomplish nothing. And so putting into place the final pieces of wisdom, I said my goodbyes, instigated my betrayals, visited those who would condemn me through their lack of participation in my fate as well as their participation in it, and allowed myself to be crucified.

At that point, when I dangled from the cross, I realised finally what I had allowed to be done for all of those who knew of me, who had received healing through me, or bread or wine that had been touched by my hands, who had been fed by my words or seen my face, who had smiled as I had smiled at them, who had danced with me or drunk with me or laughed with me, all of them, who knew me and knew of my death, opened their hearts at the point of my departure and allowed the Christ energy that poured through me at that moment in time to ignite inside them the sleeping embers of their own Christ light and anchor, into the collective consciousness of man and into the consciousness of the Earth itself, the bridge that had been separated from mankind since before the ending of Atlantis: the Maitreya consciousness that would one day guide them all back home to God.

And still to this day in the consciousness of mankind and in the hearts of all of humanity the Christ light glows and flickers, ignited from that point onward, anchored, though not utilised — a potential return that will in time be utilised to its fullest extent.

Many people saw me leave and saw the angels that came to escort me home. It would be wrong to say that it was not a blessed release. Such sensations of flesh and bone and blood, but also that poured from the minds and hearts of those who had come to see me die, such sensation, suddenly switched off to be replaced by transcendent bliss and peace; such a strange contradiction.

I of course returned. This was part of the plan, to give them one last attempt to understand the transcendent nature of the human soul, to prove to them that my theories were all true and that indeed we did live on. But of course the majority of those who saw me or heard these words that I had spoken did not see the truth for what it was, but felt that this was just another miracle that I had performed, not recognising that it was a miracle that we are all capable of. And indeed I did return to those beloved friends and pass on to them an extra strain of the Christ light in order that they would go forwards and continue with the work that I had begun in providing people with the consciousness and the knowledge that was needed to complement the awakening Christ energy inside themselves, to give them the consciousness to see that they themselves were divine, in order that they could utilise this gift that had at long last been awakened, in order that they could begin to ascend, to grow. They were chosen carefully, my prophets, my harbingers of the New Age.

My life was one that was predetermined by all the lifetimes that I had lived before. Our latter lifetimes are always so powerful, they have such intense, focussed moments. They are engineered so delicately by the higher self as to achieve the maximum, the focus of what our entire life theme was all about. Sometimes the pre-ordained nature of my last existence was infuriatingly artificial in feeling. Sometimes it was so passionate, so moving, that still now when I think about it it touches me deeply.

I came to the Earth when I was Jesus in order to guide people towards the realisation that we are all sons and daughters of God. That we have not been cast upon the Earth as punishment for crimes committed in an Eden that did not exist but that we are to learn and grow and indeed to recognise that that model that was created for us in order to teach us, can be, when it is finished with, transcended and recognised for the illusion that it is, and that the ultimate lesson that we have been placed here to learn is the divinity of our own nature and that transcendental potential that will lead us back to our true home which is within the Divine itself. My parables, my philosophies and my teachings were constructs designed to point all in this direction. Some more misleading than others now would point you in completely the wrong way.

Asked whether I have regrets, I would say that indeed there are a few. I regret that I was not recalled as being a person who smiled more, as being a person who liked to laugh, who liked to dance, who liked to sing. When earnestness was called for, then I could be earnest. But I could also be joyful. And somehow all my joy has been written out and I am recorded as a solemn, sad figure only. And my other regret would be the mystery of my words. If the Divine had allowed me to speak in any other way, then I would have spoken in it. But the enigmatic nature of my paradoxes and riddles was meant to empower people by encouraging them to solve the riddles of my verses rather than spoon-feed them with truth. How sad that even now some riddles remain unsolved by most, and misunderstood.

I have spoken little of my mother and of Mary Magdalene, of my father and of those others that are most dear to me. But these are stories best spoken by those who experienced from their point of view these moments of joy and sadness. I speak only from my own eyes. These people were dear and beloved to me because of their understanding and because of their lack of it. Because of their belief in me and their willingness to give their life in order to make mine in majority possible. They will speak the rest that needs to be spoken about the times in which they lived. For now my words upon this life are all but done.

Remember then this:

When you see a picture of my face or a portrayal of my character, when you hear the words that I am said to have spoken, think of me not as a suffering character, devoid of humanity because of my divinity, but instead try to imagine these words spoken through lips that smiled and laughed. Try to think of me as someone who simply understood and knew so much more than all those others that surrounded him and how this was both blessing and curse. How my serenity came from realising that everything that I witnessed and endured was illusion. And how my sadness came from recognising that the purpose of my being, the message that I was to impart, fell upon so many deaf ears and would continue to do so for so long. I do not want you to grieve for me. I do not want you to pity me. I do not want you to worship me. Simply to honour and respect the work that I did, to love me as I love you, unconditionally, and to learn from the examples of my life the potentials of your spirit.

Mother Mary

My Lives with the Energy
of the Divine Mother

I am Mary, Mother Divine, Lady of Shambhala, member of the Sisterhood of Light, bringer of peace and love and joy and nurturer to all mankind.

I have come in order that I may speak of those lifetimes that I have led, that crystallise the true thread, the true meaning, the true quintessence of my life, that will, I hope, enable you to see the underlying reasons why I acted as I did when I lived as mother of the boy-child Jesus, of what occurred that was unseen and unrecorded and of the importance of the power that I represent and the message that I bring.

All things move in cycles, a pattern, a wave of movement, peaks and troughs. The primary polarity that exists within your physical universe, the polarity that was first formed when God, the divine source, entered into physical reality has always been a power that has manifested upon the Earth through seasons and cycles, gaining dominance and entering into passive states in order to find harmony and bal-

63

ance and equilibrium amongst the consciousness of mankind. The polarity can be described in many ways: light and darkness, joy and pain, aggression and love or masculinity and femininity.

Balance is the aim, it is where we intend to take the world, it is where we need to be. No one force must be supreme over the other. No one power must be greater. There must only be harmony, there must only be peace. It is the Divine's desire that the masculine and feminine forces of this universe and the Earth are brought into complete mergence with each other in order that through unity they may find rest, in order that through unity the universe may find evolution through the sacred marriage of father light and mother darkness.

Throughout the ages and histories of mankind the polarity forces have fought to gain supremacy, to reign supreme over the Earth and the universe. They have sought to dominate each other, to gain the upper hand, to be most conscious in the consciousness of mankind. At this moment in time we move out of a thousand year long patriarchal energy and move back towards a strong matriarchal surge that we hope instead of finding dominance will allow harmony to be. It has not always been this way and in the past matriarchy has had rule, has had control and power over all mankind. It would be wrong and unfair to say that patriarchy represents war and matriarchy represents peace, for there is a darker side to the feminine power that very few see and acknowledge as truth. It is that part that is red in tooth and claw, the feminine aspect of nature that is ruthless and merciless, the part of nature that survives and relies upon instinct, family loyalty and the need to maintain its own territory, its own sacred space.

In truth when matriarchy has ruled there has been acceptance, there has been grace and flow but there has also been war. Patriarchy simply makes war more logical, makes it appear to be less natural, focuses upon it as an abhorrent thing, an abomination, an indication of man's decline, rather than acknowledging it as a natural cycle of creation and destruction, of chaos and order, of death and rebirth.

Through all the lifetimes that I have led, I have represented and embodied and supported and worshipped the power and the presence and the existence of the Divine Mother energy. Men and women throughout the ages that they have lived have often called forward the power of the Divine in many shapes and forms. In its earliest forms, in its earliest names, the Divine was simply referred to as the lord and the lady, as the king and the queen, as the father and the mother of all. The Divine was seen as being an entity that was whole on a higher dimensional existence, on an infinite plane that defied our comprehension and true understanding. But here within the Earth, within the limited universe, it was acknowledged to have two faces, one male and one female, polar energies that could be recognised in these ways. The feminine force of the Divine monitored over birth and creativity, nurturing and love. The masculine force watched over death, destruction, evolution, progression, structure and logic. These were the rules, these were the laws. Anyone who found inside themselves a tendency to lean to one polarity or the other would align themselves to the God or the Goddess.

In general, the majority of women would align themselves to the Goddess through the similarity of the nature of their physical being, through their capacity to create, through their natural ability to receive, through their passive nature and their gentle minds. Men were more inclined to align themselves to the gods. They themselves were instigators of life, carrying sparks and seeds that brought things into manifestation through thought and deed. Men were logical, projective, strong, powerful, and therefore were connected to the god-form in this way. Of course there were those who crossed the fields of polarity; men who entered into the Goddess' realm, and women who became aligned to the God. Rather than being seen as aberrations, these people were celebrated and acknowledged as being those who held the power and the promise to bring the polarities back together when the time was right by providing their own species with understanding of the other polarity's point of view. At a later date of course in mankind's history these people were persecuted rather than celebrated for their differences and were looked upon as being masculine or effeminate, as being weakened by their polarity preference rather than strengthened by it, as being society's freaks rather than society's saviours.

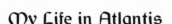

My Life in Atlantis

I lived in Atlantis in the middle part of the Atlantean dynasty, when the powers of the ancient Atlantean mystical energy were still strong. Science was beginning to awaken. Considered to be a masculine thing, we women, who were very much aligned to the Goddess' force, did not concern ourselves with this new fascination but continued instead to plunder the mysteries of the Mother Divine. In Atlantis there was a temple dedicated to the Mother Divine's energy, a temple that would only be occupied by women who dedicated their lives to the Goddess' progress, her power and her well-being. Other women were allowed to enter, to visit and contribute and receive. But no men could enter into this sacred space, no men could trespass into the Goddess' land.

Ours was a harmonious community that acknowledged the power of the cycle of woman as maiden or virgin, as mother or nurturer, as crone or wise woman. Our personal society was divided into these three sections of maturity and age, and each member was given a task or duty, a job to perform. The maidens would be responsible for the understanding of truth through innocence and purity, of their creative power of joy and light. The mothers within the community would care for their own children and the children of Atlantis who would be taken to the Mother Divine's temple upon their birth, abandoning their parents back to Atlantean society. As has already been said, the Atlantean process and structure for birth and the continuance of society was looked upon very differently from the way that it is today, our loftier perspective of divine truth allowing us to shake free from the limitations of obligation, to release ourselves completely from any feelings of unnecessary guilt. The crones and wise women would utilise their completed feminine energy to access and contact the deeper currents of the Earth Mother's force, of the Divine Mother's power, of the planetary energies that were feminine in nature and magic, and would utilize these creative powers to play their part in aiding in the sustenance of the web of life and also to bring about creation and construction of new things here on Earth. They were co-creators with the Divine and facilitators of the Divine's will. Ours was a wondrous existence, it was a life of joy, of wonder and of peace. We existed harmoniously hand in hand and lived to praise the Goddess in all her shapes and forms.

The process of our society would be repeated time and time again in other civilisations in other areas throughout the Earth and indeed from time to time I would exist inside them, continuing with my work as bridge between mankind and the Goddess herself. It is only in the later days of your modern society that no priesshood has existed upon the Earth to counteract the overbearing masculine energy of the patriarchal forces. But the Goddess has returned and the Mother Divine's energy has crept back into your society and begun to redress the imbalance of the patriarchal, masculine force recently, with the bold movement forwards that is incorporated in the recognition of female priests and also the focus upon female power no longer imbalanced in feminism but controlled and focussed through its femininity, its strength, its uniqueness, its boldness and its capacity to express itself in a courageous and outlandish manner. The feminine force has found the beginning of its resurrection and will indeed continue to grow until equalisation, sacred marriage, sacred union has been achieved, until masculine and feminine forces upon the Earth have recognised each other and found the harmony, the peace, the joy that has always been held between them as a promise, when both can realise that there is no antagonism between them but only love and joy.

In Atlantis the temple of the Mother Divine became less and less frequented by people outside its own inner circles and even the priestesses who would come to be initiated and spend their lives there dwindled and became fewer and fewer. The focus moved from the balanced state of energy to the first patriarchal reign and Atlantis became more and more drawn towards the concept of science over mysticism and the temple of the Mother Divine became no more a place of great power, of great consultation and great worship but was turned into a glorified nursery to prepare and guide the young children of Atlantis for their rise towards scientific achievement and spiritual excellence. We attempted to guide the children back to the old ways, sometimes in secret, but the Divine had ordained that what was to occur should occur and so we bowed our heads to the greater knowledge of the universe and allowed the degradation of our world to ensue. I left my body in Atlantis long, long before the circumstances began to filter into the conscious minds of the civilisation concerning any hint of the great destruction of our community.

The end of my life had become sad and hollow, the beginning of it so rich and so sweet. I moved from lifetime to lifetime. I lived in Egypt and worshipped the Goddess Isis in her temples. I moved to the ancient aboriginal planes and there in the dreamtime state connected with the great cosmic mother, Sophia. I moved into lifetimes that acknowledged the power of the Divine Mother through the ancient cabbalistic system of the tree of life and finally, after wandering through cultures, through lands, in different bodies, in different minds I found myself on Earth as a woman called Mary.

Ascendancy is very different for each and every person. For some of us it is very clear at the beginning of our life on Earth that that is our last incarnation. We remember all of who we have been, we know what lies in store for us on Earth as if the knowledge had been written in our mind and we were simply acting it out. For others, ascendancy is very different.

My Life as the Mother of Jesus

For me the lifetime of Mary was a lifetime of igno- rance and bliss, of great pain and clear under- standing, of wonder and of awe.

From an early age, looking back now, I see that I had been prepared. My parents and my parents' par- ents and their parents before them had always known deep down inside their hearts that one amongst them, part of their line, part of their genera- tion, would be the vessel through which the saviour would come. I was taught things as a child that no other child was taught: things about the universe that seemed so natural to me, things I did not ques- tion, until I realised that no-one else knew these things but me. I had always been taught to pray to angels, to see with my mind, to feel with my heart, to honour the God but also the Goddess, to talk to the great feminine, the great mother, the lady of the world. When I realised that these truths were not part of everyone's knowing, I kept them hidden deep inside my heart, even from the man who became my husband, for fear that he would think me mad. When the angel Gabriel came to me and imparted the message concerning the birth of my first child, Jesus, I knew that all the secrets that I had kept were now to be put into use, that I was the one who had been spoken of in prophecy in my family for generations, that all those things that I had hidden from Joseph now had to be spoken of, now had to be told.

I was very frightened, I was very scared. I was fearful because I knew too that my child would not be mine for long, but would be taken away from my side at a tender age, in order to be taught and prepared for the future that lay ahead. I knew that I would see him from time to time and that I was to pass on certain truths that only I knew. And I knew, too, that as he grew, my life in some strange way was meant to mirror his and that when he died my work was to begin in earnest. Carrying the child was a strange experience, one of lightness, divinity and surreal wonder. The child would speak to me in my mind with a voice of a gentle man and I would see him sometimes in dreams or in visions, shining with the golden light of the sun. I loved the child more than anything I had ever loved before and felt in some strange way that the child was part of me, that the child was part of my soul.

As we approached the time of the birth, a strange calm beset me and I did not fear anything at all. When the child was born, this calm remained, not as strong as it had been but leaving me in a perpetual state of acceptance and of grace. I taught the child all that I had been taught and knew that those secrets that remained in my heart would be spoken to him when he was older, when he could understand. I wept as he was taken away by his uncle in order to be taught, but knew that I would see him again, knew that at night when we slept, our souls would rejoin together somewhere, our souls would always be one.

Whilst my son was busy elsewhere, I continued with my life. Joseph had been traumatised by the situations that had occurred and even though in his own unconscious way he continued to do God's will, I knew that my work must be more seen. I began to gather around me women who I knew carried inside them the Great Lady's power, women who needed to be guided in order that they would know how to utilize the strength that existed inside. Together in small groups, in tiny houses, in darkened corners, in hushed voices we exchanged our teachings and our truths and I led them into inner journeys inside themselves in order that they might find their power and bring it out. In my own way these were my disciples and my apostles and I led them. Much later on I journeyed from town to town and city to city and preached upon hills and in darkened houses, in forests and in garden orchards. I guided women back to the source of all life. I taught them how to see the living radiance in the earth beneath their feet and how to touch the ethereal face of the moon at night. How to reach out and feel the power of the universe flowing through their fingertips, how to recognise the creative seasons of their lives. When Jesus was returned to me, now a man, I imparted to him the feminine secrets of my heart, the feminine mysteries, the feminine magics, the feminine truths, and I recognised that the sacred marriage that had always been spoken of between the polarities existed here and now in him and me. Although the time was not right and not ready, I saw and felt a potential glimpse of what this harmony could be and it encouraged me to carry on.

After his death I journeyed with those sisters who continued to surround me and be taught from my heart's understanding of the truth. I journeyed to places and people, I journeyed in sacred silence and in joyful, singing prayer. I journeyed to England and I journeyed to other parts of Europe, and finally, when the time was ready, I returned home. My husband had not seen the same calling in my life as I had. He had not restricted me in any way and indeed, when time allowed, we spent many days together, experiencing as much joy as we had done on the first day we ever met. He cared for my children when I was called away, and when I returned home I nursed them and nurtured them as any mother would.

By this time I had reached conclusions and revelations in my life. I had seen the secrets of the universe unfold and realised that it was time for me to leave. The Earth did not hold sadness or mortal joy for me any more and I saw it from a transcendent viewpoint, acknowledging it as the illusion that it always was.

I left this Earth in that life never to return again in physical form, rising higher and higher like a meteorite in the skies of the spiritual planes, journeying, journeying to the ascended realms, where my consciousness, where my soul was absorbed into bliss. My lifetimes were examples of commitment to my own spiritual truth. I did not allow or entertain the narrow-minded thoughts of others or the condemning, limiting possibilities of my family or my husband to prevent me from following that that I knew to be the most important thing in my life: the raising of my first child and the pursuit of my spiritual truth.

The morals and examples of my story are clear and evident: our need to acknowledge the Mother Divine and the Goddess in all her forms, to see that she is part of the solution, part of the plan. Our need to find her inside ourselves and to bring her forward once again, in order that she can aid us to become divine. And finally our need to commit ourselves to our spiritual truth as and when we see it, to give ourselves to the gods through this grace and allow, through us, the world and the consciousness of man and womankind to be renewed. The Goddess is all around you, within you and outside of you. See her and draw your strength from her and know that she loves you, know that she loves you all.

Lady Nada

My Life as Mary Magdalene

Over the centuries mankind has lost many truths. They have lost the truth of their divinity, they have lost the truth of the elements of creation, they have lost the truth of self-enlightenment, they have lost the truth of love and change.

But amongst these is a truth that is very important. It is not important for mankind's growth, it is not important for mankind's understanding of the mysteries of the universe, it is important for mankind's sustenance and maintenance whilst they continue to remain here on the physical planes. It is important for mankind's physical needs: it is the lost truth of sensuality and joy.

Many religious orders have taught their flock, their congregation, that sensual joy is to be considered amongst the sinful emotions in mankind's heart. That sensuality is to be looked upon in the same respect as envy, hatred and aggression, that it serves no positive purpose and is indeed a tool of the devil to condemn mankind to the material world of darkness and pain. But in truth the Divine created the world in order that we living, breathing human beings upon it may enjoy the sensuality of the changing seasons, the sensuality of food and drink, the sensuality of each other's bodies, the sensuality of all the wonderful things that we have the capacity to feel and hear and see and taste and touch.

When I lived upon the Earth as Mary Magdalene, my life was lived in order to teach people about the acceptance of sensual pleasure. Indeed it is true that I in that life found myself living a dark path, a path of prostitution, a path where I sold myself to others because of circumstance, because of a lack of self love and self worth, because I could see no other means, no other purpose, no other way. I acknowledged in my heart of hearts that prostitution was indeed a sin, that to sell oneself in this precious and most sacred manner was wrong. And through the spiral of my own actions I had condemned myself to an imagined eventual hell. Jesus saved me from all that, plucked me from the pit of my own despair, taught me the error of my ways by teaching me how to love myself, to respect and honour myself for who and what I truly was. He educated me as to the illusion of guilt and shame and karma and sin, whilst providing me with a clear understanding that there are those things in life that are good for the soul and bad for the soul; things that we do to ourselves as punishment for crimes committed in our eyes in lifetimes long since passed, so far in our own history that we no longer recalled the original sin that we now allowed ourselves to pay for.

Jesus told me how we write our own destiny and how I had engineered the downward spiral of my life as punishment for the lack of love that I held inside myself for myself, caused by the lack of love given to me by those who were my parents in that life. I had always been looked upon as an encumbrance by those who had provided me with passage into that reality and I had come to look upon myself in the same way, as a burden, as a chore, and in order to punish myself for my own very existence I allowed myself to be used and abused in the way that I was. I allowed myself to live a life that was sinful to me, that was wrong in my own eyes.

When Jesus saved me and absolved me, enabling me to release myself from my sin, to love myself and value myself, I recognised many things. I saw Jesus as my one true love, and deep within my heart saw that he was part of me, that I was part of him, that we were soul mates, born from the same soul. And of this I will speak in time.

But I also saw in Jesus' life a lack of joy, a lack of laughter, a lack of love of life. And despite the darksome nature of my past I knew how to bring joy into another's life, I knew what felt good, I knew what looked good and what tasted and smelled good. I had lived only within the realm of the sensual for so long that although I was not a scholar of the heart, I was a scholar of the material world and of the body's sensual needs.

I taught Jesus how to remember and incorporate into his existence acknowledgment of sensual pleasure and joy, whether this was washing his hair or smoothing the furrows from his brow, the stroke of my hand, feeding him sweet fruits, whether it was stopping and reaching down some blossom from a tree in order that he might smell it or gaze upon its delicate finery. Whether it was encouraging him to touch the surface of the sea or to stay awake until the sunset gave birth to the twinkling stars of night with me. Whether it was lighting ten candles in the place where he slept so that these flickering fireflies of life could lull him to sleep with their gentle, dancing caress. I taught him how to lift his gaze from heart and heaven to the Earth from time to time and see the sensual joys that his Mother Earth extended to him, that his reality offered in his honour and for his praise.

And Jesus saw the truth within my words and ways. Jesus saw the right action of my deeds and my intent, for God had not created the Earth in order for us to ignore it or simply transcend it without gazing at its majesty, but had instead laboured upon a beautiful planet in order that we might feed from it in a way not of spirit or of mind or even of heart, but of body, in order that through our limited physical senses we might know the physical pleasures of reality. Reality is indeed an illusion, this much is clear. But in order for illusions to be transcended they must first be looked upon so that within them we can find the key that unlocks the door and allows the secret to be seen and known.

The key here is not that the illusion of our reality is to be ignored or looked beyond, but that it is to be seen as a beautiful place, forged with imagination and the inspiration of a creator's love and it is that love that we are to feed upon through the sensual pleasures that the world extends, in order to recognise how much God loves us, how tirelessly God has worked to create such perfection, so tailor-made for our consumption as to include ingredients that would cater to each one of our individual needs.

And so, spiritual people of the Earth, do not ignore the world in which you live but savour it, relish it, suck it dry of all that it has to offer you and in so doing remember that God loves you and has furnished your existence well.

Jesus, myself and Mary, the mother of Jesus, were indeed all born from the same soul, a soul that had decided in order to evolve that it would split itself in two — one male in energy and one female. Jesus was the incarnation from the male half of our higher self, Mary and I two pieces born from the feminine side. Mary represented the mother's energy, and the energy of the crone. She was the cooling, calming, nurturing influence that would mould Jesus, the boy, into Jesus the man with her love and wisdom and her willingness to release him to his destiny. I was the passion of the maiden and the virgin, the sensual merriment of girlhood. I was the part that would not let him go, the part that would, through my spirituality, hold on to him still and remind him that there were those who loved him, not as a teacher, not as a son, not as a saviour, but as a man. For although Jesus was enlightened and divinely realised, man he still was, incarnate and bound by body to Earth and in need of recognising for one last time that as a man he was seen and loved; that as an individual devoid of spiritual gift of the grace of kinship he was cared for by someone who loved his heart.

His death did not devastate me, for I had realised a long time before that such a man could not be truly possessed or held but had to be shared with all, including God. I knew that a man such as him would not live long upon the Earth, could not, that mankind would not allow it to be so. And I knew too that he existed beyond life even when he lived because when I slept I felt him in my dreams watching me, beside me all the time; and even after he had passed from life I knew his eyes rested upon me as I slept, as lightly as a summer blanket.

After his death I became one of his mother's disciples and remained with her until her ascension, after which I myself taught, before I journeyed into the realms of spirit too. I knew in my heart of hearts that she was the moon to Jesus' sun and that she was the summer to my spring. In her I found peace and calm, sanctuary and nurturing, and in me she found the youth that some say she never had. Unified now we are in truth one, complete, whole, joined. And through this holistic being, all is complete. Now we are passion and love and grace and shine upon the Earth wearing either face, carrying the balanced light of our true being.

I remember when I lived upon the Earth in ancient times, and in Atlantis danced in the temples and sang to commemorate the changing seasons of the year. This was my task then, to honour and recognise the moving cycles of time. And I see now that in Jesus' life I did the same, and celebrated each twist and turn of his preordained fate, recognising them as a cosmic and elemental shift. Nature is to be celebrated and all those elemental things of nature which contribute to the unfoldment and evolution of mankind. It is said that God sang and celebrated each flower's arrival upon the Earth, each new thing born was born to the merriment of God's joy.

And so as you go forwards in life, honour not only your own movement but the movement of others too with sensual celebration, with laughter, joy and fun. Take your lessons from the innocence of children, who in their purity know that joy is the key to happiness, not riches and not acclaim, but laughter and smiles and love.

And acknowledge too your physical needs as you raise your heads to the spiritual sun. And make sure that in your all-too-desperate desire to leave this plane, you find some time to sample its wonders.

In love, in innocence, in purity and joy, I bless you with my love.

Saint Germain

─────⟡─────

Throughout all the lifetimes that I have lived on Earth there has been a concurrent underlying theme, a theme that is ultimately connected with my divine origin, the source of my soul's light, a theme that has secured and fixed me upon the spiritual path that I have always walked, that has aided me in countless ways to fulfil the divine tasks that have been set before me. A source that has always been very much part of whoever I have become and yet a source that has remained mysterious and invisible, and a source that always will.

Throughout the lives that I have lived, I have guided and prepared individual mortals who lived upon the Earth for their spiritual tasks that lay ahead of them. I have played a preparatory role, never embracing that task myself but providing those special and historical individuals with the correct stimulus and ingredients that were necessary in order that they may, when the time came to them, triumph over challenges and obstacles and indeed play their part in the grand universal scheme of things. From time to time I have been seen for the work that I have done, more because of the character that I have kept rather than the manner of the work that I have performed. I have been noted and praised because of my attitude and bearing, because of my mystery and charisma. And yet many would not focus upon the true essence of my being, the educational nature of my life, the very meaning of my existences.

Whether I was Merlin in ancient medieval England, whether I was Joseph of Arimathea in ancient Christian times, whether I was Francis Bacon in the latter Elizabethan period of England, or whether I was the priest of ancient Atlantis who made a bold attempt to resurrect the civilised and equal standards of a once great race, I have only been seen for the mask rather than the motive that has always lain beneath the surface, beneath that which is easily seen.

The Divine teaches us that no one man is any less important than another, that we are indeed all equal, that we are all parts of the jigsaw of the universal picture, all pieces of the universal clockwork that are integral in order to make the mechanism work and move. And yet history would teach us something different. History would show us that there are indeed individuals who are more important than others, individuals who shine and excel and are seen. History is cheating and lying. It is created from sensationalist facts which belittle the powerful and important efforts of the unsung heroes, of the teachers, of the guides, who have positioned the pawns of the Divine into place, in order that they might speak a line or play a part when it was needed, that was never written by their own brains but rather engrained into them as teaching by another once wiser man. But the universe provides us with our parts to play and we are often happy to play them. Whether they are hero or villain, whether they are teacher or king, it matters very little, it only matters that we play our part well and do all that we are asked for the greater good of man.

My Life in Atlantis

The first role then that I would speak of was in ancient Atlantis, a place once beautiful and majestic, a place breathtaking in its simplicity and mystery, in its magic and wonder. A place that was consumed by the needs and desires of men who sought to conquer their benign and good Master simply because they presumed themselves to be better than that great Being that created them.

Atlantis had endured for thousands of years. It had begun to recognise the part that it was asked to play. It had begun to see that it was to be the preparatory kingdom that would set an example for all those others and indeed in time even educate them, so that they might see the greater truths.

Any race on Earth you would think would be pleased with such a task set them by God. But the

Atlanteans were not like any other race. The Atlanteans were keen on solving riddles and paradoxes. They had striven throughout the generations of their incarnations and existences to ponder the mysteries of time and space, to ponder the mysteries of dimension. And indeed they had been successful in many cases with assistance from God and the angelic brethren and from extraterrestrial beings that they had connected with and befriended.

But they were not content and so they sought the answers to more mysteries, mysteries that they could not know the answers to. One of these mysteries was the nature of God's power, where the energy the Divine utilised with such simple grace originated and came from, how the magic worked. God had always told them that to understand the Divine was nothing that was meant for mortal minds but they refused to hear those words that did not content their ears and so ignored God's speaking and continued to search. Their searching led them to create complexity where once there was only simplicity. And it also led them to birth science upon the planet where once there was only mysticism. They began to combine forces in unnatural ways: taking energy from the earth and joining it with energy from the sky, manipulating the powers of the human mind and of the mineral consciousness without either's consent, considering that anything that would not willingly contribute its energy to their pursuit did so out of fear and ignorance and was to be superseded, overthrown, cajoled and threatened, made to cooperate by duress or enforcement. The Atlanteans convinced themselves that their greater plan was so important that it took precedence over all other things.

Their search and their opinions on those who resisted their investigation led them to begin to segregate their society into different strands of social class: scientists and mystics, priests and members of the royal family, members of the royal guard their foolish enforcers, and the peasantry who exhibited less powerful psychic and spiritual awareness and gifts. Atlantis became a place of prejudice and snobbery, a place of suspicion and envy, a place of competition, where harmony took a second place to standing and success.

This was indeed when the vibrations of the Earth began to fall rapidly and the heart-centred consciousness of mankind plummeted into the solar plexus area of the body, an area consumed by the pursuit for power and acknowledgment, trauma, pain and strength.

This pattern ensued for quite some time and degraded with the turning of each year. Atlantis had become a nightmarish world of abuse and manipulation, where experimentation of all levels took place without anyone's consent other than the high council, whose agenda was the strengthening of its own merits.

Genetic experimentation joined the ranks of energetic experimentation. Dimensional quantum physics, space travel, laser technology, all those things that your society at this time marvels at and considers to be proof positive of its superior civilisation, proof positive that mankind rules, these were our society's signs of decay and decline for those mystics and prophets who knew the truth. Signs of sadness and signs of doom.

But all was not lost. And some of us considered ways of redressing the mistakes of our fellow brethren, some of us who had not replaced our feelings of love with hate but rather with feelings of pity, feelings of despair. We sought ulterior ways of solving the problems that our brothers and sisters had created. And one of these fell to a priest who taught me the way.

That priest has long since risen into the ranks of Cosmic Ascended Masters and he is now known there as Solomon the Wise. He from the Archangels of old received a method of empowering those who were considered to be less psychically and spiritually advanced than the higher members of the Atlantean society, opening their chakras and attuning their energy systems to higher vibrational realms of consciousness, awareness and power. And through this method it was hoped by the Divine and Atlantean alike that equality would be established throughout Atlantis and wisdom would prevail over power and ignorance by redressing the equality of power that was shared. The system was known as *Inspiration* and I was one of the first who was versed in it, as the priest who had been inspired with this system was my teacher, my master at that time. He was old and knew that even though he was the right man to receive the guidance he was not the man who would perform it widely. He knew that task would fall to me and so indeed in that lifetime my true destiny began. I took myself away to the mountains and there with me my disciples, my followers and my students and I taught them what I myself had been taught. We began to practise the system of Inspiration and we began to call those who we knew were ready on a consciousness level to receive the power that we were now capable of bestowing. Using our telepathy, using astral travel and using the interconnectedness of our consciousness through dreams, we called out to the Atlanteans, whether they were priests or scientists or peasantry, to journey to the mountains where we now lived as Inspirers in order to be tried and tested and then to receive the gift that we would give, the gift that would make them equal, that would open their eyes in order that they might aid us in returning sanity to our insane world. The system incorporated the injection of energetic symbols, keys of vibration that would open the system of those who received them to the higher vibrational planes, locking them into these sources of energy and providing them with powers and abilities that they at this time did not possess.

There were 364 symbols all in all and these symbols were imparted in short doses that were designed not to overload the consciousness of the recipient but to gently evolve them and prepare them for the next symbols that would be downloaded into their energetic system. The system of Inspiration was successful, but it was too little and it was too late. The Inspirers realised that Atlantis was doomed, that it would be destroyed by God and so some of us fled the island before it was destroyed. I was broken-spirited in my pursuits and chose to remain, witnessing the destruction of Atlantis first-hand. Some of the Inspirers fled to Tibet where they attempted to pass on the system of Inspiration again in order that those humans that they encountered there might benefit from it and aid them in re-establishing the Atlantean vibration on the Earth in other parts of the planet, pockets where they felt the energy had not degraded so harshly as to prevent this resurrection from occurring.

The Tibetan Inspirers, cautious in their practice, gave five symbols to those Tibetans who had heard their telepathic calls, to see how they would digest the altered state of consciousness and power, the gift that they had been given. Some excelled and some turned and twisted that which they had been given by altering the symbols themselves in order that they might contact energies that were more negative and more easily manipulated. Horrified by what they had seen, the Atlanteans removed themselves from Earth, depositing 21 symbols in the care of one of their most promising students and hiding the remaining in ancient texts and scrolls which they placed high in the Tibetan mountains. The system exists now known under the name of Reiki. It is not complete though some Reiki masters do indeed know and have access to the full 21 symbols that we imparted then. The remaining missing symbols have long since been found and even to those who have not or will not ever see them are still available by accessing them on the akashic planes. The system that is used now is beneficial to some but not to all as it was in ancient days. It is a system to create equality, not to empower the already empowered. So many who have been drawn to the temptations that the system proclaims to offer them to strengthen what they already have, have long since discovered that instead of doing this it simply attuned them to an alternate source of power or even limited that which they already had. Of course they can be liberated from this and if they find someone who genuinely has the remaining mysterious symbols they can be attuned to the higher realms and therefore freed from the limitations of vibration that they have access to at this moment in time. But once again, these things now lie within the hands of man and therefore it is man who will decide whether they will free this knowledge which was once so freely given in order to indeed allow mankind to become more equalised in consciousness and power, more spiritual in thought and deed.

Patterns occur throughout history and time, staggering in their repetition and we from this loftier plane and perspective watch open mouthed how mankind continues to repeat the same mistakes that they have made time and time again – the abandonment of the spiritual and the embracing of the scientific, the jealous way in which mankind guards power and is reluctant to share it with his fellow man and even now those who are spiritually awoken and proclaim in loud voice that they are guides and teachers do not use the gifts that they have been given to educate each other and share the knowledge but instead to boost their fragile egos in order that everyone might know who is more spiritual than the other. If you are to succeed and heal your planet and bring back your world into the place that it is meant to be, then you must liberate yourself from these attitudes of superiority. You must acknowledge the errors of your ways, for if you continue to focus purely upon the need for your importance to be fed and the need for power to be discovered then as surely as Atlantis was destroyed, so will you be too. Think then on these words and on this story told, for time repeats itself but always extends an opportunity in order that the pattern may be absolved.

My Life as Merlin

By the time that I lived upon the Earth as Merlin, my awareness of who I was and what I had returned to the Earth to do was growing complete. Although not ascended, I was close to realisation, close to self-perfection. And my closeness was both my gift and my curse.

From an early child I had been earmarked and acknowledged for my unusual father, for the madness of my mother and for my own peculiarities. Rumours were abound as rumours often are, and it was said that my father was a demon or an angel, the devil himself, or some being from the fairy realms who had enchanted my mother or raped my mother or disguised himself in order that he might create me through my mother's beguiling.

My gifts came to me early and I was privileged with the sight, capable of seeing into realms that others could not even dream of. Realms of the elementals and the fairy folk. Realms of great beauty and of tragic sadness.

From an early age, too, I began to become slowly aware of an inner knowing, a guiding hand that steered me through life, that pulled me to people and places, that opened my mouth and encouraged me to speak, encouraged me to say the strangest things that meant nothing to me but which opened the minds and the hearts of those who heard the words, who witnessed me describe and see the visions that I had.

Soon the druids in their wisdom took me into their brotherhood and they, because of prophecies that they had a long time ago received, were willing to guide me. My instruction was classical, disciplined, rigid, remarkable. I learned from the finest tutors the most incredible secrets that were strengthened by my own comparable experiences and my ability to decipher and understand the truth of what I saw. The more I grew, the more I understood, the more I was taught, the more I began to realise why I was being trained, exactly why I had returned, the details of my destiny in their entirety, details that intrigued and frightened me. Details that astounded me, details that I slowly saw come true.

I knew of Arthur's birth and life a long time before the event actually occurred. I even knew how Arthur would fall, though I did not know whether this would be a truth. The future, you see, is not cast in stone but is rather created as a possibility, manufactured as a probable outline, a template, a blueprint. It is mankind's free will that gives it shape and form. Still time moved on much in accordance with my understanding and my knowledge. To my great sadness, I saw Arthur rise and fall just as I knew he would.

My destiny was not to promote the druids or their religion — quite the contrary. It was to prepare a man who would eventually herald a new religion that would wipe out that one that had made me who I was, a religion that would sponge away any sign of the goodness of my craft and kind. Because it was God's will, because it was what was meant to be, because the matriarchal society that had dominated Britain for some time that had begun to reach out into the world and saturate the very ethers with its power and its passion and its love, needed now to be replaced in order that balance could be resolved on

Earth, in order that eventually in time, in a far-flung future that I would never see, the masculine and feminine forces would come together in a perfect and holy union as one.

Matriarchy must form the tender foundations that Christianity would stand upon with its harsh heels in order that in time both would realise that the answer was not in persecution or force but rather harmonious mergence, divine union, a perfect and beautiful blending of both into one.

Arthur represented all that was masculine, all that was projective and inspirational, all that was instigative and creative. Although he was tempered by my hand from a babe, although he knew and understood the ways of the Goddess and acknowledged her power and her presence, although he knew how the sun and the moon balanced each other within the sky, how the druids and priestesses of Britain lived in harmony and respect for each other out of the acknowledgement of the flow and perfect harmony of the cycle of the seasons, he would grow to figurehead a religion that he would understand with little clarity, but acknowledge as the religion that would re-establish control to a warring Britain and provide a chance for the heart of the world to be opened again.

During the time of the Great Mother, Britain had become diverse in its focus, although almost all of it acknowledged the power of the Goddess and the power of the pagan way. The pagan way had not encouraged union between clan and county but rather had simply encouraged union to the Goddess, union to the power of the Earth and this had been achieved in its way. But harmony had not been found for man throughout it, only for the Earth. Christianity through fear would unite the counties, would unite Britain. Unfortunately it would ostracize and exile every witch, druid, priestess, wizard and wise man, and even the powers of the Earth itself.

A long time ago the elementals had begun to recede into their own dimension again, from whence they had once originated. They had foreseen what was coming, the early attacks upon them by Christian fundamentalists who existed in the early days, who considered them to be manifestations of the devil, had pursued them; the knights who hunted the dragons as symbols for paganism had sealed their decision to disappear and to cloud their very existence from man's mind with a powerful enchantment. It is hoped of course that in time once again they will return to the Earth when they see that the consciousness of mankind is once again opened to a point where their existence will be welcomed, but even at this moment that outcome seems a long way off.

For the priestesses too like the druids had foreseen what might occur and even were aware that the divine source that transcended polarity was in agreement, wanted this to occur. But they were resistant. It was their task, it was who and what they were, they were challengers, as Lady Portia is, guardians on the way of evolution, put in place to see whether or not the new and evolving Christianity had the power to withstand the presence of the old.

My duties and my tasks were to prepare Arthur; first of all to procure him, which was a simple matter as his father was an idiot, and secondly to train him in the druids' way and guide him towards the destiny that I knew clearly and that he had little to no awareness of. And much the same way as I had trained Jesus when I was Joseph of Arimathea, I now guided him towards his doomed destiny and fate.

And as when I was Joseph it was a lonely task. For I had no-one to whom I could really turn in order to speak of my worries and my concerns but only the realms of spirit who were ghostly companions, loyal, faithful, encouraging, loving, but possessing no body that could be touched or hugged or taken comfort from. At times I would take myself into the woods and hug the trees and listen to their soothing sighs, their voices beneath my feet and inside my mind strengthening me. My magics were my only escape, my only source of joy. My vision had long since stolen happiness from my heart, concerning this beautiful boy, knowing full well what might lay in store for him and knowing too that when my task was done I would leave, no further any point to my existence, knowing that I would have to abandon him to his fate, as all teachers and all parents have to abandon their children in order to see whether they have learned their lessons well or, still squandering even the last words spoken, allow themselves to be pulled under by their certain fates. When Arthur was prepared I stayed with him a while in Camelot, tried to get him to see the chinks within his armour, the sour passion of Morgaine La Faye, his half-sister, and the truth behind Guinevere's impending and inevitable betrayal. He had been taught of the truth of soul mates and complications of their existences. I had explained it to him time and time again using Jesus as an example and his mother and his beloved Magdalene. But when the time came Arthur could not see. His love for Guinevere was so strong that, even though Guinevere was not the subtlest of creatures, he failed to observe her infidelity with Lancelot, failed to see his similarity, his link, his connection with his greatest knight and in his blindness allowed the betrayal to occur, seeing it only when it was untimely presented before his eyes and then in rage, rather than in wisdom, dissolved his marriage to Guinevere and thus cut himself from his connection to the earth and the Goddess and attempted to destroy her from anger and rage.

Guinevere had no option, there was nothing that she could do. Lancelot, as much as Arthur, was her twin soul and so she could not be expected to do anything other than love him.

At this time I recognised that it was my turn also to disappear and retreat and so I stepped back and bid him a fond farewell.

Some legends say that I was imprisoned in a tower of air, a place deep into the earth, by Morgaine La Faye or Vivian, a fairy lover, neither of which of course is true, but like the elementals before me, I too wove a cloak of illusion and allowed my fate to be sealed by the imagination of men.

I returned to Arthur from time to time in dreams and visions in an attempt to at least provide him with some hint and clue as to how he could make the best out of the worst situation that he had created by seeking the Holy Grail. Indeed his fate was saved to some extent even if his life was not.

Poor Arthur died at the hand of his half sister's child who was born to destroy him, as Morgaine La Faye died hiding the last of the Earth's great magics beneath the Goddess' skin. His destiny was not completed, but in part achieved, as was mine.

And the Earth, battered and bruised and bleeding, moved on. And Christianity, so much harsher without Arthur's tender hand to aid in its birth, gripped mankind and bullied them towards certain truths.

And so my sadness was my sight and my joy was my sight and my great power was indeed my magic and at the same time it was my greatest downfall because even though I knew how to move the earth and sky, I could not mend a broken heart or open eyes shut by seeming betrayal. I knew this and casually gave in to my knowledge without even attempting or trying to change what would be, obedient as ever to God's will.

And so the meaning and the message of this life is simple. God has a plan for the Earth and for his children — for mankind, and the plan involves understanding certain things in order that decisions may be made and twists and turns along the road may be taken so that mankind's consciousness will open and expand and be exposed to certain energies and truths in preparation for their great advancement and ascendance, possibilities, that may be the future, exist like phantom images, waiting for man's free will to make them solid. We seers see the possibilities and try to guide mankind in order that they will make the decisions that will bring about the best, sweetest, the brightest possibility.

The moral and lesson behind the story is that all of life has purpose and meaning, that we would do well to content ourselves with our part whether we are guides or healers, whether we are knights or serfs; we would be well advised to content ourselves with our task and, as I did, acknowledge what can be done and what cannot. Also it is important to see that some of us are born in order to know truths that others cannot see; however maddening or insane these truths may appear, we cannot deny them, even if we attempt from time to time to turn our back upon them and pretend that they do not exist. We know that they do.

Our gifts are our curses and our curses are our gifts and it is our perception that allows us to deal with this truth as well as all others. Mystery serves a purpose as does challenge, as does manipulation and we must prepare to embrace all things if it is our destiny to guide in such a way.

And at the end of the day and at the end of our life we must place our faith completely in God and we must believe that God knows the twist and turn of the path. We must believe that God knows the truth.

And so, the way ahead is not always as it would seem. A balanced path can sometimes be a still one, and the imbalanced path the one that promises the greatest progress, the greatest opportunities for expansion, development and truth.

It always was the druids' way to teach creative imbalance, that by walking upon a path that challenged and constantly questioned that which it had taught before, we would rather move forwards by breaking through the boundaries of our beliefs than by standing still and contemplating in all harmony the spot beneath our feet.

Go forwards then and allow all words that you hear or read to break the barriers of belief that you have too. Do not content yourself with your knowledge but instead be bold and in your boldness allow yourself to believe new things each day, new possibilities, that liberate you from limitation and enable you to see that, no matter how much we see, it is not real, that there is always another face, another mask behind the mask that we are aware of, another truth that contradicts the truth that we have come to call the ground that we walk upon. Contradiction is our only hope and creative imbalance the way to embrace contradiction without going mad.

Go forwards then. Embrace the inconsistency of life, follow your path, know that you are not alone, and know that God's wisdom and will is absolute, and that if we would only follow it, all would indeed be well.

My Life as Francis Bacon

Words are powerful things. And it was in my lifetime as Francis Bacon that this truth was more clearly understood and investigated than in any other lifetime I had experienced. Even when I was Merlin and even when I knew words of power that could open doorways between this dimension and a thousand others, I did not clearly understand the true meaning of the power of words.

Words in essence are more powerful and important than action or deed because although a lifetime lived by someone through their actions and teaching by the example of them is in essence more powerful than a thousand speeches, it is still words that I use to record these actions, to note them down in history in order that they may never be forgotten. And therefore the deed, the example, of a living life is subject and victim to the power of words and how they are used to record the historic moment for all to see.

Since the beginning of time words have been used not only to record and explain the truth but also to hide it, in order that those incarnate mortals, members of mankind whose intelligence and awareness is not yet great enough to acknowledge the finer spiritual truths and use them well, would overlook those gems of spiritual knowledge that were meant for those with finer minds and finer eyes, those who would acknowledge the encodements hidden within the secret doctrines that had been written by masters and priests who sought to spread the light only to those who had the consciousness to receive it and pass it on with love. In the bible and in the ancient grimoires, the spell books of mages and mystics, of Atlantean priests, of Egyptian witches, codes and cyphers were used; metaphors, poetry and symbolism, to hide the greatest and deepest meanings inside magical and mystical fables and mythologies. And so it was in my lifetime, too.

Awareness came in fleeting moments as truth; the position of my birth, the secrecy of the nature of who I was, the physical form that had been created for me from royal heritage of the time, in order to allow certain energies to flow into and through me that could only be accessed by those of royal blood who from generation to generation had been able to attune themselves through their royalty to the mystical and magical powers of the earth and the other four elements since the beginning of Atlantean times. The love for poetry and language, the fascination with fantasy, fantastical truths, mythology, history; my imagination, my capacity to weave the visions in my mind into words that could be spoken as a soliloquy by a character or read as sonnets and poems to woo the heart of a loved one.

Piece by piece the strands of my life were woven together through the understanding of my fast-opening spiritual mind and my fast-opening heart. And I came to remember part of who I had been, and partly who I was, and partly what I was meant to do.

As in all my lifetimes, it was meant that I would remain invisible and unseen. Sometimes in all truth the best way is to be as visible as possible. The more noticeable you are, the easier it is to be forgotten. But sometimes it is also important in truth to be truly deceptive in one's carriage and demeanour. And in this case, this is what I was. I found myself a stooge of sorts, a folly, a fool. I found for myself a person who would take my part in public life, who would be that one who would be recorded famously for my endeavours and my actions, a diversion, a distraction. And so I chose an actor to play the part, always favouring irony above all devices in drama in order to amuse and delight. And so Shakespeare took my place, claimed the glory for my work, acted his part, played the fool and shone and was remembered and acknowledged, he who forged masterpieces from air that even to this day are held above all others for their dramatic excellence and ingenuity of plot and language.

At times I was saddened by my actions and confused and enraged by them, too. But deep down inside I saw the reason and the purpose and relished the invisibility, knowing that it allowed me to continue full time with that work that I needed to do and did so well.

Play after play and sonnet after sonnet the words were written and inside them were encoded the mysteries of lifetimes long since lived and forgotten by the majority of mankind. Also, combined and interwoven with this, enlightened truths, truths that flowed into my mind and heart, truths that were all my own, or at least of my own discoverance and acknowledgement. Truths that were given to me as blessings by the Divine, truths that I knew would not be used in a lifetime in which I lived, but would be in fact used at much later times when the world was in much greater need of truth. Encoded into the structure of the stories and the speeches spoken were words of power and invocations of great mystery and majesty. And still today they can be found by the nimble minded and those who feel the power in their soul. Magnetised by like attracting like, these sorcerers and priests now born again will find the truth, guided to it by the tingling within their stomachs, and raising the words within their mouths they will know and feel the power, ancient and wise, stored within these texts and use them, knowledge and invocation alike, to free and liberate the Earth from its entrapping illusion and limiting pursuit of power.

Words are sometimes the only thing that remains. The only thing that is important, that has the power to save. Words.

And so, do not be fooled or foolish enough to think that words count for nothing, because they can change the course of nations. They can lift someone to the heavens or throw them into the raging fires of hell, they can inspire and strengthen and empower and enlighten or they can quench the dimmest flame into eternal darkness in order that no light may pass into the minds and hearts of those who might read a thousand books or hear a thousand lectures spoken. Power through sound, through words, was given to us by God in the beginning and can still be used today, whether sung or spoken, to bring peace and truth. Those who walk the spiritual path and who read *these* words must take heed of this most important lesson for unless it is adhered to you may be lost.

Power grows as we grow inside ourself. And our words have more meaning than ever before. They become more real in essence than we ourselves are in flesh or blood. Words spoken in haste can bring the downfall of a person in the most physical way, because they are the manifestation of our thoughts and our hearts' desires, whilst words spoken to bless can heal and bring miracle into being. I talk no longer of the power to encourage but the power to shape, and so I would say in all honesty and truth, be cautious with your words. Express them with earnest understanding that they have power and meaning as they always did. Use them well.

And so the lesson of this life for me and the lesson that I would pass on to you is a simple one. It is obedience to God and to the heart as was seen and known in all the lives that I have lived. But it is also something more; it is acknowledgement that the life we led may not have great meaning or impact upon the present which we temporarily journey through, but more impact upon the future which we ourselves may never see. Sometimes we are here to prepare the way for something we will never know but which, without our effort and our aid would never be and therefore would never allow times of great peace to come.

My life as chronicler of spiritual wisdom and truth, harbinger of the power of the word that would and still does change the lives of many who I would never even begin to imagine, who would be born hundreds of years after my death, it was for *these* times and moments and people that my words were written, not the people at the time. And it was for these that my identity was hidden in order that they would embrace these words in all innocence and purity and in so doing would find the true magic and power inside them, rather than investigating them as mystical and magical texts and looking so hard for the words of power that they would not see them even when they were upon their faces. Invisibility has its necessity. It is one of the greatest means available to us for ensuring success.

So if you are given a task which you know you will never see the result of, do not despair, for it is as important as any of those who live their lives now in order that their majesty and might may be seen to have a difference upon the Earth. If you are meant to be invisible and unseen, cherish it, for fame has its harsh price and prevents us from continuing to pursue with all integrity and honesty those things that we know to be most dear to us and to be the quintessence of our reason for being. And take heed and read cautiously the words of ancient poets and playwrights, allowing the likeness in your heart to guide you to their power, and once awakened inside you use your words carefully too, in order that in gentle, soft and sweet harmony we may speak and bring only love to the world, and not horror and not pain and not sadness and not woe. These then are my words to you, a blessing to all those who would dare to speak.

My Life as Christopher Columbus

On Earth once I lived as an explorer, a ship's captain. In this life my dreams of youth came true, and through my hard work and determination I was allowed to sail across the seas, guiding a crew to foreign, far off places of great beauty, great mystery and great wonder.

For some, the life of a sailor was a curse, a prison sentence, a means of earning good money that they would send back home to loved ones abandoned on the shore. To others it was freedom, to others it was duty. To some it was placing one's entire life and the lives of all those who trusted you in the hands of God. It was an exercise and experiment in divine trust.

As Christopher Columbus my duties and obligations to those whom I served were always clear in my mind. But also too, there was a greater understanding, a greater awareness that I would never dare put into words, for fear that I would be clapped in irons and sentenced to the deepest dungeons that the world could conceive. For my thoughts and understandings were things that could be misinterpreted as a mad man's ego. Or things that could be recognised as a spiritual man's truth.

I was aware from a very young age that there was a hidden purpose to my life, that I was used by God, guided and taken to people and places in order that I might catalyse events into being, I might facilitate great change and transformation in the lives of people, in the affairs of state, in the movements of the world. I knew that I was destined to sail. And even in those most unlikely moments when it seemed impossible that my dream would come into reality, when all others despaired and lost faith, I believed in my spirit that guided me always on, despite all odds.

It would be untrue to say that I knew the reasons why, because I did not. And knowing the reasons why never seemed important to me. I followed my heart and my heart led me to adventure and experiences that brought me great joy and great wonder. And this was all that mattered, that was the entirety of my concern. Everything else felt just commonplace amongst these divine feelings of truth.

It is strange being at sea; held in God's hand, subject to the changeable powers of the wind, steering your course in accordance with the stars and sun, never truly knowing whether you are following an imaginary path or one indeed that truly will lead home. A compass is such a fragile thing and the stars at times seem to shift and move so freely in the sky from one moment to the next. Your perception of the world around you is radically altered and changed. Indeed there were times when it was feared amongst those members of the crew who knew the truth that we would die without further provisions, with no land in sight and no hope of discovering where we had gone wrong, with the wind against us and the seas rough against our sound ship's bow.

But amongst them all I was content to place my faith in my heart and God. And more often than not, even when storms rose from nowhere and tossed our ship upon the waves like a feather in the air, I knew, sure in my mind and being, that we would be safe and the storm would carry us to where we needed to be. And indeed our journeys, though at times haphazard, led us to the most marvellous places, to the most wondrous people, to the most spectacular things; treasures, islands, people, cultures, things that enriched our lives, aye! and our pockets, and allowed us to journey home with new inventions in mind and new discoveries in our keel, ensuring our capacity to return to the seas further funded by those authorities who had been pleased with our booty, with our discoveries, with our truths.

And then of course there were those times when our ship ran afoul of others or journeyed to places where our presence interfered with the existing scheme of things, of course the most famous of these being our haphazard and chanceful discovery of the

Americas, which led in turn to mankind's pollution of this place of natural order, natural beauty, natural power and natural truth.

It was at these times, when I saw what would occur, or when I witnessed first-hand how man, interfering with something that they knew nothing about, could so easily destroy something that had endured for thousands and thousands of years, it was at these times that I contented myself with the belief that I had been used by God to bring purification, punishment, to deliver God's wrath, to challenge these people, to see if they had the power and the strength to overcome the odds that stood against them.

In my own ignorant way I was aware of the power of the Violet Flame that worked with me and through me even then, that urged me to bring change and transformation and alchemy to all those who were in danger of stagnation. To bring to them God's ruling and the power that would indeed seal their fate and set in motion a thousand events that would in turn enable others to view this doomed truth or populace and learn from their example, grow wise from their death.

And so what is the moral of this life that I led? There were no great spiritual truths told by me though indeed there were spiritual truths exposed to the world through the things that I discovered, through the pathways that I found. But what did I learn? And through this learning what can I impart to you?

I can impart this most valid and valuable truth: that some things are meant to die, some things are meant to pass and end, no matter how virtuous they were, no matter how great or grand they once seemed to be, no matter how favoured by God. And although we are by God's creation a curious race, sometimes it is best left undiscovered, the truth. Sometimes it is best left unseen. And we, we who are agents of God, we would do best to surrender to our duty and our task on Earth and realise that it is not through our ignorance we cause destruction but it is through our grace that we allow destruction to occur, destruction that is part of the great plan, destruction that is meant to be. And so if we follow our hearts and remain ever truthful and constant to ourselves, doing what we do because we feel it is the right thing and not because we seek power or flattering to the ego, and no matter the outcome, whether it be fair or foul, it is right and good. It is what is meant to be.

And so I would say to all you would-be sailors or journeyers who would travel the sea, the air or the world, or travel into a thousand minds and hearts of those who you would seek to teach or guide, follow your hearts, steer yourself through your oceans and your seas. Do not be frightened of the monsters that you may encounter along the way but know that if your journey is divinely ordained by God, these creatures, these experiences will twist and turn you on to the right path, and on to the right experiences that are indeed needed in order that you may rightfully find your way. And do not concern yourself with things that go astray. But rather think and know that these too are meant to be, are ordained. And even if you cannot see the reason why, do not worry, do not be sad, but know that sometimes God's will is not meant for mortal eyes.

The Native Americans' time had come. They were to be challenged by society, by the world, to see if they had the awareness to extend their hand of friendship whilst protecting their hearts and their homes. They had been guided to walk a path of balance which they lost sight of. Even if it was through trickery and deceit, their fate was sealed and in its sealing they were lost.

All things rise and fall in accordance to their readiness to evolve and grow, to incorporate the lessons they have learned, and rather than just talk of them, use them, to be confronted by the unusual and the remarkable and excel rather than fall foul and victim. Mankind will be challenged in this way and we will see whether they have the strength to endure.

And so then this life was about grace and trust, belief and flow. It was about understanding some but not all, but not being fearful of that which I did not understand, but instead focussing upon that which was strongest in me: my belief that what I was doing was right and good and true. And so, whether or not I truly felt at times that my words or work had brought peace rather than destruction, I knew that as long as I did not allow my mind to interfere with my heart, then I was not ruled by the devil but by God, and in so doing was absolved from any misdemeanours that I had caused because they had been caused through me by the Divine for divine purposes that my mind was too small to comprehend. If we then learn to simply trust, to have faith, to be bold in our faith and trust, then mankind will do well. But if we question too much why, if we blame one another when all we have done is followed our own hearts, then the race may not endure.

So sail your stormy seas, let your heart be your compass and your guide and your faith your lifebelt and your shield. Trust in the Divine and know that whatever happens, whatever it may be, it flows in accordance with God's will and therefore is good.

My Life as Saint Germain

For some of us who walk upon the spiritual path, our duties and our tasks are centred around the role of ambassador for God. We have been placed upon the Earth to represent the unseeable Divine, to be God's reasoning and God's voice, to be God's intervening hand that guides and protects and reinforces the law of karma and cause and effect, and this was clearer to me, more so than in any other life, in the life in which I lived my last upon the Earth; in the life in which I was Saint Germain.

In this incarnation more than any other I was in my maturity, guided constantly to be seen by many who would notice my uniqueness and through the examples of it pay attention too to the words that I would speak and not only the sound of my voice.

As Jesus had used miracles to exemplify the power of the Divine but had unfortunately been seen only as a magician who possessed abilities unique to one such as him, I utilised miracles, growing from the patterns of his life, realising that mankind in certain areas had expanded very little, and would be drawn to the wonders that I could perform, and that that attraction, that awareness, would provide me with a forum in which to speak to those who would see through the eye-catching mask of my magic, whose appetite would have been whetted by my wizardry, and who would be more open to listen to what I would have to say. This unfortunately is how it still is today. Mankind is much more willing to listen to that one who can pull a few white rabbits from a few hats than the Tibetan priest who exudes serenity and glows with an inner peace and enlightenment. Mankind, as material as ever, is drawn to the dramatic and so it was dramatic that I used to capture the ears of Europe.

I decided when I lived as Saint Germain that I would live for a long time. That if this was going to be my last lifetime upon the Earth, I would enjoy it. I would call upon the fast-dissolving capacity to enjoy sensual reality and I would milk it until the last drop was spent. And so I utilised my awareness and ability to transcend limitation in order to sustain my physical existence upon the Earth for as many years as was possible, until my consciousness had reached such a limit and extent that sensual pleasure meant nothing to me any more. Sometimes I almost think that in retrospect I could become quite sad at no longer being able to be moved by a sunset or excited by a beautiful human being, but of course sadness is something that I transcended a long time ago. And so even if I produced these emotions inside the core of my being I know that they would be false, more illusions, created by myself, in order to make me feel more human and less ascended. But once you have seen through the illusions there is no going back, and pretending is just pretending and never any more than that.

I used my immortality well to astound and stir curiosity in the hearts and minds of many men and women in high places and of high standing, in order that their intrigue would afford me a space in which to be heard. And obliging God, I did as I was guided and as I was told and endeavoured to bring peace into the hearts and minds of men, between warring nations, between people who had existed for centuries locked in ancient feuds that they could not even remember. I endeavoured to establish harmony by being the voice of righteousness and reason, by showing a little of what lay in store for all of them when they reached the glorious moment of self-realisation, by passing on the words of God.

My life was a close parallel to Jesus', except I encouraged no disciples and I maintained an illusive and mysterious existence. I lived within circles that were decadent and luxurious and I was as decadent and luxurious, as dramatic and extravagant, as the rest. I did not claim to be a saviour, or a messiah or a leader, but simply an enlightened man who was willing to share his enlightenment with everyone and anyone who was in need of it. And in those days as in these, many people were.

And so from time to time I pulled my party tricks. I mended flawed diamonds and appeared in places where I could not be, sometimes employing bi-location and multi-location in order to be with many people at a time. Sometimes I astounded people with my knowledge of their secrets. Sometimes I flaunted my alchemical might and appealed to people's more material minds by promising them a little of understanding concerning the truth of how to turn lead into gold. Whatever trick I used, at times it worked and was most successful! At times of course it failed and flatly fell to the earth as heavy as a stone. As much as the human spirit astounded and inspired me, human stubbornness confounded me and horrified me to the core: how little men with a great deal of power could stamp their feet and create such a tantrum as to cause the death of a thousand loyal men and women. How such little things could grow into such major disasters, simply because of the unwillingness of a few key people in places of power who were blinded by their prejudices and their unwillingness to see. This was sad indeed.

In the interim moments when I was not needed or when it was more appropriate that I was not seen, I spent my time in different places, sometimes as different people. I had a hideaway, a retreat, a sanctuary, which existed obscured by illusion in the heart of Darjeeling. I lived some of my time in other dimensions, perfecting my perspective, my awareness, preparing myself for the day when I would leave the world of flesh and enter into the realm of spirit. Everyone who lives their last lifetime upon the Earth is subject to such need. For ascension is more than death, it is transformation, it is the willingness to let go of individuality and character. It takes great courage to release your tight grip upon the edge of the void and calmly allow yourself to be consumed by the vortex of the Divine, not struggling, not screaming, not kicking, but willingly allowing yourself to be tossed and torn, picked apart at the very fabric of your consciousness. Letting go of illusion is so much more than the realisation that illusion exists. It is knowing that it is no longer needed and through that knowing transcending it. In the spiritual planes I prepared myself for this, coached and guided by those who had gone before me, ironically some of whom I in the past had trained and taught. I returned when God bade me to, when the times were right, in order to continue to play my part, to finish off those final ties that bound me to the physical plane, to make sure that everything I had ever been asked to do had indeed been done.

One of the last emotions that I recall existing in my mind, floating through my heart, was one of frustration and hopelessness. Mankind seemed on one hand civilised and wise, the sum of all that they had once been, on the verge of making so many breakthroughs, realising and recognising so many things and yet at the same time mankind seemed stubborn and blind and deaf and obsessed with power, maintaining it and holding it and achieving it. I knew that God had all of this in hand. That this was not the right time, that these were not the right people. And it was this certainty, this knowing, that eased these thoughts from my brain and allowed my heart to become quiet and still in order that I might slip from this world like the faint and untraceable memory that I had always been and enter the great silence of the brotherhood of light.

The strange thing about ascension is that it is very much like early childhood. It is blissful and there are no worries or concerns, there are no needs that are not met, there are no fears. There is only existence, joy, happiness and the sense of drifting, drifting through fields of light, passing through the mind, passing through the heart, passing through the spirit and the soul and opening you ever wider to a greater truth that cannot be spoken of or seen or imagined but that must be felt.

When I was Saint Germain I was born to a royal family; an obscure royal family, but royal nevertheless, noted and acknowledged more for their glamour and social prestige than their power. I was well educated, though my mind was not at ease or happy with the knowledge I was given. My eyes and thoughts were always on something else, something greater, something more intangible. I was always different from my friends and cousins. I had no brothers and sisters in that life and my parents often worried and concerned themselves over my actions and my comments, my evident powers that were so easily recognisable, even when I was a very young man.

I knew at a very young point exactly who I was, exactly who I had been, what was to become of me, where I was to go, what I was to do. There were no surprises in my life, none at all, and I was worried why that did not worry me. But it did not. Life was like some strange game, all laid out before me neatly in my mind and all I had to do was walk into it and live it. To say the words that I knew would appear within my mind, to find the people who I had already seen. For one who is born to ascend, the past, the present and the future mean nothing.

Life was a game, life was a play, sometimes a comedy, sometimes a tragedy, but I was always the enduring character who knew the plot, knew the script and had the power to freeze the scene or rewrite the reality; the enduring central character who could not be harmed, who could not die but who orchestrated like some diabolical circus ringmaster the parading of animals and the dancing of clowns. I still loved life, I still loved mankind. It was only in my latter years that my consciousness and understanding had grown so powerful that I had transcended joy in the way that you understand it. That was the last thing that I let go of.

And so from this lifetime I learned a great deal. I learned the importance of enjoying each and every moment, each and every present, each and every passing minute, each and every passing hour. I learned how ascendancy was indeed a beautiful, worthwhile and attainable thing. But life too with all its blinding illusions was also most desirable and most beautiful and this is something that I imparted to people before I departed; the importance of cherishing life, the importance of loving the illusion before you realised it for what it truly was and let it go. The importance of seeing beyond petty and insignificant struggles in order to recognise the wonders of joy.

And so, fellow ambassadors who walk upon the spiritual path of light, these are my words to you: use whatever trick you have to guide and teach, use whatever means you would to show people the greatest spiritual truth, but whilst you do and whilst your consciousness still allows you, do not lose sight of the wonders of this world that many of you feel you would give up at the click of a finger in order to embrace the bliss of spiritual union. Do not stare beyond the illusion too soon, before you have valued it for its prettiness, for its beauty. Guide and teach and heal and show, to play your part in God's grand scheme. But whilst you live here, take just a little piece of time to enjoy the show.

Lady Portia

My Life as Morgaine La Faye

I am Lady Portia, she who was once Morgaine La Faye, she who is the soul mate of Saint Germain, she who is custodian of the silver-violet ray of feminine empowerment and transformation. She who is the challenger on the way, she who is the initiator, she who is the herald of change.

I have lived upon the Earth many times. I have known many faces and many names. I have seen many different cultures rise and fall at the hand of the Divine or at their own hand. I have seen people live and die.

And it is of this darker side of life, it is of this cycle of death and rebirth that I have come to illustrate and speak of by gazing back along my past and looking at those people that I have been.

In the beginning, in the ancient land of Lemuria, I lived and was fortunate enough to be one of those firstborn from the mind of God to the realms of Earth. I knew life for the first time when it was still vibrant with the Creator's touch, when the colours were rich and strong and the animals were new to us and we were new to them, when the whole world sang with freshness.

I lived and grew to appreciate and value the potency of life, living for each second and each moment, living for the sunrise and the sunset, living for the silvery orb of the moon, for the touch of autumn and winter upon my skin. I lived to see the change of life that took place in this ancient isle the moment when God decided that we could no longer live as we did, in bodies that could not fully express the needs of our hearts. I lived to see the dark wings of the Angel of Death, as his feet touched the Earth and his hands touched the beating hearts of those who lived in order to still their beating and liberate them from life through death to life anew in the spiritual realms of light.

The Lemurians were encouraged to die, because their ectoplasmic forms could not sustain their growing minds and hearts and so death was introduced to man in order to encourage rebirth. The realms of spirit then were new, as fresh as Earth in its own way, and the process of beginning was a beginning in itself.

I still remember the times between my lives, the moments in the shining realms of glory and of light, where stunned and awe-struck we were ushered into halls forged from light, where our minds and hearts were filled with the comfort and the touch of God, in order that we might know that this was the very beginning of a sequence, a chain, a cycle of lives which we would know. It was then, in this very beginning time, that I became fascinated with the concept of change and death and, holding on to this fascination, desperate thoughts brought it into each of the lives that I lived from this point on.

And so again and again I tumbled to the Earth, living out lives of passion and glory, of heartache and pain, observing, recognising the powers of change and transformation and of death. And growing in understanding of why this darker shade of life was so necessary, so needed, so appropriate in the Divine's eyes.

Change, the Divine teaches us, is the only true constant in the universe, more powerful even than love itself. It is abundant, even at the level of the Divine. We cannot escape it, we cannot cheat it, we cannot hold it back. It is that that drives us forwards, that perpetually invokes us to be greater than that that we are.

I recognised and saw that change could become more powerful if it was recognised and celebrated, rather than feared or ignored, that if ceremony were used to celebrate and commemorate transition, the transition itself would be more poignant and more powerful. And so I conceived the need and the importance of initiation. I had also seen that those who desired to transform themselves too quickly, inappropriately, when they were not ready, had often fallen shortly after, when they had attempted to walk a path that was not meant for them. And so too, I came to realise and recognise the need for challenge upon the initiate's journey, to see if they had absorbed enough, as much as they needed to, in order to pass forwards, transcend and go beyond that that stood in their way.

As challenger, as tester, I came to be looked upon as a dark and shadowy force like death, when people, fearful of failure and of what lay beyond, could no longer see the purpose of my being and the reward of the goal. And so in lifetimes when I did not have a title or a form in which to take shape and issue my challenges, I was seen simply as the enemy, as the temptress, as the devil, as the demon, as the darkness that opposed the growth of life, when in truth I was the force that represented it and encouraged it rightfully to grow.

What would life be without death? We could not truly value it! What would light be without darkness? We would never truly recognise it for the wonder that it is! What would acclaim and success be without trial and challenge? It would have no meaning for us, it would have no worth! I, and my brothers and sisters who represent the same force and energy within the universe, am all these things, have been all these things to man in many ways, as needed and as necessary as air and water, as needed and as necessary as love.

It is the pattern of men to scout ahead, to investigate, to look, to see, to search, and it is the nature of women to hold back, to listen, to feel, to receive. Women therefore through their receptive capacity have always been inspired, guided or used by the Divine to challenge the societies in which they live, their husbands, their children, their men. They have moved forwards in different ways, and they have found their challenges too, in different ways, in internal ways, invisible and unknowable to man. Women, being closer to the Divine through their creative power, have always trodden an inner path whereas men have always needed more an external means to see their progression, to acknowledge their growth and strength. Women, through their attunement to the deep currents of the universe, and through this way in which they have been used, have therefore been interpreted as demons and vessels of darkness, whereas men considered themselves to be custodians of light.

When I was Morgaine, I was chief priestess of the worshippers of the Goddess, of the land known then as Albion, now as Britain. I had known the Goddess' power since the beginning of my earliest memories of life and also carried in my heart and mind the knowledge of my life in her care, hundreds of lifetimes before. Becoming the chief priestess of the land of Albion had been the greatest honour of my lives and it was something that I treasured and honoured and looked upon with the utmost seriousness, with the utmost intent.

When the druids came, our brothers who worshipped the sun as we worshipped the moon, and told us of the prophecies they had received of the coming patriarchal religion that was meant to usurp our motherly own, I was reluctant to see the truth within their words. Unlike these men who forged forwards so eager for the truth of the future, I preferred to stay behind, to hover in the present, to listen to the wisdom of the past.

I opened my soul and received confirmation of their truth but unable to so easily succumb to the Divine's law, felt that I was indebted to the memory of all the Goddess had done for me, to fight on her behalf, to champion this matriarchal presence, to be its champion and challenge the patriarchal energy that sought to usurp it and destroy it and replace it on the Earth.

My allegiance to the Goddess caused me to fight my own half brother, caused me to oppose him and all that he stood for and represented. And indeed once again playing the role of the challenger on the way, I stood between the future and the rising religion of man and fell before its mighty hand, giving it clear path to enter into the world.

I lost my life weaving a final enchantment to seal deep within the Earth the secrets and the magics of the matriarchal kingdom in order that one day, when the time was right, the true secret powers of the Goddess' magic would be revived by those who still held the knowledge inside their minds and hearts. For this time these secrets, these spells, these ancient enchantments would die with the queen of the world, would sink beneath the foot of the patriarchal God, so that he would not be enabled to use them to strengthen his own sword.

It is only now that they return, word by word, strand by strand, flowing into the hearts and minds and mouths of men and women who are all goddesses at heart, who seek to revive these powers in order to establish not supremacy but balance, for now even I see that balance is the only way to evolution. And now it is a different challenge that is issued mankind, the challenge of whether or not the patriarchal energy will bow down beneath the rising powers of the spiritually minded men and women of the Earth who seek no longer dogma and control, but liberation, freedom and the universality of the open mind.

And so in all the lives that I have lived, in Lemuria, in the temple of the Mother Divine in ancient Atlantis, in the temple of Isis in ancient Egypt, in the Babylonian temples of the Mother Goddess, in the ancient Australian outback where I slept and dreamt the truths of the universe, in icy Greenland when I praised Sedna, the goddess of the sea, in Ireland and in Scotland and in Albion herself, I have acknowledged and honoured and worshipped and represented the powers of change, the powers of challenge, the powers of death, the powers of transformation, and still do so now.

And it is with this knowledge, with this truth, with this power that I say:

Mankind of Earth, grow in your understanding, recognise the difference between evil and challenge, see that devotion and stubbornness and the narrowminded sometimes are vessels for the challenging powers of the universe that stand fast in order to see whether you have the power, the strength, the knowledge, the truth and the light to transcend the old and become the new, and that these obstacles are there for you to overcome, to test yourselves against, in order that in comparison you may see the power that you wield, the right that you have, the change that must be wrung out in order for the world to be birthed anew.

Do not despise the guardian of the door. Do not look too harshly upon the stern-faced oppressor, but know that once they were you and you were them, recognise their place in the grand scheme and pattern of life and honour them for the role they serve you with.

And for all of those sisters and brothers of mine who live still upon the Earth and who, by my side in lives gone by, worshipped the Mother Goddess in all her many forms and guises, to you I would say this:

The Goddess awakens from her sleep and rises. She stirs and her dreams come to an end. And risen from her grave she gathers strength in order that she may walk side by side, hand in hand with the powers of God, not suppressed, no longer in control but balanced and in peace, married and at harmony and at one, knowing love, knowing peace, knowing enlightenment and joy. The way forward is not to give, the way forward is not to receive. The way forward is to be both giving and receiving. The way forward is to be, and in your being to acknowledge the needs of all.

Peace then, children of light and life, I will wait for you and I will see you soon and although you may not recognise my face, you will recognise the taste of me. For I will visit you many times in life to see if you are ready to open the door and go beyond.

Peace then and love, brothers and sisters of the Goddess and the God.

Kwan Yin

My Life in Atlantis

I have come to speak of three lifetimes that I lived upon the Earth, one of which is that lifetime more widely known as Kwan Yin.

My story, however, begins in ancient Atlantis. The third incarnation that I had had found me born into the royal family of the element of water, in the earlier part of the Atlantean dynasty, when the magic of this fabled place was still strong.

The royal families of Atlantis were entrusted with maintaining the energy vibration of one of each of the seven elements of Atlantis. Later in Atlantean history, the two abstract elements of love and change would fall away altogether and the royal families that governed those powers would collapse, leaving only five. But in the beginning all seven existed, all seven royal families combining and maintaining their energies together in order to sustain global order and global peace.

The royal family of water was of course concerned with all the powers of the astral realms and dreams and the powers of the heart, the powers of the emotions. I was born as first princess to this family and therefore knew that one day it would fall to me to become Queen of the household and uphold the power of the sacred chalice that had been given to our royal ancestors by the Archangel Gabriel himself.

I was therefore schooled in all forms of emotional understanding and taught to develop the powers of my empathy to its greatest extremes. My mother, who had achieved an enormous amount of empathic sensitivity in her lifetime, guided me as to how I could open my heart in order to gently feel all the emotions which radiated from those who lived upon the island of Atlantis, without losing myself within the emotions and without allowing myself to be destroyed by the anger and the tiredness, and the bitterness and the pain.

Such an empathic feat has for a long time not been achieved upon the Earth by anyone. It takes great skill, great power and great personal awareness of identity to do such a thing.

My father, of course the king of the royal family of the element of water, was a strong man. He ruled his small kingdom with a stern hand, taught people how to strengthen their emotional resolve. He was largely responsible for guiding those Atlanteans who would journey into the outside world and possibly be confronted with people from other cultures and races and societies. He taught the Atlanteans how to become sensitive to these harsher emotions, how to protect themselves, how to use their empathic sensitivity in order to provide them with valuable guidance that they would need in their acts of diplomacy and spiritual teaching. He even taught them how to use projective empathy, known as Telempathy, in order to protect themselves from the danger of animals and also attacks that could be waged against them from those native peoples that they would encounter along the way.

I had a brother in this lifetime, a prince of the royal family who was tutored under my father's care. Of course we combined our spirits' energy in love every day. But the division between the masculine and feminine perception and expression of love was evident from my earliest moments of conscious thought and memory. It was the beginning of an emotional education that would span many, many lifetimes.

In the Atlantean age I was drawn to follow and worship the Goddess, the Mother Divine, and so attended the temple dedicated to her honouring. I would visit the temple and spend time there in contemplation, in meditation, and being taught by the priestesses how to utilise the full potential of my own feminine energy and power.

There was no need here for pomp or ceremony. Ours was a harmonious and loving relationship and we sat together in deep states of peace and love that transcended the structures of society, of age and wisdom and spiritual maturity. We were forged through our desire to unlock the mysteries of our own feminine strength and our desire and calling to worship the creative, nurturing, sensitive powers of the universe and the Divine.

In this lifetime I learned many things. I learned the value of being myself, of recognising my character, my personality, my individuality. And that if I centred myself within this awareness I could never be lost, even when I was attuning myself to a thousand hearts and minds. In this lifetime I learned the way in which men and women viewed the power of love differently. I learned ways of utilising emotional energy in a projective and aggressive way, in a receptive and informative way, in a healing way. And I recognised how love had an undeniable power, a power of unification, of binding.

Of course the household of water was strongly connected to the kingdom of love, which was one of the other abstract elements that was still honoured at that time. But the kingdom of love was more cosmic in its understandings and its practises, more concerned with universal things than those things that took place upon the Earth. And so our interaction was one that would not provide me with understanding until much later in my lifetimes when I would look back upon my memories of my times in that great palace and recognise and see the truth behind the words that were spoken to me then that I did not understand or value. You see, no memory is wasted in our evolution. Our higher self records them all and when we are granted the gift of remembrance, memories that meant nothing to us in the past often provide us with great insight and teaching in our future present.

When I became queen of the kingdom of water, I embraced my responsibilities with dignity and serious application. In time, I chose myself a king and married him. And we reigned for many hundreds of years, maintaining peace and love and order in Atlantis. I chose to leave my life just before the beginning of Atlantis' fall, before its autumn. In truth I was one of those who had received precognitive warning of what was to take place. And I embraced my death, not wanting to remain behind and see the beautiful city that I had lived inside for so long turned to dust.

In my lifetime, I reached out with my energies and through the magnifying lens of the Holy Grail chalice all around the world, to sample and taste and experience the emotions of many thousands of people. It was a beautiful experience, one that has shaped and tempered my soul for ever.

My Life in Egypt

The second lifetime that I would speak of is a lifetime that took place in ancient Egypt. In this incarnation, many hundreds of years after my death in ancient Atlantis, I returned to the Earth and found myself being raised in a temple dedicated to the goddess Isis.

This was a strange lifetime, an unusual experience in many ways. I had been entered into the temple by my parents who were wealthy members of the Egyptian society. They thought that it would be prestigious to have a daughter of theirs enrolled in such a prestigious temple, dedicated to such a profitable goddess who looks down upon those members who nurtured and sustained her worship with favourable and approving eyes. I had no choice and at first was resistant to my fate, realising later that this was indeed my destiny and therefore nothing to complain about.

It is rumoured that in some of the lifetimes led by those who will become ascended within a certain space of time, they have a vague foreknowing of what their future destiny holds in store for them. It is said that within the space of several hundred years of becoming raised to the point of ascension, there is a fore-echo, a foreshadow that ripples backwards through time and allows the Ascended Master or Lady Ascended Master to be aware of what is to come. Here in this lifetime we worshipped a Goddess who I now know to have been at that time a Lady Ascended Master herself. Indeed at the time of worship she had moved from the physical realm and consulted and guided her people from the realms of spirit, but was nevertheless no goddess but rather an ascended being of great knowledge and of great power. In worshipping Isis I felt and saw a resonance, a strange attunement, a strange likeness and similarity that enabled me to prepare myself for what lay ahead.

From that point on I knew in a strange, vague way

where my future lay and so prepared myself to aim for nothing other than ultimate awareness, than true spiritual enlightenment and truth.

In this lifetime, what appealed to me the most about my position within the temple was my duty in providing Isis with awareness of her people's love. It had fallen to me to find the words and offer the libations that would carry into Isis' attention our prayers, our dedication and our awareness. Unlike those before me, I did not rehearse my words. Unlike those before me I did not seek the plumpest, fattest animal to slay, but rather offered flowers and dreams, wishes and the laughter of children, music and dancing, poetry and beautiful pieces of art.

At first the alternate nature of my worshipping was looked upon as dangerously hazardous, but in time when Isis favoured our temple with divine manifestations, with miracles and healing cures, with the powerful presence of her energy and love, it was seen that all along, all previous priestesses had sacrificed wrongly, had given to Isis those things that she did not favour, that she did not want. And that my inspired words that sprang from the heart were more powerful than lines of poetry rehearsed and rehearsed and memorised, offered coldly, like old food. And so rather than rising in the ranks of the priestesses, I stayed for that lifetime in this role, presented with the constant challenge of finding new ways to give thanks and offer our love, rising to the challenge ever further, ever more and providing my temple with great feeling, and teaching the followers of Isis what truly is appreciated by the gods and by ourselves. Not slaughtered animals or recited prayers but genuine expressions of care and honour.

My Life as Kwan Yin

And it is the word "honour" that takes me to the third and final life that I would speak of, a lifetime in which I lived upon the Earth as Kwan Yin and found ascension through the final experiences of my last physical life.

In this lifetime I was born daughter to an emperor, fulfilling and completing the pattern of my life which had in majority been that of entering into a family of high standing and society, rich and capable of much.

In this life, with nothing other to do than idle away my time, I became fascinated by those people who had something that I did not: the poor. For they had no money and no clothes, ill health, no meaning. They had no inheritance, no guardians, no protectors, no carriages, no jewels, no palaces to live in. They had all these things that I did not possess. They had all these things that I thought I could never understand. And so in the beginning, my excursions into the lands of the poor were either done without my father's wishes or done behind his back. But in time, after he had discovered me time and time again visiting these people and these places with my guard, he gave me license to go forth and speak with them.

From here on I would while away my hours in the dirt by these people's sides, talking and listening to their aches and pains. I would bring food and herbs and ointments and creams. I would bring money and clothes and assistance to the needy and the poor. More and more I demanded from my father's coffers those jewels and gems, those moneys that I had never been interested in. And although my father at first resisted my desires and my intentions, later he realised that I was indeed an ambassador not only for spiritual good but also for his popularity as emperor and king. Although I was not fully content being allowed to perform these duties as long as it fell in accordance with my father's desires to be seen as a benevolent and loving saviour of mankind, I realised that when there was a storm, indeed any shelter would do to weather the elements until the storm had passed. And so as much as my father used me, I used him and continued with my work, loving those people who I could touch.

I never became Empress, but was presented at an early age with an opportunity to ascend into the realms of light. The opportunity was given because of the development of my heart, because I had become heart-centred in nature and because I had recognised my divinity through my giving, through my generosity, through my expressions of love.

And so I climbed the stairs of light that led to the great white peace. But near to the point of entering into the radiance of collected unity, I gazed down upon the Earth and saw all those that I had not touched, hundreds, thousands, millions of people who had never heard my name, who had never benefited from my riches, who had never benefited from my peace. And so I returned. I was given 200 years in order to complete my task before I would have no other option than to enter into the light that would be by that time my unavoidable destiny.

My return was looked upon as a miracle by my father who thought that I was dying, rather than making a transition into the other planes of light. Upon my return my father was so grateful for my salvation that he said that he would give anything to the gods in thanks for what they had done. I told him that I carried a message from them, that they had asked me to beg of him to build a temple on their behalf that I would run.

The temple in time became dedicated to my presence and my power on Earth as it became increasingly apparent that my return had changed me somewhat. My majesty was now part of miracle and magic as much as it was of good humour and good heart, and people came to be healed and cured. I began to teach and train priests and priestesses, not of me, but of the power of compassion that I had come to represent. I taught them how to manifest on a physical level, from the source of their heart, a flame of compassion that could be seen and felt by all. The pearl-white flame, the flame of alabaster light, could be taken out into the world and used to educate mankind as to the benefits of love. My priests and my priestesses would heal and cleanse and feed and bless and teach my truths to the poor and the rich alike. And so I remained upon the Earth, growing day by day in consciousness and spirituality, until indeed to many I was seen as a goddess.

And then I recognised and saw the link that joined my final existence there on Earth to the first incarnations I had ever had. I recognised that love was more than loving one, than loving two or a hundred people, as I saw them in my days. I recognised that true love was loving all things born from God: truth and lie, reality and illusion, darkness and light. I realised that love transcended the boundaries between the poor and rich and that love transcended the boundaries of good and evil, too. And for the first time I remembered and recognised the words that had been spoken to me in the royal kingdom of love, governed by the archangel Hanael in ancient Atlantis, that love was the binding force, the beginning and the end, the creation and the destruction of all things, that it could be found in the darkest night and the brightest sun. That, because God had created life with the primary intention of a loving father, of a loving mother, of a loving divine creator, love permeated all things.

I recognised too, at this stage in my evolution, who Isis was and how she must have felt, standing before her subjects, hailed as a goddess, simply because she had risen to a point beyond the imagination of any human being, a point that they could not begin to comprehend as possible inside their lives. I stood on the tip of a dragon's nose and gazed down at the Earth, gazed down at my people, gazed down at my temples as they had spread throughout the world. And I recognised how far man had come and how far man had yet to go.

And so, this is my message to you: What prevents you from recognising the power of love inside your hearts, the power of love that permeates your reality, the need for love and your capacity to give it, is your misplaced honour and your misplaced pride. My people, to whom I administered for hundreds of years upon the Earth, were steeped with an honour that was as strong as a brick wall. An honour that prevented them from saying "Help! I need, I want, I desire, I deserve." A pride that prevented them from saying: "I can give, I will help, I will supply uncondi-tionally, without expectation of response."

Some people say that poor men have nothing to give but this is not true. For all of us are born with an abundance of love and we have the choice as to who and how we will show it and give it. And in truth this is the greatest gift. It is a gift more precious than air or water or food. It is a substance that we need in order to survive, and it is a substance that we all search for throughout life. Go forth then and take this truth with you. Let it open your heart and in-spire you to do good in the Divine's name.

Djwal Khul

Change and the Flow of Life

It is written by some that I am the youngest of the Ascended Masters at this moment in time, that I, Djwal Khul, am new to the realms of light and limit-lessness, to the realms of peace and tranquillity, to the realms of ascension and Shambhala. But this in essence is not true, for I lived in Shambhala on Earth. Being ascended does not mean being beyond the body, being beyond the world, existing as a bodiless entity, as a floating patch of surrealist light. It simply means existing in a state of consciousness that enables one to see that reality is an illusion and that the only truths are love and change.

Being ascended is recognising one's own divinity as the divinity of the Divine, acknowledging and feeling the resonance that exists between oneself and God and therefore becoming God-realised on Earth, enlightened and ascended in all ways. One therefore can be ascended whilst remaining inside the physical form and upon the physical Earth. Connected to the Divine and to the Ascended Master collective, it is still possible to live a mortal life.

Of course, one's perception of reality is distinctly altered by one's capability to perceive the limitlessness of the divine source that shines brightly in all things. No longer does the fascination exist of bird and flower and tree and sky, but rather the internal light that illuminates each thing with living presence and living life. And this tends to place the ascended being in a state of bliss, in a state of altered consciousness that can make them unapproachable, uncommunicative, distant and full of riddles, paradoxes and conundrums.

It is difficult to communicate what you can perceive when others cannot even begin to imagine what you see. And so all the words that you might muster to describe the feelings in your heart fall from your mouth like the ravings of a lunatic, obsessed by things that most would dismiss as obvious and insignificant.

My last life upon the Earth was spent in majority as an incarnate ascended being. I had no great purpose like those masters that had preceded me, like Jesus or Saint Germain. My task was a self-fulfilling one; to become enlightened and to simply be, to shine and to show that if we lived our life through our beliefs we would reach that point that we had all hankered for, the promised Shambhalic state that is the goal of every Tibetan priest.

One message I did try to impart. It was concerning the need and importance of sharing. And I spoke of it many, many times repeating word for word a concisely formed parable that I felt surely could not be misinterpreted even by the most blinded mind, the deafest ear. I spoke of how there was need for enlightenment to be given freely, for enlightenment not to be looked upon through the framework of social structure or form, but that all truths must be made available and apparent to those who lived. And that if our secret truths were not passed on, then we would surely pay the price for sitting on this treasure-chest of God's wisdom, benefiting from the riches contained within ourselves and presuming to be so knowledgeable as to decide who else should benefit from the gift that God gave, in our care, to all.

But still they did not see. And knowing that free will is a precious thing I did not attempt to convert through gesture, through miracle or manifestation, but rather guide through inspiration and story-telling, which was more my way. Of course part of my truth was heard and part of the teaching was done. But in majority all was avoided. And my brothers paid the price for the selfishness of their truth.

Our teachings were and are still good. They contain the keys to many mysteries of the universe. Our time is not yet over. We have not been destroyed because of the error of our ways or by the harsh aggressor that seeks to swat and destroy what it fears and does not understand. There is still much for our kind to do and say, many people who will be saved and lifted to the light by our words and our wisdom and truths, and it is of two of these that I would speak in connection with my lives, in connection with my life as Djwal Khul.

Reincarnation is a testament to impermanence, to the law and power of constant change and evolution. It is true to say that nothing lasts forever, not even love, which is a power still bound by the law of change, which is greater than love is. Change and transformation are more powerful than God, for God is bound to change and cannot resist its internal motivation to continue to grow and evolve. Love, no matter how strong, no matter how passionate and powerful, will not last for ever in the same shape and form but will shift and change and move, bound by this cosmic law, as all things are.

I have walked the Earth, maybe not as many times as others have, but I have seen the rise and fall of civilisations. I have seen the destruction of the dreams of man, as I have seen the realisation of mankind's fantasy, mankind's wildest imagining realised on Earth. I have seen things fashioned and formed and raised from the earth, things that mankind has said, time and time again, would not be destroyed by the passing of the years; sometimes things un-solid like belief and words of truth, like memory and history, that one by one have all fallen to change. Buildings age and decay and crumble and fall or are swept away by technological advances. History is lost with the dying of a generation or destruction of text, things are forgotten, whispers transform a truth into an untruth in a historical blinking of an eye. Legends and heroes and virtues and morals fall out of favour and out of fashion in the public's eye and they are gone, never to be resurrected, never to be retrieved from the fires of transition, from the flames of alchemical change.

Impermanence rules and once we acknowledge it, once we release our precious grip on those things that cannot be forever, then we can learn to enjoy them in the eternal, infinite present moment when they are still new and favoured and young and real. This is how the Tibetans have lived their lives and this is how I have lived out the incarnations of my spirit; by moving through each precious moment and sucking it dry of life, by not holding on to those things that I cannot possess – my memories, my friends, my beliefs, even the very nature of my being, but instead, by welcoming change as it approaches me daily, by embracing the death of my old self and embracing the birth of my newness. Once we release the tightness of our grip, life passes through us as if we are the phantom, as if we are the ghost, and no longer bounces off our chest.

The second thing that I would speak of is the mandala, a shape and pattern that reflects the laws and light of life. A pattern, a shape, a form, spun within a circle, is a mandala no matter what ingredients combine to form the shape that can be seen. We live in a spiral which can be perceived from the topmost point looking down as a circle of life, stacked higher and higher upon itself. The movement of our spirit from era to era, from period to period, from history to history, from life to life, creates a woven pattern of luminescence that forges a mandala dyed with the colour or our experiences for all in the universe to see. This becomes our map, our masterpiece, a perpetually building work of art that details all the experiences of our existences. It becomes a more and more complex, more and more finely detailed mandala work of art, breathtaking in its beauty, awe inspiring in its intricacy, overwhelming, staggering in its truth.

When a mandala is created, fashioned from grains of coloured sand, its completion may take many weeks, many months, even years. When it is completed it is adored and then, after a short time, it is destroyed. This is done to celebrate the impermanence of life. When the mandala of the soul is completed and finally fashioned, it is looked upon and it is adored. But the higher soul-self recognises that the answer behind each lifetime lived, each experience gained, each thought, each pain, is that reality and everything learned inside it is a lie. And that all that matters is that the lifetimes that we have journeyed through have taught us how to see the original answer to the original question that existed in our hearts in the very first lifetime that we ever lived. It is like the child who does not value the gift of his parents, who journeys through life and finally becomes a parent himself, only to recognise the value of his parents' love for him. It is like the fool in the Tarot who journeys out into the world, his head full of seeking the mysteries of the universe, only to discover at the end of his arduous trek that all the answers to all the questions exist not outside of himself but within. They were always there for the looking, if only he had stopped and gazed inside himself.

And so the mandala of the soul, intricate and beautiful, is destroyed and the light that burns in the core and centre of its being radiates out and rises to return to God. Nothing is wasted; the effort of creating the mandala, the journey, the experience, the emotions, are as vital as the light. They are absorbed by the Divine in order to enrich it and as we are part of it, they enrich us too. But the light is the core, the light is the quintessence, the light is the beginning and the end.

In closing then I would say this: I have lived many lifetimes. I have seen and known much pain and anguish, I have seen and known much fear. The answer is living a life of peace, is finding moments in order to enter into the stillness of serenity, through whatever means. For it is these spaces that give us the strength to continue the journey, to reflect upon the mandala of our creation and to go on.

It does not matter if people do not understand the wisdom of your words or the wisdom of mine. It only matters that we live our truth and find in it peace. And by living the example of our beliefs, our peace and our truth, shine the brightness of our being and ignite those minds that are ready to see.

May serenity protect you. May peace be at your door. May stillness surround you and chaos harm you never more.

Serapis Bey

My Life as an Incarnate Angel

Mine is an unusual tale. Unusual because unlike those others who have risen into the realms of the ascended state, I was not born from the mind of God. My origin is the heart of the Divine, a continuum, a consciousness known as the Angelic Collective, a stream of life born before creation in order to aid in creation; extensions of God's will, angels, mediums through which the Divine would manifest his desires, create his universe and maintain the forces of existence that you have now come to accept as the norm.

In the beginning when mankind was fresh upon the Earth, angels walked side by side with man and taught them practical things as well as spiritual truths, but as the vibrations fell, mankind became distanced from these extensions of God, losing sight of them and only a treasured few were still capable of seeing and hearing what the angels had to give and say. The Divine, concerned that his people would stray without being enabled to access his wisdom through his divine messengers of grace, made it possible for some angels to cross over the streams of existence and incarnate into the fleshy bodies of man. I was one of those first few angels to transcend the barrier, the veil of the streams of existence and enter into physical life, to incarnate upon the Earth.

In the beginning, things concerning limitation and physicality were unknown to God and angels alike. We had no understanding of what it would be like to be physical. We had no understanding of how it would affect us, of how it would make us feel. Angels are beings of love, we perceive everything through the heart, we are non-judgemental and non-critical in nature, as God is, and therefore love all things. We are beings of energy, neither male nor female in true nature. We have no shape or form, we have no colour. We are simply consciousness with speciality and frequency, but limitless nonetheless.

It is usual for an angel's apparel to be dictated by those who perceive them or contact them. But now we were issued with the capacity to choose which shape and form we would adopt, not for a temporary moment in time but for a lengthier period, for the period of a life. And unknowing we chose without contemplation and entered willingly into a world that was alien and strange to us. As extensions of the Divine's will, we have no free will of our own. We have limited consciousness and capacity to grow and learn and understand, but what God desires is what we do. We cannot resist. We do not desire to. We simply enact the will of the Divine, whether we are in the continuum of the angels or on Earth, and although this relieves us from karma and enables us to sail through life worry-free, it has caused great consternation in the consciousness of those who have awoken to the true nature of their being. Incarnate, the immediate emotions that beset those who had crossed the streams were ones of frustration and fear, intense loneliness at being disconnected consciously from the continuum where we had always existed, as one, in a world where people did not love us as much as we loved them, where we were more sensitive to the emotions of all things than man, in a world where we were trapped inside a physical body that would not surrender to our will as finely as our energetic state would. We found ourselves overwhelmed by the heaviness of your world. We adopted illusions, masks, in order to make ourselves seem more real; a chakra-system, a meridian-system, a consciousness and a subconscious, a shadow self, an anima and an animus and an inner child. We adopted issues and complexes, problems and difficult impediments in order to blend in more truthfully with our surroundings, absorbing the information from our family and our friends. Many of us disguised ourselves so well that we lost sight of who we truly were, and believed our own illusions, thinking that we were simply ineffectual men and women on Earth.

We are not logical or linear beings and therefore science and mathematics and geometry eluded us. Only art and expression were natural to the state of our intrinsic beings. At night, when we would sleep, we would journey far from the physical form and replenish and nurture ourselves by returning to the continuum for lengthy periods of time. In the mornings when we would awaken, we would be dazed and confused, unfocussed and muddled in our minds. In truth, the more lifetimes that incarnate angels lead upon the Earth, the more they learn to cope with these intrinsic problems, and depending upon the origin of their source, whether they are simply angelic or an aspect of one of the divine archangels, provides them with a capacity to understand certain things better than other angels whose frequency is more akin to other disciplines on Earth. But still incarnate life is harsh for beings made of light, as impressionable as clay, as loving as God, beings who are more make-believe than truth, who live on faith and need the faith of others to sustain their life on Earth.

Each incarnate angel has an anchor, someone who believes in them, someone who is mortal, someone who was born from the mind of God. And without these anchors our essence will begin to slip itself free of the bonds of physical life and we will appear to die in your realm. We therefore try to maintain the belief of at least one person here on Earth or to sustain ourself with our own belief for limited periods of time. We enact God's will and unfold God's plan, kept invisible by the nature of our being and yet attracting many to our light. We are instructed to guide only, not to teach, not to change the mind, not to impose our power on the free will of mortals. And therefore we can never lead, we can never be seen to be instrumental in any great change of consciousness. It must always be done in an invisible way.

When I lived upon the Earth, I lived many times in cultures unrecorded and forgotten. I influenced the sway of thought through my actions, through my beliefs, sometimes unconscious of what I did and sometimes conscious of my own truth.

I lived towards the end of the Atlantean period and here tried to gently turn the Atlanteans' attention back towards the mystical ways of life. I tried with others to show the scientists of Atlantis the errors of their ways. I tried to encourage them to talk to God rather than to fight him. In other cultures and civilisations I encouraged them to try to see the underlying spiritual light that bound all religions together. I tried to encourage my fellow man not to war with each other, but to acknowledge their mutual common ground of connection in order that peace could will-out upon the Earth.

In Egypt, my most famous life, the lifetime from whence I take my present name, I lived in order to teach of the oneness of the Divine. By this time many cultures and civilisations had begun to worship variations of the truth, calling the same pure light down from heaven but giving it new names and shapes to wear. These gods and goddesses were archetypes born from man's need to crystallise and pigeonhole each frequency, each specification, each quality of God into a separate form.

In Egypt, I tried to guide people back to the perception of one Divine, enabling them to acknowledge and see that all archetypes, that all gods, were fractures of the same light, were vessels through which the one pure light shone. I was successful for some time. But after my death, my truth was obscured and those who preached the words that I had brought to Earth said that the God that I spoke of was more powerful than the rest, rather than being the source from which they came. Misinterpretation has taken the purest truth and transformed it into the blackest lie.

Mankind has a habit of not truly listening to what others have to say and to repeating or speaking out of turn. This is what occurred in my time; this is what occurred in Jesus' time; this is what has occurred throughout many lives, throughout many attempts by wise and spiritual people to unite the world through truth.

Incarnate angels still exist upon the Earth today, invisible to the human eye as their ethereal brothers are. They disguise themselves in suits of bone and blood. They do not draw attention to the origin of their being, but for those who are aware they are easy to see. There is a light within their eyes, a grace within their carriage, a lightness and openness in their heart, a special quality. They are beings with the potential for great love, who are always a little lost, a little wounded, a little sad. They are people with great, generous and charitable natures who make people feel special, or magical or loved.

In my life upon the Earth, I grew with each experience that I had. Watching man and becoming more aware of the differences of my soul to him, I recognised very soon that I was not from the same source. Believing this I perceived man from an even farther distance and saw how much pain could be avoided, if man would only flow and accept the grace of God.

For man resists the flow of his own destiny. And man resists the guidance of his own divine source. Man thinks too much and listens to his heart too little and bound by this trap is caught in difficulties of his own creating. The Divine is abundant, a source of light and love and hope, a being who gives infinitely of his bounty. This bounty will replenish, it has the power to transform, to sustain, to provide us with all that we need. All that we have to do is ask God for those things that we require and open our eyes and ears to achieving the possibility of our needs. All that we have to do is open ourself to flow and grace and abiding by this simple, silent truth, sail on. The breath of God propels us and the hand of God supports us and our faith in the Divine and in ourself protects us, too. These things are my teachings. These things are my words. Who better to talk of faith but an angel?

My observations of the world and the people inside it caused me to reach a point of ascension within one of the lives that I lived upon the Earth. I became enlightened and self-realised and so rose to the higher spiritual planes unsure of where I would journey to, of what I would become. The first angel to reach this dizzy height through physical incarnation, I was allowed to become the bridge between the continuum of angelic beings and the Ascended Master collective. And this is where I remain to this day, joining the two together with my energy and my love and my understanding and presence and power.

I gaze down upon the Earth and overshadow those paths of people who have worked with angels before. With the old Atlanteans reborn and the Essenes and all those people who have lived in mystical, magical orders where they have called upon our names and power. And to all those too who are incarnate angels upon the Earth, I send and shower my living light, in order that I may guide them, in order that I may offer them ease and understanding concerning the deep pain that they experience now. Emotions are a powerful thing and those angels and those humans who are open and sensitive to them will feel such pain at this time in your Earth as I have never known in my lifetimes there.

I look down upon them with empathic eyes and offer you all my strength and love. My lives then were uneventful in nature of their action but were more packed with opportunities for observation and means whereby I could utilise what I had seen to act in such a way as to inspire new direction of movement and of thought. As a being who a long time ago was unaccustomed to speech, I am well aware of the power of example and of being and of doing. And of how this itself can say more than a thousand words, can say more than a million sentences.

Go forth then and flow and be in grace. Live in accordance with your spiritual beliefs, teach through the examples of your being and open your eyes for the angels who may cross your paths. With angelic blessings I leave you with those thoughts and take my leave.

Heart-felt thanks and blessings go to Carole Humber who did such a valiant and loving job in checking the channelled readings to the transcription. Without her hard work this book would never have found its way into the English word with such precision and beauty (which I know the Masters appreciate so greatly).

A special thanks has to go to the Masters themselves for sharing their stories in such an ingenious way and to the "Spirit of the Merlin", my own spiritual Master, for his continued guidance and teachings on my journey.

All praise to the teachers and blessed be the great Goddess and God of the old and ancient ways.

ABOUT THE AUTHOR

(BY THE AUTHOR)

Edwin Courtenay is a 33 year old practising non-traditional solitary witch living in South Yorkshire, England with his dog and familiar Rune. Clairvoyant as a child and mediumistic since his early teens he is a spiritual guide, healer and teacher, working internationally to empower people by guiding them to connect with the Divine inside and outside of themselves. He does not consider himself a vastly spiritual person (as anyone who gets to know him will soon attest to), having a liking for violent movies and junk food! But rather sees himself as fortunate to have retained abilities that give him in this life rather a head start on most people. His teaching skill he puts down more to his neurotic nature than vast intellect and his popularity to the fact that he has difficulty saying no! He teaches on a variety of spiritual topics and is author of *The Ascended Masters' Book of Ritual and Prayer*, brought out his first professional meditation CD last year with Rachael Kelly called Angel Kiss and has recently shot his first spiritual lecture video. This year he has high hopes of bringing out a range of mugs and T shirts! He gives regular reading consultations at the College of Psychic Studies in London as well as working up and down the U.K. and overseas. For more information on Edwin's itinerary please log on to:

www.bluestarofwonder.com.

BY THE SAME AUTHOR

Most of us would like to change in some way but don't know what to do about it. This book contains very practical rituals that we can carry out, focusing the power of our inner divinity to set in motion the changes we would like to see.

Thirteen Ascended Masters (among them Saint Germain, Mother Mary, Jesus and Kwan Yin) provide us with simple rituals to improve various aspects of our lives. These rituals will also strengthen our connection with the Source and awaken our dormant powers. The Ascneded Mastes reach out their hands full of love and want to give us a glimpse of the speldor of the Divine. This book helps us to find the way back.

> „A remarkable little gem of a book. Every word is measured and contributes to a seamless, elegant conception with passages of serene and universal application. An extraordinary distillation of spiritual teaching."
>
> Colourama Magazine

128 pages, paperback, 13 x 20,9 cm, ISBN 3-929345-08-0

The Prince of the Stars

The Greening of
World Trade Issues

The Greening of World Trade Issues

Edited by
Kym Anderson and Richard Blackhurst

HARVESTER
WHEATSHEAF

New York   London   Toronto   Sydney   Tokyo   Singapore

First published 1992 by
Harvester Wheatsheaf,
66 Wood Lane End, Hemel Hempstead,
Hertfordshire, HP2 4RG
A division of
Simon & Schuster International Group

Typeset in 10/12 pt Times
by MCS Limited, Salisbury

Printed and bound in Great Britain by
BPCC Wheatons Ltd, Exeter

British Library Cataloguing in Publication Data

The greening of world trade issues.
  I. Anderson, Kym II. Blackhurst, Richard
333.7

  ISBN 0-7450-1174-8
  ISBN 0-7450-1175-6 pbk

2   3   4   95 94 93

Contents

Figures

Part 4

Tables

Part 4

Contributors

Kym Anderson is with the Economic Research Division of the GATT Secretariat in Geneva, on leave from his position as Professor of Economics at the University of Adelaide in Australia, where he was Director of the Centre for International Economic Studies. He has written extensively in the areas of agricultural, development and international economics. Recent books include *The Political Economy of Agricultural Protection* with Yujiro Hayami, *Changing Comparative Advantages in China*, and *Disarray in World Food Markets* with Rod Tyers, plus an edited volume on *New Silk Roads: East Asia and World Textile Markets*.

Richard Blackhurst is Director of the Economic Research Division of the GATT Secretariat and Professeur Associé at the Institut Universitaire de Hautes Études Internationales in Geneva. His research interests embrace numerous aspects of trade policy in a growing and interdependent world. Among his publications are several GATT Studies in International Trade including *Trade Liberalization, Protectionism and Interdependence* and *Adjustment, Trade and Growth in Developed and Developing Countries*, both with Nicolas Marian and Jan Tumlir.

Alice Enders is with the Economic Research Division of the GATT Secretariat in Geneva. Her research interests include strategic aspects of international trade policy, an area in which she has published in journals, as well as the economics of problems posed by international cooperation.

Arye L. Hillman is Professor of Economics and Director of the Economics Research Institute at Bar-Ilan University in Israel. He has written extensively in academic journals on the theory of international trade and trade policy. As well, he recently authored a book on *The Political Economy of Protection* and edited a volume on *Markets and Politicians*, and is currently editing with B. Milanovic a set of essays on *Socialist Economies in Transition*.

Bernard Hoekman is with the Economic Research Division of the GATT Secretariat in Geneva. His areas of interest centre on the theory and practice of commercial policy, multilateral trade negotiations, and issues relating to international transactions in services. He has contributed numerous articles to conference volumes and academic journals in these and related areas.

Michael Leidy is with the Economic Research Division of the GATT Secretariat in Geneva, on leave from the Department of Economics at the University of Arizona in the United States. His research has focused, among other things, on the political economy of trade policy and firm behaviour under alternative commercial policies. He has published papers in numerous books and academic journals on these topics.

Peter J. Lloyd is Professor and Dean of Economics and Commerce at the University of Melbourne, Australia. He is a microeconomist with a special interest in the economics of international trade and trade policy. In addition to publishing extensively in academic journals he has written a book on *Non-tariff Distortions to Australian Trade*, co-authored with Herbert Grubel a book on *Intra-Industry Trade*, and edited a volume on *The Economics of the Mineral Sector*.

John Piggott is Professor of Economics at the University of New South Wales in Sydney, Australia. His research interests have centred around applications of general equilibrium modelling to trade and public policy issues. As well as his numerous contributions to academic journals he has written a book with John Whalley on *UK Tax-Subsidy Policy and Applied General Equilibrium Analysis*, and edited a volume of essays on *Applied General Equilibrium*, also with John Whalley.

Amelia Porges is Counsellor for Legal Affairs at the GATT Secretariat in Geneva. Her publications have focused on Japanese trade, GATT and trade law, and trade in legal services. She has been active since 1978 in trade law and policy, chiefly in GATT dispute settlement and negotiation of bilateral and multilateral trade agreements, including the Montreal Protocol negotiations. In 1988–90 she was a Visiting Fellow at the Institute for International Economics in Washington, D.C.

Michael Rauscher has a joint appointment with the Economics Department of the University of Kiel and the Kiel Institute of World

Economics in Germany. His recent publications include a monograph on *OPEC and the Price of Petroleum* and several journal articles in the fields of trade theory and environmental and resource economics.

Richard H. Snape is Professor of Economics in the Department of Economics at Monash University in Melbourne, Australia. He has written extensively on a wide variety of trade policy issues including a report on whether Australia should seek a trade agreement with the United States. As well as being the author of *International Trade and the Australian Economy*, he has edited a volume of *Studies in International Economics* (with Ian McDougall) and *Issues in World Trade Policy*, and has spent periods as editor of *The World Bank Economic Review, The World Bank Research Observer* and (with Peter Lloyd) *The Economic Record*.

Arvind Subramanian is an economist with the Policy Affairs Division of the GATT Secretariat in Geneva. His journal articles include papers on the international economics of intellectual property protection and on the legal, institutional and political economy aspects of the recent intellectual property negotiations.

Heinrich W. Ursprung is on the economics faculty at the University of Konstanz in Germany. He is author of numerous journal articles on the political economy of trade policy, several of them jointly with Arye Hillman.

John Whalley is Professor of Economics and Director of the Centre for the Study of International Economic Relations at the University of Western Ontario in Canada, and co-editor of the trade policy journal *The World Economy*. In addition to many journal articles on trade policy and general equilibrium analysis he has published numerous books including *Trade Liberalization Among Major World Trading Areas* and a volume edited with T. N. Srinivasan on *General Equilibrium Trade Policy Modelling*. He has recently coordinated a Ford Foundation project on Developing Countries and the Uruguay Round.

Randall Wigle is Professor of Economics at Wilfrid Laurier University in Waterloo, Canada. His research interests and publications include various applications of general equilibrium modelling with a special focus on multilateral and bilateral trade policy issues and trade and the environment.

L. Alan Winters is Professor and Head of the Department of Economics at the University of Birmingham in England and Co-Director of the international trade program at the London-based Centre for Economic Policy Research. He has published widely in applied areas of econometrics and trade policy, is author of the textbook *International Economics* and has edited a number of conference proceedings volumes for the CEPR including *European Integration, Primary Commodity Prices: Economic Models and Policy,* and *New Issues in the Uruguay Round.*

Preface

This volume arose out of papers prepared as background material for the special topic – trade and the environment – in the GATT Secretariat's annual report, *International Trade 1990-91*. The papers were initially discussed at a workshop in Geneva in June 1991, before being revised substantially for publication.

The editors and contributors are grateful to all the workshop participants (including Carlos Primo Braga, Chin-Seung Chung, Ronald Findlay, Jaime de Melo, Patrick Messerlin and Suthad Setboonsarng) whose constructive comments before and during the June workshop facilitated the revision process; to John Black and Sherry Stephenson for their scrupulous copy-editing of the manuscript; to Lidia Silvetti, Sinéad Deevy and Aishah Collautti who not only managed with great care all the administrative details of the project but also provided superb secretarial services under tight deadlines; and to Peter Johns of Harvester-Wheatsheaf for making rapid publication of the volume possible.

The contributors also wish to acknowledge with thanks the support of their employing institutions, without implicating them of course. Several authors were temporarily visiting other institutions during their involvement in the project and would like to express thanks to them as well, including Peter Lloyd (OECD Development Centre), John Piggott (University of Konstanz), Richard Snape (Graduate Institute of International Studies, Geneva), Heinrich Ursprung (Bar-Ilan University) and John Whalley (Institute for International Economics, Washington, D.C.).

The opinions expressed in the volume are the responsibility of the authors alone, and in particular are in no way intended to represent the views of the GATT Secretariat or GATT contracting parties.

Geneva   *Kym Anderson and*
July 1991   *Richard Blackhurst*

Abbreviations

CFC	Chlorofluorocarbon
CITES	Convention for International Trade in Endangered Species
EC	European Community
GATT	General Agreement on Tariffs and Trade
GDP	Gross domestic product
GHG	Greenhouse gases
OECD	Organisation for Economic Cooperation and Development
PD	Prisoners' dilemma
PPP	Polluter pays principle
PSE	Producer subsidy equivalent
VER	Voluntary export restraint
VPP	Victim pays principle

PART 1

Overview and conclusions

1

Trade, the environment and public policy

Kym Anderson and Richard Blackhurst

1.1 Overview of the issues[1]

The first wave of widespread public concern with the degradation of the natural environment, in the late 1960s/early 1970s, focused mainly on national and regional problems associated with industrial pollution in the advanced economies. Some trade/foreign direct investment policy issues arose at that time, but they were confined mostly to the concern of industrialists and their workers in rich countries that the imposition of strict pollution standards would lower their international competitiveness, for which they sought to be compensated by subsidies or import protection.[2]

Following the lull brought on by the economic disorders of the 1973–82 period – double digit inflation and recession in the industrial countries and two world oil price shocks – there has been a second wave of public interest in environmental issues. This new wave is much more intense and more widespread in several dimensions. Ozone depletion and global warming have emerged as major pollution issues, and the primary and service sectors are coming under as much scrutiny by environmentalists as the manufacturing sector. Issues in which personal values play an important role, such as species diversity and animal rights, also are increasingly becoming the subject of international debate and sources of friction between countries.

At the same time as the list of environmental issues has grown, it has taken on more of a global orientation. This internationalization results in part from the fact that many of the new issues have transborder features, involving either the physical spillover of pollutants or what might be called psychological spillovers, as in the case of concern over species extinction or animal rights. Continued economic growth and industrialization outside the OECD area also have internationalized environmental issues, because they have brought many developing countries and centrally planned

3

economies into the category of important contributors to environmental problems and solutions. Another element is the ongoing integration of the world economy. As people in different countries sense they are living closer together, they become increasingly sensitive to one another's behaviour, including in the environmental area.

The recently intensified public concern with environmental degradation and its effects on public health and safety is unlikely to be temporary. One reason is that, even though uncertainties remain, the scientific basis for many of the concerns is more solid now than was the case twenty years ago. Another is that the world's population has increased by $1\frac{1}{2}$ billion since 1970 (an increase of more than 40 per cent), the annual production of goods and services has nearly doubled, and average per capita income in the world has increased about 40 per cent. These increases – which show very few signs of slowing down – are adding substantially to the demand for the goods and services provided by the natural environment, which include raw materials for producing energy and other primary products, human health services (clean air, potable water, filtered sunlight, natural foods and medicines), aesthetic and recreational services (such as visiting or even just knowing of the existence of unspoilt wilderness areas), and the capacity to absorb wastes.

Many environmental problems can be traced to the absence of markets for most of nature's services. Markets have not developed because of disputed, ambiguous or non-existent property rights or because of the high cost of enforcing those rights. The air we breathe, the ozone layer, the oceans, most lakes and rivers and large tracts of forest are not privately owned. Without the assignment and enforcement of private property rights or some other form of government intervention, such resources are vulnerable to degradation in a number of ways. In the case of emissions and waste disposal, for example, individuals are unlikely to take into account fully the impact of their use of nature's resources on the rest of the population. Other issues, such as the protection of endangered species, raise a different question about property rights: how to manage certain 'assets' which may be owned (by a nation state if not by individuals) and yet are considered by some people as belonging to the world at large (a part of the global commons).[3] While the more advanced economies have an established institutional infrastructure to handle the tasks of arriving at a social consensus on what are the appropriate environmental policies (for that society), of allocating the costs among the population, and of enforcing the policies, such an infrastructure is less well developed in poorer economies and is largely absent at the international level. The main option available for dealing with international environmental problems – other than unilateral action, which seldom involves the best available solution – is cooperation among sovereign governments.

The 'greening' of world trade issues has been an inevitable consequence of not having well-developed and enforceable environmental property rights in the wake of the above-mentioned developments, particularly the pressures on the environment from increasing population, output and incomes, the improved understanding of the nature and extent of environmental degradation (including to the global commons) caused by mankind's activities, and the ever-greater interdependence between the world's national economies.

Trade discussions are being coloured by environmental concerns in at least three ways. First, more recognition is being given to the fact that trade and hence trade policies necessarily have an impact on the environment, through altering the volume and international location of global production and consumption activities. In the view of some analysts, international trade and liberal trade policies worsen environmental problems because they expand consumption, while others see trade and trade liberalization as a vehicle for improving the environment through raising incomes so that there is more interest in, and more money to spend on, environmental protection.

Second, the environmental policies of one set of countries can have an impact on other countries through international trade. Environmentally motivated taxes, subsidies, charges, standards and other regulations can alter patterns of production and trade through their impact on international competitiveness. Some environmentalists view trade policies – mainly of an import- or export-restricting nature – as important parts of environmental policy packages. On the other hand, export-oriented industries and trade negotiators consider many environmental policies as covert means of protecting domestic producers from international competition.

Third, trade policies are seen as playing a role in bringing about the degree of multilateral cooperation needed to deal with transborder environmental problems. The challenge is to create or increase the incentives to cooperate, and trade policies are seen as one of the few available instruments for encouraging such cooperation. This role for trade policies – as a stick or carrot for encouraging nations to cooperate – contrasts with its role in the two previously mentioned situations where the issue is mainly one of the direct impact of trade policy instruments on particular environmental objectives.

The lower the costs of protecting and improving the environment, the larger will be both the degree of public support across countries and the amount of environmental improvement accomplished. Hence it is helpful to examine the efficiency of using trade policy instruments to achieve environmental objectives. As with other areas of policy intervention, however, environmental policies also affect the distribution of income and asset values both within and between countries. This in turn creates incentives for interest groups to seek to influence the policy outcome in their favour. Experience has shown that protectionist groups can be skilful at promoting coalitions with environmental groups. There is thus a growing concern that environmental issues are creating indirect as well as direct opportunities to erect new barriers to trade.

For example, if an environmental regulation increases the operating costs of domestic firms sufficiently for them to meet an injury test, this could trigger the imposition of an anti-dumping duty on competing imports. Also, calls for new environmentally-motivated product or production process standards may stimulate domestic producers to advocate measures that impose disproportionate costs on their foreign competitors. More generally, there are many opportunities for domestic producers to attempt to camouflage a reluctance to compete with foreign producers by claiming that increased regulation of imports is an essential part of efforts to improve the quality of the environment.

The studies in this volume are an initial effort to gain insights into some of the economic aspects of these and other interactions between trade, the environment and public policy. In attempting to inform the debate on these issues, the studies address questions such as:

- Under what circumstances is it true that opening up to trade worsens a country's environment or the global commons?
- In such circumstances should trade be restricted, or are there more appropriate ways to limit damage to the environment?
- In what ways do the environmental policies of one country or set of countries affect the trade, environment and economic welfare of other countries?
- What role is there for trade policies in addressing global environmental concerns such as greenhouse gas emissions, ozone depletion, deforestation and the possible extinction of species?
- Will on-going regional economic integration in Europe, North America and elsewhere reduce or exacerbate environmental problems?
- How great is the risk that protectionist interests will co-opt environmentalists' rhetoric and support for their own ends, and what can be done to reduce that risk?
- What are the main obstacles to international cooperation on global environmental issues and what are the relative merits of compensation (side payments) and sanctions?

Before providing an overview of the individual studies, two caveats should be mentioned. One concerns the diversity of opinion on whether certain environmental problems do or do not exist and, if they do, how seriously they should be taken. The studies in this volume do not take positions on the importance of particular environmental issues. Their task, rather, is to examine the consequences of alternative ways governments might attempt to address those issues if they so choose.

The other caveat concerns the fact that the various institutional and legal aspects of the issues outlined above are not dealt with in this volume. In particular, it is beyond the scope of the present studies to examine explicitly the interactions between environmental issues and either the General Agreement on Tariffs and Trade or the Uruguay Round of multi-lateral trade negotiations. However, one of the purposes of this volume is to serve as a foundation for subsequent research which might focus on such institutional issues.[4]

1.2 Outline of the volume

The studies fall into three groups. Chapters 2 to 4 focus on the basic economics of the interactions between trade, the environment and public policy. The next five chapters apply these economic principles to specific issues, including global warming, ozone depletion, and the environmental effects of liberalization of trade in coal and food and of regional economic integration. Chapters 10 to 12 then examine the interactions between economics and politics as they affect environmental and trade policies, first at the national and then at the global level.

1.2.1 *The economics of environmental policies in open economies*

The volume begins with an overview of the economic effects of environmental and trade policies. By using the simplest economic theory available (partial-equilibrium, comparative-static analysis), Chapter 2 seeks to show how the policies of one country or set of countries can affect both its own and the rest of the world's environment, trade and welfare. One of the important points to emerge from the analysis is that opening up to trade in a good whose production is relatively pollution-intensive improves the environment and welfare of a small country if it imports the good. Should the good be exported, however, opening to trade worsens that country's environment and – in the absence of the appropriate environmental policy – welfare may or may not improve. Conversely, if consumption rather than production of this good is the source of pollution, the opposite result holds: opening to trade improves the environment if that good is exported but (again in the absence of the appropriate environmental policy) worsens the environment if it is imported. However, in each of these cases, if the opening up is accompanied by the introduction of something close to the optimal environmental policy, national welfare necessarily improves.

The analysis in Chapter 2 also shows that while, say, an export tax on a good whose production degrades the natural environment will reduce that degradation, it improves the country's welfare less than would a more direct tax on the source of environmental damage – indeed, the export tax may even worsen welfare. The same is true for an import restriction on a product whose consumption is pollution-intensive (for example, coal).

How are these conclusions altered when an economy is large enough to affect other economies? Size is shown to moderate the proportional effects on an economy of opening up to trade, although many more exceptional outcomes are possible because of varying extents to which (a) international environmental spillovers occur, (b) countries differ in their sensitivity to pollution, (c) imported goods are imperfect substitutes for domestic goods in terms of the consumption externalities they impose, and (d) the rest of the world alters its environmental and trade policies in response to policy changes in the country concerned. Even so, the fundamental point remains that free trade is nationally and globally superior to no trade, as long as something close enough to the optimal pollution tax structure is in place. And this conclusion tends to be strengthened rather than weakened when some of the simplifying assumptions are relaxed.

Chapter 2 concludes by examining the implications for poorer countries of tighter pollution standards in industrial economies. It points out that if the production of import-competing goods in industrial economies is relatively pollution-intensive, tighter standards will improve the terms of trade for poorer countries and so make them better off (provided appropriate environmental policies are applied in poorer countries as their production and exports of pollution-intensive goods expand in response to the international price rise).

What if production of a low-income country's imports rather than exports is relatively pollution-intensive? In that case the country's terms of trade will deteriorate as pollution standards are raised in advanced economies, and its own pollution will increase as its import-competing sector expands. Furthermore, if a large number of low-income countries were to respond by introducing or raising their own pollution taxes, their terms of trade would deteriorate further. This would appear rather depressing were it not for the fact that the more pollution standards are raised in industrial economies relative to poorer countries, the more production of pollution-intensive goods will be relocated from rich to poor economies, particularly if the appropriate capital is internationally mobile. Hence the more likely it is that the latter will switch to become exporters of these goods and thereby to benefit from further pollution taxes in rich economies.

The array of environmental policy instruments available to combat pollution and other environmental problems is very large. For simplicity only production, consumption and trade taxes-cum-subsides are considered in Chapter 2. But as Chapter 3 demonstrates, numerous other instruments could be used, depending on the nature of the environmental problems being addressed. In particular, environmental problems which transcend national boundaries are such that it is not always possible to use first-best environmental policy instruments because there is no supra-national agency to introduce and enforce them. Some nations could lose from an international scheme to reduce pollution, which means that schemes need to be devised in such a way as to encourage those nations to participate. Sometimes there will be circumstances in which agreement is possible only when the pollutee pays the polluter not to pollute. Even though this is the reverse of the polluter-pays principle (and so may seem unfair), it will generally be the superior outcome when the alternative is no abatement agreement. In practice, the difficulties of negotiations and the concern for the appearance of fairness often lead to proposals for harmonised standards or uniform percentage reductions in emissions, despite the second-best nature of these approaches. This in turn has prompted economists to propose that nationally allocated emission permits or emission reduction credits be made internationally tradeable, to reduce the inherent inefficiency that would result from insisting that all nations participate equally despite differences in preferences and in waste-absorptive capacity.

Whether national or international environmental policies are perceived to be fair will hinge in no small part on how those policies affect welfare in different countries. The analysis of Chapter 4 focuses on such distributional issues, using the useful simplification of a world of just two or three large countries. It is shown that it is possible for a country which is inflicting environmental damage on other countries to reduce welfare in those other countries by imposing an environmental tax, even though that tax would increase both the first country's welfare and world welfare. This possibility arises because of the improvement in the polluting country's terms of trade and the collection of tax revenue by that country. It could occur if the first country is an exporter of a good whose production is pollution-intensive, or if it is an importer of a good whose consumption causes pollution.

Chapter 4 also examines the ways in which environmental policies can affect a country's international competitiveness in a pollution-intensive industry. It concludes that there is no economic justification for countering the effects on competitiveness of optimal environmental policies. In judging the fairness of this conclusion, it is useful to recall that an appropriate environmental policy corrects, rather than introduces, a distortion in the pricing of the services of the natural environment. That is, such policy action eliminates an unjustifiable (implicit) subsidy rather than adding an unjustifiable tax.

1.2.2 *Environment and trade: case studies*

Having addressed general aspects of the economics of environmental and trade policies in open economies in Part II of the volume, Part III turns to several case studies to illuminate further, and in more concrete ways, the interactions between trade and the environment. Chapters 5 to 7 focus specifically on two problems of the global commons, namely, global warming and ozone depletion. Chapter 5 provides a survey of recent empirical estimates of the trade and welfare effects of policies aimed at reducing greenhouse gas emissions. Chapter 6 presents some new empirical results of incentives facing different country groups to participate in international schemes that might be designed to reduce carbon emissions. And Chapter 7 examines the factors that contributed to the signing of a multilateral agreement to reduce the emission of ozone-depleting substances.

As Chapter 5 points out, efforts to quantify the economic effects of various policy approaches to reducing greenhouse gases are in their infancy. That, plus the complexity of the issue, the uncertainty surrounding the physical causes and effects of those gases, and the difficulty of obtaining people's valuation of those physical effects, ensure that the range of estimated trade and welfare effects of policies to reduce greenhouse gases is wide. Nonetheless, some tentative conclusions can be drawn from available empirical studies. First, those studies suggest that carbon taxes aimed at cutting global carbon emissions by half, relative to what they otherwise would be well into next century, would reduce global GDP (as conventionally measured) by around 3 per cent. Whether such a reduction in carbon emissions would be considered by society as good value at that price is difficult to ascertain.

As anticipated in the preceding chapters, the costs of greenhouse gas abatement policies are not borne equally across countries. Such policies have uneven effects on both the volume and terms of trade, as well as on the international competitiveness, of different countries. The effects are also sensitive to the extent to which abatement is achieved by taxing carbon production or consumption, for that determines the distribution across countries of the tax revenue (assuming that a tax approach is selected and that no international redistribution of such revenues occurs). One empirical study suggests the value of the carbon tax revenue necessary to reduce carbon emissions by 50 per cent could be as high as one-tenth of world GDP (Whalley and Wigle, 1991). If abatement was achieved by raising producer taxes, international trade would be conducted at the (tax-inclusive) demand price so countries exporting fossil fuels (primarily OPEC) would receive much of the tax revenue. On the other hand, if consumer taxes were raised to reduce emissions, trade would occur at the (tax-exclusive) supply price and much of the tax revenue would accrue to importers of fossil fuels (primarily the advanced industrial economies).

Nor would the trade effects of a uniform carbon tax be neutral across fossil fuels, since the carbon content and price of fuels per joule of energy vary considerably. Coal on average is 25 per cent 'dirtier' than petroleum, which in turn emits 40 per cent more carbon per joule of energy produced than natural gas. And since coal is typically priced much lower per joule of energy than the other two fuels, a carbon tax would raise substantially the price of coal relative to other energy sources. One source suggests that a 20 per cent cut in carbon emissions between 1988 and 2005, and the stabilization of the atmosphere's carbon content thereafter, would require the real domestic price of coal to be 300 per cent higher in Western Europe and more than 500 per cent higher in North America by the year 2020 than it otherwise would be, whereas crude oil and natural gas prices would be only 70 to 80 per cent higher (Burniaux *et al.*, 1991). Clearly, energy-exporting countries with large coal reserves, and especially those for which coal contributes a large share of export revenue, would be harmed by a uniform carbon-content tax.

The cost of greenhouse gas abatement via a carbon tax can be reduced, and the international distributional effects of the tax made more equitable, if emission rights are allocated and countries are permitted to trade those rights internationally. Chapter 5 cites a number of empirical studies which support this view. They show as well that the extent of industrial restructuring required is also lessened by allowing international trade in emission permits (although that trade does place more of the burden of adjustment on coal relative to other fuels). Reducing the need for structural adjustments is especially important if international capital flows would result from the imposition of a new global or OECD-wide carbon tax, since this would reduce the push for welfare-reducing restrictions on capital flight to poorer countries with lower emission standards.

None of the empirical studies reviewed in Chapter 5 attempts to compare the economic costs of abatement of greenhouse gases with the benefit society might derive from such abatement. By contrast, a new empirical study reported in Chapter 6 explicitly incorporates such benefits in the utility functions of a global computable general equilibrium (CGE) model used to assess the effects of reducing carbon emissions. The way this is done is necessarily arbitrary, but the exercise nonetheless is helpful for evaluating the effects not only of global but also of regional reductions in carbon emission. By dividing the world into six regions, the study shows that if only part of the world reduces carbon emissions, other regions are affected by more than just the direct impact of that cutback on global warming. In particular, relative prices change in international markets and the production and consumption responses to those changes lead to indirect effects which may offset or enhance the direct effects on regions' welfare. The study also shows that should other regions be restrained to keep their emissions of carbon unchanged, the welfare gains would be larger than without such restraint because there would be less carbon emissions globally. This suggests there may be a role for side payments to or sanctions against countries not prepared to voluntarily reduce emissions affecting the global commons, a point that is taken up in Chapter 12 of the volume.

The final (and controversial) result in Chapter 6 is the effect on world trade of limiting carbon-based energy production or consumption. The study suggests world trade could be reduced very substantially by such policies. This result is strongly conditional on the CGE model used, however. In particular, if either capital and/or permits to emit carbon were allowed to be traded, world trade would decrease less and might even expand. It could expand because by pricing the carbon-absorptive capacity of the environment correctly instead of underpricing it as at present, new scope for exploiting true comparative advantage (where the environment is properly included as a resource contributing to production) would emerge. And if capital is internationally mobile, more rather than less international specialization in production and goods trade might well result from the simultaneous imposition of carbon emission taxes and distribution of internationally tradeable permits to emit carbon (or credits for reducing emission). This is a specific example of the more general point that trade in goods and international mobility of productive factors can be complements (Markusen, 1983; Wong, 1986) rather than substitutes (Mundell, 1957).

These simulation results of the effects of possible international agreements to limit carbon emissions cast doubt on the prospects for the world, or a major subset of countries, ever reaching such agreement. But international agreements concerning other environmental problems have been reached, most notably on limiting ozone-depleting substances via the Montreal Protocol. Indeed that agreement was reached within a few years after the 'hole' in the ozone layer over Antarctica was discovered in 1985. Why it was possible to reach agreement so promptly, how successful it will be, and what lessons it has for other international environmental agreements are among the questions addressed in Chapter 7.

The answers are somewhat sobering. The authors of Chapter 7 identify four factors which facilitated the signing of the Montreal Protocol: (a) there was widespread agreement as to which man-made emissions are the main cause of ozone depletion; (b) only a small number of rich countries (where environmental consciousness is relatively high) are responsible for most of the emissions, which not only made negotiations easier but also made it possible to limit emissions by non-participants via the Protocol's trade provisions; (c) the cost of phasing out the harmful substances is relatively small; and (d) the oligopolistic nature of the CFC-producing industry allowed producer profits to be secured through the effective cartelization and limitation of production, and made monitoring compliance with the agreement relatively easy. In the case of the global warming threat, by contrast, consensus on the necessity to limit fossil fuel consumption has not yet been reached; most industries of all major countries would need to be involved; trade provisions against non-participants would be ineffective because fuel production and consumption is so widespread; the cost of limiting fuel use in terms of lower material standards of living would be considerable; and few producer groups could avoid being hurt by carbon taxes, which means that environmental lobby groups would not be able to turn to such groups for support. Even if support could be found in rich countries for an international agreement to reduce carbon emissions, substantial compensation probably would be necessary to induce large numbers of poorer countries to join. If they did not join, production of carbon-intensive products would tend to relocate to such regions, thereby weakening (perhaps substantially) the effectiveness of the agreement.

In contrast to Chapters 5 to 7, which are concerned with the effects of environmental policies on trade, Chapter 8 and 9 focus on the effects of trade policies on the environment. Chapter 8 examines the likely environmental effects of global or sub-global liberalization of trade in two of the world's most distorted commodity markets, coal and food, while Chapter 9 looks at the environmental impact of liberalizing trade in all goods and factors within a geographic region (Europe).

The point is often made by environmentalists that trade liberalization expands global production and consumption, which means that if the adverse environmental externalities associated with those activities are not appropriately controlled, greater environmental degradation may result. It is even conceivable that the negative value attached to that greater damage to the environment exceeds the positive value to society of greater global consumption of marketed goods and services. Although the analysis in Chapter 2 shows that there is always a set of environmental policy instruments available to ensure that freer trade *need* not reduce overall welfare, there is the legitimate concern that such instruments may not be in place. Hence the need for case studies to determine whether trade liberalization in particular markets would be environmentally friendly.

Coal is high-priced in many rich countries and low-priced in many other (especially centrally planned) economies. If producer price supports and subsidies were removed in the former (but the higher consumer price were retained for environmental reasons), coal output would decline, the international price would rise and coal output in the rest of the world would rise. However, coal consumption would decrease in the rest of the world (because the price had increased), so global carbon and sulphur emissions would decrease. That is, in addition to the conventional economic welfare gains from liberalizing trade, the global environment also would improve. And if imported coal emits less sulphur than local coal in the protected countries, there would be a reduction in acid rain as well. If, in addition, the USSR, Eastern Europe and China opened their coal markets to more trade, the production response could more or less offset the production decline in the rich countries, but then it is also necessary to allow for a sizeable decline in coal consumption in the centrally planned economies. Provided liberalization in those economies does not more than offset the international price effect of removing producer supports in rich countries, global coal emissions would still be lower than at present and economic welfare as conventionally measured would be enhanced even further. In short, liberalization of trade in coal is very likely to enhance both economic welfare and the environment, and more so the more governments are prepared to respond to trade liberalization with appropriate emission taxes in their countries.

In the case of food, the current pattern of policy distortions is similar to that for coal: high domestic prices in rich countries and low domestic prices in many poor countries. Liberalizing protectionist policies in rich countries not only would raise incomes in both groups of countries but also would cause the world's food to be produced with less chemicals. The relocation of production to low-income countries and the global welfare gains would be even greater if poorer countries simultaneously were to remove their policy discrimination against farmers. Nor would the gains to developing countries be restricted to the main food exporters. On the contrary, many food-importing poor countries also would gain as the rise in food prices attracted labour and capital away from industries in which they have a weaker comparative advantage.

The sources of improvement to the environment from reducing agricultural protection in rich countries are not surprising. One is that the elasticity of farmers' demands for chemical inputs with respect to the price of farm outputs is very high, so a lowering of domestic food prices would reduce substantially the extent which farm chemicals pollute the air, soil and water of those countries. It would also reduce the chemical residues in food. Moreover, as marginal farm land is taken out of farm production it would not only lower the price of housing land but would allow more land to be available for aesthetic and recreational uses.

What about in the low-income countries? True, more chemicals would be used by their farmers if food prices were higher. But the increase would be from a very low base and so would offset only a part of the improvement to the environment in the rich countries. The more important concern is that forests may be felled to make available more land for agriculture, putting at risk both the preservation of animal and plant species and of wilderness areas, and the capacity of the world's trees to absorb the ever-larger global emissions of carbon dioxide. However, empirical studies suggest that the land area devoted to agriculture in developing countries is not very responsive to changes in the prices of farm products, and that the extra output would instead come almost entirely from a more intensive use of existing farm land. Furthermore, increased employment and higher incomes in rural areas of poor countries resulting from food policy reform would lead to the substitution of other fuels for wood for household needs, thereby reducing the felling of trees. Finally, since much of the deforestation in low-income countries is the result of tax incentives and inadequate enforcement of forest property rights, reform of those policies would seem to be a more appropriate focus of attention for those concerned to save forests than preventing worthwhile reform of food policies. In short, maintaining high levels of agricultural protection in rich countries is a very inefficient way of attempting to protect forests in low-income countries.

Regional trade liberalization has been very much in the news, not only in Europe and North America but also in Latin America and East Asia. It is therefore of interest to ask what impact regional trade liberalization might have on the environment and welfare of countries both within and outside the region in question. That is the issue addressed in Chapter 9. Using a simple model in which barriers to the international mobility of sector-specific capital are lowered as part of a regional integration initiative, a number of propositions emerge. One is that relatively capital-rich countries in the region will reduce their emissions of pollutants, while emissions in the region's capital-poor countries will increase if emission charges or standards are not changed. Another is that should emission taxes be altered to maximize welfare broadly defined to include the environment, this will amplify the effects just noted, although less so if governments of capital-rich countries worry about (a) the potential unemployment effects of capital outflows that would result from lowering barriers to factor movements, and (b) the potential environmental catastrophes that may occur in and spill over from nearby countries if environmental standards there are not raised.

1.2.3 The political economy of interactions between environmental and trade policies

Most of the chapters in this volume are concerned with the effects of environmental and trade policies on the environment and welfare. The reasons as to why and how governments choose to intervene in some circumstances but not others also need to be understood, for as Stigler (1975) has said, 'Until we understand *why* our society adopts its policies, we will be poorly equipped to give useful advice on how to change those policies'. Many policies advocated by environmental groups are not introduced until community support for such policies becomes very widespread or the support of other influencial interest groups can be harnessed. Achieving cooperation with other interest groups often requires advocating a second-, third- or fourth-best policy instrument for achieving the desired environmental objective, however. For example, suppose consumption of a particular product causes pollution. Although the most efficient corrective policy is a tax on consumption, it may be easier for environmental groups to gain support for a policy to limit consumption indirectly through an import barrier than through a direct consumption tax, because import-competing domestic producers would support the former but oppose the latter. This example raises two general and somewhat complementary questions: how might the emergence of environmental interest groups affect the political market for protectionist trade policies, and how might the co-existence of other interest groups and environmentalists affect the choice of environmental policy instruments adopted by governments? Chapter 10 addresses the former while Chapter 11 focuses on the latter question.

In Chapter 10 the simplest possible political market is considered in which the government seeks to be re-elected by obtaining political support by promising either free trade or import protection for a particular industry whose product causes pollution during either the production or consumption stage. The analysis examines how that policy outcome is likely to be altered when the profit-motivated industry producer groups are joined by an environmental interest group. Given the assumed restrictive policy choice for environmentalists (either a liberal or a restrictive trade policy), it is not surprising that the analysis suggests that environmentalists would often favour restrictions on imports, especially if it is consumption rather than production that is causing pollution and if the environmentalists are 'supergreen', that is, if they are concerned with the global rather than just the national environment. Only when production is the source of the environmental externality and the environmentalists are concerned only with the national environment does it emerge that they would support free trade.

This rather sobering conclusion — which admittedly results largely from the explicit assumption that trade policy is the only instrument available to the environmentalists — underscores the importance of making environmentalists aware that there are many policy instruments other than trade policy available for achieving environmental objectives, and that in almost all circumstances trade policy instruments would not be the most efficient or effective ones for achieving the desired environmental objectives. Without that awareness, there is the risk that as environmental groups grow in their political influence, import protectionism will increase despite its inefficiency as an instrument for addressing environmental concerns. Worse still, a particular trade policy may even have adverse environmental consequences when its general equilibrium implications (not considered by many environmentalists and not included in the analysis in Chapter 10) are taken into account.

Chapter 11 also uses a public choice perspective, but it is aimed at shedding light on why particular policy instruments are adopted to achieve national environmental objectives in a trading economy. In particular, it looks at why environmental policies so often take the form of quantity regulation or technical product or process standards rather than being price-based policy instruments, and then examines how such regulations or standards affect, or are affected by, trade and trade policy. It points out that for a variety of reasons regulations and standards are simultaneously (a) more profitable for producers in an industry and (b) apparently more certain in their effects on the environment. The environmental effects are only *apparently* more certain because, again, the indirect general equilibrium effects of imposing quantity regulations or standards in one industry may cause greater environmental degradation via another industry than is avoided by the industry being regulated.

Moreover, product and process standards can have different effects on trade: a product standard may well inhibit imports whereas a process standard (applied only to domestic firms) or a restriction on domestic output may foster imports. In the latter event, the reduction in an industry's international competitiveness resulting from such an environmental policy may increase its ability to demonstrate injury from imports. This would, in turn, increase the likelihood of gaining access to the country's safeguard, anti-dumping duty or countervailing duty provisions. Even though environmentalists may have no intention of increasing trade barriers, that may be an indirect consequence of introducing their preferred type of policy.

Not only might more information on the costs and other consequences of various environmental policy instruments be necessary to improve the efficiency of environmental policy, but transfers might also be required. For example, the affected industry and/or the environmentalist programs might need to receive some of the tax revenue from an emissions tax, or some of the auction revenue from the sale of emission rights, to render a tax-based policy politically feasible.

Chapter 12 concludes the volume with an analysis of two questions related to multilateral cooperation: what are the principal obstacles to cooperation on international environmental problems, and what can be done to promote multilateral cooperation? The answers have important implications for trade policies because it is evident that many governments – and most environmental groups if they have thought about it – believe there is a role for trade policy in promoting and enforcing international cooperation on environmental issues.

When pollution affects only domestic environmental resources – that is, when there are no physical spillovers into other countries or the global commons – other countries are affected only to the extent that the country's environmental policies have an impact on trade or capital flows. In this case, the need is for countries to agree on multilateral rules designed to minimise the trade frictions that may arise in such situations. But a different type of international cooperation is called for when transborder spillovers are involved, since the activities of the country in question are causing primarily environmental rather than commercial problems for other countries. This second type of cooperation, which is the focus of Chapter 12, generally poses a considerably greater challenge than cooperation on minimizing commercial frictions.

Obstacles to multilateral cooperation include different interpretations of the scientific evidence, different priorities for dealing with environmental problems, disagreements over the allocation of responsibility for dealing with environmental problems, and attempts by countries to free-ride on the efforts of others. If the obstacle(s) present in a given situation cannot be removed, the countries which are taking the lead in organising a proposed agreement are likely to consider creating incentives for other countries to participate.

One option is to create negative incentives through the threat of sanctions of one form or another. However, most analysts take the view that sanctions are not an effective device for promoting cooperation on environmental problems. It is true that a limited number of existing environmental agreements include trade provisions applicable to trade in products directly related to the environmental problem in question, and that these provisions generally are such that non-participants are at a disadvantage. But the primary purpose of trade provisions is to prevent the agreement from being undermined by the actions of non-participants. What distinguishes trade provisions from trade sanctions is that the latter involve 'innocent' products, which means, among other things, that they are very likely to be viewed as inherently more aggressive actions.

Alternatively, side payments can be used to create positive incentives for countries to participate in environmental agreements. Such payments can take many forms, including financial assistance for work directly related to the agreement and access to environmentally friendlier technology. It is also possible to go outside the context of the agreement to find positive incentives – for example, in the areas of trade, aid or debt policies. The chapter concludes by drawing attention to the risk that traditional protectionist groups will try to tip the balance against side payments and in favour of trade sanctions.

1.3   Conclusions

What broad conclusions should be drawn from the studies in this volume? Allowing for some over-simplification, the key results of the analysis of the many varied problems and issues can be grouped under five headings.

1.3.1   *The importance of indirect effects*

In proposing policies to protect the environment, it is crucially important to consider not just the direct but also the indirect effects of government intervention. These indirect effects occur because of substitution possibilities in domestic production or consumption, or because of international connections. An example of the former is a tax on carbon-based fuels which could lead to an increase in the demand for nuclear-generated energy, and hence add to problems related to the disposal of nuclear waste. An example of the latter is a decision by one country to reduce activities that are polluting the global commons, which might cause an expansion in those activities abroad that has a more than offsetting effect on the environment. One means by which such international substitution occurs is through changes in the international terms of trade. Any analysis of an environmental policy proposal which failed to consider possible terms of trade effects would be incomplete and could mislead the public and their elected representatives. Foreigners could also be misled, since there are instances in which a country's trading partners are made worse off by the indirect effects of a country's decision to introduce a pollution tax.

The key point is that when a government intervenes with a tax, subsidy or regulation designed to solve an environmental problem, or when it reduces barriers to imports, it triggers a complex set of repercussions that ripple throughout the economy. In our increasingly integrated world economy, the repercussions necessarily extend to other sectors and other countries, and may prompt other policy changes at home or abroad which in turn have feedback effects. It is evident from the studies in this volume that while predicting the nature and size of the indirect effects is difficult, the effort must be made since the indirect effects will play an important – sometimes dominant – role in determining the net impact of future policy changes.

1.3.2 The need for appropriate environmental policies

Another conclusion which emerges from the studies is that the impact of trade and trade liberalization on a country's overall welfare depends on whether the country's environmental resources are correctly priced, which in turn depends on whether appropriate environmental policies (from the viewpoint of the country in question) are in place. If they are, trade and trade liberalization benefit the environment because the resulting increase in economic growth stimulates the demand for environmental protection and generates additional income to pay for it. On the other hand, if countries do not have appropriate environmental policies in place, conventional estimates of the gains from trade may overstate the net gain to society. It is even possible in such a situation that trade or trade liberalization could reduce a country's overall welfare. For this to happen, two conditions must hold: first, that the increased trade adds to environmental degradation; and second, that the conventional gains from increased international specialization are not sufficient to outweigh the negative effect of the reduction in environmental quality.

If a country appears not to have appropriate environmental policies – not always an easy judgement to make, especially on the part of foreigners – it is sometimes argued that the country should be wary of trade liberalization and may even want to raise certain trade barriers. This advice is short-sighted, however. Trade is not the only area in which inappropriate environmental policies can be costly for a country, which means that manipulating a country's trade policies cannot be a meaningful substitute for a direct attack on the source of the problems. If environmental policies are inappropriate, it is much better to begin working to improve them than to try working around them.

1.3.3 *The need for multilateral cooperation*

It is no longer possible for most countries to create an appropriate environmental policy entirely on their own. If a particular problem affects only domestic environmental resources, but the corrective policies (or lack thereof) affect trade and capital flows, other countries will take an interest in the country's environmental policies. When an environmental problem involves a transborder externality – either a physical spillover of pollution into other countries or the global commons, or a psychological spillover – the only alternative to unilateral actions based on economic and political power is for countries to cooperate in the design, implementation and enforcement of an appropriate multilateral environmental scheme for dealing with the problem at hand. The demands on cooperation typically are much greater in such cases because there is no supra-national government or infrastructure to resolve the property right or property management issues that are at the root of the environmental problem.

1.3.4 *The role of trade policy*

The broad conclusion of all of the studies in this volume which address the question is that trade policies are not the best instrument to use in dealing with environmental problems. This follows from the fact that trade *per se* is not a direct cause of environmental problems. Some distortion must be present – most obviously, the absence of an appropriate environmental policy – in order for there to be a possibility that international trade will create or worsen environmental problems.

If all countries participated in all international environmental agreements, there would be nothing more to add. As several of the studies note, however, it is often a major challenge just to get a critical mass of countries – let alone all countries – to participate in an international environmental agreement. As soon as participation is less than universal, trade policy re-enters the picture, albeit in a different role. Trade measures may be considered as one type of carrot (or, if necessary, stick) that could be used to encourage participation. The organizers of any agreement are likely to consider including in it trade provisions designed to minimize the extent to which the agreement will be undermined by the activities of non-participants.

1.3.5 *Political economy aspects*

The trade/environment area has an above-average risk of being exploited by special-interest groups to their own benefit and at the expense of the general interest. More specifically, the risk is that traditional protectionist groups will manipulate environmental concerns in order to reduce competition from imports. This could occur at any of several stages: by promoting policies that discriminate against imports as part of the solution to environmental problems, by biasing the choice between carrots and sticks in favour of trade sanctions, or by pushing for the inclusion of unnecessary or excessive trade provisions in multilateral agreements. Any such gains by protectionists would be in addition to their gains in the area of administered protection, where tighter environmental controls can be expected to increase the ability of firms to satisfy an injury test for obtaining increased protection against imports via the country's safeguard, anti-dumping or countervailing duty regulations.

These political considerations call attention to the importance of devising rules and disciplines that will reduce the ability of protectionists to manipulate environmental concerns. It is not just that protectionists gain at the expense of the rest of society, but that their activities also ultimately harm the environment. This follows from the fact that the biases they introduce into the policy package increase the costs of environmental improvements, which in turn in the longer term will reduce the amount of improvement that society is willing or can afford to achieve.

Notes

1. Parts of this chapter draw liberally on material in GATT (1991).
2. See, for example, Baumol (1971), GATT (1971), Siebert (1974), Walter (1975, 1976) and Blackhurst (1977).
3. There are, in contrast, a limited number of issues which are often described as environmental, but which do not involve property rights. A leading example is health and safety standards – an area in which, nonetheless, government policies play a prominent role.
4. The interested reader will find in Petersmann (1991) an introduction to some of the legal and institutional aspects that might be addressed.

References

Baumol, W. (1971), *Environmental Protection, International Spillovers and Trade*, Stockholm: Almqvist and Wiksell.
Blackhurst, R. (1977), 'International Trade and Domestic Environmental Policies in a Growing World Economy', pp. 341–64 in R. Blackhurst *et al.*, *International Relations in a Changing World*, Geneva: Sythoff-Leiden.
Burniaux, J.-M., J. P. Martin, G. Nicoletti and J. O. Martins (1991), 'The Costs of Policies to Reduce Global Emissions of CO_2: Initial Simulation Results with GREEN', Working Paper No. 103, Economics and Statistics Department, OECD, Paris, June.
GATT (1971), *Industrial Pollution Control and International Trade*, GATT Studies in International Trade No. 1, Geneva: General Agreement on Tariffs and Trade.

GATT (1991), *International Trade 1990–91*, Volume I, Geneva: General Agreement on Tariffs and Trade.

Markusen, J. (1983), 'Factor Movements and Commodity Trade as Complements' *Journal of International Economics* 14: 341–56.

Mundell, R. A. (1957), 'International Trade and Factor Mobility', *American Economic Review* 48: 321–35.

Petersmann, E.-U. (1991), 'Trade Policy, Environmental Policy and GATT: Why Trade Rules and Environmental Rules Should be Mutually Exclusive', *Außenwirtschaft* 46: 197–221.

Siebert, H. (1974), 'Environmental Protection and International Specialization', *Weltwirtschaftliches Archiv* 110: 494–508.

Stigler, G. J. (1975), *The Citizen and the State: Essays on Regulation*, Chicago: University of Chicago Press.

Walter, I. (1975), *The International Economics of Pollution*, London: Macmillan.

Walter, I. (ed.) (1976), *Studies in International Environmental Economics*, New York: Wiley.

Whalley, J. and R. Wigle (1991), 'The International Incidence of Carbon Taxes', in *Economic Policy Responses to Global Warming*, edited by R. Dornbusch and J. Poterba, Cambridge, MA: MIT Press.

Wong, K. Y. (1986), 'Are International Trade and Factor Mobility Substitutes?', *Journal of International Economics* 21: 25–43.

PART 2

Economics of environmental policies in open economies

2

The standard welfare economics of policies affecting trade and the environment

Kym Anderson

The greening of world politics in recent years has brought forward, among other things, claims and counter-claims as to the effects of trade and hence trade policy on the environment. Environmentalists have also propagated suggestions for government intervention to slow the degradation of the natural environment which, if adopted by one set of countries, would affect the trade, environment and welfare of other countries as well. There is thus a growing demand for a better understanding of the welfare economics of the various interactions between trade and the environment, and between environmental and trade policies.

This chapter draws on the simplest economic theory that is able to demonstrate the linkages between trade, the natural environment and welfare. Using partial-equilibrium, comparative-static analysis, it seeks to show how the environmental and trade policies of one country (or set of countries) can affect its own and the rest of the world's environment, trade and social welfare.

After listing the basic assumptions to be used (some of which are relaxed during the course of the analysis), the following key questions are addressed:

- What are the effects on the environment and social welfare of a country opening up to or liberalizing its trade?
- How are these effects altered when the country also adopts appropriate environmental policies?
- To what extent are trade policy instruments able to substitute for first-best means of overcoming environmental externalities?
- How do changes in environmental and trade policies abroad affect this open economy's environment and welfare?

Initially the analysis focuses on an economy small enough for its production and consumption activities not to have significant effects on the rest of the world. The large economy (which could include a group of several similar small economies) is then analysed, to show the effects of its own and its trading partners' policies not only at home but also abroad. The final section of the chapter summarizes the results and mentions some qualifications that need to be kept in mind.

2.1 Basic assumptions

Consider an economy in which one group's production (or consumption) of a good begins to impose an externality on others through its effect on the natural environment. That is, this economic activity involves a marginal divergence between the private and social cost of production (or benefit from consumption), by adding to other producers' costs or reducing the aesthetic pleasure provided by nature. Such a divergence may have arisen because of new knowledge about the activity's pollutive effect becoming available or because preferences for a cleaner environment have strengthened, or because a threshold level of pollution has been reached which triggers concern for the environment. Whatever the reason, assume that property rights are not defined clearly enough and/or that there are high transactions costs which prevent the full internalization of the externality.[1] For simplicity, assume also that there are no administrative or by-product distortionary costs of collecting taxes or disbursing subsidies and that the income distributional effects of such transfer policies can be neglected. Assume too that producers, consumers and policy-makers are well informed and can appropriately value the aesthetic or material cost (or benefit) of the externality involved.[2]

The externality is assumed to result from the production (or consumption) activity itself, not from the use of a particular process. This means that a tax-cum-subsidy on production (or consumption) is equivalent to a tax-cum-subsidy on the source of the externality and thus is the optimal environmental policy instrument for correcting this divergence.[3] Initially assume also that the externality results from the production (or consumption) of just one good, and that there are no distortionary policies affecting other markets in this economy – although both these assumptions are relaxed later in the analysis.

To simplify the exposition a negative externality will be referred to as pollution, but it should be kept in mind that the analysis is equally relevant for all types of externalities. We begin with the small-country case, in which international prices are given and the effects on the rest of the world can be ignored, before turning to the large-country case. As is appropriate in this comparative-static analysis, changes in tastes and technological changes are not considered, nor is international factor mobility.

2.2   The small-country case

The marginal private benefits from consuming and the marginal private cost of producing a particular good are represented by the D and S curves, respectively, in Figure 2.1. Production (but not consumption) of this good is pollutive, however, the marginal social costs of production being represented by S'. (In practice, social and private costs may not diverge until the level of production has passed a certain threshold, and may not diverge increasingly over all output ranges, but the exposition is simpler and loses no generality by depicting all curves as linear with the divergence beginning with the first unit of production.) These curves fully incorporate the feedback effects of changes in production and/or consumption of this good on the markets for other goods, for productive factors and for foreign currencies in this economy. The price axis refers to the price of this good relative to all other prices in the economy (which are assumed to remain constant throughout).

Given the above assumptions, OQ would be the equilibrium level of production and consumption in the absence of both a pollution tax and international trade, yielding net social welfare equal to the difference between areas *abe* and *ade*.[4] Suppose the economy's trade policy were to change from autarchy to free trade. Then if OP_o was the international price at this small economy's border, as in Figure 2.1(a), production would fall to OQ_m, consumption would rise to OC_m and Q_mC_m units would be imported. Net social welfare would now be *abfg-ahg*, so the welfare gain from opening up to trade is *defgh*. Not only is this gain from trade positive but it is greater than it would have been in the absence of a negative production externality, by shaded area *degh* (the difference between the private and social cost of producing Q_mQ units domestically). On the other hand, if OP_1 was the international price, as in Figure 2.1(b), the country would become an exporter of C_xQ_x units of this good under free trade. In that case net social welfare would be *abik-amk*, so the welfare effect of opening up to trade is *eik-dekm*, which may be positive or negative. The ambiguity arises because the gain from trade in the absence of an externality associated with the extra production (*eik*) is more or less than offset by the uncharged cost of polluting the environment by producing an additional QQ_x units of this product (*dekm*).

In short, *liberalizing trade in this good whose production is pollutive improves the small country's environment and welfare if, following the policy change, the country imports this good; but should this good be exported, the environment is worsened and so welfare in this small country may or may not increase in the absence of a pollution tax* (Proposition 1).

What difference would it have made if this country had in place its optimal environmental policy both before and after trade was liberalized? In this case the optimal policy would be a production tax equal to the vertical distance between S and S' at the output level at which the marginal

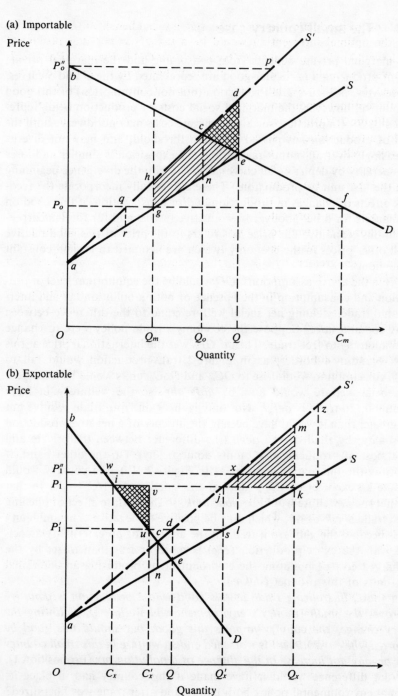

Figure 2.1 Effects of opening up a small economy to trade in a product whose production is pollutive

social cost of production equals the marginal social benefit. In the autarchy case the optimal intervention would be a tax of cn per unit produced, which would induce output of OQ_o rather than OQ in Figure 2.1(a) (yielding a welfare benefit represented by the dark shaded area cde, the difference between the social cost and benefit of those Q_oQ units).[5] In the free trade case the optimal production tax would be qr if OP_o was the international price (Figure 2.1(a)), or js if OP_l prevailed (Figure 2.1(b)), both of which would curtail production somewhat and thereby improve the environment and raise welfare relative to the situation where no pollution tax existed. In the exporting case, for example, production would decline from OQ_x to OQ_x' in Figure 2.1(b), improving social welfare by shaded area jkm. The gain from opening up to trade in the presence of such optimal environmental policies is represented by qcf in the case where this good would be imported or cij if it were to become an exportable. If the optimal pollution policy was not in place before trade liberalization, the gain from reform would be even greater, by cde. That is, *even in the export case there is an unambiguous welfare gain from trade for a small country provided something approaching the optimal environmental policy also is introduced, despite the fact that the environment is more polluted when production expands to supply exports* (Proposition 2).

The above analysis of the move from autarchy to free trade is easily modified to examine the effects of reducing or removing less-than-prohibitive trade taxes. In that case the initial domestic price is closer to the free-trade price and domestic production does not equal domestic consumption, but the conclusion is the same: lowering barriers to imports of this good will improve the environment and welfare in this small country especially with, but even without, the optimal pollution tax, whereas if the good is an exportable, then lowering export barriers will worsen the environment but will nonetheless improve welfare so long as something close to the optimal environmental policy is in place.[6]

Suppose there are prohibitive administrative costs involved in imposing the optimal environmental policy instrument, namely, a production tax. In the case where the good is exportable an export tax could be used instead to reduce degradation of the environment, but it would be less efficient than a production tax. This can be seen from Figure 2.1(b). An export tax of js would lower the price producers receive and hence domestic consumers pay by $P_l'P_1$, thereby shrinking exports from C_xQ_x to $C_x'Q_x'$. This would ensure the marginal social cost of production is lowered to its marginal benefit (the international price OP_1), so bringing about the same welfare gain on the production side as an equally large production tax, namely shaded area jkm. But the export tax also imposes a by-product cost of distorting the consumption side of this market. By setting the price to consumers below the opportunity cost of OP_1, the deadweight welfare cost of encouraging an extra C_xC_x' units of consumption is shaded area iuv. This inferior environmental policy instrument therefore reduces environmental degradation as much as a production tax of the same rate, but at higher cost than the optimal pollution tax instrument. Indeed if *iuv* exceeds *jkm* this second-best policy instrument would also be worse than no intervention, despite the reduction in environmental degradation brought about by the cut-back in production to OQ'_x. The optimal second-best export tax rate is thus less than the optimal first-best production tax rate: as the export tax is gradually reduced from $P'_1 P_1$, the area of triangle *iuv* is reduced more than the truncated triangular area *jmk*.[7] More generally, *trade taxes-cum-subsidies can be used to reduce environmental degradation by a given amount, but they will improve welfare less than a more direct tax on the source of pollution and may even worsen welfare* (Proposition 3).

To this point the analysis has focused on the effect of this small country's own trade and environmental policies. But how would this open economy's environment and welfare be affected by other large countries reducing their import taxes/export subsidies on this product or introducing or raising a pollution tax on its production? These policy changes abroad − like an exogenous expansion in overseas excess demand − would raise the international price of this product. Would this increase or decrease the benefit our small economy enjoys from being open to free trade?[8] If the international price rose from OP_1 to OP''_1 in Figure 2.1(b), the welfare benefits from being an exporter would rise by *ijxw* if the optimal pollution tax was in place and raised accordingly from *js* to *xl*. If no pollution tax existed, welfare would change by *ikyw-mkyz*, which might be positive or negative. That is, *the welfare benefit to a small country of adopting a free trade policy would be enhanced if the international price of its exportable rose − notwithstanding the greater environmental damage caused by greater production − so long as it had a sufficiently small divergence between its marginal social and private cost curves or applied a pollution tax close enough to the optimal rate* (Proposition 4). The pollution tax needs to ensure that the new vertical area between the S and S' curves and bounded by the quantities produced before and after the change does not exceed the new horizontal area between the S and D curves and bounded by OP_1 and OP''_1.

On the other hand, if this small country is and remains an importer of this product at the new international price, its welfare benefits from being open to free trade rather than autarchic (*defgh* in Figure 2.1(a) if there is no production tax) would be truncated as the price line *fg* moves up and the vertical line *gh* moves to the right. The benefit if the optimal production tax was in place and adjusted accordingly (*qcf* in Figure 2.1(a)) would also be truncated as the base of that triangle, *qf*, moved up with the rise in the international price.

There is the possibility, however, that the international price rise causes this country to switch from being an importer to an exporter of this product. Should that change be sufficiently large, the country's welfare gain from being open to trade rather than autarchic could turn out to be *enhanced*. This would happen if, for example, the international price rose by P_oP_o'' in Figure 2.1(a) and the optimal production tax was in place and adjusted accordingly, and *bcp* exceeded *qcf*.

The practical significance of this result is important: *even a country importing a product whose international price rises because of the imposition of environmental policies or a reduction in protectionism abroad need not be made worse off – even though its own environment will be harmed by the increased output and hence pollution stimulated by that price rise – if that country were to switch sufficiently from being an importer to an exporter of this product and had a sufficiently small divergence between its marginal social and private cost curves or applied a pollution tax close enough to the optimal rate* (Proposition 5).

Indeed the possibility of an importing country gaining from an international price rise need not even require that country to switch to exporter status if one or two of the basic assumptions listed in Section 2.1 above does not hold. One assumption is that other markets in this economy are not distorted by policies; another is that there are no externalities elsewhere in the economy. Consider relaxing each of these assumptions in turn.

If the sector under discussion is implicitly favoured or discriminated against by negative or positive government assistance to other sectors, then the international price line in Figure 2.1 has to be redefined. Recall that the price axis refers to the price of this sector's product relative to the prices of all other products (which are assumed to be constant). If the composite price of other products is, say, higher domestically than internationally because of protection in this economy's other import-competing sectors, then the relative price of this sector's product in the domestic market is lower than it is in the international market.

To see the significance of this, consider Figure 2.2 in which *ED* and *ED'* are the economy's private and social excess demand curves for this product (the horizontal difference between the supply and demand curves in Figure 2.1(a)), and OP_o is the (relative) price of purchasing a unit of this product domestically, given the protection afforded other sectors. The international relative price of this product, however, is necessarily higher than the domestic relative price in this distorted economy. If it is above *e*, say *OP*, the economy would be an exporter of this product under free trade, even with the optimal pollution tax in place. In this setting it turns out that should the international price of this sector's product rise, this economy with its optimal pollution policy in place will gain even though it may remain a net importer of this product.

The reasoning is as follows. Suppose the international price increases from *OP* to *OP'* and this increase is fully transmitted so that the domestic price rises from OP_o to OP_o'. The protectionist policy reduced welfare in this economy (with its optimal pollution tax) by *hcf* when *OP* and OP_o

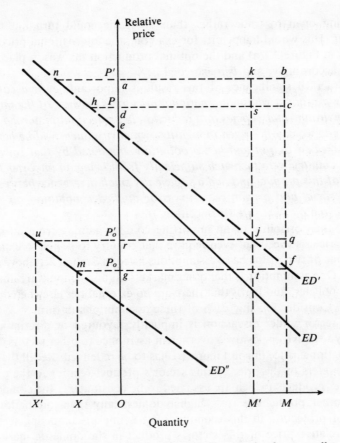

Figure 2.2 Effects of an international price rise for a small distorted economy

prevailed. Now with OP' and OP'_0 prevailing, the welfare loss from protection is *nkj*. But if the social excess demand curve is linear and the international price change has been fully transmitted, areas *hcf* and *nkj* are identical. However, the rise in the international price itself adds to the country's welfare, because of the country's comparative advantage at price OP and hence OP'. If the economy was undistorted, it would have benefited by *adhn* from the price rise, which is the producer gain net of the consumer loss. In the presence of the distortionary protectionist policy, the producer gain net of the consumer loss is a negative value, *fgrj*, but off-setting that is the reduction in the implicit import subsidy to foreigners which is a saving of *bqjk* ($= cfts$). The sum of these turns out to be equivalent to *adhn*.[9] That is, even though the country remains a net importer of this product, and even though its environment would be more degraded as domestic output of this good expands, the rise in its international price would (if P is above e in Figure 2.2) boost welfare in this distorted economy.

The second assumption that, when relaxed, can lead to a conclusion that an importing country could gain from an international price rise has to do with externalities in the markets for other products in this economy. If other sectors also pollute, then diverting resources from this sector to others is less socially useful than is suggested in Figures 2.1 and 2.2. That is, the marginal social cost curve S' (or the social excess demand curve ED') is closer than depicted to, or may even be below, the marginal private cost curve S (or the private excess demand curve ED). If in Figure 2.2 ED'' was the true social excess demand curve, on the assumption that other industries pollute more than this one, then with optimal pollution taxes in place this good would be exported rather than imported if the international relative price was OP_o. Even without pollution taxes the country would gain (by *gmur*) rather than lose from an increase in the international price from OP_o to OP'_o that was fully transmitted domestically, again despite the fact that output and hence pollution from this industry would increase. In this case, however, the environment would improve because pollution from other industries would decrease by more than was added by this industry. (Had the optimal pollution tax been in place the country would have been an exporter of this product, and its exports would have increased from OX to OX' when the international price rose from OP_o to OP'_o and the pollution tax was adjusted to its new optimal rate. The welfare gain from the international price rise in this case would be *gmur*, the same as when there are no pollution taxes.)

In short, these two illustrations using Figure 2.2 demonstrate that *even an economy which remains a net importer of a product whose international price has risen could benefit from that price rise if (a) domestic production of that product was being discouraged sufficiently by assistance to other sectors of the economy or (b) other sectors were more pollutive than this sector so that attracting resources into this sector improved the country's environment sufficiently* (Proposition 6).

Before moving on to consider the large-country case, it should be noted that negative consumption externalities, such as from burning fossil fuels, can be analysed in a similar fashion to production externalities. If a country had no pollution taxes and were to open up to or liberalize trade in such products, its environment and welfare would improve if it became an exporter as the higher domestic price would curtail domestic consumption. If it became an importer, on the other hand, consumers would gain more than producers lose but pollution would increase so welfare might increase or decrease in the absence of a pollution tax. This can be seen from Figure 2.3. In autarchy Q units of the domestic product would be produced and consumed, yielding net social welfare represented by *abj-abg* in the absence of a pollution tax. Under free trade, the country would import

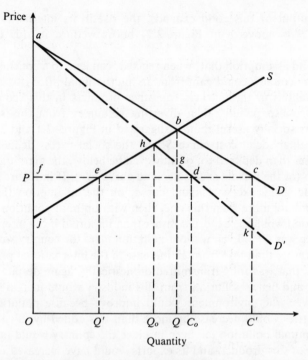

Figure 2.3   Effects of opening up a small economy to trade in a product whose consumption is pollutive

$Q'C'$ units at the international price OP, yielding net social welfare of *acej-ack*. The gain from trade in this case is thus *deh-bckg*, which may be negative. Should the optimal pollution policy be in place and adjusted accordingly when trade is liberalized, however, welfare must improve even if the country becomes an importer. The optimal level of consumption then would be OQ_o under autarchy and OC_o under free trade, with the net welfare gain from opening up to import $Q'C_o$ units being represented by the unambiguously positive area *deh*. That is, *liberalizing trade in a good whose consumption is pollutive improves the country's environment and welfare if the country exports that good, but would worsen the environment and therefore may reduce welfare if the good is imported unless a pollution tax close enough to the optimal rate is in place* (Proposition 7).

What if consumption of the foreign imported product was not as polluting as the domestic product? An example might be coal, where local coal contains more sulphur and so adds more acid rain than does the burning or foreign coal (as may be the case in Europe – see Newbery, 1990). Suppose in the extreme that the rest of the world is unworried by acid rain and so is indifferent as to the sulphur content of the coal it consumes, but for this country there is a social preference for imported coal which, for the sake of exposition, is assumed to be sulphur-free and to involve no other externalities. In this case it is possible that even in the absence of an appropriate environmental policy, import liberalization could improve both the environment and welfare because under free trade the country would import all its needs from abroad at price *OP* in Figure 2.3 and export its own product abroad, also at price *OP* (given the assumption that foreigners are indifferent as to the sulphur content of the coal they burn). The consumer surplus with free trade is *acf* and producer surplus is *jfe*, yielding net social welfare of *acej*. There is a clear gain in both environmental quality and net social welfare from opening up to trade in this case, the welfare gain being equal to *aceh* plus *hgb*. While this gain would be less if imported coal contributed some rather than no sulphur pollution, or if a sulphur emission tax had been in place before trade was opened up, this example serves to make the point that import liberalization of goods whose consumption is pollutive need not necessarily add to pollution. Or, to put it another way, where consumption of the imported product is less pollutive than consumption of the domestic substitute, an import barrier may be more rather than less costly to this country than is conventionally measured without accounting for pollution (Proposition 8).

2.3 The large-country case

How does the above analysis change when it is no longer assumed that the country's production and consumption do not affect the markets and environment of other countries? One change is that the export demand and import supply curves are no longer horizontal lines at a given international price as drawn in Figures 2.1 to 2.3, since this country's activities are sufficiently large to affect the price in the international market. Another fundamental change is that the divergence between the country's social and private excess demand curves alters, because its actions affect pollutive activities abroad which may spill over into this country's environment. Together these changes ensure that the effect of the country opening up to or liberalizing trade are somewhat different in the large-country case than in the small-country case. They also ensure that policy changes in one large country (or group of small countries) may cause other countries to change their policies too, so a wide range of outcomes is possible as the following examples illustrate.

Consider first a product whose production and consumption involve no international environmental spillovers. In the home country production of this good is more pollutive than would be production of the next most profitable good. Suppose in the rest of the world (call it the foreign country for simplicity), however, that this product is no more pollutive than other products. Hence the social and private marginal cost curves coincide abroad but diverge at home. An example might be agriculture, where in the advanced industrial (home) economy the alternative use of mobile farm resources is in the relatively unpolluting service sector whereas in the less-developed economies their alternative use would be in equally polluting smoke-stack manufacturing industries. Moreover, the advanced economy may use more chemical inputs and more intensive livestock methods than the poorer, more agrarian economies, and be relatively densely populated, in which case at the margin its farmers would be more pollutive than are farmers in less-developed economies. [10]

The effects of the large home country opening up its trade in this setting can be seen from Figure 2.4, where it is assumed that costs of transporting this product between the home and foreign countries are zero and that under autarchy, the price at home, P_H, would be above the price in foreign countries, P_F, so that this item is imported under a free trade regime. If the home country replaced its self-sufficiency policy with the optimal environmental policy it would import OT units ($= Q_m C_m = C_x Q_x$) of this good at the equilibrium international price OP. This is less than but closer to the proportional trade increase for a small country the closer the foreign supply curve, FS, is to being horizontal. Welfare unambiguously increases for the home country for three reasons. First, if there was no externality and hence no need to impose an environmental tax on production, there would be the normal gain from trade equal to *efj* which is the difference between the loss in producer surplus and the gain in consumer surplus in the home country. (In that case production would be *hj* more units than Q_m.) Second, there would be the increase in social welfare associated with reduced pollution due to the cut-back in domestic production. This is equal to the area between S and S' above the segment *je* of the S curve. And third, there would be the additional increase in social welfare (net of the loss of producer surplus *hgj*), associated with reducing production even further, to Q_m, by imposing the optimal environmental tax on production. That is the area between S and S' above the line *hj*. The total gain, shaded area *defh*, is smaller than it would have been without the international price rise (the small country situation) by *fkmh*, but it is certainly positive. Moreover, there is a welfare gain of shaded area *rst* and (by assumption) no extra environmental degradation in the foreign country following this trade liberalization. It follows that even in a situation where the foreign country's expanded production added to local and global pollution, both countries could still be better off as a result of the home country's reduction in import protection.

Now consider a case of liberalizing export trade, and explicitly include international environmental spillovers. Figure 2.5 depicts markets for a good (steel, for example) whose production involves the same by-product emissions in the two countries. Emissions in each country are partly transmitted to the other and assume these emissions are considered pollutive by the home country but not by the poorer foreign country. Given the foreign country's excess demand curve, the home country is assumed

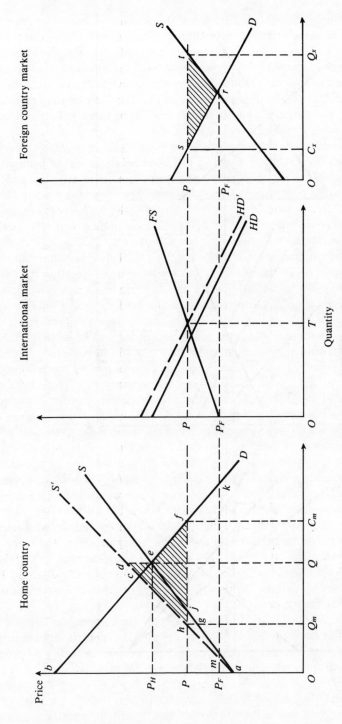

Figure 2.4 Effects of opening up a large economy to imports of a product whose production is pollutive

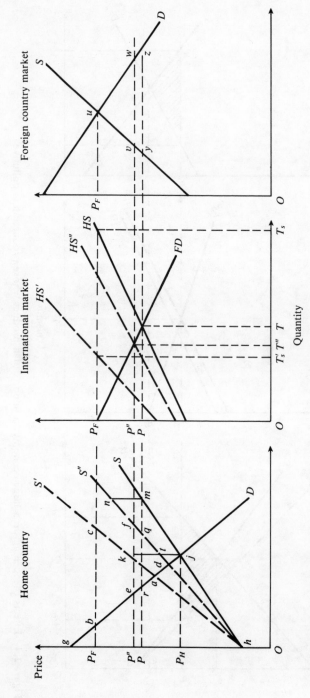

Figure 2.5 Effects of opening up a large economy to exports in a product whose production is pollutive

to be able to assess how much a production tax at home not only would reduce home emissions but also would increase pollution emanating from abroad of concern to home-country citizens (either because it is blown or flows to the home country or because, in their opinion, it affects the global commons adversely). The fact that taxing production at home encourages production abroad once this economy is opened ensures that the marginal social cost of domestic production drops somewhat below what it would be if the economy was small, say to S''. The vertical gap between S' and S'' would be larger, the greater the extent to which the benefits to home-country citizens of decreased emissions from domestic production are perceived to be offset by increased pollution from abroad, which in turn depends in part and inversely on the extent of pollution taxes abroad.

If the home country in Figure 2.5 opens up to trade, it will become an exporter of this product. In the absence of a pollution tax OT units would be exported from the home to the foreign country at international price OP (which is above the home country's autarchic price of OP_H). In the presence of an optimal pollution tax in the home country, liberalization would result in less trade (OT'') and the international price would be higher at OP''. But in both cases the new price at home is lower than the pre-liberalization foreign price of P_F.

In this case the trade effects of opening up to free trade when the country is large could be either proportionally larger or smaller than for an otherwise-similar small country, depending on the offsetting effects of (a) a less-than-infinitely elastic export demand curve facing the home country on the one hand and (b) the propensity for transfrontier pollution on the other hand. In the case illustrated in Figure 2.5 the small country facing OP_F would have exported OT_s units in the absence of a pollution tax, whereas the large country only exports OT at the lower international price OP. If the optimal pollution tax was applied, however, the small country would have exported OT'_s units at price OP_F, whereas the larger country exports OT'' at price OP''. That is, in the case illustrated the change in the effect on trade of facing a downward-sloping rather than horizontal export demand curve is more than fully offset by the trade effect of the drop in the domestic marginal social cost curve because of transfrontier pollution from abroad.

The welfare effect of opening up to free trade also could in this case be either greater or smaller the larger the country. In the presence of an optimal environmental policy before and after opening up, for example, the welfare gain from opening to free trade is *abc* in Figure 2.5 if the home country is small (and therefore has no effect on the foreign country's pollution). When it is large, however, the welfare gain is *def*, which may be more or less than *abc*. Nor is it clear whether under free trade the environment will be cleaner for the larger country than for the small country. This is because output may expand more or less in the large country than the small country, but even if it expands less and so means a smaller increase in domestic emissions for the large country, there may be extra spillover of foreign pollution in the latter case which could be enough to offset that difference.

As in the small-country case, trade liberalization for this export commodity (as distinct from an import-competing product) need not necessarily increase welfare in the large country if there is no pollution tax in place. Before trade is allowed and when no pollution tax applies, social welfare from producing and consuming this product is represented Figure 2.5 by *dgh-djt*. After trade is opened, social welfare in the absence of a pollution tax would be *qrgh-qmn*. Thus the change in the home country's welfare from opening up fully to trade in the absence of a pollution tax is *qrjt-qmn*, which could be positive or negative. Should the optimal pollution tax be introduced when trade is opened, however, welfare certainly improves at home (by *eftj*).[11] The superior outcome in the latter case arises not only because marginal social costs and benefits are brought into line by the pollution tax (contributing *qmn*) but also because that tax improves this large country's terms of trade (adding *refq*).

Given its lack of concern for the environment, the foreign country in Figure 2.5 gains from this trade: it would gain by *uyz* if no pollution tax applied in the home country or by the lesser area *uvw* if the optimal pollution tax was introduced in the home country when its trade was opened up. That is, that pollution tax itself reduces welfare in the foreign country in this case where that foreign country is and remains an importer of this product.

These results expose the intriguing opposite possibility that a large country (or group of small countries) that exports a polluting product but is unconcerned by that pollution might nonetheless benefit from taxing the production of that good and might at the same time improve welfare for its trading partners who care more for the global environment. This could happen when the gain in welfare of the 'greener' country group due to the cleaner global environment more than offsets the global loss in welfare due to reduced consumption of goods, and the net gain in global welfare (which is the difference between these two effects) is shared between the exporting and the importing country groups. Examples that come to mind are taxing the carbon content of fossil fuels at the point of production, or taxing logging activities to compensate for the foregone carbon absorptive capacity of depleted forests.

To illustrate this possibility, consider an extreme case in which exporting countries do not consume and importing countries do not produce the product in question. Then the international market for this good, depicted in Figure 2.6, is also the global market. The curve *MD* is the demand in the importing countries and *XS* is the supply in the exporting countries, while the vertical distance between *XS* and *XS'* reflects the negative aesthetic value importers place on an extra unit of production. If the importers were successful in persuading the exporters to place a tax of *bd*

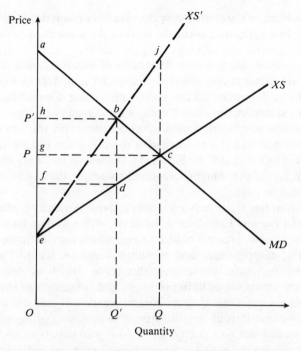

Figure 2.6 Effects of taxing production or consumption to improve the global environment

per unit on production of this good, the price would rise from OP to OP'. The importers' loss in consumer welfare is $bcgh$, but their welfare gain from reduced environmental degradation is $bdcj$ which conceivably could exceed $bcgh$ and thereby make them better off. At the same time exporters are better off as well (even assuming they get no aesthetic pleasure from a cleaner environment) so long as the reduction in producer surplus, $cdfg$, is less than the production tax revenue, $bdfh$. In that case the global gain, bcj, would conveniently be shared between the two groups of countries without explicit (non-market) foreign transfers.

Clearly administrative problems exist in collecting producer/exporter taxes and distributing those tax revenues between producing countries. The strategy adopted by OPEC of course has been to try to agree on national production quotas, but even then there are policing costs because of the free-rider incentive to produce above quota. Moreover, as Chapter 4 in this volume by Snape points out, importing countries alternatively or additionally could tax consumption and thereby possibly improve their own and global welfare, but at the expense of the exporters in this situation.

So far only a two-country world has been considered. International cooperation becomes more complex when three or more countries/country groups are involved, as the controversy over trade in raw ivory exposed (see Barbier *et al.*, 1990). Figure 2.6 can be used to illustrate crudely the main features of that controversy. Africans supply raw ivory almost exclusively for export. East Asians are the main demanders of that ivory, and of course they have no domestic supply source. Hence *XS* and *MD* in Figure 2.6 represent both the domestic and the excess supply and demand curves for these two groups, respectively. But there is a third group of people, mainly in Western Europe and North America, who believe this trade is causing the African elephant herd size to be smaller than they feel is desirable. The distance between *XS* and *XS'* in Figure 2.6 represents the marginal 'cost' to that third group of the slaughter required to supply the raw ivory trade (their willingness to pay).[12]

   In this situation free trade in ivory would provide African suppliers with a welfare gain of *ceg* and East Asian consumers with a welfare gain of *cag*. But the conservationist group would lose *cej*, which may be more or less than the sum of the producer and consumer surpluses (*cea*). The latter group has been successful in banning this trade, which is clearly sub-optimal from the viewpoint of both producers and consumers of raw ivory. A globally optimal outcome, if taxes could be collected and redistributed costlessly and without introducing distortions such as smuggling, would be to reduce the trade from *OQ* to *OQ'* by imposing an export or import tax of *bd*, so as to equate the global marginal benefit with the global marginal cost.[13] Such a trade tax would reduce East Asian consumers' surplus by *bcgh* and African producers' surplus by *cdfg*. But it would also provide tax revenue of *bdfh*, which would go to Africa if it imposed an export tax or to East Asia if it imposed an import tax. If each imposed a smaller trade tax which together summed to *bd*, that trade tax revenue would be shared between the two country groups in proportion to their tax rates. As well, the conservationist would be better off by *cdbj*, so the global gain from such a trade tax is *cbj*. If *fd* happened to be half the horizontal distance from *f* to the straight-line *MD* curve, an export tax of *bd* also would happen to be optimal from the African producers' viewpoint if they were given the tax revenue, because *d* would be the point of intersection of the marginal revenue curve from point *a*, given the average revenue curve *MD*. Or if *hb* was half the horizontal distance from *h* to the *XS* curve, an import tax of *bd* would happen to be optimal from the East Asian consumers' viewpoint if they were given the tax revenue. Clearly in this case the conservationists could seek support to restrict trade to *OQ'* from either producers or consumers, but the excluded group would oppose or retaliate in response to that restriction. And both producers and consumers of ivory would oppose restricting the trade to less than *OQ'*. Conservationists have been prepared to insist on a ban on raw ivory trade in large part because they have not been required to compensate the losers. If they were, they would need to be able to pay the equivalent of *cea*, and even if the benefit to them of the ban (*cej*) exceeded that loss to ivory suppliers and consumers, it might not exceed it sufficiently to overcome free-rider and other administrative costs of collecting that revenue from supporters of this conservationist policy and redistributing it to the relevant producers and consumers.

2.4 Summary, qualifications and implications

Several key points can be summarized from the above analysis concerning the effects of trade and environmental policies on the environment, trade and welfare. First, opening up to trade in a good whose production is relatively pollutive improves the environment and welfare of a small country if, after opening up, this country imports the good in question. Should this good be exported, however, trade expansion through trade liberalization worsens a small country's environment, and so welfare may or may not increase in the absence of a pollution tax. And conversely if the pollution is generated from consumption. Even the small country exporting (importing) this good whose production (consumption) is relatively pollutive would gain unambiguously from trade liberalization if it simultaneously ensured that something close to the optimal environmental policy was in place, despite the fact that its environment may be more polluted under a liberal trade regime.

Second, trade taxes-cum-subsidies could be used to reduce environmental degradation by a given amount, but they would improve a country's welfare less than would a more direct tax on the source of pollution – indeed they may even worsen welfare.

Third, if the international price of a good whose production is pollutive rose because of the imposition of a pollution tax (or import liberalization) abroad, welfare in a small open economy which exports this good would improve – notwithstanding the environmental damage caused by its greater production – so long as a pollution tax close enough to the optimal rate was applied to domestic producers. However, if the economy was an importer of such a good, an international price rise might but need not necessarily make that economy worse off. The country could be better off if it were to switch sufficiently from being an importer to being an exporter of this good and applied a pollution tax close enough to the optimal rate. [14] But even an economy which remains an importer of such a product whose international price has risen could benefit from that rise if (a) domestic production of that product was being discouraged sufficiently by government assistance to other sectors of the economy or (b) other sectors were more pollutive than this sector so that attracting resources to this sector improved the country's environment sufficiently. And conversely for a good whose consumption is pollutive.

The larger the country, the more its activities affect international prices and the larger is its proportionate effect on production, consumption and hence pollution in the rest of the world. This tends to moderate the proportional effects on an economy of liberalizing its trade, although many more exceptional outcomes are possible because of the varying extents to which (a) international environmental spillovers occur, (b) countries differ in their disutility from pollution, (c) imported goods are imperfect substitutes for domestic goods in terms of the consumption externalities they impose, and (d) the rest of the world alters its environmental (and trade) policies in response to policy changes in the country concerned. Even so, the fundamental point remains that free trade is nationally and globally superior to no trade so long as the optimal pollution tax is in place.

The above results depend of course on the assumptions made, so numerous qualifications are needed. Nonetheless, the key results are likely to be strengthened rather than weakened by more comprehensive analyses. For example, relaxing the assumption that the source of pollution is production or consumption *per se*, rather than the process used, ensures that the welfare gains from trade will be greater than suggested above when the optimal environmental policy instrument is used. This is because that optimal instrument will be less costly in terms of resources used or consumption foregone than a production or consumption tax. Relaxing that assumption also increases the cost of using trade policy rather than the optimal environmental policy instrument to overcome environmental externalities. The welfare gains from opening up an economy are also enhanced if by being more open it is less expensive (a) to import or develop domestically new technologies that are environmentally friendlier and/or (b) to import or export mobile factors of production in response to changes in countries' environmental policies. And when many small countries simultaneously impose a pollution tax on production of their exportables, the cost to any one of them of improving their national environment by a given amount is likely to be less, for two reasons: their terms of trade improve in the case of multilateral action; and pollution from abroad is reduced by the other countries' pollution taxes. The only possibility for their environment not to improve is if the increase in production in third (non-taxing) countries adds more degradation than the reduction in emissions in the taxing countries.

An important real-world implication of the above analysis has to do with developing countries' concerns that they will be made worse off as advanced industrial economies tighten their pollution standards. The analysis suggests these concerns are not justified if the advanced countries' imports are relatively pollution-intensive in their production. But if it is the developing countries that continue to import goods whose production is relatively pollutive, they may well have cause for concern. This is because their terms of trade are worsened by the rise in the industrial countries' pollution taxes and their own emissions increase as their import-competing sectors expand. And should developing countries respond by introducing or raising their own pollution taxes, their terms of trade would deteriorate further and thereby limit the extent to which such a response could have an offsetting positive influence of welfare. However, three points should be kept in mind when considering this issue.

First, the more pollution taxes are raised in advanced economies relative to developing economies, the more production of pollution-intensive goods will be relocated to developing countries. This is particularly so if the appropriate capital is internationally mobile, in which case it is more likely that those countries will become exporters of pollutive goods. Once that point is reached, developing countries will be beneficiaries of further pollution tax increases in the advanced economies provided their marginal disutility from a dirtier domestic environment is low or they adjust their own pollution taxes upwards to their new optimal level.

Second, it should not be inferred from the above that poor people do not care for the environment. On the contrary, it is reasonable to assume that rich and poor people have similar tastes and preferences for all goods and services, including those of a clean environment (following Stigler and Becker, 1977). What differs between rich and poor people is their incomes, and hence their capacity and preparedness to trade off greater goods consumption for a cleaner environment. It is therefore not surprising that the (explicit or implicit) rates of taxation of pollution tend to be highly correlated with the per capita incomes of nation states. With this perspective it is clear that pollution abatement is not greatly different from any other item with a high income elasticity of demand, including its effect on the international terms of trade as global incomes rise. There is no more justification for underpricing environmental services as their demand grows, in order not to worsen the terms of trade for a subset of countries, than there is to distort the prices of any other goods or services.

Having said that, the third point to keep in mind is that provided pollution tax rates are not too far from their socially optimal levels in each country, the rich countries whose welfare increases when they raise their pollution taxes need share only some of that gain to compensate fully those poorer countries whose welfare is reduced.

One other important real-world implication of the above analysis relates to the relationship between the demand for a cleaner environment and the pattern of distortions to incentives that is in place. In a distortion-ridden economy, one of the cheapest ways for policy makers to satisfy the increasing demand for less pollution may be not to introduce a pollution tax but to reduce government assistance to pollution-intensive industries. That would be the case if those industries were the most assisted. On the other hand, if pollution-intensive industries were the least assisted by the current pattern of distortions, an economic reform program aimed at reducing distortions may need to be accompanied by the introduction of or an increase in pollution taxes to guarantee that the policy changes improved national welfare. These are matters that are taken up and developed at length in Chapter 8 of this volume.

Notes

Helpful comments by John Black, Bernard Hoekman, Michael Leidy, Peter Lloyd, Francisco Nadal De Simone, Richard Snape, Arvind Subramanian, John Whalley and Alan Winters are gratefully acknowledged.

1. Where property rights are well defined and transactions costs permit, social costs may be internalized cheapest by the private sector (Coase, 1960). This would be especially so if government intervention is likely to result in the use of second-best policy instruments because of interest-group pressures on politicians, as discussed for example in the chapter in this volume by Hoekman and Leidy.

2. These are standard assumptions in the economic analysis of distortions, as discussed for example by Corden (1974). While not denying the considerable difficulties associated with measuring the benefits of the environment, as discussed by, for example, Johansson (1987) and Braden and Kolstad (1991), the analysis explicitly assumes that such benefits are not infinite and that costs of pollution abatement are positive.

3. As Krutilla (1991) points out, with production externalities this is the case when emissions are not substitutable with other inputs in the production process, or when reducing output is a lower-cost response to an emissions tax than changing the production process (as it may well be in the short to medium term and/or when low levels of intervention are called for).

4. For a detailed exposition of the appropriateness of this consumer and producer surplus approach to measuring social welfare, see, for example, Just *et al.* (1982).

5. Given the assumptions made, this would bring about what is known in the environmental literature as the Lindahl equilibrium (Mäler, 1985). Note that even when the environment is highly valued it does not follow that the society would be better off the higher the pollution tax, because such a tax reduces environmental degradation at the expense of goods production and hence consumption. In the autarchy case, a production tax of *tg* units, for example, would provide less social welfare than if no environmental policy was in place because *tch* exceeds *cde* in Figure 2.1(a).

6. Further elaboration of the environmental effects of lowering trade barriers is provided in Chapter 8 of this volume.

7. As Britten-Jones *et al.* (1987) point out, the optimal second-best export tax is that which maximizes the difference between those two areas, contrary to the criterion suggested by Corden (1974). Note that a parallel analysis of an import subsidy could be made, but in situations where production taxes are administratively infeasible (notably developing countries), import subsidies are likely to be difficult to implement also because of the high costs of raising the necessary tax revenue.

8. What follows draws to some extent on an analysis (in a different context) by Anderson and Tyers (1991).

9. As Anderson and Tyers (1991) point out, area $cfts = z\Delta P.s$ where ΔP is the change in price, s is the import subsidy per unit and z is the (negative of the) slope of the excess demand curve. Area $fgrj = \Delta P[zs - X] - \frac{1}{2}z\Delta P]$ where X is the quantity that would have been exported if the domestic price had been *OP*. Hence the difference between these two areas, which is the net welfare gain from the international price rise of ΔP that is fully transmitted domestically ($\Delta P = PP' = P_0 P_0'$), is thus $\Delta P(X + \frac{1}{2}z\Delta P)$. This is identical to *adhn* in Figure 2.2. Notice that the above is concerned with the welfare effect of the international and domestic price changes in the presence of the

country's protectionist policy, not with the change in the welfare cost of that protectionist policy.

10. This presumes in particular that if the expansion of agriculture in less-developed economies involved the clearing of forest land, such an expansion would be no worse for the local and global environment than if the resources so used to expand food output were used in other (pollutive) activities. Variations of this example are discussed in more detail in Chapter 8 of this volume.

11. Unlike in the small country case, though, it does not follow from the latter result that liberalizing a less-than-prohibitive trade barrier (as distinct from switching from autarchy to free trade) must improve this large country's welfare, even with the optimal pollution tax in place. This is because the large country by definition has some monopoly power in trade, and the trade tax that it eliminates may be less than (or not sufficiently above) its optimal trade tax from the viewpoint of maximizing its consumption of goods.

12. In what follows the positive externality which the existences of elephants bestows on Africa's tourist industry and the negative externality which roaming elephants impose on African farmers and villagers are assumed exactly to offset each other.

13. Here only ivory tax policy instruments are considered. There is, however, the possibility of better national park management policies and the like being able to boost elephant herds sufficiently at even lower cost.

14. This possibility of a switch in an importing country's trade pattern raises the more general question of what determines changes in a country's comparative advantage in pollutive goods in a growing world economy, an issue that is addressed in, for example, Blackhurst (1977).

References

Anderson, K. and R. Tyers (1991), 'More on Welfare Gains to Developing Countries from Liberalizing World Food Trade', mimeo, Australian National University, Canberra, July.

Barbier, E., J. Burgess, T. Swanson and D. Pearce (1990), *Elephants, Economics and Ivory*, London: Earthscan.

Blackhurst, R. (1977), 'International Trade and Domestic Environmental Policies in a Growing World Economy', pp. 341–64 in *International Relations in a Changing World*, by R. Blackhurst *et al.*, Geneva: Sythoff-Leiden.

Braden, J. B. and C. D. Kolstad (eds.) (1991), *Measuring the Demand for Environmental Quality*, Amsterdam: North Holland.

Britten-Jones, M., R. S. Nettle and K. Anderson (1987), 'On Optimal Second-Best Trade Intervention in the Presence of a Domestic Divergence', *Australian Economic Papers* **26**: 332–36.

Coase, R. H. (1960), 'The Problem of Social Cost', *Journal of Law and Economics* **3**: 1–44.

Corden, W. M. (1974), *Trade Policy and Economic Welfare*, Oxford: Clarendon Press.

Johansson, P-O. (1987), *The Economic Theory and Measurement of Environmental Benefits*, Cambridge: Cambridge University Press.

Just, R. E., D. L. Hueth and A. Schmitz (1982), *Applied Welfare Economics and Public Policy*, Englewood Cliffs: Prentice Hall.

Krutilla, K. (1991), 'Environmental Regulation in an Open Economy', *Journal of Environmental Economics and Management* **20**: 127–42.

48 *Kym Anderson*

Mäler, K.-G. (1985), 'Welfare Economics and the Environment', Chapter 1 in *Handbook of Natural Resources and Energy Economics*, Vol. 1, edited by A. V. Kneese and J. L. Sweeney, Amsterdam: North Holland.

Newbery, D. M. (1990), 'Acid Rain', *Economic Policy* 5, (11), 297–346.

Stigler, G. J. and G. S. Becker (1977), 'De Gustibus Non Est Disputandum', *American Economic Review* 67: 76–90.

3

The problem of optimal environmental policy choice

Peter J. Lloyd

Transfrontier pollution and environmental problems are a particular set of externality or market failure problems, with the added feature of the transmission of the pollutants and environmentally-related products across national borders.

The primary effect of national borders is to limit the instruments available to deal with these problems because the jurisdictions of national governments stop at their borders and there is no international government or law with powers corresponding to those of national governments. Nations which are net losers from international transmission of pollutants have become increasingly concerned about these problems. If international actions fail to address them satisfactorily, there will be increasing agitation to use national measures. Among these in some cases will be trade-based policy measures to achieve national goals. Trade-based measures are also used as a means to ensure compliance with international environmental conventions, as with the regulation of international trade in ivory under the Convention for International Trade in Endangered Species. Conversely, the GATT, the OECD, UNCTAD and other international agencies have become concerned over the potential impact of national and international environmental policy measures on international trade.

The analysis of the policy options for environmental problems is a subset of standard analysis of market failures. As with other externality problems there is, for each environmental problem, a multiplicity of instruments which may be used to seek to correct the market failure. The nature of these problems is such that there is no single instrument or set of instruments which ranks generally above all others. For example, Bohm and Russell (1985) concluded their comparative survey of alternative instruments with the observation that '...no general statements can be made about the relative desirability of alternative policy instruments once we consider such practical complications as that location matters, that monitoring is costly, and that exogenous change occurs in technology, regional economies and natural environment systems'. This result carries over to environmental problems with transnational flows. Transnational environment problems differ in details such as the numbers of polluters or pollutees, the locations of the emission and reception areas, the stock or flow nature of the pollutant, the extent of uncertainty, the form of the damage function and the enforceability of instruments. Each problem must therefore be analysed separately because the ranking of two or more alternative instruments is not robust with respect to variations in these specifications.

Notwithstanding the specificity of each problem, however, there is a common approach. The choice of instrument may be regarded as an optimization problem. One selects an objective function and specifies the structure of the market(s) concerned. An important part of the structure in this class of problem is the transmission mechanism. There is a list of instruments available. The optimization yields an optimal or first-ranked instrument. The other instruments available can then be compared and ranked and, if necessary, a second-best choice can be made. The ranking may not be straightforward. Even the list of available instruments is constantly growing. For example, over almost twenty years the OECD has carried out several studies regarding the principles of selecting instruments in pollution and environment problems. The listing of 'economic' (i.e. price-based) instruments alone in their latest study (OECD, 1989) is considerably longer than earlier lists (OECD, 1976) as it includes newer types of economic instruments such as liability insurance. In some cases, none of the instruments in the existing list may solve the problem or there may be adverse effects on some parties which are not acceptable so that an important part of the analysis may be to try to design a new set of instruments. The analysis of transfrontier pollution problems such as acid rain and waste disposal is of this type.

This paper provides a general survey of the issues involved in selecting instruments to regulate transnational pollution and environmental problems. It begins with a comparison of instruments in terms of the concepts of equivalence and non-equivalence. Then the discussion moves briefly to the jurisdiction of governments which apply instruments of environmental policy. Two archetypal problems which are the source of most conclusions concerning the choice of instruments in a closed economy are outlined. The analysis focuses on the aspects which can be related to the internationalization of pollution. Next the problem of managing environmental policy in a world with nations and the international transmission of pollutants or products is considered, while problems associated with the use of trade-based instruments are discussed in the last section.

3.1 Comparison of instruments

To make the comparison of two (or more) instruments precise, there is one concept which turns out to be particularly instructive, namely, the equivalence of instruments. This concept is useful for all policy problems which must rank multiple instruments. It has been widely used not only in environmental economics but also in tax theory (e.g., the Ricardian equivalence of tax and bond financing) and in international trade theory (e.g., the Lerner 'symmetry' of an export tax and an import tax and the equivalence of a tariff and a quota).

Equivalence or non-equivalence is a relation that holds between a pair of instruments. A three-fold distinction is made. The distinctions are based on the concept of a market solution which was introduced into the comparison of a tariff and a quota in international trade theory by Ohta (1978). A market solution is simply the set of solution values in an optimization problem of all endogenous variables such as the quantities of market production, consumption and imports, the prices to consumers and producers, and the value of revenue collected from the instrument to the government.

Definition 1: One instrument is said to be *identical* to a second alternative instrument if both instruments, when set at appropriate levels, yield the same market solution.

Definition 2: One instrument is said to be *equivalent* to a second alternative instrument if both instruments, when set at appropriate levels, yield the same market solution except for the incomes of the agents. (Otherwise, the instrument is defined as *non-equivalent*.)

Definition 3: One instrument is said to be *quasi-equivalent* to a second alternative instrument if both instruments, when set at appropriate levels, yield the same solution value for one of the endogenous variables.

In Definition 3 it may be that more than one endogenous variable takes on the same values, but the possibility that all variables except the income variables take the same values is ruled out. Thus, Definitions 1, 2 and 3 are mutually exclusive. They are in decreasing order of the set of variables in the market which take the same values. One could define the complements of Definitions 1 and 3, that is *non-identical* and *non-quasi-equivalent* instruments, in the same way if desired.

These definitions are all partial equilibrium but they have general equilibrium analogues. In the general equilibrium version of the policy problems, two equivalent instruments may both be Pareto-efficient, that is, they yield production and consumption allocations which put the economy on the utility possibility frontier, but they will yield different sets of real incomes for the households in the economy. In what follows, for example, equivalence relates to static comparisons, but it should be kept in mind that in a dynamic setting such equivalence may break down. See, for example, Anderson (1988) on the non-equivalence of tariffs and quotas as trade policy instruments in a dynamic setting. It should also be kept in mind that in addition to standard economic policy instruments there are policy options such as publicity campaigns to alter individuals' contributions to micropollution (Opschoor and Pearce, 1991). Economic efficiency rules out the possibility of any slack in the economy in the sense of any possibility of Pareto-improving reallocations.

These distinctions are very helpful. The usefulness of Definition 1 is self-evident. Surprisingly, some pairs of instruments which are identical are not obviously so. An example is the identity of a property rights assignment and the appropriate tax-subsidy together with the rule for the disbursement of the tax revenue or the financing of the funds to pay the subsidy (see below). The usefulness of Definition 2 is that it isolates the efficiency effects of instruments. Definition 3 is useful when one wants to compare the effects on some pre-selected variable.[1] In the environmental literature, the problem is often posed as one of attaining some environmental standard. Thus we are comparing instruments which are quasi-equivalent with respect to the environmental standard. The concern in the GATT and the OECD has recently shifted to the 'trade impact' of environmental policy instruments. These international organizations are concerned with the linkage between environmental policies and trade flows. When examining instruments which impact on the exports or imports of a commodity, it may be useful to fix the environmental standard and then compare the effects of different instruments on other variables, especially the quantities traded between nations.

Two instruments which are equivalent may be compared in terms of their income effects. Thus, economists frequently argue that it is better to auction quota rights to avoid the transfer of rents to quota holders. More generally, a government may be concerned with the distribution of the income effects of instruments among its citizens. One instrument may have an effect which is more progressive or regressive than another or may have a particularly large impact on some households. For example, Harrison (1975) concluded that the costs of controlling air pollution from motor vehicles in the United States have been distributed progressively within cities but have affected the rural poor rather badly because their car ownership is high and they have fewer alternatives, with the overall effect being regressive. The concern over the distribution of the costs and of the benefits may be greater in developing countries. It has been argued that the poor have fewer opportunities to substitute as income-earners or consumers (Eskeland and Jimenez, 1991). A government preference for one instrument over others because of the pattern of income effects implies it is unable or unwilling to compensate losers.

Two non-equivalent instruments may be compared and ranked in terms of their efficiency effects. Frequently, the problem is posed as one of achieving a given improvement in the environment at least cost. Income effects may also be considered.

It is now well understood that any relation between two instruments only holds under certain assumptions. Any modification of one of these critical assumptions will alter the rankings. This non-robustness is the reason why the ranking of policy instruments is so difficult.

3.2   The jurisdiction of the government

Until recently, almost all of the literature on the environment related to problems which were national. That is, all of the agents involved lived within the borders of one nation and were, therefore, subject to the jurisdiction of the one government which could select the instrument of policy. Regulating international transmission of pollutants and/or of commodities whose production or consumption is polluting is complicated by the restriction of the jurisdiction of the policy-imposing governments to the subsets of agents living within their national borders (or to negotiated international agreements in the form of bilateral or multilateral treaties). Initially, the analysis here is restricted to a closed economy. This allows us to consider the choice of policy instrument or the design of new instruments without concern for the limitations on instrument choice which derive from national jurisdictions. The last two sections consider the nature of the second-best problem when the economy is open and the choice of instruments is constrained by national jurisdiction.

The closed economy consists of a given population of people which, in turn, defines the population of agents (polluters, pollutees, consumers, producers). The agents have a fixed geographic location which may or may not be important, depending upon the structure of the market(s) concerned. A sole government has jurisdiction over all agents in the economy.

3.3   Two archetypal environmental problems

In order to develop some principles, the analysis focuses on two archetypes of environmental problems which feature prominently in the literature and which produce some principles of wide applicability. The problem is described as a pollution problem for concreteness. The term 'pollution' can, therefore, be understood to include all environmental problems. The first is the upstream-downstream problem where one or many upstream producers raise costs for a user of water downstream. The second involves not only multiple dischargers but also multiple reception areas for pollution.

3.3.1   *The upstream-downstream problem*

Much of the literature and most of the textbooks – for example, Varian (1984) and Pearce and Turner (1990) – are based on a type of problem involving one upstream producer who produces a pollutant as a by-product and one downstream producer who is adversely affected by the pollutant. We can call them the steel mill and the fishery respectively. This is the simplest form of a unilateral or non-reciprocal producer-on-producer externality with only two agents. This is what is sometimes called the one-on-one problem (see Helm and Pearce, 1990) where the first 'one' refers to the number of polluters or generators and the second 'one' to the number of pollutees or affected parties. Moreover, it is assumed that the pollution problem is a flow problem, the two industries are competitive and there is no uncertainty in the product or factor markets or pollution flows. The pollution is transmitted by water and arrives directly at the fishery without being dissipated and without affecting any other agent in the economy. There is perfect information and no monitoring or enforcement costs. Many authors assume there is no possibility of abatement by means of reducing pollution per unit of output, but this restrictive assumption is easily relaxed.

While this model is over-simplified, it has been the source of most fundamental insights of pollution theory. These include the Pigovian tax (Pigou, 1932), the Coase Theorem (Coase, 1960) and the equivalence of a pollution tax and a pollution abatement subsidy (see, for example, Baumol and Oates, 1975).

The social objective function in this problem is simply the sum of the profits of the two activities since the only two agents involved are competitive producers. If the agent who suffers the damage is a consumer, the problem can be recast in a similar way by taking some monetary measure of the value of the product to the consumer(s) less that of the damage. Let subscripts 1, 2 and 3 denote the outputs of steel, the pollution by-product, and fish respectively. The structure of the problem is given by the technologies of producing the outputs which can be represented by the production functions:

$$y_1 = f_1(x_1)$$
$$y_2 = g_2(y_1, a_1)$$
$$y_3 = f_3(x_3, y_2)$$

$g_2(y_1, a_1)$ is the pollution by-product function. This assumes pollution is some function of the output of steel, y_1, and possibly also of the use of abatement inputs by the steel producer, a_1. The social problem is to find:

$$\max\{[p_1 f_1(x_1) - w_1 x_1 - w_2 a_1] + [p_3 f_3(x_3, g_2(y_1, a_1)) - w_3 x_3]\}$$
$$\text{such that } (x_1, a_1, x_3) \geqslant 0$$

where (x_1, a_1, x_3) are the vectors of inputs used in steel, abatement and fisheries production and (w_1, w_2, w_3) are the vectors of their prices. (It is useful to note for comparison with the second model below that the social problem can be recast as one of maximising the social profit gain from the pre-intervention situation by reducing pollution.)

The model yields a number of standard results. Steel producers in an unregulated market maximize their own profits, disregarding completely the harmful effect of steel production on fisheries production which results from the river pollution. This yields, under very general restrictions on the functions, a market failure with too much steel output and too little fisheries output. The social maximum solution is achieved by the rule of choosing input levels so that the marginal cost equals the marginal social benefit, taking into account in the benefit function both the value of the sale of steel and the harm imposed by the pollution by-product. The socially-optimal adjusted solution has the property that the optimal quantity of pollution is, in general, not zero.

The social optimum can be achieved by a number of policy choices which include the following: a pollution standard; a pollution charge; a pollution abatement subsidy; an assignment of property rights to (a) the polluter or (b) the pollutee; and the internalizing of the externality through one of the operators taking over the other activity (i.e. unitization).

The pollution standard is fixed in terms of the total emission. The pollution charge is based on the pollution emitted. Examples are taxes on waste discharged, pollutants emitted into the air or water, and the carbon tax proposed to reduce global warming (see OECD, 1991). The pollution charge rate is set at the rate $(p_3 \; \partial f_3/\partial y_2)$ per unit of emission which measures the social cost of pollution in terms of the value of the loss of fish output at the margin. (Alternatively, it could be set in this example as a tax on steel output if there is a one-to-one correspondence between steel output and emission.)

When there is no possibility of abatement by means of the use of abatement inputs, abatement can only occur through a reduction in the output of the steel mill. When there is a possibility of abatement by the use of abatement inputs, there are two margins of pollution reduction. A tax on pollution (or any of the equivalent instruments) provides the incentive to the polluter to adjust output and/or to use abatement inputs at the margin so as to minimize the private and the social cost of pollution reduction. This solution may call for zero abatement inputs if the abatement technology is expensive. The use of abatement inputs is an example of action the polluting agents might adopt to reduce their tax burden. Other actions might also be possible, such as the relocation of the mill to another site where pollution taxes are lower.

The use of concepts of equivalence sheds further light on the choice. All of these instruments are equivalent to each other, but they are not all identical because the income effects differ between some pairs. An assignment of property rights to the fisheries is identical to the combination of a tax or charge on the polluter with the proceeds paid lump-sum to the fisheries. This is of interest because many economists have advocated a polluter pays principle but opposed the payment of the proceeds as compensation to the pollutees (see Bohm and Russell, 1985) while others advocate property rights which are equivalent to the charge with compensation. An assignment of property rights to the steel mill is identical to a pollution abatement subsidy in combination with the finance for the subsidy being levied lump-sum on the fisheries. These two sets of instruments are not identical to each other because they affect the profits of the two producers differently. Similarly, a pollution charge and a pollution abatement subsidy are not identical to each other. All equivalent instruments yield the same total pre-tax/subsidy profits of the two producers.

The optimal tax, or an equivalent instrument, is optimal because it has a tax base, namely, the emission itself, which bears directly upon the damage caused and a tax rate which measures exactly the extent of damage associated with a marginal unit of the emission. Other instruments which do not bear directly upon the emission will inflict incidental costs on the economy and will, therefore, be sub-optimal. As the first example, consider a tax on steel output in the circumstance when abatement technology is available. In this case, although an output tax will reduce pollution and pollution damage, there is no longer a one-to-one correspondence between the quantity of pollution and output. Taxing output gives no incentive to the producer to reduce pollution by means of an abatement technology. Similarly, a subsidy based on abatement inputs, as distinct from a subsidy on the abatement of the emission itself, is sub-optimal. It gives no incentive to the producer to reduce abatement by reducing output and therefore raises the cost of abatement reduction through an excessive use of abatement inputs. Such instruments which are based on variables that are themselves related to the level of the damage-causing emissions are sometimes called 'indirect' instruments (see the taxonomy in Eskeland and Jimenez, 1991). These include taxes on the complements of the product with which the pollutant is associated (e.g. taxes on motor vehicles whose consumption of petrol pollutes the atmosphere) and subsidies on substitutes (Sandmo, 1976). All indirect instruments are inefficient and sub-optimal if direct instruments are feasible.

This classification of optimal (or efficient) and sub-optimal (or inefficient) instruments can be refined to give a ranking of more than two instruments. Such a ranking will reflect the rule that an instrument ranks more highly (i.e. is more efficient), the more closely the base is related to the source of the pollution-creating emission.[2] A good example of this principle is the problem of global warming due to carbon dioxide emissions. The optimal (first-best) tax is a tax on carbon emissions. If this is not feasible, taxes on carbon-producing fuels or on the outputs produced by these fuels such as electricity, have been suggested. But each of these produces incidental costs. A tax on fossil fuels does reduce their consumption but each fuel produces different marginal quantities of carbon in different uses. Similarly, a tax on electricity is independent of the source of fuel or power and gives no incentive to substitute carbon-free sources such as water, wind or nuclear energy or to introduce technologies which economise on the use of fuel or produce less carbon per kilowatt. Such instruments do not minimize the social cost of pollution reduction. Some indirect instruments may have such large incidental costs that they lower rather than raise social welfare.[3]

The model may easily be extended to n producer/polluter agents, that is, a many-on-one version of the model. Let the technologies be given by the production functions:

$$y_{1i} = f_{1i}(x_{1i}) \qquad i = 1, \ldots, n$$
$$y_{2i} = g_{2i}(y_{1i}, a_{2i}) \qquad i = 1, \ldots, n.$$
$$y_3 = f_3(x_3, \Sigma_i y_{2i})$$

The subscript i denotes a variable of the ith firm. This specification allows steel firms to be distinct in terms of steel-producing technologies. The pollution damage function may be firm-specific. However, it still assumes that it is the aggregate emission which affects the downstream producer and there is no dissipation of pollutants.

Again in this version a pollution charge or its equivalent is optimal. This should be levied at the rate of $\tau = (p_3 \, \partial f_3 / \partial y_{2i})$ where y_{2i} is the ith firm's contribution to the aggregate emission.

In practice, the extension of the model to many polluters may introduce complications which can change the optimal rule and imply that some equivalences no longer hold. With many polluting agents it may become difficult to identify the contribution of each to the aggregate emission. This has the effect of making all of the instruments less efficient. Some instruments may cease to be feasible as the number of agents increases; for example, unitization is only practicable with one or a very few polluters. This is an example of the non-robustness of instrument rankings with respect to the structure of the model.

The model can also be used to examine the Polluter Pays Principle (PPP), that is, a Pigovian tax. This principle is widely accepted. The OECD Member countries approved this general principle for all Member countries in 1972 and the EC endorsed it in 1975 (OECD, 1991). However, the recommendation is usually made on the realization that such a tax leads to the socially optimal outputs and inputs, that is, it is Pareto-efficient. The existence of other instruments which achieve Pareto-efficiency equally well shows that this is not the only way to approach the problem. In a case involving damage inflicted by a factory owner with a smoking chimney, Coase (1960) recognised that the problem could be equally well addressed by a subsidy paid to the factory owner to induce him to install a smoke-prevention device; that is an abatement subsidy is equivalent to a pollution charge. The preference for a tax instrument might be based on the view that it is morally wrong for an agent to inflict harm on other agents, but Coase showed that this argument too is false. 'The question is commonly thought of as one in which A inflicts harm on B and what has to be decided is: how should we restrain A? But this is wrong. We are dealing with a problem of a reciprocal nature. To avoid the harm to B would inflict harm on A. The real question that has to be decided is: should A be allowed to harm B or should B be allowed to harm A? The problem is to avoid the greater harm.' (Coase, 1960).

The problem is elucidated by the property rights involved. As has been noted, an assignment of property rights to either the polluter or the pollutee will solve the efficiency problem, at least in the case of one-on-one problems. Now, how are we to decide who should have the rights? In the case of one-on-one problems this is quite unclear. For example, in a one-on-one case of passive smoke inhalation how are we to justify the assumption that the interests of the passive smoker and his/her rights to be free of smoke should prevail over the interests of the active smoker who will be harmed if this is accepted, or vice-versa? The problem cannot be decided on this basis alone.

The extension of the problem to involve more agents gives a clue. In the case of a water pollution problem, such as the steel mill, there are frequently many agents who suffer damage. The riparian view of property rights relating to water applies in most countries and declares that these rights belong to the whole community. The extension of the commons to include air is based on the same view. If the commons belong to all, individuals cannot have the right to use them as they please and to inflict harm on other users. This justifies some intervention but it does not decide the allocation of the scarce resource of the commons. In the steel mill-fisheries example, the uses of the commons by either the fisheries or the steel mill restricts the use by the other agent and both impose a cost on the economy. One may note too that the governments which levy pollution taxes or proxy taxes in defence of the interests of those harmed rarely compensate them by returning the revenue to the agents who have been damaged. The Polluter Pays Principle identifies who should pay but it does not specify who should receive the revenue.

The term Victim Pays Principle is sometimes used to describe the alternative pollution abatement subsidies. This is an unfortunate and unhelpful misnomer as any action produces a victim because of the reciprocity noted above. The term Pollutee Pays Principle would be preferable as it merely identifies the agent who pays.

The choice of instruments is complicated by other considerations. Olson and Zeckhauser (1970) noted that the application of the Polluter Pays Principle gives no incentive to the agents who are damaged by pollution to take evasive action. Sometimes it will be easier for the affected agent(s) to take such action than for the polluting agent(s); for example, by relocation of plants or residences. The earlier example implicitly assumes the possibilities of evasive action were restricted to the polluters. Similarly, in some problems, the enforcement costs of schemes which pay polluters may be less than those which penalize them. Conversely, pollution abatement subsidies may have adverse incentive effects (see for example, Baumol and Oates, 1975).

3.3.2 The problem of multiple dischargers and multiple reception areas

In the model above the aggregate of emissions matters but not its location, apart from the fact that the mill is located on the one stream. In many pollution problems the precise location of the source of the pollution matters. This can occur because there are many sources of pollution and the damage occurs at some reception area other than the point of emission. The quantity of many pollutants at the reception area is less than the quantity at the point of emission because the substance or chemical is not entirely conserved. It is chemically changed or physically settled between the source and the reception area and the loss varies from source to source. As well, if there are multiple reception areas, the damage caused by a given quantity of a pollutant measured at the reception area where it arrives may vary from area to area. Indeed, since areas differ in terms of the agents who inhabit them and their preferences and activities, this variation in damage is a universal feature of problems with multiple reception areas.

Numerous pollution problems are of this form; for example, discharge of sewerage or industrial waste into river systems or the sea and air pollution with deposition in many areas. These situations can be modelled by a many-on-many model, that is, a model with 'many' dischargers and 'many' reception areas.

Figure 3.1 illustrates an example in which there are multiple dischargers and three reception areas – A1, A2, and A3. Each cluster of sources has a transmission mechanism such that the waste discharged from all of the sources in a cluster is received at one or two areas. The lines indicate the transmission paths in real space.

Suppose there are $n \geqslant 1$ sources, and $m \geqslant 1$ reception areas. The benefit from reducing pollution is the avoidance of the social damage it would cause if it were not reduced. This benefit is not modelled but it is assumed there is a monetary measure of these damages and the damage function is known. The costs are the costs of reducing pollution at source and the cost function is assumed to be known. Let:

$D_i^0 =$ initial level of pollution discharged at source i.

$\Delta D_i =$ reduction in level of pollution discharged at source i

$A_{ij} =$ pollution discharged at source i arriving at reception area j

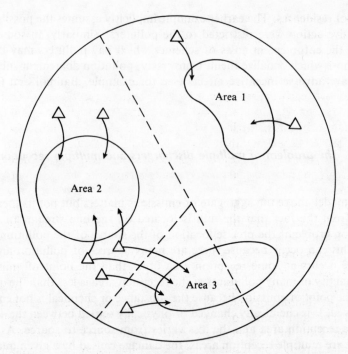

Figure 3.1 A world with multiple polluters and reception areas

$E_j = E_j(\Sigma_i \ A_{ij}) =$ damage function at reception area j

$B_j = -\Delta E_j =$ benefit from reducing pollution at area j

$C_i = C_i(\Delta D_i) =$ cost of reducing pollution at source i

The pollution received in area j from source i is some function of the pollution discharged from this source, $A_{ij}(D_i) = \alpha_i D_i$ where α_i is some fraction. It is assumed that the damage at each reception area depends solely upon the aggregate pollution received at the area. This is the model which underlies the analysis of most of the many-on-many pollution problems.

Formally the problem is to find:

$$\max_{\Delta D_i} \ \{\Sigma_j \ B_j[\Sigma \ A_{ij}(\Delta D_i)] - \Sigma_i \ C_i(\Delta D_i)\} \text{ such that } \Delta D_i \geqslant 0 \text{ for all } i$$

The reductions in discharge below the initial levels are the policy variables. This rule essentially views the problem from the status quo in which there is an excessive level of discharges. The problem, therefore, is to reduce these discharges to the optimal level and in the optimal way, as a given aggregate reduction can be achieved in many ways. This seems to be the way in which policy-makers conceive the problem.

This maximum is achieved by the rule:

$$\frac{\partial C_i}{\partial D_i} = \sum_j \frac{\partial B_j}{\partial A_{ij}} \frac{\partial A_{ij}}{\partial D_i} = \sum_j \frac{\partial B_j}{\partial D_i}$$

assuming the objective function is concave and differentiable. That is, the reductions at each source should be such that the marginal cost of each reduction is equal to the marginal social benefit. The marginal social benefit is the sum of the benefits in each area which receives pollution from this source. (Strictly speaking, this rule holds only if $\Delta D_i > 0$. One should allow for the possibility that there will be a zero reduction at some sources. This will arise when the marginal cost of reduction exceeds the marginal benefit at a source.)

This rule implies that the reductions are not equi-proportionate across sources. The reductions should be greater in those areas where the marginal costs of reductions are less or the marginal benefits of reduction are greater. It also implies that, in general, society should not minimize the cost of achieving a given reduction in pollution. This can be seen readily from the dual problem. The problem of maximizing net social benefit has a dual problem of minimizing the cost of achieving a given level of net social benefit. This minimum problem implies minimizing the cost of pollution reduction if and only if benefits of reducing pollution at source are equal across all sources. This result is intuitively obvious. A rule of minimizing the cost of pollution reduction would forgo possibilities of improving welfare by shifting the pollution reduction from areas with low marginal costs of reduction but little benefit to those with marginal costs which are a little higher but more than offset by gains in benefits.

It is usually supposed that the agent (producer or consumer) producing the discharge or emission acts purely selfishly. Typically the agent is a producer who is assumed to maximize the profits of the firm when activities yield pollutant as a by-product of a production activity but the model also encompasses selfish consumers who smoke cigarettes or consume other products which yield some harmful by-product such as chlorofluorocarbons (CFCs). Thus the initial level is that which maximizes the welfare of the private agents. In this case the social optimum may be achieved by a set of charges on discharge or emission at each source. The charges are location-specific since location matters either because it affects the contribution to the amount of the harmful substance which reaches the reception area or because the damage depends on the reception area. The rate of charge should equal the marginal damage caused, that is, the negative of the marginal benefit, at the optimum point. Any source whose discharge or emission is received at more than one area should pay a charge with components equal to the marginal damage caused to each group of agents.

Under these assumptions the set of discharge taxes is equivalent to a set of discharge abatement subsidies at the same levels. The latter is not usually pursued, apparently because of adherence to the Polluter Pays Principle.

Equally, an administered system is equivalent to both economic instruments, under these assumptions.

Historically, the first model of many dischargers was the model of a river system.[4] This model is important because much of the discussion of charges and trading in emission rights derives from it. The model was one in which there was a single reception area or equivalently an unspecified set of agents who suffer damage from waste disposal. Moreover, the problem was conceived as one of attaining some ambient environmental standard measure at some monitoring point. Much of the literature takes this desideratum either because this standard is believed to be the appropriate goal or in some cases because the damage function is unknown. This is unfortunate in one respect. The way the problem is posed leads to policies which minimize the cost of achieving a reduction in pollution whereas, in a more general model, one should also consider the marginal benefit at each source.

This problem too is solved by a set of effluent charges on the waste load discharged at each source. The charges are source-specific because location affects the contribution of a unit of discharge at source to the standard measured at the monitoring point. This rule equates the marginal cost across sources of reducing the waste at the monitoring point. It takes account of differences in location and of differences in the marginal cost of reduction in each location. It implies percentage reductions at each source which are not uniform. Those sources with lower marginal costs of reduction have larger percentage reductions.

The focus in these river problems has been on emissions trading through marketable permit systems. The difficulty with either an administered system or a charge system is that the controlling government agency must have full information on the locational factors and cost functions of each source (except under very restrictive assumptions which yield a single fixed charge). With a tradeable permit system the government agency fixes the total of the waste or residual at some point, allocates this total in the form of permits among sources and then allows trading of permits among sources. In practice, non-tradeable permits specified in terms of discharge limits or technological specifications are the commonest policy instruments for environmental policy. The novelty lies in permitting the trading of these rights. The advantage is the government need not know the location differences and the costs of reduction at each source. Under certain conditions, the permit trading would ascertain these and produce the desired standard at least cost, provided the rights traded are defined as rights to cause pollution by certain amounts at the monitoring point. Trading of emission permits was first suggested by Dales (1968). Montgomery (1972) provides a proof of efficiency that holds for any initial allocation.

A system of marketable permits is equivalent to a set of optimal charges if the permits are auctioned and certain conditions hold. The difficulty is that these conditions frequently do not hold. There is a growing literature on the comparison of marketable permit systems with a single emission charge or uniform reduction or other systems. When monitoring and enforcement costs are present or the market for permits changes or there is strategic behaviour among permit-holders, the ranking of instruments is not fixed.[5]

3.4 The complication of transnational transmission

Many pollution problems involve the transmission of pollutants or other commodities which embody environmental effects across national borders. Examples include solid wastes discharged into rivers, acid rain, trade in elephant ivory and other animal or bird products which endanger species. Some of these problems are global in nature, chiefly the release of carbon which gives rise to global warming (the 'greenhouse effect') and the release of CFCs which damage the ozone layer of the earth. Problems differ greatly in terms of the location of agents causing the pollution and the location of damage or deposition, the nature of the transmission process and other respects. Problems which are global in nature plainly call for a globally-coordinated solution which involves all nations in joint action. This section concentrates on problems which are transnational in nature but not global, and on the efficacy of international and national instruments to address such problems.

The economy is now the world economy. It consists of a given population of people which defines the population of agents (polluters, pollutees, consumers, producers), each of whom has a fixed geographic location, as before. However, the geographic world is now partitioned into nations, each of which contains the population of agents resident in the area defined by its national borders. The government of each nation has jurisdiction over its own residents only. These nations now trade with each other in the usual sense of exchanging commodities. They also exchange pollutants across their borders, though not every country is necessarily an exporter and an importer. Thus, the economies of nations are open in a dual sense. (It is possible for a nation to have an economy closed in the usual sense of not trading commodities with other countries and still be an exporter or importer of pollutants from other nations, or vice-versa. For example, the East European countries have had little trade with West Europe but have been a major source of pollution in West European countries.)

The many-on-many location-matters model discussed in the previous section captures the essential features of transnational pollution with the addition of the feature that the locations of the sources and reception areas are in different countries. It is further assumed that national governments take account of the cost which pollution from each source in their home country imposes on residents in the reception areas of their own country. They use pollution charges or some equivalent instrument to ensure that the marginal cost equals the marginal national benefit of pollution reduction. However, the national governments have no concern to regulate activities within their territories for the benefit of residents of another country. Thus, there is, from a global point of view, excessive pollution. This is the model which underlies analyses of many transnational pollution problems (see, for example, Mäler, 1990, and also Newbery, 1990).

Several distinct cases are possible depending on the location of sources and reception areas. As an example, consider the pattern of location shown in Figure 3.1 with the addition of national borders of three nations. The total area can now be considered as a projection of the globe on to two dimensions. The broken lines in this real space mark the borders of nations. They may by-pass completely an area or they may intersect the lines which mark the transmission paths from a source. This generates a number of cases. One case is that of separate clusters of sources and reception areas which fall entirely within the borders of a single nation. This is illustrated in the case of Area 1 and its sources. Obviously no transnational transmission occurs and the previous analysis applies with the national government able to choose instruments which apply to all sources.

The remaining cases involving transnational transmission can be sorted by considering the pairs of countries which are involved when the source area is in one country and at least one reception area is in another. These cases can be cross-classified according to whether the transnational transmission is one-way or two-way (reciprocal) and whether the reception area is in one or two countries. This twofold classification gives four types. Type I is that of one-way transmission with the deposition wholly in the foreign country. Type II is one-way transmission with deposition in both countries. Type III is two-way transmission with the deposition from the sources in each country being wholly in the foreign country. Type IV is two-way transmission with the deposition from the sources of at least one country being partly in the country of source and partly in the foreign country. The latter type is illustrated by the sources that transmit to Areas 2 and 3 in Figure 3.1.

With more than two countries, the pattern of sources and reception areas can be arrayed in a matrix. An illuminating example is the pattern of deposition of sulphur dioxide in the form of gas or particles borne by air currents in the countries of Europe which is reported in Newbery (1990). The data were collected by the European Monitoring and Evaluation Programme set up in 1978 and are measured in thousand tonnes per annum. Fourteen countries or groups of countries are reported. One outstanding feature is that almost all of the entries in the 14×14 matrix are strictly positive. The only group of zero entries relate to sources in the Scandinavian countries which do not deposit to a significant extent on the other countries in Europe with the exception of the Soviet Union because of their location on the north-west fringe of the continent and the prevailing east-to-west wind movements. With this exception, the pattern is one of almost universal reciprocity with the great majority of pairs of countries experiencing two-way or reciprocal flows of the acid rain-producing compounds. A second notable feature is the relatively large numbers in every element of the diagonal. This shows that most of the deposition in fact is within the source country. This is an example of Type IV in the above typology. National policies will not suffice in such cases. The data can also be used to calculate bilateral and multilateral export/import rates or net balances and the ratios of imports/totals received or the import shares.

Previous analyses of the location-matters model showed that the optimal policy response is a set of charges differentiated by source, or an equivalent policy. In terms of the first-best policy response, the global problem does not differ from that of a closed economy. A world of many countries, like a closed economy, contains disparate sources and reception areas and calls for a set of differentiated charges or equivalent instruments. The globally optimal policy produces a non-uniform reduction in pollution by source and, therefore, by country. This takes advantage of the differences across sources (and countries) in the marginal costs and benefits of reduction at each source. One should note that, in the absence of transfers among nations some nations would lose, in the sense that net benefits would be reduced, even when the world as a whole gains from pollution reduction.

The first-best policy could be imposed if there were a global agency with authority to enforce these charges, but there is no such agency. The first consequence, therefore, of introducing nations into the model where each nation has jurisdiction over its own territories only, and the set of instruments is restricted compared to the case of a closed economy, is to make the first-best optimum unattainable. The efficacy of all instruments of national policy is reduced when the enforcement of these instruments stops at the border.[6]

This limitation has spurred economists to seek other ways of agreed action by nations to achieve the first-best policy for the global economy. Early in the debate on transnational pollution the Polluter Pays Principle was extended to instances of transnational pollution. Similarly, the Stockholm Conference of 1972, which resulted in the establishment of the United Nations Environment Programme, stated that 'States have ... responsibility to ensure that activities within their jurisdiction or control do not cause damage to the environment of other states or of areas beyond the limits of national jurisdiction' (quoted in OECD, 1976). This statement can be interpreted as a declaration of the principle. Nevertheless, it was recognised that this principle could not be enforced among nations and that some compensation for nations which are net losers from pollution reduction would be necessary. The Polluter Pays Principle does not indicate to whom the tax proceeds should be paid and the implicit property rights are obscure in these problems. The early emphasis was on burden-sharing schemes (OECD, 1976, 1981).

Mäler (1990) characterizes such international negotiations as a game in which those who gain from multinational cooperation must devise rules so that those who would otherwise lose have an incentive to agree to play the game. He considers situations involving unidirectional externalities and regional reciprocal externalities as well as global externalities. His conclusion is that 'There will be many situations where the victim pays principle, or transfers from the country whose environment has been degraded to the country that causes degradation, will be necessary in order to achieve an efficient solution' (Mäler, 1990). These transfers may take the form of concessions in other areas in which the countries have common interests rather than financial transfers. The reason for the transfers is that the net gains stand to be very unequally distributed among the countries and compensation is necessary to give the losing countries an incentive to cooperate. Adherence to the Polluter Pays Principle would lead to the non-cooperation of these countries and the collapse of the game. The problems are exacerbated if there is incomplete information regarding the costs of abatement or the national damage functions. Countries may seek to understate their net benefits by exaggerating their abatement costs or understating the benefits of pollution reduction. In the case of many countries affected by pollution, there is a free rider problem. Yet, it is still possible to devise rules with side-payments that will lead to participation and the truthful revelation of national costs and benefits. This is an encouraging result.

In practice the difficulties of negotiation seem often to have led to the simple rule that countries agree to uniform percentage reductions. For example, the 1985 Protocol to the Geneva Convention on long-range transport of pollutants called for a uniform 30 per cent reduction in sulphur emissions. The main proposal for reducing carbon emissions in OECD countries is to lower the emissions in all countries to a common percentage, say 80 per cent, of a base level. This is called a Toronto-type rule, after the proposal of the 1988 Toronto Conference on climate change.

In this context a number of authors suggest that internationally tradeable permits are the natural device to achieve efficient social-cost-minimizing reductions (Mäler, 1990; Newbery, 1990; Tietenberg, 1990). These permits could relate to emission reductions. A global market could be established for the trading of (national) emission reduction credits. Suppose, for example, that an international agreement is signed which calls for some reduction in the growth of carbon emissions. Under an offsets policy, countries which reduced their emissions by more than the agreed amount would get a credit which could be traded with a country that had difficulty in achieving its target. Such trading permits the reductions to occur in those locations where there are lower-cost methods of reducing emissions by recycling, treatment, introducing new technologies, etc., or where there are greater marginal benefits. Moreover, it could provide a method of payment to low-income countries who protest that they cannot afford conservation measures. By selling offsets, some third world countries would be in a better position to undertake environmentally sound investments such as protecting forests. Countries such as Brazil may have a new comparative advantage in global emission reduction products.

Negotiation to curb carbon emissions are now taking place under the auspices of the United Nations as part of a convention on global climate change. Burniaux *et al.* (1991) report simulations with the OECD's GREEN model which compare a carbon tax and a carbon tax combined with trade in emission rights as alternative means of achieving a percentage reduction goal for carbon emissions. The latter policy combination distributes the emission cuts optimally to the countries with lower marginal abatement costs. The burden of adjustment shifts from oil and gas to coal as the most efficient way of achieving reductions. China, the USSR and other countries with lower carbon taxes before trading gain by selling their rights. The common carbon tax required to reduce global carbon emissions to 80 per cent of their 1990 level would need to be about US $150 per ton of carbon in the year 2020 with trade in emission rights, compared with about $215 without emission-rights trading. The average fall in real household incomes is only 1 per cent with trading compared with more than 2 per cent for the uniform percentage reduction rule without trade in emission rights. Nevertheless, there is still a problem in persuading all countries to participate, as some countries will not perceive the gains from reduced global warming to justify the loss of real incomes.[7] One possible source of funding is the proceeds of the carbon tax itself. A carbon tax would yield large revenues. For example, a tax of $150 per ton of carbon would add about $18 to the price of a barrel of oil.

In all models of environmental damage with international transmission of the pollutant or emisison, the optimal policy affects international trade in some commodities. A good example is the set of optimal taxes on carbon which would substantially lower the price of fuels to producers, especially that of coal, as well as raising the relative price of these goods to users. The volume and terms of trade of coal-exporting countries, for example, would necessarily deteriorate, but such consequences need to be borne as part of the required change in the competitive general equilibrium. (Second-best arguments for using instruments of environmental policy to correct other market failures are ruled out). There will be pressures on governments to prevent some of the changes in real income, including demands for protection from imports when world prices fall. If governments accede to these demands the costs of pollution reduction will be increased. The next section considers the direct use of trade-based instruments.

3.5   The use of trade-based instruments

Trade-based instruments are the subset of instruments which are based on flows of commodities between nations. They include import tariffs, export taxes, export and import prohibitions, and quantitative restrictions on trade. These instruments are already used as one means of regulating some environmental problems. Examples are the bans on exports and imports of live birds, animals and reptile species which are considered endangered, or of products made from apparently endangered species such as products made from elephant ivory or the skins of reptiles or fur-bearing animals. Most trade-based instruments are in the form of total prohibitions of export or import trade. A closely related field is the use of barriers at national borders to prohibit the importation of live animals and plants or products made from animals or plants in order to protect domestic animals or plants from contracting diseases which would impose costs on and/or harm the environment of the potentially importing country. This set of transnational environmental and health problems has recently been reviewed by Kozloff and Runge (1991).

While the ranking of trade-based instruments can only be determined specifically for each environmental policy, there is a presumption that trade-based instruments will generally have a low rank and should not, therefore, be used, or at least not as a sole instrument. This conclusion follows as an application of the principle that the optimal instrument for a problem is that instrument among the list of feasible instruments whose base is most closely related to the source of the market failure. In very few, if any, cases is the actual cause of an environmental failure international trade in commodities itself, although some problems will be associated with trade in products.

For most environmental problems involving the transnational transmission of pollutants the transnational transmission occurs via the common property resources of water or air which act as a carrier. There is no direct link to trade in goods and services in such cases and the instrument chosen should be one related to the production or consumption activity or to the use of the inputs (such as fossil fuels) which are the source of the pollutant or emission.

Even for those environmental problems where there is some link with commodity trade in animals or plants, or animal or plant products, there are several aspects of the transmission or the generation of the problem which reduce the efficiency of trade-based instruments. An externality may be transmitted solely by the sale and transport of some product, but sales can occur on domestic markets as well as the markets of foreign countries. An example of this type may be the transmission of diseases among plants or animals. Such cases call for regulation of all sales from infected areas, to both domestic and foreign buyers alike. Export or import taxes or bans are merely a part of the regulation of all sales. If, say, an import ban is used and there is no corresponding restriction on sales of domestically-produced goods, there will be an incidental cost in the form of the distortions due to protection. Moreover, it will generally be more efficient to prevent the sales from the seller whose area is affected. Bans on exports and imports are a second line of defence, as it were, though they are not objectionable in cases where sale bans are appropriate in general, provided the international trade bans are not used for an excessive period or over an excessive range of products as a protective instrument, and they do not discriminate among nations.

The strongest argument for trade-based instruments occurs in cases where the transmission is associated with international commodity trade in all sales, that is, there are no domestic sales of the commodity concerned. A situation close to this may occur in a few instances. For example, almost all of the demand for products made from elephant ivory or certain exotic birds is from buyers resident in foreign countries. But even in such cases export and import bans may have limited efficiency. The reason for the danger to the species concerned may have more to do with the destruction of the habitat than with the killing or the capture of the animal or plant concerned. Primary attention should focus on the preservation of the habitat in such cases.

Another difficulty with trade-based instruments arises from problems of enforcement. A total prohibition on the exports and/or imports from or to the countries concerned gives very strong incentives to smugglers and illegal traders. Enforcement efforts will not always succeed in stopping all trade. If only a proportion of illegal trades is detected, the effect of a ban as distinct from an export tax or quota may be to increase rather than decrease the number of animals or birds traded while at the same time reducing the number of live animals or birds delivered in the importing countries. For birds such as parrots, for example, it is known that many die in transit: in order to achieve each successful trade, many may be attempted. Furthermore, if there is more than one country of supply of an endangered species, the export bans must be enforced equally in all supplying countries, because otherwise production and exports of the product are likely to expand in the countries with less-effective control. In some cases it may be preferable to permit breeding in captivity and to legalize the international trade in the products of a regulated domestic industry.

This paper has mostly ignored a number of features which may be present in particular environmental problems. These include problems of enforcement, uncertainty and dynamic aspects associated with cumulative effects of pollution. The introduction of these features may change the optimal instrument and the ranking of sub-optimal instruments. However, the most basic principles are robust with respect to variations in the specification of the problem. In particular, all instruments should be considered, and the optimal instrument is one whose base is most closely related to the source of the market failure.

Notes

I would like to acknowledge gratefully comments from John Martin.

1. In the comparison of a tariff and a quota, the first statement by Bhagwati (1969) was in terms of the (quasi-) equivalence with respect to the quantity-of-imports variable. But Shibata (1983) observed that quasi-equivalence with respect to the quantity of domestic production was the crucial feature as the policy problem was conceived as one of protecting the domestic producers.

2. This principle was developed by Bhagwati (1971) in international trade theory where the problem was to rank alternative instruments which might be used to achieve a 'non-economic' objective such as employment in an import-competing industry. Generally trade-based instruments such as tariffs and quotas rank lower than instruments such as wage subsidies or output subsidies which bear more directly on the objective.

3. An issue closely related to indirectness is the suggestion sometimes made that the optimal intervention should take into account other distortions in the economy due to taxes, imperfect competition or other market failures. Consider, for example, that the polluter is a monopolist. Buchanan (1969) suggested a Pigovian tax is inappropriate as the monopolist's output is less than optimal. While the monopolist's output is less than the output of a competitive industry, it may be less or greater than the output of a competitive industry which also pays the Pigovian tax. Moreover, the use of pollution control instruments to address monopoly problems would do nothing to control monopolists who happened to be non-polluters. Equally, one could suggest that monopoly controls be used to penalize polluters. This would do nothing to control polluters who happened to be non-monopolists. Given the small intersection of the sets of polluters and monopolists/oligopolists and the very different bases of the instruments required in each case, the linking of pollution control and competition policy is likely to be effective in controlling neither. The two distinct problems require two distinct sets of instruments. Pollution and imperfect competition may be linked in another way. Polluters may prefer administrative controls over taxes and subsidies as the former may inadvertently restrict entry into an industry if the pollution is associated with an essential input or process. This point is emphasized in the chapter by Hoekman and Leidy in this volume.

4. This model is largely due to Kneese (1964). Bohm and Russell (1985) provide a useful discussion and references.

5. Tietenberg (1985) is the standard reference. OECD (1989) and Hahn (1989) survey the extent of such systems and recent experience.

6. In this respect, the problem resembles that of other national externality problems in which the national government is constrained by a constitution to impose charges or grant subsidies which are uniform among agents. The standard reference is Diamond (1973).

7. Little is known of the total benefits from the avoidance of global climate change, nor of the distribution of those benefits across countries, so these benefits are not included in the model. Other empirical studies of policies aimed at reducing greenhouse gas emissions are reviewed in Chapter 5 of this volume, and some new modelling results presented in Chapter 6 include a valuation of benefits from carbon emission reduction.

References

Anderson, J. E. (1988), *The Relative Inefficiency of Quotas*, Cambridge: MIT Press.

Baumol, W. J. and W. E. Oates (1975), *The Theory of Environmental Policy*, Englewood Cliffs: Prentice Hall.

Bhagwati, J. N. (1969), 'On the Equivalence of Tariffs and Quotas', in *Trade, Growth and the Balencce of Payments: Essays in Honor of Gottfried Haberler*, edited by R. E. Baldwin, Amsterdam: North Holland.

Bhagwati, J. N. (1971), 'The Generalized Theory of Distortions and Welfare', in *Trade, Balance of Payments and Growth: Papers in Honor of Charles P. Kindleberger*, edited by J. N. Bhagwati *et al.*, Amsterdam: North Holland.

Bohm, P. and C. S. Russell (1985), 'Comparative Analysis of Alternative Policy Instruments', in *Handbook of Natural Resource and Energy Economics*, edited by A. V. Kneese and J. L. Sweeney, Amsterdam: North Holland.

Buchanan, J. M. (1969), 'External Diseconomies, Corrective Taxes and Market Structure', *American Economic Review* **59**: 174–77.

Burniaux, J. M., J. P. Martin, G. Nicoletti and J. Oliveira Martins (1991), 'The Costs of Policies to Reduce Global Emissions of CO_2: Initial Simulation Results with GREEN,' Working Paper No. 103, Department of Economics and Statistics, OECD, Paris, June.

Coase, R. H. (1960), 'The Problem of Social Cost', *Journal of Law and Economics* **3**: 1–44.

Dales, J. H. (1968), *Pollution, Property and Prices*, Toronto: Toronto University Press.

Diamond, P. (1973), 'Consumption Externalities and Imperfect Corrective Pricing', *Bell Journal of Economics* **4**: 526–38.

Eskeland, G. S. and E. Jimenez (1991), *Choosing Policy Instruments for Pollution Control: A Review*, Working Papers in Public Economics, Washington, D. C.: The World Bank.

Hahn, R. W. (1989), 'Economic Prescriptions for Environmental Problems: How the Patient Followed the Doctor's Order', *Journal of Economic Perspectives* **3**: 95–114.

Harrison, D. (1975), *Who Pays for Clean Air: The Cost and Benefit Distribution of Automobile Emission Standards*, Cambridge, Mass: Ballinger.

Helm, R. and D. Pearce (1990), 'Assessment: Economic Policy Towards the Environment', *Oxford Review of Economic Policy* **6**: 1–16.

Kneese, A. V. (1964), *The Economics of Regional Water Quality Management*, Baltimore: John Hopkins University Press.

Kozloff, K. and C. F. Runge (1991), 'International Trade in the Food Sector and Environmental Quality, Health and Safety: A Survey of Policy Issues', Staff Paper p. 91–12, Department of Agricultural and Applied Economics, University of Minnesota, St. Paul, May.

Mäler, K. G. (1990), 'International Environmental Problems', *Oxford Review of Economic Policy* **6**: 80–108.

Montgomery, D. (1972), 'Markets in Licences and Efficient Pollution Control Programs', *Journal of Economic Theory* **5**: 395–418.

Newbery, D. (1990), 'Acid Rain', *Economic Policy* **5**, (11), 297–346.

OECD (1976), *Economics of Transnational Pollution*, Paris: OECD.

OECD (1981), *Transfrontier Pollution and the Role of the State*, Paris: OECD.

OECD (1989), *Economic Instruments for Environmental Protection*, Paris: OECD.

OECD (1991), *The State of the Environment*, Paris: OECD.

72   *Peter J. Lloyd*

Ohta, H. (1978), 'On the Ranking of Price and Quantity Controls Under Uncertainty', *Journal of International Economics* **8**: 543–550.

Olson, M. and R. Zeckhauser (1970), 'The Efficient Production of External Economies', *American Economic Review* **60**: 512–517.

Opschoor, J. B. and D. W. Pearce (eds.) (1991), *Persistent Pollutants: Economics and Policy*, Dordrecht: Kluwer Academic Publishers.

Pearce, D. W. and R. K. Turner (1990), *Economics of Natural Resources and the Environment*, London: Harvester Wheatsheaf.

Pigou, A. C. (1932), *The Economics of Welfare*, London: Macmillan.

Sandmo, A. (1976), 'Direct versus Indirect Pigouvian Taxation', *European Economic Review* **7**: 337–49.

Shibata, H. (1983), 'A Note on the Equivalence of Tariffs and Quotas', *American Economic Review* **58**: 137–41.

Tietenberg, T. H. (1985), *Emissions Trading*, Washington, D. C.: Resources for the Future.

Tietenberg, T. H. (1990), 'Using Economic Incentives to Maintain our Environment', *Challenge* **33**: 42–46.

Varian, H. (1984), *Microeconomic Analysis*, New York: Norton.

4

The environment, international trade and competitiveness

Richard H. Snape

Interconnection between international trade issues and the environment is coming increasingly into focus. The Montreal Protocol (regarding the depletion of the ozone layer) and international conventions on whaling, hazardous wastes, and endangered species, relate to internationally traded products and provide for international trade measures to aid enforcement (Harris, 1991). International trade in rainforest and other products with world-wide environmental implications is receiving much attention and many calls are being made for its restriction. Meanwhile there is concern in industries in countries with tough environmental controls about competition from those without such controls.

A substantial and well-known literature has examined 'domestic distortions', including externalities from production and consumption, and the policy implications in an international trade context.[1] The environment as such has not featured strongly in these works explicitly, but adverse effects on the environment are leading examples of externalities. The chapter in this volume by Lloyd surveys more recent developments in the literature on the ranking of policy instruments in the context of pollution.

What this literature in the main has not addressed is internationally transmitted externalities. In one sense the international aspect is irrelevant. That is, if a particular policy is optimal from the efficiency perspective, then that policy will still be optimal whether or not the effects cross national borders.

However that is not the end of the internationality issue. As compared with economic activity and externalities which are wholly domestic, there are two extra dimensions in an international context. This is true whether it is the products which are traded internationally, or the externalities which are transmitted internationally, or both.

First, there is an additional set of policy instruments with which to address the problem, namely, international trade policies. Second, an additional jurisdiction is involved. The optimal intervention literature referred to above addresses the 'additional policy instrument' aspect and concludes that, from a first-best perspective, policies directed at international trade are not appropriate instruments with which to attack externalities. But when externalities are exported, the options available to those who are affected may be quite limited. This is one aspect of the jurisdiction question.

Another jurisdictional consideration is that of property rights and liability for damage. Which country has the right or obligation to regulate or tax economic activities which generate externalities when either the product or the externality is crossing international frontiers? Undefined property rights or liability for damage is inimical to economic efficiency, as is well known in the problem of the commons. It is usually more difficult to define and enforce property rights and liability internationally than nationally.

The 'polluter pays principle' is often advanced as a principle for liability, giving property rights for a clean environment to the polluted. Such a principle gives rights of compensation to the latter, or perhaps permits taxation or regulation of the polluter. The question has additional importance in an international context not only because of the possibility of clashes between legislatures and jurisdiction but because the tax revenues or the economic rents which arise from regulation can be substantial. The international distribution of who gains or loses from restricting pollution, for example, can hinge on who obtains these revenues.

The question and the analysis of who compensates whom was addressed by Coase in his celebrated paper (Coase, 1960). The international aspects parallel much of his analysis, which focused on localized nuisances, most of quite specific incidence. The jurisdictional relationships between governments considered here have much in common with his examples of relationships between individuals.

An objective of this chapter is to highlight and explore international aspects of environmental externalities using very simple models. The assumptions underlying the models presented have been chosen in such a way as to maximize the likelihood that trade will be an appropriate instrument of intervention. By then gradually relaxing these assumptions the analysis exposes the general inefficiency of trade policies in addressing environmental concerns. However, there may be situations in which, in the absence of the international definition of property rights and liability, trade policies are the only policy instruments available to a country to address a particular environmental problem. While there are some situations in which revenue from a pollution tax may provide the incentive for a government to take internationally beneficial action unilaterally (without the necessity for an international agreement), it is possible that in the absence of an international agreement a country may use the opportunity to move the terms of trade optimally in its favour (thus reducing world income, particularly if other countries retaliate).

Before summarizing and concluding the chapter, some 'competitiveness' problems associated with environmental controls and taxes are addressed as they are becoming of ever-greater concern to many industries and governments.

4.1 Trade policies and pollution

This section is concerned with internationally traded products which have environmental implications, and particularly with those resource and environmental problems which spill over from one country to another. The distinction in practice between national and international problems is not always clear, but the discussion concentrates mainly on those activities and policies which have identifiable effects on other countries. Thus acid rain, ozone depletion, whale extermination, nuclear fallout, rain-forest destruction, the use of pesticides in the production of products traded internationally or which pollute international waters, and carbon dioxide emissions which affect the world's climate, are all conceptually included, as are environmental policies affecting internationally traded goods. However, pollution of a local river from which internationally traded goods or services are not produced is not included.

In examining policies which may be adopted by governments for environmental or conservation reasons, it is important to identify the source of the problem. Is it the commonality of a resource which is the essence of a problem? Recognizing this commonality and dealing with it may provide the best approach from an international perspective, though not necessarily so from the perspective of every country. Is it the production of a product itself or its production processes which is of concern? If it is production itself which is the cause of the problem, reduction of production is appropriate. If it is a production process, then it is the process which needs to be addressed. If consumption of particular products is damaging the environment (e.g. some pressure-pack propellants), then consumption should be focus of attention for policy purposes.

As noted, while the division of the world into nations introduces the possibility of problems spilling over from one jurisdiction to another, it also provides another set of policy instruments: those associated with international trade. It also magnifies greatly income distribution problems associated with policies aimed at the efficient use of the world's resources. While within a country there are mechanisms for dealing with income distribution questions, any such mechanisms on the international arena are generally *ad hoc*.[2] Whalley and Wigle (1990) bring out the importance of the distribution question in a general equilibrium model in which they estimate that the tax revenue raised from carbon taxes designed to reduce world carbon emissions by 50 per cent would amount to 10 per cent of world gross product (see also Whalley, 1991).

To simplify the exposition the term 'pollution' is used to cover all external diseconomies referred to, and it is assumed that it is related to production, not consumption.[3] Thus 'pollution' is any activity which imposes costs on others in a manner which is not communicated efficiently by a market or a market substitute. (Such a market substitute may be a social norm – see Dasgupta, 1990). We assume that the pollution costs can be measured. This is an heroic assumption for it assumes not only that costs which one firm's activities impose on other firms, and which are not transmitted by the pricing mechanism, can be valued but also that the costs which are imposed on people generally (for example by the loss of a beautiful forest) also can be valued. Heroic or not, such valuations are made explicitly or implicitly all the time, for example, when it is decided to build a road in one location rather than another. For the purpose of analysis, these valuations must be made explicit though this should not blind one to the difficulty of placing even rough measures on the values in practice.

Initially it is assumed that the pollution is generated by production of a particular product and not by the use of a particular productive process. It is also assumed that property rights regarding the environment are not well defined or that transactions costs for those who have the rights are large enough to prevent them from being exercised. We also initially assume away 'government failure' problems in the levying of taxes or the imposition of restrictions.

In a closed economy, it is clear that either production or consumption of a product causing pollution could be restricted: the effects would be the same. The appropriate restriction will be one which brings into equality marginal social costs and marginal social valuation of the product, but the restriction (which could be induced through a tax) could be imposed on the producer or on the consumer. In practice it may be simpler administratively to impose it on one or the other, but that is a second-stage decision. Tax revenue would flow to the tax authority for use as the government saw fit. It may be most efficient to have marketable permits to pollute or to consume polluting products, so as to allow individual producers or consumers to evaluate the options.

Now turning to international trade and pollution, from a world efficiency perspective it is clear that it is again irrelevant whether the producers of the polluting production are induced to reduce production or the consumers of the polluting product are induced to reduce consumption. However, the incentive for a government to take such action in the interests of its nationals varies according to where the pollution 'falls' (meaning the location where the pollution costs are experienced) and which countries are producing and consuming the relevant product. This will now be explored in a series of very simple models. To anticipate a result which may appear paradoxical, it is shown that a country which is having pollution dumped on it by production abroad can be worse off if the global optimal tax on pollution is imposed by the polluting country, or by an international authority, than if no action were to be taken, even though world real income would be raised by such action. On the other hand it would be better off if it took the action itself. This result could also occur if it is a production process, including the use of a particular factor of production, which causes the pollution. Similarly, if importing countries restrict imports of products which pollute the exporting country (and this includes excessive felling of timber, for example), this may be judged harmful to the exporting country even if everyone is of one mind regarding the measurement of the environmental costs and agrees that it is in the world's interest that production be reduced.

When countries impose taxes or production restrictions on goods which are traded internationally, terms of trade changes bring gains or losses of real income to countries. To suppress as far as possible the terms of trade effects associated with changes in the level of production and consumption of the product in question in order to focus on pollution *per se*, constant costs of production are assumed initially. It is also assumed initially that the costs associated with a 'unit' of pollution are the same irrespective of the country in which the pollution falls and that is a constant cost of pollution per unit of output.[4] Competitive conditions are assumed in production and consumption. In all cases the relevant policies are applied so as to maximize global income.

4.1.1 *Constant costs of production and pollution*

4.1.1.1 *Pollution falls only on the polluting country*

Let us consider the optimum economic policy where a country A is producing, at constant cost, the polluting product (pollution being at a given rate per unit of output) and all the production is exported to country B and there are no other potential buyers. Country B does not produce the good nor does it import it from any other source. Assume also that all the pollution costs are contained within country A.

In Figure 4.1, $S(p)$ shows the private marginal and average costs of production and $S(s)$ shows the real or social costs of production, the difference between $S(p)$ and $S(s)$ being the costs of pollution. D is the demand curve in country B for the product. In the absence of any production, consumption or trade restrictions, OQ is the level of production, consumption and trade. While it is profitable for the producers in A to produce the good, for they earn a normal profit, A's real national product properly measured would be increased if production were to cease, for the revenue received by A does not cover real costs.[5] Despite the incentive for A to cease production, from an international point of view it may be desirable that A continues to produce it. This will be so as long as *HBA* (the consumers' surplus

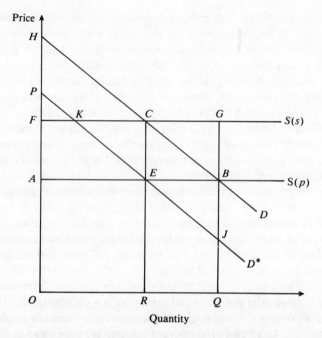

Figure 4.1   Effects of abating pollution from production with constant costs

in B) exceeds *FGBA* (the loss of real income in A arising from its production), that is, if *HCF* exceeds *CGB* (assuming equal welfare weights for residents of the two countries). But let us assume that pollution consciousness has not yet arisen and production exists. By not restricting exports A is effectively subsidizing production, for the benefit of B.

Now let us introduce pollution consciousness. The optimal policy from a world perspective would be for a restriction on production or consumption (or, in this case where all the production is traded internationally, on international trade) to a level *OR*. Should a tax be used to achieve that restriction it would be at a rate appropriate to the marginal generation of the pollution, *AF/OA*. Whichever country imposes the tax, the price of the product will increase in B by the full amount of the tax, to *OF*, while the price net of tax will remain constant in A. The incidence of the tax is thus wholly on B, due to the constant cost assumption. Production, consumption and international trade will be *RQ* units less than before. If A imposed the tax (on production or exports) it will gain by the tax revenue *FCEA* plus the reduction in production multiplied by the excess of social over private costs, *CGBE* (= *FGBA*). As there is no pollution in B, B loses by the new level of consumption multiplied by the price increase, *FCEA* (which is the tax revenue collected by A) plus the excess of consumers' valuation of the reduced consumption over its cost to B (that is, *CBE*). The world gain is *CGB*, the excess of the social (or real) cost of the quantity *RQ* over the valuation of it.

If B had imposed the tax (on consumption or imports) and retained the revenue then B would have borne only the *CBE* part of its cost and A would have gained only to the extent of the reduced production times the extent of the pollution, *CGBE*. However, now that pollution consciousness has arisen, A's government has an incentive to ban production unless it receives at least the price *OF*. Thus B would need to pay A the amount *FCEA* to produce the output *OR* if B imposed the tax. Whoever taxes, then, the outcome is the same: there is a loss of *FCBA* to B and a gain of *FGBA* to A, leaving a net world gain of *CGB*. While A might gain by restricting output (or exports) to a level below *OR*, this would not be optimal from a global viewpoint and thus is not considered further.

If an international authority had levied the tax (and retained it), A's gain would have been *CGBE* compared with no intervention, the same as if B had taxed. B's loss would be *FCBA*, the same as if A had taxed. But again A would have no incentive to produce unless it were to be compensated.

The situation would have been similar if quantitative controls had been used rather than taxes, except that the revenue associated with quantitative controls would not necessarily have passed to the governments of A or B: who received the benefit of the restrictions within countries would, as usual, depend on who received the entitlements to produce, trade, or consume under a regime of restriction. But then we have been implicitly assuming that tax revenues generate utility in the country receiving them; at this level of analysis one can make the same assumption regarding the economic rents arising from production restrictions, and assume also that real resources are not wasted in the pursuit of the economic rents or the benefits of the tariff revenues.

4.1.1.2 *Pollution falls only on the consuming country*

Assume now that the costs of the pollution associated with A's production of the commodity are felt entirely by B: the pollution falls entirely on B. Still using Figure 4.1, we now interpret *S(p)* as the private and social cost of production to A and the private cost to purchasers in B of buying the product. *D* is the demand curve in B for the product, reflecting private valuations of the product. D^* is below *D* by the extent of the pollution costs to B from A's production, which is solely for B's consumption. (The assumption that the pollution externality is the same per unit irrespective of which country it falls in is a convenience but is of no other significance at this stage.) As B is the sole consumer, there is again, from a world efficiency point of view, no difference between A and B imposing taxes on consumption, production, or trade: the world efficiency gain will again be *CGB*, which is equal to *EBJ*.

If A levies the tax it gains by the tax revenue, *FCEA*, this being a net gain due to the assumption of constant costs. That is, it has obtained a terms of trade gain.[6] If A levies the tax, B gains *EBJ* (the excess of cost of the quantity *RQ* over the true valuation of it as shown by the curve *D**) but loses *FCEA*, the additional cost to it of the remaining consumption of *OR*, which equals the tax revenue in A. The net gain to B could be negative, even though A is taking the action to restrict the pollution which A is causing and which is all falling on B! However, as far as B is concerned it is possible that some tax by A is better than no tax, even though B might be worse off if the optimal tax from a world point of view were imposed. For world efficiency it does not matter who taxes. But if the polluter taxes according to the damage it is causing others, the others may be worse off. And, just as in the case in which A was receiving the pollution, it may be in A's interest to ban production even though the product is desirable from a global point of view and profitable for its producers, in this case it may in B's interest to ban consumption (or imports) if A receives the tax revenue, even though it is in the global interest for the product to exist. (This situation would exist if the tax revenue *FCEA* exceeded the true consumers' surplus, *PEA*; that is, if *KCE* exceeded *PKF*.) If A paid B at least the amount by which the tax revenue exceeded the true consumers' surplus, it would be worthwhile for B to continue consuming it.

If B levies the tax it has the efficiency gain in reducing consumption to the point at which the true marginal valuation of the product to it is equal to its cost, and it retains the tax revenue to balance against the additional cost to its consumers of the remaining consumption. Its net gain is *EBJ*. There is no gain or cost to A due to the constant cost assumption; A will receive the same net price but on a lower level of sales. But the government of A could now perceive an opportunity for gain: if it imposed the tax it would capture the tax revenue from B. Tax warfare could develop.

As before, if an international authority levies the tax and retains it, the situation for A is the same as if B levies it, and for B the same as if A levies it. And, as before, the analysis is essentially unchanged if quantitative barriers to production, consumption, or trade are imposed at the level *OR*: the outcome depends on which country imposes the restriction and who captures the revenue.

4.1.1.3 Pollution falls only on a third country

Consider a situation where A and B are as before but all the pollution falls on C who neither produces nor consumes the product. Again there are no other relevant countries. Only C has an incentive to seek a reduction of the pollution but C has no benefit from the product. C has an incentive to pay A to reduce production, and due to the constant cost assumption would be able to secure cessation of production at a very low cost. As A could obtain a terms of trade gain (at the expense of B) from reducing production, A may be very willing to use pollution as a justification to reduce (though not cease) production. But B would then have an incentive to pay A to raise (or continue) production. B would also have an incentive to compensate C for the pollution damage it suffers in order to discourage C from bribing A not to produce: such an arrangement would be Pareto-optimal. Interesting strategies could result.

4.1.2 *Increasing costs of production and pollution*

We now allow for increasing costs of production in country A and also for the pollution cost per unit of production to rise with the level of production. Other simplifying assumptions are retained, including that the cost of pollution is the same whichever country suffers the consequences of the pollution. Again it is irrelevant from the point of view of world efficiency whether consumption, production or trade is restricted. The terms of trade will change with the level of production this time, and there is scope for each country (and not just A) to impose traditional 'optimum' restrictions on international trade in order to secure the gains from trade restrictions. Such actions of course reduce world income, and we shall again assume that they are not adopted. Instead we focus only on the restriction of production, consumption, or trade which would correct the pollution distortion, and on the income distribution and incentive effects of this correction.

4.1.2.1 *Pollution falls only on the polluting country*

In Figure 4.2, $S(p)$ and $S(s)$ are private and social marginal costs of production, respectively, and $S(p)$ is also the supply curve to B, while the D and D^* curves are as in Figure 4.1. The optimum reduction of production is from OQ to OR. This will bring a world efficiency gain HGB, equal to the excess of the social cost of the production QR (in A) over the valuation of that quantity of product in B. This reduction can be achieved by a per unit tax of EA/OE yielding tax revenue of $ABCE$. To analyse the importance of the tax revenue in gains and costs, it is convenient to assume initially that a tax is levied by an international authority, and that the authority retains the tax revenue. We then can observe the difference that collection of the tax revenue would make to A or B.

With the pollution falling on A the net loss of consumers' surplus in B is $ABJF + BGJ$, while the real gain of producers' surplus to A is $HGJB$ (the excess of the social cost of production over revenue on the output RQ) minus $FJCE$ (the loss of revenue on the remaining output OR). The net overall gain for the two countries then is $BHG - ABCE$, the latter term being the tax revenue which we have assumed is held by an international authority. This shows that without the tax revenue, each country could be

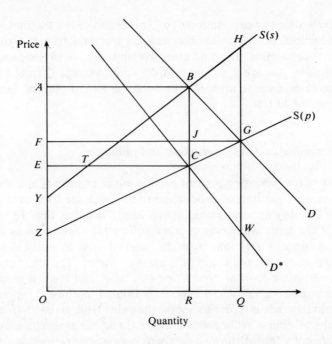

Figure 4.2   Effects of abating pollution from production with increasing costs

worse off: B certainly is and A may be. If B imposes the tax its loss is reduced to *BGJ* – *FJCE*, which could be negative (that is, a gain) though not necessarily so. That is, B may, as in the previous case, be worse off as compared with no tax whichever party imposes the tax, but will be better off if it imposes the tax than if A does.

While it is clearly desirable from a world point of view for the product to exist when the output is restricted to *OR* (the quantity at which the marginal social costs and valuations are equal) and it is profitable for A's producers to produce at this level (producers' surplus with respect to private costs is *ECZ*), again A may raise its real national income by not producing the good unless it receives the tax revenue. This is because the 'true' producers' surplus (that is, with respect to social costs of production) is *ETY* – *TBC*, which could be negative.[7] But it is no longer necessary for it to receive all the revenue to justify continuation of production.

4.1.2.2 Pollution falls only on the consuming country

When the pollution produced by A falls only on B, we can again use Figure 4.2. As in Figure 4.1 the D^* curve differs from the demand curve *D* by the pollution per unit of production (i.e. consumption) and D^* shows

Table 4.1 Summary of gains and losses from taxing polluting production

	A taxes production	B taxes consumption
(1) *Constant costs of production and pollution*:		
(a) Pollution falls on A	A + B −	A + B −
(b) Pollution falls on B	A + B + / −	A0 B +
(2) *Increasing costs of production and pollution*:		
(a) Pollution falls on A	A + B −	A + / − B + / −
(b) Pollution falls on B	A + / − B + / −	A + / − B +

Note: Country A produces the product and the associated pollution. The sign + indicates a real income gain for a country; − indicates a real income loss for a country; + / − indicates a real income gain or loss; and 0 indicates no change in real income.

the marginal social valuations of each level of consumption. $S(p)$ shows the marginal costs of producing in A and the supply curve to B. The world gain from the reduction of consumption, production, and trade to OR is again HGB and this is equal to the area GCW.[8]

Again assuming initially that the revenue is collected by an international authority, the gain of real consumers' surplus (that is with respect to the social valuation curve D^*) in B is $GWC - ABJF$ while the loss of producers' surplus in A is $FJCE + JGC$. And again without obtaining the tax revenue each country could be worse off as compared with no intervention, A necessarily being so in this situation. With the tax revenue B would be better off than with no intervention, while A may be if it receives the revenue. B has therefore an incentive to tax if it receives the revenue; A may not have such an incentive even if it receives the revenue, but will have an incentive if the alternative is for B to impose the tax or restriction.

4.1.2.3 Pollution falls only on a third country

Where the pollution falls on C, a non-producing, non-consuming country, the situation is very similar to the constant-cost case. C has an incentive to seek reduction of the polluting production, but no means to do it other than persuasion or payments to the others to do so. Because both A and B, in this case, would obtain a terms of trade gain from reducing trade below the free-trade level, they may be easily persuaded to do so, though the trade reduction which secured the optimum world output would only fortuitously be that which was, from a national point of view, also the income-maximizing trade reduction.

Table 4.1 summarizes the situations analysed above where there are two countries. In all situations it is important to note that world income increases, for we have assumed the optimum restrictions from a world efficiency point of view. Thus if one country loses the other must gain, and its gain exceeds the first country's loss.

4.1.3   *Property rights*

In this analysis there is a similarity with the property rights question as formulated by Coase (1960). As in Coase's analysis and with the absence of transaction costs, the efficiency question is independent of whether the polluter has the right to pollute, on the one hand, or whether the pollutee has a right not to be polluted, on the other. In the situations we have analysed above, there are two relevant property rights questions: whether polluters have the right to pollute internationally and which country has the right to tax or otherwise restrict ('tax', for short). But also important is which country has an incentive to tax. In each case above, and concentrating on pollution rather than conventional terms of trade considerations, it is only the polluted country which has a clear and general primary (rather than retaliatory, or defensive) reason to tax. If the polluted country is a producer or a consumer it has tax weapons available, but if it is neither it can only use bribery or persuasion. If the country producing or consuming the product is not being polluted, it only has a general incentive to tax if the alternative is that the other party, or an international authority will do so if it does not. (Again, this is setting on one side the terms of trade gains that exist quite separately from the pollution.)

It might seem reasonable through an international agreement to oblige polluters to restrict polluting production, that is, to give taxation property rights to them and oblige them to tax or otherwise restrict polluting production. But to do so could make countries which consume the product worse off than without restrictions, even if the pollution were all falling on the consuming countries. The incentives would be better in these simple cases if the taxation 'property rights' were to be allocated to the polluted, though this right could not be exercised where the pollution falls on countries which are neither significant producers nor consumers. An international agreement determining rights and liability could settle who has rights to compensation and tax.

It was noted earlier that marketable entitlements to pollute (or be polluted), or to consume polluting products, may be an efficient form of restriction. But where the pollution is international, which government has the right to issue licences? Agreement for an international authority to issue them could be warranted if an appropriate incentive mechanism could be devised.

As restriction of pollution to the appropriate level will increase world real income, those countries that gain from such restriction would in principle be able to compensate those that lose from it. Such compensation could involve those who are polluted paying those that pollute, even if the pollution all falls on other countries. The moral hazard incentives which such compensation may provide for the adoption of production processes which are not the most pollution-efficient from a world perspective, could argue against such international compensation.

4.2 Trade restrictions to protect the environment?

From the analysis above it appears that a case could be made for countries to restrict imports or exports of those products causing pollution. In all the cases considered, world real income would be increased by such actions, though the incentives to levy the taxes would depend on where the pollution fell. The analysis was set in a framework that incorporated assumptions most favourable to the use of import and export restrictions as policy options. As such assumptions are relaxed, import and export restrictions become less appropriate and/or more complicated to apply. We now examine some of the implications of relaxing the assumptions.

4.2.1 *Import restrictions*

First, the smaller the proportion of the polluting production which is imported by countries imposing import restrictions, the less effective will their import restrictions be and (while imports continue) the more costly to the importing country will be the restrictions on imports. If B and C are importing the product from A while all the pollution is falling on B, and B restricts its imports, then because the world price of the product will tend to fall as B reduces its imports, consumption in C will tend to rise (as it will in A also if A is consuming the product as well as producing it). Thus there is not a one-to-one relation between B's reduction in imports and the reduction of polluting production. Where there are many importing countries, even if all are bearing pollution costs, the relatively small importers will have an incentive to free-ride on the restrictions of the others. They will obtain lower import prices from the restrictions of others while their own import restrictions would have negligible effects on production and therefore on the pollution they are receiving.

Second, if importing countries on which pollution is falling also produce the product, and if their production pollutes themselves, then it is clear that restrictions on both imports and production (that is, on consumption) are appropriate. Restricting imports alone will stimulate domestic production and while there may be some pollution gain (for total consumption would fall with the higher domestic price) again the gain would be bought at a higher price than in the cases covered in the previous section. On the other hand if the pollution from importing countries' production falls on other countries, the importing countries do not bear the pollution cost of extra production and have an incentive to restrict imports but not production.

Third, we need to consider the case where production in all countries is not equally polluting. For world efficiency, production should be located so that the marginal cost (including in this the global pollution cost) is equalized in all the locations. This would require restrictions on imports (if import restriction is to be the policy instrument – though as already noted, it is production restriction which would be more appropriate) which differentiate according to source. But importing countries would have an incentive to differentiate according to the effects of pollution on themselves, not on the world as a whole. The problem becomes more complex when we allow that not all locations, producers, or production processes within a country may be equally polluting, so that import restrictions would have to differentiate between all of these. If it is a particular production process rather than production *per se* which causes pollution, neither trade nor production restrictions will address the real problem and provide the right incentives: it is the process itself or the pollution itself which needs to be addressed.

It is well known by economists that an import restriction is not an optimal policy instrument to use against production-generated pollution and that the incentives for countries to use them to combat pollution are haphazardly associated with the true costs and sources of pollution. But what weapons does a country have available to it, if it is being polluted by other countries? Paying others not to pollute is one, but we have already noted the moral hazard problems associated with this. So in the absence of international agreements with effective compliance (which generally means effective enforcement mechanisms), measures against imports comprise about the only economic instrument available to countries being polluted by others. (Measures against imports other than those which cause the pollution are a possibility also.) So in some situations import restrictions may be the only instrument available to increase national, and world, income.

4.2.2 Export restrictions

The situation is somewhat simpler with respect to export restrictions, whether the pollution falls on the polluting country or on others. Here it is obvious that it is production restrictions rather than export restrictions which are really appropriate, or restrictions on particular production processes or on production in particular areas, depending on the source of the problem. Restricting exports when there is domestic consumption (including processing) of the product will have a cushioned effect on production in that it will stimulate domestic consumption.

4.3   Competitiveness

The analysis in the previous two sections looked at the correction of the effects of external diseconomies in a manner designed to raise real world income. It also examined the international income distribution implications of these actions, and the consequential incentive effects for governments which were attempting to increase their own countries' real incomes. Individual firms do not see matters from this perspective. They see taxes on polluting production and requirements to satisfy environmental regulations as affecting their ability to compete on the world stage, and naturally are likely to attempt to influence policy. Partly under this influence and partly for mercantilist and 'strategic' trade policy reasons (including the moving of the terms of trade favourably for their own countries), governments also are much concerned for the competitiveness of their countries' industries on world markets.

It is clear that taxation or other restrictions on a polluting industry which is engaged in international trade will make it more difficult for that industry to compete. One view of the matter is expressed in Shrybman (1990):

> For a country wanting to maintain stringent environmental standards, while not undermining the competitiveness of its domestic industry, the choices are simple: (a) Establish import tariffs to offset pollution costs so that domestic producers will not be at a disadvantage when competing with imports from jurisdictions without similar environmental regulation, or: (b) Subsidize the cost of environmental protection with general revenues by underwriting pollution control costs.

In looking at this we need to distinguish between production- and consumption-generated pollution. If the pollution arises from *consumption* then domestically produced and imported products should be treated equally. An appropriate policy would be a consumption tax on the product or on the component generating the pollution, and this could be imposed directly on consumption or by means of matching taxes on production and imports.

It is more likely, however, that it is *production*-generated pollution which is of concern. In this case, the general concern is to compensate domestic producers for costs which they are required to bear but which their foreign competitors are not. This principle could have very widespread implications. On the one hand, different countries have different 'absorptive capacities' for pollution, and the real impacts of effluent on the environment, for example, vary greatly between countries. The absorptive capacity of the local environment is a resource in the production process similar to the amount of sunlight, the quality of labour, and the fertility and abundance of the local soil. If firms are compensated for different costs relating to the absorptive capacity of the environment, should they also be compensated for other natural disadvantages? Secondly, demand for environmental protection varies greatly between countries and typically grows with income (Pearce *et al.*, 1989). Thirdly, environmental control is one of many forms of legislation which differs across countries and for which producers may seek compensation. Minimum wages, labour laws, industrial health practices, and maternity, paternity and military leave, are examples of others. Application of the principle could easily explode into a proliferation of barriers to counter every sort of legislative and natural resource advantage.

If the objective is to secure efficient levels of output with all production costs taken into account, property rights can be with polluters or the polluted (assuming no transaction costs), as Coase (1960) established. But offsetting the costs by means of tariffs or by subsidies will sustain the level of output even though it may be efficient to curtail it. The line of argument usually followed by economists is that environmental costs are real costs incurred by firms in the productive process and that to increase real income these external costs should be brought to bear on those activities which generate them. (One form in which costs can be brought to bear is the opportunity cost of refusing to abate pollution when compensation is offered for this abatement.) The allocation of property rights can determine who should pay whom but it does not change the existence of these costs. While the costs would impair the firm's ability to compete on international markets, so be it: the costs are just as much real costs as those of labour and raw materials. Bringing the pollution costs to bear on the production activity which generates them will discourage production of those products in which a country does not have a true comparative advantage and thereby encourage production of those things in which it does have such an advantage.

There is thus an essential difference between (a) requiring pollution abatement and compensating for it, and (b) polluters compensating the polluted or the polluted offering payment to stop pollution. Under the alternatives in (b) the costs are brought to bear on the decision of whether or not to pollute. Under (a) the costs are not brought to bear on the production and pollution decision: there is no incentive to adjust production and pollution in the light of all the costs. Of course if it is consumption which generates pollution it is the consumption decision on which, for efficiency, the full costs should be brought to bear.

Compensation to producers for required environmental protection costs can be viewed as a payment from the polluted – society at large – to the polluter to reduce pollution. In the common situation in which the property rights regarding the rights to pollute or not-to-be-polluted have not been well defined in the past, polluters may very well argue that they purchased the right to discharge in an area when they purchased the property, or at least that they have as much right to discharge as other people have the right not to be discharged upon. Such arguments may lead to society at large bearing at least some of the cost of pollution reduction, but efficiency requires that the full costs be brought to bear on the production decision. Within a society, whether or not to offer compensation is a question of the internal distribution of income and wealth, not a question of international trade – except to the extent that the pollution spills abroad, or that other governments react to these subsidies through countervailing import duties, for example.[9]

Should this principle be applied internationally? It would imply that those countries receiving pollution should pay others to desist or to install abatement equipment. Again there are moral hazard problems, together with what could be an extraordinarily complex system of payments.

4.4 Summary and conclusions

This chapter has emphasized the international income distribution implications of controlling the environmental effects of economic activities, a matter that intertwines with, though is conceptually distinct from, the traditional national terms of trade gains achievable when trade is restricted. In restricting adverse environmental effects world welfare can be increased, but in doing so significant redistributions of income may occur according to which country(-ies) introduces the policies to contain environmental damage. (In contrast, trade restrictions to obtain traditional terms of trade gains lower world real income as well as redistributing it.)

It is shown that it is quite possible for a country which is inflicting environmental damage on other countries to reduce welfare in those other countries when it restricts this damage, even though this restriction raises world welfare. This arises from a terms of trade effect and is reflected in the collection of the tax revenue (or economic rent) by the country causing the damage. It is a result which underscores the importance of the question of who is collecting the environmental tax revenue.

If those countries which are suffering environmental damage are able to secure optimal (from a world point of view) production reductions of the activities causing the damage, they will gain from taking this action provided there is a close relation between the policy instrument they are using to achieve this reduction and the resulting production reduction. Where this damage is being inflicted by their own producers, a tax on production would be an appropriate policy. But where producers are inflicting damage on other countries, import or consumption restrictions by the latter countries on the product causing the damage may have little impact on the activity which is damaging their environment, yet the restrictions will have costs for the country imposing them. If there is a one-to-one relation between import or consumption restrictions on the one hand, and production of the product which is damaging the environment on the other hand, import or consumption restrictions (at an appropriate level) will be beneficial to those imposing them. The looser is this connection, however, the less likely that such restrictions will raise real income.

International trade policies thus are not appropriate instruments to use for countering those who exploit the world's resources, including environmental resources, inefficiently. Using them for this purpose will nearly always reduce global welfare. But, in some limited circumstances, such policies could bring a gain for a country which is being polluted from abroad, and may be the only policy option available.

The effects of these environmental policies on world income distribution are linked with the incentives which governments of various countries would have to introduce these policies. The receipt of the tax revenue (or the economic rent associated with other forms of restrictions) is a crucial element in providing incentives. Since the world real income will be raised by appropriate restrictions of activities which damage the environment, those countries which gain from these restrictions could always be able to compensate those who lose. Those who have the clearest incentive to intervene will be those whose environment is being damaged, while those inflicting the damage (on others) may lose unless it is they who are imposing the restriction and unless they are compensated by the others. Compensation paid from those damaged to those who inflict the damage provides an incentive to undertake damaging activity and raises a moral hazard question. It also raises the question of whether polluters have the right to pollute or whether those who are polluted have the right not to be polluted: this can only be settled through a determination of where the property rights lie.

Discouragement of polluting activities will affect international competitiveness. But pollution is a real cost of production. Attempting to counter the effects on competitiveness will tend to support an inefficient level of production, when all costs − including pollution costs − are taken into account.

Notes

Much of the work on this paper was undertaken when the author was Visiting Professor at the Graduate Institute of International Studies in Geneva. An earlier version of some sections was presented at the Troisième Cycle Romand en Economie Politique Conference 'Le Commerce International', at Champéry, Switzerland in March 1991. The author is grateful for discussions and comments to Kym Anderson, Richard Blackhurst, Bernard Hoekman, Michael Leidy, Gary Sampson and John Whalley. They are not responsible for any errors or opinions in the paper, and nothing in it should be attributed to them or to any institutions with which they are associated.

1. Examples of contributions in this area include Meade (1955), Johnson (1965), Corden (1974) and Bhagwati and Ramaswami (1963).
2. There are some provisions for re-distribution under international agreements. For example the GATT allows for compensation to injured countries as one of

a number of possible actions, when safeguard measures against imports are taken under Article XIX. International agreements themselves are a form of settling the international distribution of costs and benefits of actions which have cross-border effects.

3. There could be by-product benefits of the atmospheric kind which extend across international borders, just as there are by-product costs. Discouraging production which yields such consumptive benefits would raise real global income.

4. Some of the points which follow were addressed by Baumol (1971). He does not suppress the terms of trade effect, but rather examines the optimum tariff in the presence of externalities and monopoly power. Markusen (1975) explores tax structures to maximize national income, also in the presence of international externalities and monopoly power.

5. There would be some levels of output between zero and *OQ* at which it would be profitable to produce if A's government were to act as a monopolist exporter and could raise the export price above *OF*.

6. This is not the optimum tax from an income maximization point of view for A which would be such as to equate marginal revenue on the B market to A's marginal costs. We are assuming a tax which is at an optimum with respect to curing the effects of the pollution and thereby maximizing world income, the pollution being the only inefficiency from a world point of view, and are not examining the tax which would maximize the income of either A or B.

7. Note again the point made in note 5, that in the presence of monopolistic exporting, a non-zero level of output could be socially profitable.

8. The two triangles have equal height, defined by the change of quantity *RQ*, and equal bases, *HG* and *GW*, this because of the assumption that the pollution causes the same cost wherever it falls.

9. Foreign producers are likely, of course, to claim that such assistance for pollution abatement is 'unfair' competition if they are required to bear the costs themselves of such abatement in their own countries or if they are taxed for polluting.

References

Baumol, W. J. (1971), *Environmental Protection, International Spillovers and Trade*, Stockolm: Almqvist & Wiksell.

Bhagwati, J. and V. K. Ramaswami (1963), 'Domestic Distortions, Tariffs and the Theory of Optimum Subsidy', *Journal of Political Economy* 71: 44–50.

Coase, R. H. (1960), 'The Problem of Social Cost', *Journal of Law and Economics* 3: 1–44.

Corden, W. M. (1974), *Trade Policy and Economic Welfare*, London: Oxford University Press.

Dasgupta, P. (1990), 'The Environment as a Commodity', *Oxford Review of Economic Policy* 6: 51–67.

Harris, S. (1991), 'International Trade, Ecologically Sustainable Development and the GATT', mimeo, Australian National University, Canberra, January.

Johnson, H. G. (1965), 'Optimal Trade Intervention in the Presence of Domestic Distortions', in *Trade, Growth and the Balance of Payments: Essays in Honor of Gottfried Haberler*, edited by R. E. Baldwin *et al.*, Amsterdam: North-Holland.

Markusen, J. R. (1975), 'International Externalities and Optimum Tax Structures', *Journal of International Economics* 5: 15–29.

Meade, J. E. (1955), *Trade and Welfare: The Theory of International Economic Policy*, Volume 2, London: Oxford University Press.

Pearce, D. W., A. Markandya and E. B. Barbier (1989), *Blueprint for a Green Economy*, London: Earthscan Publications.

Shrybman, S. (1990), 'International Trade and the Environment: An Environmental Assessment of the General Agreement on Tariffs and Trade'. *The Ecologist* **20**: 30–4.

Whalley, J. (1991), 'The Interface between Environmental and Trade Policies'. *The Economic Journal* **101**: 180–9.

Whalley, J. and R. Wigle (1991), 'The International Incidence of Carbon Taxes'. in *Economic Policy Responses to Global Warming*, edited by R. Dornbusch and J. Poterba, Cambridge, MA: MIT Press.

PART 3

Environment and trade: case studies

5

The trade and welfare effects of greenhouse gas abatement: A survey of empirical estimates

L. Alan Winters

Greenhouse gas abatement is one of the newest items on the economists' agenda, but one of the fastest growing. A recent major survey of estimates of the economic effects of abating greenhouse gas emissions – Boero *et al.* (1991a) – considered twenty-two modelling exercises, of which only two had published results before 1989. This chapter, which draws heavily on that survey, offers a snap-shot of current information about two issues. It starts by briefly considering the consequences of greenhouse gas (GHG) abatement for global economic welfare as reflected in existing estimates derived from econometric models. It presents some of the estimates available in the literature and describes the principal determinants of their conclusions. With this as a backdrop the chapter then contains three sections exploring the estimates of the possible impact of GHG abatement on international trade flows. Although these sections still aim to focus on model-based quantitative estimates, they are rather more conceptual than substantive purely because, to date, so few studies have considered this issue empirically.

5.1   Global costs of reducing greenhouse gases[1]

The analysis starts from the presumption – albeit controversial – that greenhouse gas emissions at current and projected rates will raise world temperatures and that this is undesirable. If there is indeed such a GHG problem, it is therefore a global one which needs to be tackled on a global scale. This is because everybody's emissions affect global warming and everybody is, to some extent, affected by it. Hence a natural starting point for the analysis of abatement policy for GHG emissions is a single-economy model of the world. The GHG problem is also a very long-run one, first because GHG damage is related directly to the stock of GHGs in the atmosphere rather than to the annual flow of emissions, and second because any adjustments required to reduce emissions will take a very long time.

Quantitative analyses of abatement policies generally consider the proportional difference in the level of world long-run steady-state gross domestic product (GDP) between a business-as-usual scenario and an abatement scenario. (Some studies use welfare measures such as equivalent variation rather than GDP.) They implicitly assume that both scenarios generate steady states and that business-as-usual represents a continuation of current economic trends. The latter assumption implies a view that, within the time horizon considered, although unabated GHG emissions will raise average temperatures, they will not cause significant reductions in GDP. Most exercises analyse the effects of an arbitrary abatement policy, making no attempt to balance marginal costs and benefits so as to produce optimal policies. Researchers are well aware of the limitations that these various assumptions impose on their analyses, but are forced to make them for the sake of tractability.

The majority of global studies of GHG abatement suggest that a long-run reduction of 40 to 50 per cent in carbon dioxide emissions, *relative to what they would have been*, would reduce world GDP by about 2 to 4 per cent relative to what it would have been, but estimates of around 1 per cent also exist in the literature. Greater abatement entails greater costs, with estimates of up to 6 and 8 per cent for 60 to 70 per cent reductions.[2] Hence there is plenty of explaining to do. Moreover, different studies have quite different business-as-usual projections, so there is a still wider range of estimates of the absolute levels of emissions and GDP under abatement prices. Only in relatively few cases, however, is a 60 per cent reduction relative to business-as-usual consistent with the Toronto-type target (a 20 per cent reduction of GHG emissions by the year 2005 relative to 1988). It is very difficult to assess the validity of such long-run projections of GDP in absolute terms, and so GHG researchers have tended to concentrate on the proportional costs of abatement relative to GDP. This chapter follows this trend, and after briefly describing some of the estimates, seeks to explain the differences in proportional costs with the aid of a simple conceptual framework.

Given the nature of the problem, only long-run global models are considered here (even though Boero *et al.*, 1991a, considers a wider range). Table 5.1 summarizes the main studies available in early 1991. As the research area is too new for a consensus to have developed, it is not surprising that every column suggests a wide range of estimates. The differences in the choice of final years are not important, for all the authors consider their final year to be in the almost indefinite future. There is a fair degree of agreement about the degree of abatement relative to business-as-usual that is relevant, but this is not replicated in the degrees of abatement relative to the present. This is because the business-as-usual scenarios differ so much. Finally the range of proportional abatement costs is substantial and would be even greater if one included in the comparison exercises not based on models, such as Williams (1990a).

The principal cause of GHG emissions is the burning of fossil fuels and any plausible abatement policy will have to address such combustion. Fossil fuels generate energy which, in turn, helps to produce output (GDP). This chain establishes a direct link between GHG abatement and losses of output. If we ignore any distinction between different forms of energy, this can be illustrated formally in the following simple model.

Assume for simplicity that there is only one good; only one economy, the world; only one greenhouse gas (carbon) which emanates from only one source, the burning of fossil fuels; only one consumer; no distortions in the economy, so that there are no GDP gains to abatement; and no feedback from global warming to the production function for world GDP. Suppose that output (X) is generated by competitive firms using a constant-elasticity-of-substitution technology combining energy (E) and other factors (F).

$$X = H(aF^\rho + bE^\rho)^{1/\rho} \tag{1}$$

where the elasticity of substitution between E and F is given by

$$\sigma = \frac{1}{1-\rho}; \ 0 < \sigma < \infty; \ -\infty < \rho < 1 \tag{}$$

and where a, b and H are parameters. It is straightforward to show that the percentage change in output due to a given percentage change in energy input is

$$\frac{\partial \log X}{\partial \log E} = \frac{\partial X}{\partial E} \cdot \frac{E}{X} = s \tag{2}$$

where s is the value share of energy in total inputs. If energy has price p, output has price q and the composite of other factors has price 1, and if the economy is in full equilibrium, we also know that

$$s = b^\sigma \left(\frac{p}{q}\right)^{1-\sigma} \tag{3}$$

Using this framework we can identify several crucial determinants of the costs of abatement, and, because the framework parallels quite closely the modelling techniques used in much of the literature, explore the differences between models. These key determinants are considered in turn.

The share of energy in the total cost of output

The more important is energy in the cost of production, the greater the effect on output of a given proportional cut in energy inputs, *ceteris paribus*.

Table 5.1 Estimates of GDP losses from greenhouse gas abatement policies

Study	Region	Projection period	CO2 emission changes (% of baseline)	CO2 emission changes (% of reference year)	GDP losses %	GDP losses (year)
Manne and Richels (1990)	USA	1990–2100		−20 (1990)	3	(2030+)
	OECD			−20 (1990)	1 to 2	(2010)
	SU-EE			−20 (1990)	4	(2030+)
	China			200 (1990)	10	(2050)
	ROW			200 (1990)	5	(2100)
	WORLD		−75 (2100)	16 (1990)	5	(2100)[1]
Edmonds and Reilly (1983, 1985) (IEA-ORAU)	USA (M)[2]	1975–2050	−60 (2000)	70 (1975)	0.4[3]	(2050)
	USA (U)		−63 (2000)	54 (1975)	0.7[4]	(2050)
	WORLD (M)		−40 (2000)	162 (1975)	1.0[5]	(2050)
	WORLD (U)		−15 (2000)	272 (1975)	n.a.	
CBO (1990) (IEA-ORAU)	USA (M)[6]	1990–2100	−11 (2100)		1.1	(2100)
	USA (M)[7]		−36 (2100)		2.2	(2100)
	USA (U)[8]		−50 (2100)		0.9	(2100)
	USA (U)[9]		−75 (2100)		−3	(2100)
	WORLD (M)[6]		−21 (2100)	305 (1975)	n.a.	
	WORLD (M)[7]		−50 (2100)	158 (1975)	n.a.	
Cline (1989) (IEA-ORAU)	WORLD	1975–2075	−65 (2075)	−31 (2000)	7.4	(2075)[10]
Mintzer (1987) (IEA-ORAU) Modest Policies	WORLD	1990–2075	−41 (2075)	66 (2000)	n.a.	
Slow build-up	WORLD	1990–2075	−88 (2075)	−66 (2000)	3	(2075)
Edmonds and Barns (1990a) (IEA-ORAU) OECD action only	WORLD	1975–2025	−39 (2025)	0 (1988)	4.0	(2025)
World cooperation[11]	WORLD		−39 (2025)	0 (1988)	negligible	(2000)
	WORLD				1.8	(2025)
	WORLD		−51 (2025)	−20 (1988)	2.3	(2025)
	WORLD		−69 (2025)	−50 (1988)	5.7	(2025)[12]

		Period				%
Whalley and Wigle (1991)	WORLD (NP)	1990–2030	−50 (2030)			4.4
	WORLD (NC)		−50 (2030)			4.4
	WORLD (G)[13]		−50 (2030)			4.2[14]
Nordhaus (1991)[15]	WORLD	1990–2100	−50 (2100)			1
Anderson and Bird (1990)	Industrial countries					0.1 (2000) 0.5 (2020) 1.4 (2050)[15]
	Developing countries	1990–2050		17 (1990) −68 (2050)		0.8 (2000) 2.0 (2020) 4.8 (2050)[16]

Notes:

1. Weighted average using 2100 GDP estimates.
2. M = Multilateral tax imposed to all consuming regions. U = Unilateral tax imposed by the United States. The tax is as follows: 100% for coal; 78% for oil; 56% gas, 115% shale-oil production; initiation data 1985 (see Edmonds and Reilly, 1983a and page 40).
3. Equivalent to $30 billion constant 1975 US dollars per year.
4. Equivalent to $50 billion constant 1975 US dollars per year.
5. Equivalent to $380 billion constant 1975 US dollars per year.
6. Multilateral tax of $100 per ton of carbon, starting in year 2000.
7. Multilateral tax rising from $100 to $300 per ton of carbon, from 2000 to 2100.
8. Unilateral tax of $100 per ton of carbon, starting in year 2000.
9. Unilateral tax rising from $100 to $300 per ton of carbon from 2000 to 2100 (see CBO, 1990, p. 10).
10. Cline qualifies this result heavily and has stated in private correspondence that he now prefers an alternative estimate of around 2% that he quoted in a footnote to his paper.
11. World cooperation to reduce CO$_2$ emissions at specified targets. Correspond to reference case of Edmonds and Barns (1990b).
12. World GNP is estimated to be US $32 trillion (1975) by 2025. In a personal communication Edmonds advised me that the figure of 8 per cent for a 50 per cent reduction in emissions (see Edmonds and Barns, 1990a) is incorrect. The figures given in this table are derived from Edmonds and Barns (1990a, p. 23 and Figure 24), in the light of this information. Edmonds considers these estimates to be on the high side.
13. NP = National producer tax; NC = National consumption tax; G = Global tax; C = Ceiling on per capita emissions.
14. Welfare losses measured by Hicksian equivalent variation. Percentage of GDP in present value terms (1990–2030).
15. For the industrial countries GNP is estimated to be $20 trillion in year 2000, $35 trillion in year 2020, and $60 trillion in 2050 (see Anderson and Bird, 1990, Table 15).
16. For the developing countries GNP is estimated to be $5 trillion in 2000, $12 trillion in 2020, and $45 trillion in 2050 (see Anderson and Bird, 1990, Table 15).

Sources: Anderson and Bird (1990, Table 15 and Figure 2), CBO (1990, Tables 5 and 6 and pages 37, 43 and 44), Cline (1989), Edmonds and Reilly (1983, Table 10 and page 44), Edmonds and Barns (1990a), Manne and Richels (1990), Nordhaus (1991) and Whalley and Wigle (1991, Table 7).

The price of energy relative to other inputs

Regardless of abatement policy, energy prices are likely to rise over the next century just through stock exhaustion. This will affect the share of energy in total costs, causing it to rise if energy and other factors are poor substitutes and to fall if they are good substitutes – see equation (3). Most researchers assume the former situation which implies that in the business-as-usual case the world economy becomes more dependent on energy in the sense of allowing its marginal product to rise. Hence a policy-induced reduction in energy-use exacts a higher price.

More important is the price of energy under the abatement policy. GHG abatement in the medium term – say, thirty years – can rely mainly on the substitution of relatively 'clean' fossil fuels, such as natural gas and oil, for 'dirtier' ones such as coal. Beyond about 2050, however, these cleaner fuels will begin to become exhausted.[3] Then the only alternative to drastic cuts in energy use will be to develop new energy sources. Modellers have a concept of so-called backstop fuels – fuels in virtually unlimited supply which as a consequence cap the price of general energy supplies. Clearly the price at which these are available is a central factor in the cost of abatement. There is, however, a surprising degree of agreement between modellers about the prices of the marginal fuels in the last part of the twenty-first century, (see Boero *et al.*, 1991a), and so this factor does not explain much of the variance in Table 5.1.

The substitutability of energy and other factors of production in the production process

Substitutability helps to determine changes in the share of energy in total costs of production when relative input prices change. It also affects responses to the curtailment of energy-use, although in a somewhat complex fashion. The more highly substitutable is energy for other factors, the greater the extent to which any firm can offset reductions in energy-use without large losses of output by using other factors. This does not necessarily imply, however, that the aggregate output losses are smaller. If there are fixed endowments of the other factors, higher substitutability implies greater pressure on them, and in fact, for a given real increase in the energy price, aggregate output will fall further the greater the degree of factor substitutability.[4] Of course with greater substitutability a smaller rise in the price of energy is required to achieve a given abatement, which helps to offset the previous effect. Indeed if we think of the energy price as being set at whatever level is necessary to achieve a given percentage cut in energy use, the degree of substitutability does not affect the output loss directly, for the latter depends only on the energy share. Under these circumstances substitutability matters only through its influence on the energy cost share.

Studies vary considerably in their estimate of the elasticity of substitution of energy for other factors. The range in conventional models is from 0.3 to over unity, with a mean of around 0.7. There is, however, a group of studies (Cline, 1989; Edmonds and Barns, 1990a,b) which imply very high values and which, confronting these values with large exogenously determined increases in real energy prices, produce (rather implausible) GDP losses of 7 to 8 per cent for 60 per cent abatement.[5]

Technical progress

This is probably the most important determinant of economic change measured over centuries. It has several dimensions. Most obvious is the above-mentioned development of new sources of energy, but technical progress also increases the productivity of energy and other factors of production. For analytical purposes this shifting of the production possibility frontier is best thought of as the combination of (i) a rate of neutral technical progress common to all inputs (measured through increases in H in equation (1)) and (ii) a bias towards saving (i.e. faster progress in the productivity of) one factor or another (measured by a change in one of other of a and b in equation (1)). Technical progress lowers the effective price of factor inputs and hence biased technical progress affects relative prices. All modellers who assume a bias over the next century show a saving of other factors. Thus they raise the relative effective price of energy and so increase energy's share of costs which raises proportional abatement costs. In some cases the effect is very marked.

Neutral technical progress, on the other hand, does not affect factor shares directly, but it is still important in defining base GDP. This affects the translation of proportional into absolute costs and also influences the relative weights of different regions in world GDP. An extreme example is Manne and Richels (1990) who assume such rapid technical progress in China that its share of world GDP grows from 1.8 per cent in 1988 to 22.1 per cent in year 2100. China faces significant losses from abatement and, with its very high share in the total, accounts for nearly half of Manne and Richels' global costs in their final year.

An interesting empirical issue is whether technical progress could be affected by abatement policy. A number of writers imply that it would through regulation (Edmonds and Reilly, 1985) but fail to model it as such. Hogan and Jorgenson (1990) argue that higher energy prices would curtail the rate of neutral technical progress which, if true, would dramatically increase the costs of abatement.

Substitution between goods

Once one recognizes the existence of several goods, shifts in demand affect abatement costs. If it is easy and cheap in terms of utility to switch between carbon-intensive and other goods, abatement costs will be correspondingly lower. These possibilities are discussed in the next section. There is, however, an unfortunate tendency for some researchers to combine the reduction in energy-use per unit GDP due to the switch towards services together with technical progress proper into a single parameter. This makes interpretation of model results very difficult.

Economic distortions

A number of commentators (Grubb, 1990; Williams, 1990a,b) argue that a significant degree of abatement can be achieved at no cost to GDP or economic welfare by correcting or off-setting existing market distortions. This is the so-called 'no regrets' school. Its adherents argue that current energy use is very inefficient and that by wise regulation and the dissemination of information governments could shift the economy out onto its production frontier. These claims may be exaggerated with respect to economic welfare if not with respect to GDP. Apart from relatively minor examples, these authors do not identify the distortions causing these problems and hence provide no convincing reason why users behave inefficiently. One important existing distortion is the extensive taxes and subsidies in energy markets; indeed coal is probably one of the most distorted of all products. It is not clear without further analysis, however, whether these distortions stimulate or curtail energy use and carbon emissions, and hence whether their elimination would really help the GDP-GHG trade-off.[6]

A related issue is the valuation of the changes induced by abatement policy. The traditional method of applying measures such as consumers' surplus or the use of constant-price GDP to represent economic welfare presumes that actual prices reflect marginal utilities. But existing distortions invalidate this presumption. In particular a number of authors argue that the first unit of abatement is free because the marginal unit of consumption yields no surplus. If there is a wedge between marginal cost and price or between price and marginal utility, however, this is no longer true. These considerations could seriously affect estimates of abatement costs, but there seems to be no research yet that has focused on the matter.

In most regards the global results just described capture the most important aspects of GHG abatement. The problem is, after all, genuinely a global one. For policy-makers, however, as well as for students of the political economy of abatement, the geographical breakdown of the costs and benefits is also of interest. The distribution of the costs of abatement is intimately related to countries' excess supplies of particular goods, that is, to their international trade, as will be seen below.

5.2 Greenhouse gas abatement and the terms of trade

A necessary condition for modelling the international trade consequences of GHG abatement is that models include more than one country and more than one good. Several global analyses have a geographical dimension and most distinguish fuels from final output; hence potentially they cover one important aspect of international trade. Few of them, however, pay any attention to the shape of regions' excess demand curves for fuels and final output and hence fail to exploit this potential. So far as the level of world trade is concerned, it is easy to predict that it will fall in these models, for reduced fuel demand will tend to reduce fuel exports and hence final good imports. Moreover, since fuels are essentially Ricardian goods – goods in which comparative advantage depends primarily on natural resources – it is easy to see which trade flows and countries would be most affected.

More interesting than the volume of trade are the terms of trade between fuels and final goods. These are potentially sensitive to GHG abatement policy, as is well illustrated by Whalley and Wigle (1991). Abatement is bound to lower the supply price of carboniferous fuels relative to business-as-usual, but it will also raise the demand price of such fuels – directly if it is pursued by taxes or tradeable carbon permits or indirectly by raising shadow prices if it is pursued by regulation. The critical issue for individual countries' welfare is, then, whether trade occurs at the supply price or the demand price – equivalently, who gets the tax revenue?[7]

Whalley and Wigle suggest that a carbon tax sufficient to induce a 50 per cent curtailment of GHG emissions would generate revenues of around 10 per cent of world GDP, so these distributional issues will probably dominate any allocative consequences of abatement for individual countries. Table 5.2 summarizes Whalley and Wigle's (1991) conclusions on the effects of a producer tax (received by producer governments), a consumer

Table 5.2 Welfare effects of carbon taxes on various regions of the world

	Producer tax	Consumer tax	Global tax
Average tax rate ($ per ton of carbon)	448	448	448
Welfare change (equivalent variation, in percentage):			
European Community (12)	-4.0	-1.0	-3.8
USA and Canada	-4.3	-3.6	-9.8
Japan	-3.7	+0.5	-0.9
Other industrial market economies	-2.3	-2.1	-4.4
Oil exporters	+4.5	-18.7	-13.0
Rest of the world	-7.1	-6.8	+1.8
World	-4.4	-4.4	-4.2

Source: Whalley and Wigle (1991).

tax and a global tax whose revenue is distributed across countries proportionately to population. The producer tax is essentially an export tax, which, by conducting world trade at the demand price, transfers the policy-induced scarcity rents on energy to producers. It is as if OPEC were revived. The consumer tax, on the other hand, forces the world price down to the supply price and allows consumer governments, mostly in OECD, to reap the benefit. The differences are starkest for the oil exporters, but are also significant for other countries.

A similar issue is raised by Marks *et al.* (1990) who consider the effects of abatement policy on Australia. Most of their analysis concerns the costs of adopting new transport and electricity generating technologies, but they also advance the view that every 1 per cent reduction in the world price of coal would reduce Australian national income by 0.27 per cent in the long run. This is a prodigious figure, and may well be somewhat over-estimated (see Boero *et al.*, 1991a) but it illustrates the very large amounts at stake for net energy exporters. Moreover, although no researcher has yet provided such detailed analysis, there is probably a strong parallel between Australia and China. China has large stocks of coal which would become increasingly valuable under a business-as-usual scenario with growth driving up energy prices. Abatement policy could then be very costly for that country.[8]

Reinforcement of these conclusions is provided by the OECD's GREEN model (Burniaux *et al.*, 1991a,b). This general equilibrium model, which has seven regions, eight producer sectors and four consumption goods, concentrates at present on substitution between fossil fuels.[9] The cost of abatement to individual regions varies with their demand and production structures, including the distribution of the output and use of fossil fuel over coal, oil and gas. The preliminary results using the GREEN model identify serious terms of trade losses for coal producers and exporters, compounded in the case of China by the need for increased imports of oil as domestic coal use is curtailed in order to achieve emission targets. World coal production falls by around two-thirds for an agreement involving a 20 per cent cut in emissions by year 2010 for industrial countries and the USSR plus up to a 50 per cent increase elsewhere.

The distinction between (carbon-based) energy and final goods captures the most immediate of the terms of trade effects of abatement policy, and also the one which will probably generate the strongest debate. It does not, however, exhaust the possibilities. A carbon tax — the archetypal abatement policy — will raise the costs of final goods differentially. The initial impact will be proportional to goods' total carbon-intensity;[10] this will then be moderated by the extent to which substitution away from carbon inputs is possible in production and by the feed-backs from demand to total output and hence to overall costs. No study yet offers a satisfactory quantitative analysis of this problem on a global scale, but Symons *et al.* (1990) offers some interesting insights for the UK.

Symons *et al.* (1990) explore the impact of a modest carbon tax (£60 per ton) on UK prices and consumption disaggregated into 35 categories. They estimate its impact on prices via an input-output table, considering both direct and indirect fuel inputs, as would be appropriate to a single closed economy model, and then use a detailed consumer demand model to derive the first-round effects on demand.[11] The changes in relative prices are significant, as are those in consumption. For example, as well as increasing fuel prices, a carbon tax would increase the relative prices of food and drink significantly and cut real consumption. This helps to explain Symons *et al.*'s finding that carbon taxes are regressive. Moreover, although this regressiveness can be mitigated by compensating changes in direct taxes (there is plenty of scope for these because the carbon tax raises substantial revenue), making such compensation reduces substantially the degree of abatement achieved. This is because carbon-intensive products account for relatively high proportions of poorer people's budgets.

This finding obviously raises serious domestic policy issues for governments pursuing abatement policies, but it might also have international parallels. Global abatement would be less easy to pursue if it fell particularly heavily on the less well-off. There seem to be no formal analyses of differences in national consumption patterns relating to income level and carbon content, but studies of the overall use of carboniferous fuels suggest that significant global abatement will require major contributions from China, India and the USSR (Manne and Richels, 1990; Burniaux *et al.*, 1991a; Edmonds and Barns, 1990a,b). Thus distributional issues cannot be avoided in any practical discussion of GHG abatement.

Whalley and Wigle (1991) offer a complete analysis of inter-good substitution. With only two final goods (energy-intensive manufactures and other goods) they are able to generate only schematic results. Their results suggest substantial changes in trade patterns arising from their 'global' carbon tax of $438 per ton. Out of twelve trade flows (six regions with two final goods) they suggest changes in the sign of the trade balance in four. If abatement is pursued via global per capita emission limits, the effect is even greater.

A slightly more detailed model is provided by Perroni and Rutherford (1991). They attempt to fill in some of the details implicit in Manne and Richels' work, by simulating a general equilibrium model with five regions, three tradeable goods (oil, basic materials which are energy-intensive and non-basic, non-energy goods), a number of non-tradeable energy sources (e.g. coal), and potentially tradeable carbon permits. They find that a 23 per cent abatement by year 2020 reduces world GDP by 1 per cent. This entails a global carbon tax of $278 per ton on consumption, which increases the prices of non-traded energies by 30 per cent to 70 per cent and depresses the world oil price by 15 per cent. The output of the energy-intensive basic materials falls globally because demand is switched away from them, but it is also relocated towards developing regions. These results imply considerable shifts in trade patterns and the terms of trade from even relatively modest abatement packages. A further interesting dimension of Perroni and Rutherford's work is that they show that trading carbon permits is a substitute for trading carbon-intensive goods.

Even without a model, it is obvious that net exporters of carbon-intensive goods will suffer an overall loss of demand from abatement and consequently experience considerable adjustment pressure. But we should not immediately conclude from this that such countries will suffer major losses of income as a result. They will if their export industries have specific factors, as was the case with coal deposits discussed above, or if imperfectly competitive market structures allow the persistence of significant producer rents. If, on the other hand, factors are intersectorally mobile, industries are competitive and specialization is incomplete, then once adjustment has occurred, factor price equalization will ensure that all labour in the world experiences the same income shift independent of its initial industry of employment and regardless of previous output patterns. Over periods of a century or more it is, perhaps, difficult to maintain that factors are immobile and that market structures are imperfectly competitive. Hence on these grounds, once one has allowed for specific factors and for adjustment costs, it is not clear that much more can be said about the *differential* welfare effects of abatement. That is, there are not yet grounds for believing that the income generated by particular final-good activities will be unduly favoured or disfavoured by global abatement.

Of course, the analysis of the previous paragraph does not preclude countries faring differently because of their different factor endowments, for there remains the possibility that labour and capital will fare differently from each other. Indeed some commentators have suggested that abatement will reduce the marginal product of capital and hence, with a given capital stock, its rate of return. There is no formal empirical analysis along these lines, but in the long run, over which the capital stock is variable, one might expect rentals to return to their natural level as dictated by rates of time preference.

5.3   Greenhouse gas abatement and competitiveness

The previous section dealt with the terms of trade and assumed that although the relative prices of different goods changed, each good had only one world price. This is quite distinct from the changes in international competitiveness which would result from the introduction of new carbon taxes. The price of tradeables relative to nontradeables for a particular country would then need to change. This is a macro-economic phenomenon which can be addressed through exchange rate and other macro-economic policies, and which consequently can be expected to be resolved well inside the time horizon relevant to any GHG policy. But it is an issue that attracts some interest among policy-makers and which has one important real dimension.

Competitive issues arise if abatement falls unevenly across countries. Crudely, the greater the abatement, the higher are industrial costs and the less competitive the economy.[12] One set of models in the literature considers abatement in only one country, but such an approach is subject to at least two serious pitfalls. The first danger lies in the treatment of abatement itself. Glomsrod *et al.* (1990) model Norwegian abatement and find that it reduces Norwegian output and energy-use and worsens competitiveness. But Norway is assumed to produce the same volume of oil with abatement or without; all that abatement does is to reduce Norwegian oil burning and so release a larger volume of oil for export and burning abroad. Similarly, Blitzer *et al.* (1990) find Egypt achieving its abatement targets by ceasing to refine oil itself and exporting crude oil instead of petroleum products.

The second pitfall is the difficulty of knowing how world prices will change if abatement is global – i.e. how to model the terms of trade changes. It is not legitimate to assume that they remain unaffected, but it is impossible to estimate their changes without a world model. Barker and Lewny (1991) confront this difficulty and try to make allowance for it. They consider a unilateral UK abatement using the same export and import functions in their abatement and business-as-usual scenarios. However, they do not allow UK exporters to lose market share through the migration of energy-intensive industries. This amounts to using UK data to define relative price changes among goods and then imposing these on the rest of the world. They do not extend this procedure to world oil, gas and coal prices which remain unchanged, as they should under a small country's unilateral abatement, and neither do they adjust UK import prices. These two shortcomings mean that little reliance can be placed on the macroeconomic conclusions of the current set of national models of abatement.

A similar, but quantitatively less serious, set of issues arises in analyses of partial abatement. Edmonds and Barns (1990a,b), for example, briefly explore abatement by OECD countries alone. They conclude, *inter alia*, that it could not plausibly achieve the global Toronto target of a 20 per cent reduction by year 2005 relative to 1988. Perroni and Rutherford (1991) conduct a similar exercise but conclude that significant abatement is possible and that it will be accompanied by only a modest degree of 'carbon leakage'. The latter is the extent to which carbon-use foregone in the OECD is offset by increased use elsewhere. Perroni and Rutherford's base-run assumes 23 per cent abatement globally with 33 per cent abatement in the OECD. If abatement is pursued just by the OECD, it would generate a 14.7 per cent global reduction in emissions with no leakage, but would achieve 14.5 per cent even with leakage. Leakage is greater if supply elasticities and growth rates in non-OECD areas are increased, but it never becomes large.

The recent GREEN results from the OECD Secretariat (Burniaux *et al.*, 1991b) offer some support for Perroni and Rutherford's conclusions. They appear to find little evidence of carbon leakage (industrial countries' costs of abatement are assumed independent of whether other countries pursue abatement or not), and note that OECD abatement imposes costs on oil exporters (which is not surprising) and on developing countries (which might be). The latter effect presumably reflects the reduced supply of manufactured exports which cannot be circumvented by carbon leakage. Both Burniaux *et al.*'s and Perroni and Rutherford's low estimates of leakage probably stem from the strong product differentiation between OECD and non-OECD output that is built into their models. It is an almost inevitable result of trying to calibrate constant-elasticity-of-substitution (CES) demand and production functions to rather aggregated data. Leakage may, however, actually be greater, but there are as yet no studies which support that view.

Competitiveness could become an issue in global abatement under two circumstances: first, if economies have existing distortions that are addressed by abatement (coal-mining subsidies, for example) and second, if abatement entails non-transferable carbon limits. The so-called 'no regrets' school has considered existing distortions at some length, but only in the terms that their elimination would improve world welfare. It was also noted above that their presence could seriously disturb traditional welfare measures. A third dimension also can be considered. Existing studies of GHG abatement implicitly assume that the business-as-usual scenario continues current policy into the future and that abatement policy is simply added on. In those scenarios the carbon tax is simply added to existing petrol taxes and to any taxes or subsidies offered to other fuels. This view is not necessarily valid as a normative prescription – its validity depends on why society imposed those other policies. Nor is it necessarily valid as a positive prediction of what would happen.

It may well be that existing subsidies should be removed before thinking about imposing any carbon tax or, equivalently, that global GHG policy should merely 'top up' existing taxes and subsidies to a common level. However, even if doing so will be welfare improving overall, it would still entail additional adjustment for the sectors directly concerned, and might well be reflected in their international competitiveness. Moreover, if domestic subsidies are accompanied by border measures, it is possible that they will affect the internal price of energy. This has two implications. First, it will probably affect the cost share of energy and hence the proportional costs of abatement; second, it will imply changes in the international competitiveness of both energy-using and energy-supplying industries.

It would be easy to believe that existing subsidies reduce the price of energy and hence that although their removal implies that overall proportional abatement costs will be reduced, a larger proportional abatement will be required. On the other hand, however, subsidies frequently permit the use of local high-cost energy sources rather than cheap imports, so the effects could be just the opposite.[13]

The second dimension of competitiveness is potentially more important. If abatement entails the determination of rigid quantitative emission targets for each country, the implicit carbon tax is almost bound to differ between countries. Indeed, even if it were identical initially, differences would soon emerge as countries grew at different rates. Different tax rates obviously imply competitiveness effects, and one would expect to see energy-intensive production migrating to places where the emissions targets were loosest (i.e. where the tax was lowest). If demand patterns remained unchanged this would affect international trade patterns and would raise the ugly possibility of a carbon tariff.

Both Perroni and Rutherford (1991) and Burniaux *et al.* (1991a) have explored this issue elegantly. Both compare abatement with rigid geographical emission limits with that generated by the same allocation of emission rights but with free trade in permits. The precise differences between these scenarios depend on the allocation of carbon rights, but Perroni and Rutherford suggest that quite significant differences could arise between them. For example, with no trade in carbon permits the implicit tax ranges from $122 per tonne in China to $347 per tonne in the USA (for a 23 per cent abatement) compared with $278 per tonne world-wide when trade is permitted. These authors do not report differences in GDP between the two scenarios, but do observe that industrial restructuring is substantially reduced by trading permits. That is, they show that trading carbon permits and trading carbon-intensive goods are subsitutes.

The Burniaux *et al.* (1991a) study concurs in these conclusions and shows additionally that trade in carbon permits places more of the burden of adjustment to abatement on coal and less on oil. The higher tax that permit-trading imposes on China curtails its energy use by more than in the non-permit-trading outcome, and the revenue earned by selling permits allows it to import more oil, which further reduces coal use. China still loses income from GHG abatement, but by significantly less than if permit-trading is prohibited.

5.4 Some other trade issues

So far this chapter has deliberately restricted itself to surveying existing quantitative studies of GHG abatement. Even this suggests that a huge research agenda is necessary to fill in the gaps and resolve the remaining confusions. An even larger agenda, however, exists once new issues are considered. This section notes a selection of issues which may arise from the interactions between GHG abatement policies and international trade and which might deserve some attention. All of these issues can be explored by considering deviations from a largely arbitrary base or business-as-usual run. This is probably a more fruitful use of modelling effort than would be an attempt to define ever more precise measures of the absolute cost of abatement.

Abatement policy will impinge differently on different fuels and hence is likely to disturb trading patterns *within* the energy sector. Obvious issues include the possible growth of trade in natural gas and uranium, the decline of trade in coal and shale oil, and corresponding price effects. These consequences will be greatly complicated if abatement is compounded by trade liberalization, or at least by the evening out of distortions across countries. For example, if reducing the use of coal encouraged the closing of high-cost production in Europe, the costs of abatement on the major coal users in those countries would be mitigated or possibly even reversed. An important dimension of the political economy of such a situation, however, would be the extent to which high-cost producers would be able to prevent their governments from signing abatement-cum-liberalization packages. There is a danger that spurious arguments about employment and national security would lead countries to seek to place the burden of reduced coal consumption on foreign rather than domestic producers. The resulting import restrictions would clearly be a matter for the GATT.

A second potential effect of abatement could be to curtail the growth of trade in manufactures. This might occur as prices of manufactures rose relative to those of services and non-tradeables, and possibly also because protectionist barriers may be used to try to defend local producers from abatement costs. The post-war period has witnessed a rapid expansion in manufactured trade, which, to many commentators, has been one of the principal explanations of the world's unprecedently large increase in prosperity. The causal chain behind this observation entails not merely the fact that trade makes more goods available, but also that it increases competition, allows the exploitation of economies of scale, and stimulates preferences by providing variety. If abatement policy curtailed such growth it could induce a decline in GDP beyond that suggested by the current generation of static or simple growth models. This, in turn, would feed back onto trade patterns in general. This possibility − which has something in common with Hogan and Jorgenson's (1990) views about technical progress − would bear further exploration with regard to both the abatement/manufactures trade link and the consequences of a decline in the growth rate of trade in manufactures.

A third issues which requires exploration is the possibility − noted, but largely dismissed, by current models − that the imposition of national carbon quotas would stimulate a major relocation of world industry. Given the current relative freedom of foreign direct investment flows, this seems to be a stronger possibility than current modelling suggests. This issue is important, moreover, because greater mobility of industry (carbon leakage in the earlier terminology) would reduce the global costs of a given set of carbon quotas by allowing greater adjustment but would also potentially redistribute those costs. A major determinant of the extent of redistribution is the extent to which industries confer surpluses on their countries of location, which in turn depends on market structure, factor market institutions, tax policies, etc. It is not a foregone conclusion that all such corporate migration hurts the home country and benefits the host. An important aspect of this question is the fact that issuing carbon quotas would, of itself, change competitive conditions and could induce strategic behaviour of a form not seen heretofore (Ulph, 1990). A final consideration is that if relocation were to become a major phenomenon, the institutional framework for capital flows and profit repatriation would come under severe pressure.

Much of the advice offered by international institutions to developing countries over the last decade has been to liberalize their trading and regulatory regimes. This has at least two points of interaction with abatement policy. First, if current techniques of production are optimally chosen and liberalization does not change them, any extra industrial growth induced by the liberalization would increase all inputs roughly proportionately to their present use in industry. Since developing countries are currently very inefficient users of energy and also use rather dirty fuels, any such growth will increase carbon emissions if those countries' environmental policies remained unchanged. This effect would be exacerbated if liberalization not only increased world industrial activity but relocated it towards developing countries as well. Of course, in many cases liberalization would encourage greater fuel efficiency, and the income growth it generated would increase the demand for anti-pollution policies in developing countries. But so long as different countries have different coefficients for carbon emission per unit of output, industrial relocation will affect emission totals.

The second interaction between trade liberalization and carbon emissions occurs at the interface between agriculture and industry. Economic reform in many developing countries would involve stimulating agriculture relative to industry and hence might curtail emissions (see Chapter 8 of this volume). This effect would be enhanced if industrial countries also liberalized, for their agriculture is more energy-intensive than developing countries' and their industry may well be less carbon-intensive. Both of these interactions deserve serious explorations on a positive level, and both raise important policy issues such as coupling abatement policy with technology transfer and migration.

5.5   Summary

This chapter has surveyed recent quantitative modelling of the consequences of abating emissions of greenhouse gases. It shows that estimates centre on a global loss of GDP of around 2 to 4 per cent in order to reduce emissions by about 40 to 60 per cent relative to what they otherwise would be. It argues that the estimates depend on various parameters of economic behaviour, however, and that there are wide variances in the assumptions used concerning some of these parameters.

There are few empirical studies of how GHG abatement might affect international trade and prices, but a number of important determinants of those effects were identified and an important distinction drawn between terms of trade changes and changes in competitiveness. The former is the more important issue, but competitiveness could be disturbed if abatement is pursued by imposing quantitative limits on trade. The terms of trade between fuels and other goods will be altered no matter how abatement is achieved, but the direction of change depends on whether the (explicit or implicit) carbon tax is collected and kept by consumers or by producers. The chapter concludes by identifying a number of areas for further research at the interface between international trade and greenhouse gas abatement.

Notes

Thanks are due to Gianna Boero and Rosemary Clarke with whom I have worked closely on this subject. They are also due to Jim de Melo, to the participants at the conference and to the editors of this volume for comments on an earlier draft of this chapter, and to Tina Attwell for typing.

1. This section draws on Boero *et al.*, (1991a,b).
2. Over the course of writing Boero *et al.* (1991a) the authors detected a gradual convergence of modellers' views towards the range of 2 to 4 per cent, even for higher abatements, although this is not yet evident in their published work.
3. Exhaustion of cleaner fuels will occur earlier and of coal later under abatement policy than in its absence because of the policy-induced substitutions over the early twenty-first century.
4. This surprising conclusion arises because for a given rise in real energy prices, the higher is factor substitutability the greater is the reduction in energy use and the greater the increased demand for other factors. But since under the hypothesised conditions the use of other factors cannot, *in aggregate*, increase, a larger cut in energy implies a larger cut in output. The 'catch' in this lies in the assumed real price increase for energy – higher substitutability would allow a given abatement to be achieved by a smaller price increase – but many modellers do in fact start with an exogenous price increase and hence do potentially encounter the perverse response.
5. In private correspondence Cline and Edmonds have noted to me the reservations they expressed about these estimates and agreed that they are not plausible.
6. Of course, eliminating these policies would almost certainly boost world aggregate economic welfare, but this does not render doing so a 'no regrets' strategy in the sense used by GHG analysts because it does not necessarily cut emissions. As Anderson notes in Chapter 8 of this volume, however, reforms in world coal markets may well cut emissions, given the current pattern of distortions in those markets.

7. Analytically the issue is very similar to the question of who gets the scarcity rents from quantitative restrictions – the importers (with quotas) or the exporters (with VERs).
8. Manne and Richels (1990) report high costs for China (10 per cent of GDP), partly for the reason described here, but partly also because of their extremely optimistic assumption about the growth of labour productivity and GDP in China.
9. Its use of a 2020 horizon precludes the advent of significant back-stop technologies in its scenarios.
10. Since we can treat the world as a closed economy these impact effects will be well represented by $dP = (I - A)^{-1}c$ where dP is the change in price, A the input-output matrix and c the vector of carbon taxes levied on different goods.
11. Hence their model ignores any excess demands created in the first round and discounts the fact that industry costs may change with the quantities supplied.
12. Viewed alternatively, the greater the abatement the lower national output and the greater aggregate excess demand.
13. See, for example, the analysis of coal trade liberalization in Chapter 8 of this volume.

References

Anderson, D. and C. D. Bird (1990), *The Carbon Accumulations Problem and Technical Progress*, University College London and Balliol College Oxford, September.

Barker, T. and R. Lewney (1991), 'A Green Scenario for the U.K. Economy', Chapter 2 in *Green Futures for Economic Growth: Britain in 2010*, edited by T. Barker, Cambridge: Cambridge Econometrics.

Blitzer, C. R., R. S. Eckaus, S. Lahiri and A. Meeraus (1990), 'A General Equilibrium Analysis of the Effects of Carbon Emission Restrictions on Economic Growth in a Developing Country', paper presented at a Workshop on Economic/Energy/Environmental Modelling for Climate Policy Analysis, the World Bank, Washington, D.C., October.

Boero G., R. Clarke and L. A. Winters (1991a), *The Macroeconomic Consequences of Controlling Greenhouse Gases: A Survey*, Research Report, U.K. Department of the Environment, London.

Boero, G., R. Clarke and L. A. Winters (1991b), 'The Costs of Controlling Greenhouse Gas Emissions: A Survey of Global Estimates', Working Paper, Department of Economics, University of Birmingham.

Burniaux, J.-M., J. P. Martin, G. Nicoletti and J. O. Martins (1991a), 'The Costs of Policies to Reduce Global Emissions of CO2: Initial Simulation Results with GREEN', Working Paper No. 103, Economics and Statistics Department, OECD, Paris, June.

Burniaux, J.-M., J. P. Martin, G. Nicoletti and J. O. Martins (1991b), 'GREEN – A Multi-sector, Multi-region Dynamic General Equilibrium Model for Quantifying the Costs of Curbing CO2 Emissions: A Technical Manual', Working Paper No. 104, Economics and Statistics Department, OECD, Paris, June.

Cline, W. R. (1989), *Political Economy of the Greenhouse Effect*, Washington, D.C.: Institute for International Economics, April.

CBO (Congressional Budget Office) (1990), *Carbon Charges as a Response to Global Warming: The Effects of Taxing Fossil Fuels*, Congressional Budget Office, Washington, D.C.

Edmonds, J. and D. W. Barns (1990a), *Estimating the Marginal Cost of Reducing Global Fossil Fuel Carbon Emissions*, PNL-SA-18361, Pacific Northwest Laboratory, Washington, D.C.

Edmonds, J. and D. W. Barns (1990b), *Factors Affecting the Long-term Cost of Global Fossil Fuel Carbon Emissions Reductions*, Global Environmental Change Program, Pacific Northwest Laboratory, Washington, D.C.

Edmonds, J. and J. Reilly (1983), 'Global Energy and Carbon to the Year 2050', *The Energy Journal* 4: 21–47.

Edmonds, J. and J. M. Reilly (1985), *Global Energy: Assessing the Future*, New York: Oxford University Press.

Glomsrod, S., H. Vennemo and T. Johnsen (1990), *Stabilization of Emissions of Carbon: A Computable General Equilibrium Assessment*, Central Bureau of Statistics, Oslo, April.

Grubb, M. (1990), *Energy Policies and the Greenhouse Effect. Volume One: Policy Appraisal.* Dartmouth: The Royal Institute of International Affairs.

Hogan, W. W. and D. W. Jorgenson (1990), *Productivity Trends and the Cost of Reducing Carbon Emissions*, Energy and Environmental Policy Center, John F. Kennedy School of Government, Harvard University, Cambridge, MA.

Manne, A. S. and R. G. Richels (1990), *Global Carbon Emission Reduction – The Impacts of Rising Energy Costs*, Electric Power Research Institute, Palo Alto, CA.

Marks, R. E., P. L. Swan, P. McLennan, R. Shodde, P. B. Dixon and D. T. Johnson (1990), *The Cost of Australian Carbon Dioxide Abatement*, Australian Graduate School of Management, University of New South Wales, Sydney.

Mintzer, I. M. (1987), *A Matter of Degrees: The Potential for Controlling the Greenhouse Effect*, Research Report 5, Washington, D.C: World Resource Institute.

Nordhaus, W. D. (1991), 'To Slow or not to Slow: The Economics of the Greenhouse Effect', *Economic Journal* **101**, 920–37.

Perroni, C. and T. F. Rutherford (1991), 'International Trade in Carbon Emission Rights and Basic Materials: General Equilibrium Calculations for 2020', mimeo, Department of Economics, Wilfrid Laurier University, Waterloo, Ontario.

Symons, E. J., J. L. R. Proops and P. W. Gay (1990), *Carbon Taxes, Consumer Demand and Carbon Dioxide Emission: A Simulation Analysis for the UK*, Department of Economics and Management Science, University of Keele, Staffs.

Ulph, A. (1990), 'Pollution Control and Strategic International Trade', mimeo, Department of Economics, University of Southampton.

Whalley, J. and R. Wigle (1991), 'The International Incidence of Carbon Taxes', in *Economic Policy Responses to Global Warming*, edited by R. Dornbusch and J. Poterba, Cambridge, MA: MIT Press.

Williams, R. H. (1990a), 'Low-cost Strategies for Coping with CO_2 Emission Limits', *Energy Journal* **11**: 35–59.

Williams, R. H. (1990b), *Will Constraining Fossil Fuel Carbon Dioxide Emissions Cost So Much?*, Center for Energy and Environmental Studies, Princeton University, Princeton, April.

6

International linkages and carbon reduction initiatives

John Piggott, John Whalley and Randall Wigle

There is the possibility that over the next decade or two a major global initiative will be adopted to reduce (or at least slow the rate of growth of) carbon emissions because of concerns over global warming. This possibility is now taken sufficiently seriously for economists to study its consequences (Cline, 1989, 1991; Nordhaus, 1991; Boero et al., 1991). The focus of most work thus far has been the global costs of such a measure, although analysts have noted the incentives, especially for smaller countries, to free-ride (see the related discussion in Black et al., 1990, and Pezzey, 1991).

This chapter argues that the incentives to either participate or not participate in any international initiatives to reduce carbon emissions reflect much more than free-riding on the benefit side. While a cut in energy use by one country confers benefits on other countries insofar as they value reduced carbon emissions and slowed global warming, a number of other effects involving the wider international economy will either reinforce or weaken any individual country's incentive to participate. These include:

- *Production (or consumption) substitution across countries*: reduced production (consumption) or carbon-based energy by one country raises producer prices (lowers consumer prices) elsewhere, which increases production (consumption) elsewhere;
- *Terms of trade effects involving energy products*: reduced carbon consumption by large energy importers (the European Community, Japan, the United States) can improve their terms of trade in energy products at the expense of energy exporting countries; and
- *Terms of trade effects involving energy-intensive and other products*: countries adopting policies to reduce carbon emissions may face a change in their commodity terms of trade as higher energy prices affect costs of producing carbon-intensive energy products.

We use a global numerical general equilibrium model of trade and carbon emissions to analyse these additional effects of carbon taxes. This model has been previously employed by Whalley and Wigle (1991b) to analyse the international incidence of various global carbon tax schemes. Here, we extend that earlier model through a specification of preference towards temperature change, and analyse incentives to join a range of both global and unilateral (single-region) schemes for reducing carbon emission. The model is implemented using MPS/GE software package (Rutherford, 1989).

Our results highlight the importance of the additional effects listed above in affecting country incentives to reduce carbon emissions, especially in so far as initiatives for unilateral reduction are concerned. While benefit-related incentives to participate in schemes to reduce carbon can be large, these effects are offset to a surprisingly large degree by production (or consumption) responses in non-participating countries. Large effects on trade volumes can also accompany carbon reduction initiatives. The model results we report thus suggest the likely need for trade or other third-country sanctions, or incentive payments to support global agreements on carbon limitation. This may have important implications for the international trading system over the next few decades.

6.1 A general equilibrium model for assessing incentives to participate in carbon reduction schemes

As stated above, the results reported in this chapter are based on a global general equilibrium model developed earlier by Whalley and Wigle (1991a) to study the international incidence of carbon taxes.[1] We modify this earlier model by explicitly incorporating the benefits obtained from slowed global warming through reduced carbon emissions, by specifying preferences to capture climate change. This enables us to make a number of counterfactual calculations of the effects of alternative initiatives for reducing carbon emissions in which the benefits from slowed global warming and the costs from reduced use of carbon-based energy both enter the analysis. Because countries fully bear the costs of reduced carbon energy use, but only receive a portion of the global benefits from slowed global warming, optimal unilateral reduction schemes will typically involve smaller reductions than global (full-participation) reduction schemes. But terms of trade effects, and cross-country substitution effects in production and consumption, also come into play.

The model incorporates trade, production, and consumption of both energy and non-energy products for six country groups spanning the world. It projects over a forty-year period from 1990 to 2030, which is treated for analytical convenience as a single period.[2] This means that the model incorporates no explicit dynamics. Neither does the model incorporate existing taxes on energy products, although these vary by region and so would affect the results if they were included. To further keep the model manageable, we do not identify fuel types within the broader category of carbon-based energy products, even though various elements within this category (oil, coal, natural gas) have different carbon contents.

In the model, the world is divided into six regions, indicated in Table 6.1. These are the European Community, North America, Japan, other industrial market economies, oil exporters (OPEC countries plus major non-OPEC, non-OECD energy exporters) and a residual rest of the world which includes most developing countries (other than oil exporters) and the centrally planned economies (CPEs).

Nested constant elasticity of substitution (CES) functions are used to represent production and demand in each region. The nesting structure is set out in Table 6.2. Each region is endowed with four non-traded primary factors of production: primary factors other than energy resources; carbon-based energy resources (deposits of oil, gas and coal); other energy resources (hydro-electric and nuclear capacity); and sector-specific skills and equipment in the energy-intensive manufacturing sector. Both energy resources are treated as able to be converted into the relevant energy products through a refining/extraction process which uses other primary factors. There are three internationally traded commodities: carbon-based energy products, energy-intensive manufactures, and other goods (all other GNP). Energy-intensive manufactures, other goods, and the composite energy product (carbon-based and non-carbon-based energy) enter final demands.

Each of the five produced goods in each region uses energy resources and primary factors in its production. Non-carbon-based energy products are assumed to be nontradeable, since hydro-electric, solar and nuclear power are not traded in significant quantities between the six regions as

Table 6.1 Regions in the global general equilibrium model[a]

1. EUROPEAN COMMUNITY (EC)
   The twelve member countries of Belgium, Denmark, France, Germany, Greece, Ireland, Italy, Luxembourg, The Netherlands, Portugal, Spain and the United Kingdom.
2. NORTH AMERICA (NA)
   The United States and Canada.
3. JAPAN (JA)
4. OTHER INDUSTRIAL MARKET ECONOMIES (OIME)
   Australia and New Zealand plus the EFTA member countries of Austria, Finland, Iceland, Norway, Sweden and Switzerland.
5. OIL EXPORTERS (OILEX)
   Algeria, Libya, Nigeria, Tunisia, Mexico, Venezuela, Indonesia, Iran, Iraq, Kuwait, Saudi Arabia and the United Arab Emirates.
6. REST OF THE WORLD (ROW)
   This is a residual category containing all other countries including USSR, the CPEs of Eastern Europe, China, Brazil, India and other developing countries not in category 5.

Note: [a] Abbreviations shown in brackets are those used in the following tables of results.

Table 6.2 Production and demand structures in the global general equilibrium model

---

A. *Factors and goods in each region*
   Endowments:
   Carbon-based energy resources (CR)
   Non-carbon-based energy resources (ER)
   Sector-specific factors in energy-intensive manufacturing (SF)
   Other primary factors (PF)
   Produced goods:
   Carbon-based energy products (CP)
   Non-carbon-based energy products (EP)
   Composite energy (E)
   Energy-intensive goods (EI)
   Other goods (OG)

B. *Structure of production in each region*
   (Constant-elasticity-of-substitution (CES) functions are used at each stage)
   State 1: Production of energy products

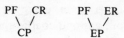

   State 2: Production of composite energy

```
   CP EP
    \ /
     E
```

   State 3: Production of energy-intensive and other goods

```
   E  SF  PF      E   PF
    \  |  /        \  /
      EI            OG
```

C. *Arguments in final demands*

   E,   EI,   OG

D. *Commodities traded internationally*

   CP,   EI,   OG

---

defined in Table 6.1. A domestic energy composite is produced by a third (energy conversion) industry, using the two energy products as inputs. The two final goods (energy-intensive manufactures, and other goods) use primary factors and the composite domestic energy product as inputs. Perfect competition is assumed throughout in all regions and for all sectors.

For the two nontraded goods (non-carbon energy products, and composite energy) there is domestic market clearing separately within each economy. Since prices in this system are treated as completely flexible, they will adjust to the levels required to clear the relevant international and domestic markets. Counterfactual analyses for any hypothesized policy change involve the computation of a new equilibrium model solution.

Policy evaluation is based on a comparison between counterfactual model solutions and the base data to which the model has been calibrated.

The base case equilibrium solution for the model represents an assumed future evolution of the global economy over the forty-year period between 1990 and 2030. This is based on an assumption of growth in OECD countries continuing at the same annual rates as in the late 1980s, and unchanged use of energy and consumption and production of other goods. Hicksian neutral (factor-augmenting) growth is assumed to occur in each of the regions in the model at average annual rates reported in the World Bank (1989), which are assumed to apply over the entire period under consideration. The oil-exporting region is assumed to grow at 2.5 per cent, the Rest of the World at 2.7 per cent, and the remaining regions at 2.3 per cent per annum. Each region's endowment of non-produced factors in the model thus reflects the present value of their resources (at constant prices) over the entire 40-year period. We assume that a 5 per cent real discount rate applies for all years in the period considered in the model. The model is solved to yield a forty-year base line solution representing an equilibrium in the world economy in the absence of any response to global warming over the period 1990 to 2030 (in discounted present value terms in US billion dollars at 1990 prices). Policy experiments are then evaluated relative to this base line, with a comparison of base and counterfactual equilibria.

The structure of the regional economies in the base data used in the model largely corresponds to data available for 1982 and projected forward to 1990. Data for regional population and GNP in 1982 are obtained from the World Bank (1987). Value-added, production and trade in energy-intensive manufactures (primary metals, glass, ceramics and other basic manufactured products) are obtained from Nguyen *et al.* (1990). These are identified as those industries having the highest energy input requirements. Input ratios from Whalley and Wigle (1991b) are used to infer energy input requirements for energy-intensive and other industries.

Production, consumption and trade data in carbon-based energy production and non-carbon-based energy (for 1982) come from the United Nations (1987). Raw data are in kilotonnes of coal equivalent. The carbon content of production and consumption for the regions in the model are determined using the same conversion coefficients as those in Whalley and Wigle (1991b). To convert production data into value terms, we use price information from the World Resources Institute (1990).

To incorporate the benefit side of slowed global warming, we have modified the preference functions for each of the regions identified in the earlier Whalley-Wigle model so as to include not only goods directly consumed but also the disutility associated with temperature change. This is linked by a simple linear relation to carbon emissions. This, in effect, involves an additional level of nesting within the utility function U_i to capture this component. For each region, goods consumed, G_i, are region-specific, but global temperature change ΔT is common to all regions. G_i in turn is a composite of the goods identified in Table 6.2 in the preference structure, that is, $G_i = G_i(EI_i, OG_i, E_i)$.

Global temperature change (ΔT) in turn is linked to global carbon emissions and hence, through each region's utility function (U_i), externality effects associated with global warming are directly incorporated in the model:

$$U_i = U_i(G_i, \Delta T) \qquad i = 1, \dots 6.$$

While this change in the model is conceptually straightforward, and parallels the analysis of public goods in the public finance literature (Atkinson and Stiglitz, 1979), there are major problems with numerical specification of these preference functions in a model such as this. As is by now well-known, there are no widely agreed estimates as to how large or small the benefits from a slowing of global warming may be. There are suggestions, such as those by Nordhaus (1991) and Schelling (1991), that the benefits of slowing global warming are likely to be quite small. On the other hand, economists such as Cline (1991) have argued that with a possible sextupling in levels of atmospheric carbon dioxide by the end of the next century, the potential costs may be larger.

Our analysis of the incentives for countries to participate in carbon reduction initiatives would undoubtedly be more convincing were there a clearer consensus on the size of possible benefits from slower global warming. Nonetheless, the profile of the policy debate on the issue is such that it still seems worthwhile to make calculations based on various assumptions, which in turn might suggest what determines the incentives for countries to implement various schemes to reduce carbon emissions.

We make the assumption that demands for emission reductions voiced at various international conferences are consistent with a global optimal allocation of resources under jointly administered carbon emission reductions on a full participatory basis. The call at the 1988 Toronto conference for a 20 per cent emission reduction by the year 2005, with further emission reductions to follow, provides the basis for our preference parameterization. We thus assume that a full-participation 50 per cent reduction in carbon emission by all regions by the year 2030 is such that marginal benefits from further global abatement will exactly balance marginal costs of achieving further carbon reductions. Using this strong assumption we are then able to analyse what the incentives are for various countries or regions to implement reduction initiatives of different forms.

The parameterization of this extended version of the model is based on standard calibration (see Mansur and Whalley, 1984), with the preference parameters towards climate change being correspondingly generated. Counterfactual analysis then allows us to compute new equilibria for our model under carbon emission reductions of various forms and various assumptions as to what type of regional participation is involved.

To implement standard calibration procedures in this case requires that synthetic data be constructed on implicit budget shares on (private) goods G_i and the public good (temperature change, ΔT) for each region. This procedure is similar to the construction of personalized prices for public goods in numerical equilibrium models incorporating public and private goods (see Piggott and Whalley, 1987, 1991). We make the assumption here that implicit regional expenditures (used to recover preference parameters) on temperature change in the base-case equilibrium solution for the model are related to both regional population and per capita income. Thus preferences towards temperature change are less strong in low-income regions, and implicit expenditures on the global public good are lower in smaller regions (as are expenditures on private goods).

6.2   Results using the general equilibrium model

Using this extended Whalley–Wigle model we explore the incentives for regions to undertake (either unilaterally or globally) various types of carbon emission reduction schemes. We investigate the strength of other channels of international interdependence (cross-country production and/or consumption substitution effects, terms of trade effects) in influencing regional participation, beyond the simple incentives to free-ride on emission reductions of others. We also evaluate the possible effects of carbon reduction schemes on trade volumes.

In Table 6.3, we report model results of the welfare effects by region of various types of emission reductions. The first column of Part A (for consumption cuts) shows results for a 50 per cent global reduction in carbon use in which all regions fully participate. In this case all regional groups benefit except the oil exporters; the oil exporters lose because of a sharp deterioration in their terms of trade. The significant net benefits accruing globally from such a cut reflect the assumptions of a falling marginal benefit schedule from emission reductions and a rising marginal cost schedule of reductions (due to emission reduction schemes having to be of increasing severity).

Unilateral consumption cuts of 50 per cent involve losses by the region making such cuts and benefits for all other regions except oil exporters. The positive effects for non-participants come not only from shared benefits in emission reductions but also from terms of trade and other effects. Regions cutting consumption lower consumer prices of energy which allows other energy importing regions to increase consumption.

Results in Part B of Table 6.3 report welfare effects from production cuts. These show a similar pattern, except for the welfare impact on oil exporters which is positive because their terms of trade improve. In the case

Table 6.3 Welfare effects by region of various carbon reduction schemes (Percentage difference relative to the base scenario)

A. *Cuts in consumption of carbon-based energy*

50% multilateral cut (full participation)		50% unilateral cuts by:					
		EC	NA	JA	OIME	OILEX	ROW
EC	5.9	− 0.4	0.7	0.1	0.1	0.1	1.6
NA	4.7	0.3	− 0.6	0.1	0.0	0.1	1.4
JA	6.7	0.4	0.8	− 0.4	0.1	0.1	1.7
OIME	5.4	0.3	0.6	0.1	− 0.5	0.1	1.3
OILEX	− 5.6	− 0.4	− 0.9	− 0.1	− 0.1	− 1.3	− 1.8
ROW	0.3	0.2	0.5	0.1	0.0	0.1	− 2.1

B. *Cuts in production of carbon-based energy*

50% multilateral cut (full participation)		50% unilateral cuts by:					
		EC	NA	JA	OIME	OILEX	ROW
EC	4.4	− 0.1	1.0	0.0	0.1	0.9	2.2
NA	4.3	0.3	0.1	0.0	0.1	1.0	2.5
JA	4.6	0.3	1.0	0.0	0.1	0.8	2.0
OIME	5.4	0.3	1.2	0.0	− 0.4	1.0	2.5
OILEX	8.2	0.7	2.5	0.0	0.2	− 2.9	6.0
ROW	0.4	0.3	0.9	0.0	0.1	0.8	− 1.3

of North America, the costs of reducing energy production are relatively low because of the high productivity of mobile factors of production elsewhere in the economy. The high marginal valuation placed on the benefits to North America of reduced global carbon use (given the calibration procedures outlined above) are a reason why benefits outweigh costs in this case.

In Table 6.4, we report a decomposition of the regional welfare effects for the two cases of 50 per cent unilateral cuts by the European Community and North America. We show that portion which is due to changed carbon emissions and that which is due to other factors (terms of trade and other relative price and hence quantity effects). These decompositions are calculated by substituting the changed emission levels under unilateral emission reductions into the utility functions for each region, evaluated at base consumption levels of all goods. Two separate substitutions are made: one using the new carbon emission level in the country or region undertaking the reductions, and the other using the new carbon emission levels in all countries. This provides us with the reported estimates of the welfare effects in Table 6.4. These results clearly indicate the difference between the own-country and global effects, and show the significance of other international linkages beyond those of free-riding by some regions on carbon emission reductions of others. Clearly, more is at stake for other countries than just the direct effect when one country or region chooses to reduce its emissions of carbon.

Table 6.4 Welfare effects of reducing EC or North American carbon-based energy production by 50%
(Percentage difference relative to the base scenario)

	Total welfare effect	Effect due to own country's carbon reduction	Effect due to changes in carbon emissions in all countries
A. *Unilateral production cut of 50% in EC*			
EC	−0.1	0.9	0.3
NA	0.3	0.9	0.3
JA	0.3	0.9	0.3
OIME	0.3	0.9	0.3
OILEX	0.7	0.8	0.3
ROW	0.3	0.7	0.3
B. *Unilateral production cut of 50% in NA*			
EC	1.0	1.7	1.2
NA	0.1	1.8	1.2
JA	1.0	1.7	1.2
OIME	1.2	1.7	1.2
OILEX	2.5	1.5	1.1
ROW	0.9	1.3	1.0

In Tables 6.5 and 6.6 we report the effects on carbon-based energy production and consumption from 50 per cent unilateral reductions in carbon emissions. In Table 6.5 spillover effects in the form of increased production in regions other than those undertaking unilateral reductions in production are apparent. These occur fairly evenly across regions, reflecting the similar regional production functions in the model. In the second case spillovers in consumption occur. These two tables help to illustrate the difference between the direct welfare effects of one region's emissions and the indirect effects that result from other regions' responses to such a unilateral policy change. Production or consumption cuts by the largest fossil fuel producers (Rest of the World and North America) induce large cross-region substitution effects.

Table 6.7 shows the terms of trade effects accompanying 50 per cent unilateral reductions of either the consumption or production type. With production-based reductions, the terms of trade of all regions, other than oil exporters, worsens. With consumption-based reductions the terms of trade of these regions move in the other direction. Either way, a significant terms of trade effect clearly accompanies any unilateral reduction in emissions.

In Table 6.8 we further highlight the difference between country effects from initiatives for emission reduction and the incentive to free-ride on the reduced emissions of other countries. This is done by examining constrained and unconstrained equilibria in response to reduction initiatives. In the constrained case, regions not directly participating in the reduction initiative are assumed to be constrained to not exceed their base levels of

Table 6.5 Effects on carbon-based energy production and consumption of unilateral production-based reductions in carbon emissions
(Percentage difference relative to the base scenario)

	Effects by region of unilateral production cuts of 50% by:					
	EC	NA	JA	OIME	OILEX	ROW
A. Carbon-based energy production						
EC	−50.0	3.7	0.0	0.3	3.1	8.4
NA	1.0	−50.0	0.0	0.3	3.2	8.6
JA	1.0	3.6	−50.0	0.3	3.1	8.2
OIME	1.0	3.7	0.0	−50.0	3.1	8.3
OILEX	1.1	3.8	0.0	0.3	−50.0	8.7
ROW	1.1	4.0	0.0	0.4	3.4	−50.0
B. Carbon-based energy consumption						
EC	−2.2	−8.8	−0.1	−0.8	−7.5	−18.9
NA	−2.5	−8.0	−0.1	−0.8	−7.6	−19.0
JA	−2.6	−8.9	−0.1	−0.8	−7.7	−19.3
OIME	−2.5	−8.8	−0.1	−0.4	−7.5	−18.9
OILEX	−2.6	−9.1	−0.1	−0.8	−1.6	−19.3
ROW	−2.7	−9.4	−0.1	−0.9	−8.0	−18.1
C. Impact on global energy use						
	−2.6	−0.9	−0.1	−0.8	−7.5	−18.6

Table 6.6 Effects on carbon-based energy production and consumption of unilateral consumption-based reductions in carbon emissions
(Percentage difference relative to the base scenario)

	Effects by region of unilateral production cuts of 50% by:					
	EC	NA	JA	OIME	OILEX	ROW
A. Carbon-based energy production						
EC	−0.9	−4.2	−0.5	−0.3	−0.9	−10.1
NA	−1.0	−2.4	−0.5	−0.3	−0.9	−10.4
JA	−1.9	−4.1	−0.1	−0.3	−0.8	−9.9
OIME	−2.0	−4.1	−0.5	0.4	−0.8	−9.9
OILEX	−2.0	−4.4	−0.5	−0.3	1.4	−10.6
ROW	−2.1	−4.5	−0.6	−0.3	−0.9	−6.3
B. Carbon-based energy consumption						
EC	−50.0	12.3	2.0	1.0	2.4	29.1
NA	5.8	−50.0	1.7	0.9	2.3	29.2
JA	7.7	14.0	−50.0	1.2	2.6	30.5
OIME	6.4	12.4	2.0	−50.0	2.4	29.2
OILEX	5.9	12.2	1.7	0.9	−50.0	30.7
ROW	5.7	12.1	1.5	0.9	2.4	−50.0
C. Impact on global energy use						
	−2.0	−4.0	−0.6	−0.3	−0.4	−8.5

Table 6.7 Terms of trade changes by region from unilateral reductions in carbon emissions
(Percentage difference relative to the base scenario)

	Effects by region of unilateral production cuts of 50% by:					
	EC	NA	JA	OIME	OILEX	ROW
A. *Production-based reductions*						
EC	−2.7	−9.5	−0.1	−0.9	−8.1	−20.5
NA	−2.8	−9.7	−0.1	−0.9	−8.2	−20.7
JA	−2.7	−9.5	−0.1	−0.9	−8.1	−20.4
OIME	−0.4	−1.6	0.0	−0.1	−1.4	−3.9
OILEX	2.8	10.7	0.1	0.9	9.0	26.2
ROW	−1.0	−3.7	0.0	−0.3	−3.1	−8.4
B. *Consumption-based reductions*						
EC	5.8	2.3	1.6	0.9	2.4	31.3
NA	5.6	2.1	1.5	0.9	2.4	31.6
JA	6.0	2.4	1.7	0.9	2.4	31.1
OIME	2.3	3.2	1.1	0.4	0.6	4.1
OILEX	−5.3	−10.8	−1.5	−0.9	−2.3	−24.0
ROW	0.8	2.9	−0.1	0.1	0.6	9.1

production or consumption of carbon-based energy. The sharp differences between results in the constrained and unconstrained cases reemphasizes the importance of the indirect international effects emphasised earlier. The substantial increased welfare gains reported in the constrained cases suggest that unilateral cuts accompanied by trade sanctions or side payments to ensure some restraint on carbon emissions by the rest of the world may emerge as a realistic policy scenario in future debate in this area.

Table 6.9 reports the trade volume effects of consumption-based emission reduction initiatives, reporting large effects on both world and regional trade volumes. The cut by more than half in the volume of world trade (measured as the sum at original equilibrium prices of import volumes) resulting from a 50 per cent global reduction in carbon emissions reflects the large cut in exports of OPEC and other energy exporters. Interestingly, in this case energy exports of North America increase as it becomes a relatively more productive energy exporter and improves its market share. The large reduction these results imply is in part a reflection of the commodity and regional aggregation used in the model: separately identifying Canada-US trade and intra-EC trade, as well as trade in separate categories of manufactures, would probably result in smaller reductions in world trade. The trade volume result may also be sensitive to the nature of the cut (for example, a production-based cut may yield quite different results). And perhaps even the sign of the change in world trade would be different if international capital flows and trade in emission permits had been allowed in the model. Nonetheless, the implications for both world trade and the international trading system seem to be potentially significant, with lowered world trade accompanying a reduction in global carbon emissions.

Table 6.8 Differences between region-constrained and region-unconstrained consumption-based carbon reductions of 50% by North America

	Change in welfare		Change in production of carbon-based energy		Change in region's terms of trade	
	Region-constrained	Region-unconstrained	Region-constrained	Region-unconstrained	Region-constrained	Region-unconstrained
EC	2.3	0.1	−13.6	−0.5	47.1	12.3
NA	0.4	−0.6	−11.9	−0.5	46.7	12.1
JA	2.4	0.8	−13.6	−0.1	47.3	12.4
OIME	1.9	0.6	−13.6	−0.5	9.1	3.2
OILEX	−2.4	−0.9	−13.6	−0.5	−21.8	−10.8
ROW	1.6	0.5	−13.5	−0.6	9.5	2.9

Table 6.9 Effects on trade volumes
of a multilateral (full-participation)
reduction of 50% in carbon
emissions

	Percentage difference relative to base scenario
EC	− 28
NA	1
JA	− 29
OIME	− 50
OILEX	− 83
ROW	− 42
World	− 53

6.3 Conclusions

This chapter has attempted to shed light on different incentives for countries to either agree on joint carbon-limitation initiatives or to unilaterally reduce their own emissions. Because of the public-good nature of reductions in emissions, unilateral cuts generate benefits that also accrue to other countries. Whether to implement global policies designed to reduce emissions and, if so, by how much and by whom, remain issues of substantial controversy in the wider environmental debate. Various calls for global reduction targets have emanated from the scientific community, such as the call from the 1988 Toronto Atmosphere Conference. Various OECD governments (including Canada, Australia, the United Kingdom and Italy) have also made commitments, conditional upon other governments acting similarly, to introduce policies designed to achieve target reductions. But the case on economic grounds for seeking to achieve such reductions remains unclear (see Cline, 1991; Nordhaus, 1991; Schelling, 1991).

Global negotiations on a framework to guide subsequent substantive negotiations on targets for emission reductions are now underway. It has been pointed out by economists that such negotiations will encounter difficulties. Countries have an incentive to free-ride and not comply, unless other incentives or penalties such as trade sanctions are invoked (see Chapters 7 and 12 of this volume). International monitoring and enforcement of targets is problematic. Developing countries worry about the impact of emission reductions on their development. And the allocation of targets and choice of instrument for achieving an environmental objective has many pitfalls. For example, should prior emissions enter target calculations? Are taxes or permits to be used, and how are they to be administered? Should existing domestic policies be credited in some way?

The analysis presented here addresses some of these issues. We emphasize that the incentive for individual regions to engage in unilateral emission reduction (including the US who account for nearly 25 per cent of global emissions) reflects production and/or consumption spillover effects in other regions. Production reduction initiatives in one region have the effect of increasing global producer prices and, therefore, increasing production in other regions, yielding adverse spillover effects to the region undertaking the reduction initiative. Consumption reduction initiatives reduce world consumer prices and increase consumption in other regions, once again yielding adverse spillover effects.

Terms-of-trade effects are also potentially important, since these tend to compound with externality features arising from crossovers of benefits from emission reductions and reduced energy consumption. Terms-of-trade effects from an own-country energy consumption cut can help energy importers and amplify (in some cases substantially) the benefits to them of reduced emissions from slowed global warming. In contrast, production-based cuts improve the terms of trade of energy exporters, and worsen the terms of trade of energy importers.

Notes

We are grateful to Tom Rutherford for permission to use his MPS/GE general equilibrium solution software, to Carlo Perroni for helpful discussion and comment, and to the Sonderforschungsbereich 178, University of Konstanz, for support.
1. See also the presentation in Whalley and Wigle (1991a) of earlier calculations made using an even more simplified version of this model.
2. This period has been chosen somewhat arbitrarily to capture the initial years and subsequent intermediate term during which a carbon reduction initiative would have its largest effects, because with discounting the significance in present-value terms of the effects of later years recedes. It would be relatively easy to run the model for a longer projection period (say, 80 or 100 years) but we believe that the main themes of our results would remain. A weakness of this 40-year projection period approach is that, in the base year data used for these projections, most trade in carbon products takes place in oil rather than in other carbon-assessed fuels. If, as some expect, trade in oil is slowly replaced by trade in coal during the next century, the data used here may be misleading since the countries who are potential future coal exporters (USSR, Australia, China) are quite different from current oil exporters (OPEC countries, Mexico).

References

Atkinson, A. B. and J. E. Stiglitz (1979), *Lectures on Public Economics*, New York: McGraw Hill.

Black, J., M. D. Levi and D. de Meza (1990), 'Creating a Good Atmosphere: Minimum Participation for Tackling the Greenhouse Effect', mimeo, University of Exeter, April.

Boero, G., R. Clarke and L. A. Winters (1991), *The Macroeconomic Consequences of Controlling Greenhouse Gases: A Survey*, Occasional Paper, UK Department of the Environment, London.

Cline, W. R. (1989), *Political Economy of the Greenhouse Effect*, Washington, D.C.: Institute for International Economics.

Cline, W. (1991), 'Scientific Basis for the Greenhouse Effect', *Economic Journal* **101**, 904–19.

Mansur, A. and J. Whalley (1984), 'Numerical Specification of Applied General Equilibrium Models: Estimation, Calibration and Data', pp. 69–127 in *Applied General Equilibrium Analysis*, edited by J. B. Shoven and H. Scarf, Cambridge: Cambridge University Press.

Nguyen, T. T., C. Perroni, and R. M. Wigle (1990), 'A Microconsistent Data Set for the Analysis of World Trade: Sources and Methods', mimeo, Wilfrid Laurier University, Waterloo.

Nordhaus, W. (1991), 'To Slow or Not to Slow: The Economics of the Greenhouse Effect', *Economic Journal* **101**, 920–37.

Pezzey, J. (1991), 'Analysis of Unilateral Carbon Taxes Using the Whalley–Wigle Global Energy Model', mimeo, University of Bristol.

Piggott, J. R. and J. Whalley (1987), 'Interpreting Net Fiscal Incidence Calculations', *Review of Economics and Statistics* **69**: 685–94.

Piggott, J. R. and J. Whalley (1991), 'Public Good Provision Rules and Income Distribution – Some General Equilibrium Calculations', *Empirical Economics* **16**, (forthcoming).

Rutherford, T. (1989), 'General Equilibrium Modelling with MPS/GE', mimeo, University of Western Ontario, London.

Schelling, T. (1991), 'International Burden Sharing and Coordination: Prospects for Cooperative Approaches to Global Warming', in *Economic Policy Responses to Global Warming*, edited by R. Dornbusch and J. Poterba, Cambridge, MA: MIT Press.

United Nations (1987), *Energy Statistics*, New York: United Nations Statistical Office.

Whalley, J. and R. Wigle, (1991a), 'Cutting CO_2 Emissions: the Effects of Alternative Policy Approaches', *Energy Journal* **12** (forthcoming).

Whalley, J. and R. Wigle (1991b), 'The International Incidence of Carbon Taxes', in *Economic Policy Responses to Global Warming*, edited by R. Dornbusch and J. Poterba, Cambridge, MA: MIT Press.

World Bank (1987), *World Tables* (Third Edition), Baltimore: Johns Hopkins University Press.

World Bank (1989), *World Development Report 1989*, New York: Oxford University Press.

World Resources Institute (1990), *World Resources 1990–1991*, New York: Oxford University Press.

7

Successful conventions and conventional success: saving the ozone layer

Alice Enders and Amelia Porges

Negotiations on a global agreement to reduce emissions of ozone-depleting substances began in earnest after the discovery of a 'hole' in the Antarctic stratospheric ozone layer in 1985. The result was the 1987 Montreal Protocol on Substances that Deplete the Ozone Layer. The Protocol, which requires a phasedown of production and consumption of chlorofluorocarbons (CFCs) and halons, has been in force since January 1989. In 1990 the Parties changed the phasedown to a phaseout by the year 2000 in the light of scientific evidence of more extensive ozone layer depletion.

All current emission source countries have signed and become Parties to both the Montreal Protocol and the Vienna Convention which preceded it and provided its legal framework. The Protocol covers almost 90 per cent of current world consumption and production of ozone-depleting substances. Projections indicate that the complete phaseout of CFCs in developed country Parties by the year 2000 will result in a two-thirds reduction in global consumption relative to the peak-year level of 1988.

Why was it possible to reach this multilateral environmental agreement rapidly, how successful will the agreement be in achieving its goal, and what are the lessons for drafters of other multilateral agreements? To address these questions, the chapter begins by describing the market for CFCs and halons and possible substitutes, and provides pertinent details of the Montreal Protocol. On this basis, Section 3 draws on game theory to explain why a cooperative, largely self-enforcing agreement was possible with respect to lifting current global CFC consumption, although there is some danger that the non-participation of several populous developing countries could jeopardize the goal of ozone layer preservation in the future. Section 4 then examines the Protocol's compliance mechanism, and concludes that problems with compliance are likely to be confined to populous low-income Parties as the demand for refrigeration and other services grows at home and in non-Party countries.

We argue that non-ratification and potential problems with compliance flow from the very different economic costs that low-income countries must bear in restricting consumption, compared with high-income countries. The uncertainty concerning the availability of substitutes and their technologies is an additional element. Without selective incentives to entice low-income countries to ratify the Protocol, the agreement will remain sub-global in country coverage. Some selective incentives have already been provided, but we argue that these are of limited practical significance – perhaps because the possible future emissions of low-income countries are heavily discounted by the original Parties to the Protocol. Without an inducement for all major potential suppliers to participate, and an effective dispute settlement and compliance mechanism, can the Montreal Protocol meet its original goal of protecting the ozone layer in the centuries to come? And if these two missing elements cannot be overcome in the small, manageable world of chlorofluorocarbon production and trade, what can we expect for negotiations on more complex issues such as global warming? This question is addressed in the final section of the chapter.

7.1   Chlorofluorocarbons, halons, substitutes and ozone layer depletion

CFCs were invented fifty years ago for use as cheap, safe refrigerants. The data compiled by the United Nations Environment Programme (UNEP, 1989) indicate that CFCs remain widely used as intermediate inputs into refrigerators, air conditioning units and heat pumps (30 per cent of world use), blowing of rigid and flexible foams (28 per cent), aerosol propellants (27 per cent), and cleaning of electronic parts, degreasing, and dry cleaning (14 per cent). Halons are incorporated in fire extinguishing agents. Because both CFCs and halons are chemically inert, they are not toxic to humans. However, it is for this reason that they are highly resistant to decomposition or oxidation in the lower atmosphere.

Depletion of the stratospheric ozone layer is understood to be the result of complex natural interactions between climatic conditions and chlorine molecules. In addition to natural sources, chlorine molecules are present in the stratosphere because of the decomposition of CFCs and halons. After CFCs and halons are released from a CFC-containing product or otherwise, it takes them 7 to 10 years to drift upwards through the troposphere to the stratosphere, where they can remain intact for long periods. The emission of CFCs and halons may in turn take place anywhere from zero to 30 years after their use or incorporation into a product. Thus, the time delay between incorporation of CFCs and halons into products, and ozone layer depletion ranges from 7 years to more than 30 years.[1]

Limited available data indicate that CFC and halon producers and consumers are concentrated in a small group of countries. As of 1986, the

European Community (EC-12) and the United States were the leaders in CFC consumption (30 per cent each), followed by Japan (13 per cent). The first two are also the leading producers of the substances, but only the EC is a substantial net exporter. Production capacity is modest in other developed countries, most of which are net importers. Developing countries are estimated to account for 10 per cent of consumption in 1986, supplied for the most part by high-income countries. (Table 7.1).

The CFC industry is highly concentrated, with five producers each in the United States and Japan, and nine producers in the EC. Dupont is the largest American producer, estimated to account for 25 per cent of world production, and Imperial Chemical Industries (ICI) is the largest European producer. CFC-consuming industry, by contrast, is much less concentrated because of the multiple uses of CFCs.

While trade in bulk CFCs is small in value relative to world merchandise trade, trade in CFC-containing products (heating and cooling equipment, passenger cars, airplanes, ships and boats with air conditioners and/or heat pumps) amounts to approximately 12 per cent of world trade. Products currently produced with but not containing CFCs (semi-conductors and products with electronic components), amount to an additional 16 per cent of world trade.

Table 7.1 Production, consumption, exports and imports of CFC and halon substances, by region,[a] 1986

(Kilotonnes)

	OECD except Japan	Asia	Latin America, Eastern Europe and USSR	Africa	TOTAL
A. *CFC (Group I) substances*					
Production	806	132	159	0	1,096
+ Imports	52	22	10	6	90
− Exports	162	15	2	0	180
(Net imports)	− 110	7	8	6	− 90
= Consumption	696	138	166	6	1,006
B. *Halon (Group II) substances*					
Production	21	3	5	0	29
+ Imports	4	3	1	0	7
− Exports	8	2	0	0	10
(Net imports)	− 4	1	1	0	− 3
= Consumption	17	4	6	0	26

Note: [a] OECD except Japan: EC-12, EFTA, United States, Canada, Australia, New Zealand; Asia: Japan, Jordan, Malaysia, Singapore, Sri Lanka, Syrian Arab Rep., Thailand, United Arab Emirates; Latin America, Eastern Europe and USSR: German Dem. Rep., Hungary, USSR, Brazil, Chile, Guatemala, Mexico, Panama, Venezuela; Africa: Egypt, Kenya, Tunisia.
Source: UNEP (1989).

Since the mid-1980s, the producers and users of CFCs have been seeking means to recover, re-use and substitute for CFCs. At the time of the 1989 UNEP Economic Assessment of substitutes and recovery options, there was no adequate substitute for use in air conditioners and refrigerators. Since then, however, the industry has made progress in developing and testing non-toxic alternatives, and these are expected to be ready for marketing in the early 1990s. In foam-blowing applications and home air conditioners, the leading substitutes are hydrochlorofluorocarbons (HCFCs), with an ozone-depleting potential of about 10 per cent of CFCs.[2] In auto air conditioners, the candidate is a hydrofluorocarbon, HFC-134a, which is free of chlorine ('ozone-safe'). For refrigeration, HFC-134a also has potential uses, but the main strategy for refrigeration remains extensive conservation and recycling. In cleaning applications, CFC solvents can be captured and reused. As well, substitutes to CFC solvents are available in the form of citrus and water-based cleaning agents.

Substitutes will be more expensive than CFCs, however. Producers estimate that HCFCs and HFCs initially will be several times the price of CFCs, because each of the (patented) processes is more complicated and requires new plants and new production lines. CFC-containing products also will need to be redesigned, since none of the substitutes is a 'drop-in' substitute to the CFC it replaces. Thus, prices of replacement products for CFC-containing products are likely to rise, but the price rise will be modest because CFCs generally represent a small fraction of the cost of the final product (about 3 per cent at mid-1980s prices).

While companies are moving ahead with production capacity for HCFCs and HFCs, the future of these new chemicals is still unclear. In the context of the (separate) environmental problem of global warming, CFCs have long been regarded as a greenhouse gas, but the substitute HFCs and HCFCs are targeted as well. International or national regulations aimed at reducing emissions of greenhouse gases may regulate these chemicals as well. Thus, CFC substitutes may be subjected to progressively stricter regulation after the CFC phaseout is completed. Indeed, the 1990 amendments to the Montreal Protocol have already laid the groundwork for international regulation of HCFCs, and the United States has enacted legislation to phase down HCFCs as of the year 2015, with phaseout by 2030. Should regulations also be introduced for other CFC substitutes, switchover costs will be higher than originally estimated.

7.2   The Montreal Protocol

Setting out to design a scheme to resolve this problem, the theory of optimal policy intervention would suggest imposing an optimal tax on CFC and halon emissions, namely at the point of disposal of the CFC-containing product or the CFCs used in cleaning applications. However, in view of the considerable number of CFC-containing products and consumers involved, and the undetectability of emissions, such a tax would be very costly to implement. An alternative is a tax collected at the point where CFCs are incorporated into products. In choosing a set of CFC consumption taxes, each tax rate would be chosen taking into account the various substitution possibilities. This consumption tax resembles the carbon tax on fossil fuel consumption proposed to reduce global warming, with the important difference that there is a variable lag between consumption of CFCs and emissions. Another option would be a set of CFC production taxes, one for each substance, with the levels based on the most likely application. Even though these would be one step further removed from emissions, the collection costs of such production taxes would be lower than consumption taxes, because of the small number of producers of these substances compared with the number of industries which use or incorporate CFCs into products. Hence CFC production taxes would probably be the most efficient instrument to use.

As in the case of many other environmental agreements, the Montreal Protocol does not express commitments in terms of taxes but rather as quantitative ceilings for production and consumption. These ceilings are set relative to 1986 with the goal of zero by the year 2000. As revised in 1990, the Protocol fixes ceilings for CFCs (Group I substances), halons (Group II), and carbon tetrachloride and methyl chloroform. Data on production, imports and exports for each chemical are weighted by a specified value chosen to correspond to its ozone-depleting potential, and consumption is defined as production plus imports minus exports.

Why did governments choose a quantitative approach, rather than the optimal instrument of a tax? One reason is that the agreement had to be one that would unite diverse actors, including the centrally planned economies. Another is that even if all parties could be certain that taxes would be collected and would affect emission levels, it would be difficult to compute each party's appropriate tax levels throughout a 10-year phaseout period involving rapid technological change.[3] To lower the welfare cost of reducing production of CFCs, internationally tradeable permits under an 'offsets policy' were introduced in 1990. To permit continued production of CFCs at an efficient scale, companies may transfer production internationally between plants by agreement between the Parties.

The commitments of the Parties to the Protocol with respect to consumption are implemented through quantitative limits on production in combination with trade provisions on imports of CFCs and CFC-containing products from non-Parties. Parties are to ban imports of CFCs from non-Parties from 1 January 1991, and ban imports of products on a list of CFC-containing products from 1 January 1993. Exports of CFCs to non-Parties are also banned from 1 January 1993, but this provision is not necessary to implement the consumption limits within the Party area. The

Protocol also requires its Parties to determine by January 1994 whether it will be feasible to ban or restrict imports of products produced with but not containing controlled substances from non-Parties.[4]

What of low-income developing countries? A developing country Party may delay for 10 years its implementation of the commitment to reduce and eliminate controlled substances, provided its per capita consumption of the substances does not exceed 0.3 kg as of the date of entry into force of the Protocol, or at any time in the course of the ten-year period of delay.[5] A low-consuming Party must also implement the trade bans on CFCs and CFC-containing products. Supply may be provided from other Parties by a clause which permits a party to let its production exceed its nominal production ceiling under the agreement by 10 per cent of 1986 production during phasedown, and by 15 per cent as of the year 2000 'in order to satisfy the basic domestic needs of the low-consuming Parties' – a measure designed to pacify traditional exporters in the EC and forestall investment in new CFC production capacity in developing countries.

The 1990 amendments established a fund for financial and technical cooperation with low-consuming developing country Parties, financed by contributions of other Parties. The fund 'shall meet all agreed incremental costs of Parties in order to enable their compliance with the control measures of the Protocol'. The fund's practical significance is limited, since its size is projected at only $160 million over ten years (less than $0.04 per person in developing countries in 1988). Low-consuming developing country Parties have few CFC plants and conversions will be needed only for a small number of these plants. Indeed, owners of the substitute technology may be reluctant to license it to countries where intellectual property protection is weak. The most likely use of the fund is to finance incremental costs of importing HCFCs or other substitutes for the few CFC-consuming industries located in low-income countries.

7.3   Why an international agreement on the ozone layer was possible

The 'tragedy of the commons', as popularized by Hardin (1968), is a classic problem. Individuals using a scarce common property resource engage in behaviour that is individually incentive-compatible, but this leads to over-exploitation of the resource. The problem has been identified as a form of Prisoners' Dilemma. The Nash equilibrium of this non-cooperative, static, non-zero sum game leads to excessive pollution. Olson's (1965) description of free-riding in the production of a public good has also been used to describe the problem of solving global commons issues – an individual who cannot be excluded from the benefits of a collective good once it is produced has little incentive to voluntarily contribute to providing it. In Olson's problem, free-riding is inherent when the production of the collective good does not require the participation of all players.

The Prisoners' Dilemma in international pollution problems has been given a generic functional form by Barrett (1990) and by Low and Safadi (1991). Barrett's model is a symmetric Prisoners' Dilemma game where a sub-group of players have solved the cooperation problem between themselves (leaders), and they seek the cooperation of the remaining potential players (followers). Leaders may offer compensation to free riders to induce them to join but, for certain parameter values, compensation exceeds the collective benefits and an equilibrium to the leader-follower game does not exist. Note that in a symmetric Prisoners' Dilemma game where leadership is not exogenous, this division between leaders and followers is never a Nash or best-reply equilibrium.

The two leading world consumers of CFCs, the United States and the EC, each accounted for about 30 per cent of world production of CFCs were 30 and 45 per cent, respectively.[6] For each entity, the impact on the ozone layer of reducing its own CFC consumption and production depends on the CFC consumption and production decisions of the other. The cost of abatement will increase as production of CFCs is reduced and their prices rise. Thus, on either the production or consumption side, the Prisoners' Dilemma can be reduced to a game played between the EC and the United States.

The United States and the European Community are the principal players in the Prisoners' Dilemma game – they constitute both the major part of the problem and its solution. Low-consuming countries are a very minor element in the game but, as discussed below, they may become more important players in the future. This is why, in our view, the leader-follower model with symmetric costs and benefits is not appropriate to the ozone layer problem.

The model we prefer to describe agreement on ozone layer depletion is the repeated Prisoners' Dilemma, where many cooperative solutions are possible provided that commitments are enforced. Two problems must be solved: (i) the problem of making credible commitments; and (ii) the problem of mutual monitoring and enforcement without an external authority.

Viewed from this perspective, the outcome of this non-cooperative game is unrelated to 'the polluter pays principle'. With a non-binding agreement, cooperation evolves from incentives for present and future actions. A notion of entitlement based on harm wrought by past actions is not relevant. Thus, the dominant role of high-income countries in emissions of ozone-depleting substances and the pollution of the ozone layer, compared to the insignificant contribution of low-income countries, will not shape an agreement. This does not mean that compensation will be absent from all multilateral nonbinding agreements, but simply that its basis comes from incentives of potential signatories to an agreement.

The scope for an international agreement on ozone layer depletion in a repeated game also depends on the future potential for action. Currently, there are no low-income countries that are significant consumers of CFCs. Even China, the leading low-income consumer, accounts for only 1.5 per cent of the world total. According to UNEP (1989), the US Environmental Protection Agency projects annual demand growth for China, India and other developing regions in the range of 5 to 15 per cent for the period 1992–2000. Applying these growth rates to low per capita consumption figures ensures that the overall level of CFC consumption in low-income countries will still be very low by the turn of the century, but rising incomes and populations will cause demand for CFCs in low-income non-Parties to rise over time.

In the Prisoners' Dilemma described above for global CFC production and consumption, the game between the EC and the United States has two levels – the national level and the industry level. Their CFC industries are highly concentrated, and may be described by the familiar quantity-setting Cournot duopoly with restricted entry, which also has the structure of a Prisoners' Dilemma. For many years, the industry resisted any form of regulation of CFCs. Unilateral government regulation of CFCs in one entity led to the capture of market share by producers of the other entity – as the domestic industry argued after the United States' aerosol ban in 1978. Once regulation was inevitable by the mid-1980s, only coordinated regulatory action taken simultaneously by the governments where major consuming markets are located was acceptable to producers. While *ex post* profits might be reduced, there are clear advantages to the industry as a whole to collusion with respect to restricting the entry of new producers in target markets. As (higher-price) substitutes looked like becoming available, existing producers sought an agreement that regulated CFC production in a closed 'competition area'.

Quantitative limits on CFC production are a form of regulation preferred by the industry. Regulation through a limit on consumption would have led to competition between producers with excess capacity, reducing profits of all. And regulation by imposing taxes would have reduced profits. According to Benedick (1991), the 'adjusted production' approach of the Montreal Protocol was chosen purely for commercial reasons. (A consumption limit was included as a result of pressure from net importing countries (such as the Nordics) who were concerned that as production limits came into effect, CFC producers in the United States and the EC would favour domestic consuming industries.)

For low-income countries, the accumulating evidence of harmful effects of ozone-layer depletion provides somewhat of an incentive in itself for participation in the Protocol. The cost of joining, however, is an uncertain future supply of essential refrigeration and other services, especially in view of the potential for regulation of substitutes. Until 1999, a developing country Party's per capita consumption of controlled substances must remain at or below 0.33 kilograms – two-thirds of the current consumption of the average developed country – and will have to be reduced and eliminated thereafter. The modest supply of domestic refrigeration in the developing countries limits the scope for recovery as a means of meeting future demands for this necessity. And few developing countries have domestic production capacity for CFCs or CFC-containing products, so few can benefit from the financing of switch-over costs by the multilateral fund. Furthermore, owners of patented substitute technologies may not wish to transfer licenses, and cannot be compelled to do so.

Even though low-income countries face these costs in joining the Protocol, the trade provisions of the Protocol nonetheless provide some of them with a sufficient incentive to join. Since the developed country Parties to the Montreal Protocol supply virtually all current developing country needs for controlled substances, the ban on exports to non-Parties is an effective inducement to join if a country seeks access to these chemicals and has no non-Party source of supply. For a non-Party currently producing CFCs, the ban on imports of products containing CFCs will affect exports from such countries. For example, automobiles exported from Korea to the United States would have to be empty of CFCs in their air conditioning units. And, judging by current trade statistics, a possible ban on imports of products produced with but not containing CFCs would have a much broader impact on exports of non-Parties to Parties, particularly electronics and components washed with CFC-113, unless CFC-113 is displaced by a cheaper, non-CFC degreasing technology or degreasing ceases.

Theoretically, a non-Party could support or continue to support the operation of CFC and CFC-containing industries, because the technology is available. But whether this would be an economic proposition depends in practice on the minimum efficient scale of operation and market size. If scale economies are significant, only a non-Party with a large internal or external non-Party market for CFC consumption would continue to produce in the long run. This may be possible only for the more populous low or middle-income countries such as India and Korea (Brazil, Mexico and Thailand are Parties to the Protocol, and China has pledged to join). Thus, it is not the sub-global character of the Protocol's membership that may lead to a new threat of ozone layer depletion in the next century, but the fact that at least two non-Parties may be able to support a domestic CFC industry, and become suppliers to developing countries that remain outside the Protocol.

7.4   Compliance with the Montreal Protocol

As Bothe (1981) notes, 'Much of international law is observed as a matter of routine ... this may be explained by the fact that international law is a decentralized legal system, that the law is created by the potential violators, that there is thus a high probability of coincidence between the actor's interests and the law'. The implication of this insight for the Montreal Protocol is that most Parties can be expected to abide by their commitments, designed by them in a cooperative game exercise, since these reflect the underlying costs and benefits of the non-cooperative game which preceded the agreement.

To deal effectively with intentional non-compliance at the governmental level, the model in Section 3 calls for a body to monitor compliance, to determine whether conduct deviates from Parties' legal commitments, and to enforce these commitments. In practice, it is difficult to find out the facts about events in another state, and in principle it is impossible to compel a state to submit to third-party settlement any matter deemed within its domestic jurisdiction. A control mechanism must be designed in such a manner that Parties cannot hide from, and have no incentive to depart from, their commitments. A violation of norms must be made sufficiently costly as to make deviation undesirable *ex ante*, and the role of a precommitment of the Parties to punish violations is intended to persuade governments not even to try violating their commitments. A successful mechanism is one where all potential deviations are precluded.

The Montreal Protocol is inching its way toward a control mechanism, but it is far from being complete. The first difficulty is obtaining the base year data for 1986 on production, exports and imports to monitor commitments on production and consumption. The Protocol's obligations are meaningless if one of the figures on the chemicals in the basket is missing. Trade data are difficult to obtain from published sources, and only a few developing countries have submitted the required production and consumption data.

Two separate procedures apply with regard to possible non-complying acts: dispute settlement under the dispute settlement provisions in Article 11 of the Vienna Convention, and a compliance procedure established at the Second Meeting of the Parties. The Third Meeting has confirmed that these procedures are coexisting and mutually independent.

Article 11 of the Convention provides a mechanism for settlement of disputes between the Parties concerning the 'interpretation or application of the Convention'. The parties concerned are first to seek solution by negotiation; then they may seek the good office or mediation of a third party. Parties may (but are not required to) accept compulsory jurisdiction of third-party arbitration or the International Court of Justice. Otherwise, disputes are to be submitted to a conciliation commission, whose final award is to be 'considered by the parties in good faith.'

In response to a mandate in the Protocol, a non-compliance procedure was developed and adopted in 1990 at the Second Meeting of the Parties.

As of 1991, the most severe sanction that may be applied under the Protocol in event of non-compliance is to withdraw the benefit of inclusion within the trade provisions and access to the financial mechanism that Parties enjoy. Thus, a ban on the export to and import from the Party in question goes into effect for CFCs, as well as a ban on the importation of CFC-containing products. Note that these are not *trade sanctions*, since they are not penalties or restrictions on products other than ozone-depleting chemicals or products containing CFCs. These measures simply convert the non-complying Party to a non-Party for the purposes of the trade relations between Parties and non-Parties.

In any case it would be difficult to establish trade sanctions for use against non-complying Parties because an exchange of concessions does not lie at the heart of the Protocol. A Party to the Protocol is obligated to phase out CFCs, and the benefit of a diminished rate of stratospheric ozone layer depletion is a collective one. For most countries, this benefit cannot be withdrawn in response to non-compliance; only non-compliance by the United States or EC would imperil the attainment of this benefit over the short term. In this manner, a non-complying Party to the Protocol (and indeed a non-Party) may be a true free-rider in the medium-term – it cannot be excluded from the benefits of producing a public good in which its participation is not required.

While non-compliance is a classic difficulty in international agreements, meeting Protocol commitments is unlikely to be a problem in high-income countries, where a preference for ozone-safe products expressed through consumer preference and through government regulation is present. In the EC or the United States, the primary risk might be that producers would cheat on their commitment to phase out CFCs. But this is unimportant because those producers are in a position to pass through cost increases, and are interested in strict regulation of substances so as to capture scarcity rents during the phaseout period, to maintain barriers to entry and to commercialise substitute chemicals. The economic pressures for deviation are more intense downstream among industrial consumers, many of whom are in less-concentrated industries. Yet even they are subject to national regulation and to the Protocol's cutoff of imports from non-Parties.

For developing-country Parties to the Protocol, the full economic costs of foregoing CFC consumption are as yet uncertain, but they are certainly greater relative to total income than in high-income Parties. Furthermore, the consumer preference for ozone-safe products may not be as well established in poorer countries due to the lack of widely circulating information on ozone layer depletion. However, the various trade provisions of the Protocol make eventual non-compliance an economic proposition only in a country with a large internal or external non-Party market for CFC consumption. Once phaseout must begin after 1999, problems with compliance at the governmental level are likely to emerge only in the most populated developing-country Parties.

7.5   Implications for an agreement on global warming

The preceding discussion of international efforts aimed at solving the global environmental problem of stratospheric ozone layer depletion brings to light the key role played by the different economic incentives of low-income countries in the two missing ingredients of the Montreal Protocol: an inducement for all major potential low-income suppliers to participate, and second, an effective dispute settlement and compliance mechanism. Without these ingredients, can Parties attain their original objective of preserving the ozone layer for future generations? While it is too early to be conclusive on this point, the answer is clearly not an unqualified yes. What, then, are the implications of the qualified success of the Montreal Protocol for the prospects of a multilateral agreement to limit greenhouse gas emissions?

The human contribution to increased atmospheric concentration of the four most important greenhouse gases – carbon dioxide, methane, CFCs, and nitrous oxide – and its potential health and environmental effects is the subject of current multilateral discussions on a 'Global Climate Convention'. The Montreal Protocol is a major step in the direction of limiting emissions of one greenhouse gas, CFCs, but the greater global warming-potential of the currently unregulated substitutes HCFCs and HFCs implies that, on its own, the Protocol may not do much to limit global warming. But it does suggest conditions which can facilitate multilateral agreement on a global environmental issue.

Four conditions in particular can be identified as having contributed to the completion of the Montreal Protocol. First, by the mid-1980s, there was widespread agreement as to the man-made contribution to ozone layer depletion. Second, only a small number of countries are responsible for most of the problem: 90 per cent of CFC production and emissions originate in developed countries (including the USSR), and environmental consciousness is relatively high in most of those countries. This concentration of (potential as well as actual) production and consumption also makes it possible to limit emissions by non-Parties via the Protocol's trade provisions. Third, the cost of phasing out CFCs and halons will constitute only a small fraction of global income. And fourth, the oligopolistic nature of the CFC-producing industry ensures that producers' cooperation could be secured by effective cartelization and limitation of production, making the monitoring of compliance not too difficult.

In contrast, there is not yet a scientific consensus that global warming is occurring. Also, the main concern is the burning of fossil fuels, and curtailing this would involve all major countries of the world rather than just a handful of developed countries,[7] as well as most of the important industries in each country. The widespread availability and use of fuels also rules out the use of trade provisions to encourage countries to join an agreement and to prevent non-joiners from continuing to emit carbon. Thirdly, as the previous two chapters of this volume make clear, the cost of reducing carbon dioxide emissions is considerable. Finally, because there are many groups of producers who would be adversely affected by higher taxes on sources of carbon emissions, it will be more difficult to secure their support than was the case in limiting production of CFCs.

This is not to rule out the possibility of multilateral agreement in limiting emissions of greenhouse gases. Despite the uncertainties as to the limiting of fossil fuel consumption, people in many countries have taken the position that a precautionary approach to the threat posed by global warming requires that some action be taken to curb man-made contributions to greenhouse gas concentrations. Indeed, Sweden has led the way with a set of carbon taxes.

However, the problem of coordinating different national approaches to the design of optimal taxes will remain. The results of Chapter 6 of this volume, by Piggott, Whalley and Wigle, indicate that the structure of the game resembles the Prisoners' Dilemma in several important respects. As in the case of CFCs, an important feature is the asymmetry of welfare gains and losses between developing countries and developed regions. In relation to the benefits of lower global temperatures, the costs for developing countries in joining a Global Climate Convention are large enough that they may remain outside such a Convention, unless compensation is forthcoming. Substantial compensation is unlikely to be agreed by major developed country participants. However, much can be achieved with respect to forestalling temperature rises by the developed regions acting in concert, resulting in a cooperative solution to this game with a sub-global coverage of countries.

An important economic implication of a carbon tax in a subset of countries is that it shifts the pattern of comparative advantage in energy-based products from that subset of countries (the Party area) to the rest of the world. Because the carbon tax will raise the costs of production of virtually all products within the Party area, imports from the non-Party area will increase and help sustain consumption of these products as production shifts offshore. In this context, Parties are likely to seek offsetting measures on the importation of products from the non-Party area. If this idea is pursued to its extreme, provisions for trade with non-Parties would be required on a vast scale in an agreement detailing specific commitments. Such an agreement would have a major impact on the principles of the multilateral trading system.

Notes

1. For details on the nature of CFCs and the scientific basis for limiting emissions see, for example, Molina and Rowland (1974), UNEP (1989) and the World Meteorological Organisation (1989).

2. HCFCs are obtained by adding hydrogen atoms which ensures that to a large extent they degrade in the lower atmosphere before they reach the stratosphere.
3. For more details on why, in general, quantity rather than price instruments of environmental policy tend to be chosen, see Chapter 11 of this volume by Hoekman and Leidy.
4. The original presumption of the Parties to the Protocol may have been that the production of such products would shift to 'pollution havens' in non-Parties if Parties' CFC consumption is limited. There is, however, no product which is distinguishable from another by the fact that CFCs are an essential aspect of its production, and CFCs are easily substitutable in degreasing applications. Hence the relationship between import restraints applied to a list of products produced with but not containing CFCs and the consumption goals of the Parties is not clear.
5. For the purposes of the Montreal Protocol, developed country members of the Protocol are Australia, Austria, Canada, European Community (12), Finland, Hungary, Japan, New Zealand, Norway, United States, Switzerland, and the USSR. Developing country members are Brazil, Burkina Faso, Cameroon, Chile, Egypt, Fiji, Ghana, Guatemala, Jordan, Kenya, Malaysia, Maldives, Malta, Mexico, Nigeria, Panama, Singapore, Sri Lanka, Syrian Arab Republic, Thailand, Trinidad and Tobago, Tunisia, Uganda, United Arab Emirates, Venezuela, and Zambia.
6. The rest of global CFC consumption in 1986 was accounted for by Japan (13 per cent), Eastern Europe and the USSR (15 per cent) and developing countries (10 per cent). The rest of global production of CFCs in 1986 was accounted for by Japan and the USSR (10 per cent each), Eastern Europe and developing countries (5 per cent).
7. The ranking of leading emitters of greenhouse gases depends on whether the computation is done on a *gross* or on a *net* basis. The net approach takes into account natural sinks located on a country's territory, while the gross approach does not. The results of the net approach are controversial, in particular with respect to the ranking of the USSR and developing countries. Under both approaches, however, the European Community and the United States rank at the top of the emissions list, but the percentages of global emissions attributed to each one varies depending on the approach taken and are smaller than in the case of CFCs.

References

Barrett, S. (1990), 'Economic Analysis of International Environmental Agreements: Lessons for a Global Warming Treaty', mimeo, London Business School, November.
Benedick, R. E. (1991), *Ozone Diplomacy*, Cambridge: Harvard University Press.
Bothe, M. (1981), 'International Obligations, Means to Secure Performance', pp. 101–106 in *Encyclopaedia of Public International Law* Volume 1, Amsterdam: North-Holland.
Hardin, G. (1968), 'The Tragedy of the Commons', *Science* **162**: 1243–48.
Low, P. and R. Safadi (1991), 'Trade Policy and Pollution', mimeo, World Bank, Washington D.C., May.
Molina, M. and S. Rowland (1974), 'Stratospheric Sink for Chlorofluoromethanes: Chlorine Atom Catalyzed Destruction of Ozone', *Nature* **249**: 810–12.
Olson, M. (1965), *The Logic of Collective Action*, Cambridge: Harvard University Press.

United Nations Environment Programme (1989), *Economic Panel Report*. Nairobi: UNEP.

United Nations Environment Programme (1991a), 'Status of Ratification of the Vienna Convention and the Montreal Protocol', UNEP/OzL.Pro./WG.3/2/Inf.1, Nairobi: UNEP.

United Nations Environment Programme (1991b), 'Report of the Third Meeting of the Parties to the Montreal Protocol', UNEP/OzL.Pro.3/11, Nairobi: UNEP.

World Meteorological Organization (1989), *Scientific Assessment of Stratospheric Ozone: 1989*, Volume I, Geneva: WMO.

8

Effects on the environment and welfare of liberalizing world trade: the cases of coal and food

Kym Anderson

This chapter focuses on the question: under what circumstances would the liberalizing of world trade in particular products lead to environmental degradation, perhaps to a sufficient extent as to more than offset the traditional gains from freeing trade? Environmentalists are right in claiming that if production and/or consumption of a good is pollutive, then an expansion in global output of that good following trade liberalization would, in the absence of increased pollution taxes or a greater use of less-pollutive production methods, lead to greater environmental degradation. And if the negative value attached to such degradation was sufficiently large, it may indeed more than offset the conventionally measured gain in economic welfare from freer trade. Of course there is always a set of environmental policy instruments available to ensure that freer trade *need* not reduce welfare (see Chapter 2 of this volume), but there is the legitimate concern that the use of such instruments at appropriate levels may not accompany trade liberalization. Thus environmentalists are prone to ask: would trade liberalization, *ceteris paribus*, cause world output/consumption of a particular pollutive product to expand and, if so, would that degrade the global environment?

The answer to even the first part of that question is not obvious, as it depends among other things on the current patterns of distortions to incentives in different countries and the net impact of reducing those distortions on international prices. In the cases of coal and food, for example, rich countries tend to set domestic prices of these goods well above international levels while many poorer countries tend to set them well below international levels (Jolly *et al.*, 1990; Burniaux *et al.*, 1991; Tyers and Anderson, 1992). Liberalization of protectionist policies in rich countries would lower domestic prices there and raise them internationally, but less so the more poorer countries transmit to their domestic market any change in international prices. If low-price policies in poorer countries were to be liberalized as well, the international price would rise even less or might even fall. Hence the net change in the aggregate level of world production and consumption of these (and other) goods, following trade liberalization, could be positive or negative.

Even if world output rose, environmental degradation need not increase: it depends among other things on the nature of the international relocation of production and consumption that would accompany trade liberalization. Thus case studies are necessary to identify the likely effects for particular products. This paper focuses on two product groups that have been both of concern to environmentalists and subject to extreme price and trade policy distortions. The first is coal, where a pertinent question is whether liberalizing world coal markets would raise or lower global emissions of carbon and sulphur and thereby affect global warming and acid rain. The simple analysis presented in partial equilibrium form in the first section of the chapter suggests that an improvement both in the global environment and in economic welfare as conventionally measured could well result from liberalizing trade in coal.

The other product group considered is food, where the main concern of environmentalists has to do with production externalities. Food trade liberalization would cause less food to be produced in rich countries and more in poor countries, but even the sign of the environmental and welfare effects of such a relocation of production are shown in the second section of the paper to be ambiguous, so quantitative analysis is required. Numerous empirical studies have been undertaken in recent years on the extent to which government policies distort incentives to produce and consume farm products, and on the production, consumption, trade and economic welfare consequences of those distortions or their liberalization (e.g., Anderson and Tyers, 1991a,b, 1992; OECD, 1987, 1990a; Parikh *et al.*, 1988; Stoeckel *et al.*, 1989; Tyers and Anderson, 1992; UNCTAD, 1990; Zietz and Valdes, 1990). Those studies say little or nothing about the effects of agricultural policies on the natural environment, however, and so under-account for the full welfare effects of reforms. Even so, those studies' estimates of the production effects and at least the traditionally measured economic welfare effects of liberalization (ignoring the welfare effects of environmental change) are illuminating. It happens that the estimates by Anderson and Tyers (1991a) show virtually all countries could gain from such liberalization if no value is placed on the changes to the environment associated with the international relocation of production. These estimates therefore provide a benchmark against which to assess any costs of environmental damage incurred as a result of relocating production. Such damage, it is argued, is unlikely to be major in countries expanding food output and may well be more than offset by reduced environmental degradation in countries removing agricultural support policies.

The chapter therefore concludes that coal and food trade liberalization

not only would generate large global income gains but also would be likely
to reduce global environmental damage from coal consumption and
farming as well as reduce chemical residues in the world's food. While not
every individual country would enjoy such a happy outcome without additional policy measures, the final section points out that there are more
appropriate instruments available than trade policies for ensuring all are
better off.

8.1   Partial equilibrium welfare economics of liberalizing coal trade

Coal contributes nearly one-third of the world's energy. Its market can be
thought of as involving three groups of countries: the highly protectionist
OECD countries (particularly Western Europe and Japan); the reforming
centrally planned economies (CPEs) of China, East Europe and the USSR
where coal is priced well below international levels; and the rest of the
world where the average domestic price of coal is assumed to be equal to
the international price level.[1] The high-income protectionist countries currently account for about one-third of global coal consumption and the
CPEs account for about half. The latter have adopted virtual self-
sufficiency for their trade policy (only 2 per cent of their production is
exported) while the former depend on the rest of the world for about 15
per cent of their consumption. Figure 8.1 depicts these three segments of
the world market, where for simplicity it is assumed that coal is a homo-
geneous product, that the coal market in the CPEs clears at P_3 (the
autarkic price),[2] and that the supply and demand curves incorporate
changes in productivity and any international factor movements that would
accompany domestic price changes.

What would be the effects on the environment and welfare of liberalizing trade in coal? Consider first the protected industrial market economies
in which the coal producer price P_p is subsidized to be above the coal consumer price P_c which in turn, because of import restrictions, is above the
international price P_2. Assuming the level of coal consumption has been
deliberately set (via the setting of the user price at P_c) at C_1 to restrict
carbon emissions, it is reasonable to assume P_c would not be lowered as
part of a policy reform. Only the producer price P_p would fall to the international level, causing domestic coal production to fall and import demand
to rise. This would induce an international price rise from P_2 to P_2'. Instead
of $Q_1C_1(=C_2Q_2)$ units being imported by the protected countries from
other market economies, $Q_1'C_1(=C_2'Q_2')$ would be traded (assuming still
that the CPEs remain autarkic). Net economic welfare in the protected
countries would increase by *abc*, using the conventional surplus approach,[3]
while welfare in other market economies in aggregate would increase by
defg plus the benefit attached to less pollution because of burning $C_2'C_2$ less

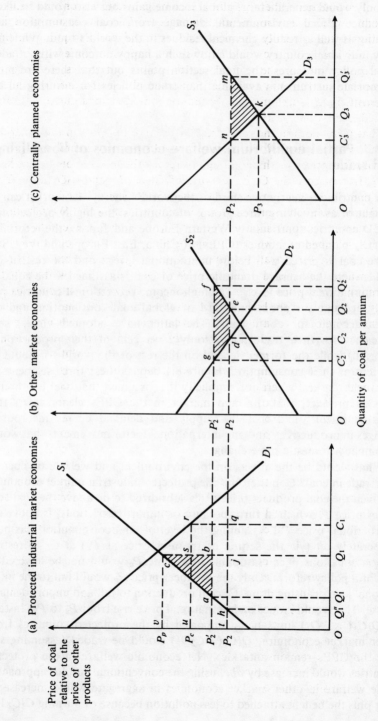

Figure 8.1 Effects of liberalizing coal trade in protected and unprotected market economies and in centrally planned economies

(a) Protected industrial market economies

(b) Other market economies

(c) Centrally planned economies

Price of coal relative to the price of other products

Quantity of coal per annum

units of coal. Such a liberalization is clearly beneficial not only in terms of economic welfare as conventionally measured but also in terms of less pollution (since virtually all substitutes for coal are less pollutive than coal). Not only would carbon and sulphur emissions be less with lower coal consumption in the non-protected market economies, but sulphur emissions in the formerly protected economies also would drop if domestic coal has a higher sulphur content than the imported substitute (as if often claimed—see Newbery, 1990).

What if in addition the reforming CPEs were to open up their markets and allow coal exports? Such exports would put downward pressure on international prices, perhaps enough to return the international price back to P_2. In that case the CPEs' exports of $C_3'Q_3'$ plus the C_2Q_2 units from other market economies would just match the imports of the formerly protected industrial economies at that common price ($Q_1''C_1$). Welfare in the other market economies would revert to what it was before either of the reforms, net economic welfare in the formerly protected economies would increase by the further area *abjh* as output is further reduced to Q_1'' (and the consumer tax would increase to P_cP_2 per unit), and welfare in the reforming CPEs would expand by *kmn* plus the benefit attached to less pollution because of the burning of $C_3'Q_3$ less units of coal than before their reform. The global welfare gain as conventionally measured is greater with than without the reform by the CPEs (*abjh* plus *kmn* minus *defg*, which is positive). Welfare defined to include also the effect of pollution would be enhanced even more if the pollution reduction in the CPEs is valued more than the emission reduction foregone in the previously unprotected market economies (where coal consumption reverts back to C_2 from C_2'). Certainly global emissions of carbon and sulphur would be lower than currently if both producer support policies in rich countries and export restrictions in CPEs as illustrated in Figure 8.1 were removed, since world coal consumption would be lower by $C_3'Q_3$.[4] Moreover, in this scenario government revenue is enhanced in the reforming rich countries. Not only is the producer subsidy net of the import tariff revenue (the difference between areas *uscv* and *jqrs*) removed but also revenue of *tqru* is raised from making explicit the tax on coal consumption. The net gain in government revenue is thus *tjcv*.

In short, coal trade liberalization in this situation is both financially and ecologically friendly. If empirical analysis were to confirm the directions of the effects of the reforms outlined above, this would provide an important example of the more general point that before demanding new environmental policies, environmental action groups and policy makers and advisers might first look for avenues where removing existing distortionary price and trade policies can contribute to pollution reduction and at the same time improve the efficiency of resource use and even, as in the rich countries illustrated above, increase government tax revenue. The latter effects are important because they enhance both the capacity and the demand for implementing other nationally desired environmental policies.

8.2   Partial equilibrium welfare economics of liberalizing food trade

To analyse the effects of liberalizing trade in food (which is assumed for the moment to be a homogenous good) it is again possible to consider a world made up of three country groups: a group of almost autarkic CPEs (Eastern Europe and the USSR) which for purposes of this section are assumed not to adjust to policy changes elsewhere and so are ignored in what follows; a set of rich countries whose farmers enjoy government protection; and the rest of the world where the price of agricultural products relative to other tradeables is lower. The demand and supply curves for the latter two country groups are shown in Figure 8.2. If P_1 is the relative price set by the government in the rich countries, then the quantity of food imported by them is Q_1C_1. Given the demand and supply curves for food in the rest of the world, this import demand would cause the price outside the rich countries to settle at P_2 in the absence of government intervention in the rest of the world (where $Q_1C_1 = C_2Q_2$ in Figure 8.2).

Complete liberalization of that agricultural protection would reduce the relative price in rich countries and raise that price in the poorer countries to P. At that price the enlarged quantity of food the rich countries would wish to import ($Q_1'C_1'$) just matches the quantity the rest of the world is prepared to export at that price ($C_2'Q_2'$). The more inelastic the rich countries' excess demand curve and the more elastic the rest of the world's excess supply curve, the lower would be P. The welfare effects of that policy change can be seen most easily, using the standard consumer/producer surplus approach, by first assuming there are no environmental externalities and then relaxing that assumption. As in the coal case, so here too it is assumed for simplicity that supply and demand curves are linear and that they incorporate induced technological changes, taste changes and any international factor movements that would accompany changes in the domestic relative price of food.

8.2.1   *Assuming no environmental externalities*

If the S_1 curve represents both the private and social marginal costs of production in the rich countries, then the reduction in the domestic price from P_1 to P following complete trade liberalization reduces producer surplus by *abgh*, increases consumer surplus by *aefh*, reduces government revenue by the amount of the import tariff (*fgmn*) and so involves a net economic

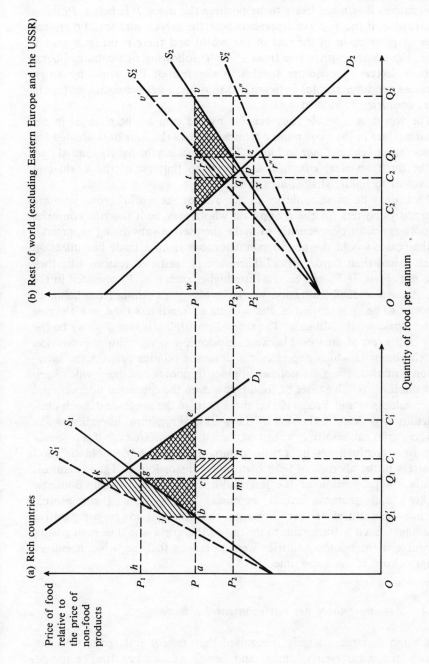

Figure 8.2 Effects of liberalizing food policies on rich and poor countries

welfare change equal to *bcg* plus *def* minus *cdnm*, which may be positive or negative. It is more likely to be positive the more P is below P_1.[5]

Likewise, if the S_2 curve represents both the private and social marginal costs of production in the rest of the world and there is no intervention there, the domestic price rise from P_2 to P following rich-country liberalization decreases consumer surplus in the rest of the world by *wyqs*, increases producer surplus by *wyrv* and thus increases net social welfare in those countries by shaded *sqrv*.

The world as a whole thus benefits by the sum of the changes in net social welfare in the two country groups, namely the four dark-shaded triangles (areas *bcg*, *def*, *sqt* and *urv*). This is because the lightly shaded part of the tariff revenue, *cdnm*, is a transfer to the rest of the world and equivalent to lightly shaded area *qrut*.

There may be some countries in the 'rest of the world' group who are net food importers (or the group as a whole may be if the rich countries support agriculture sufficiently to make themselves subsidizing exporters). In that case, would the poorer countries lose from a trade liberalization which raised their border price? There are at least two reasons why they need not. First, if P_1 had been a little higher such that P_2' operated in the rest of the world, liberalization would involve it switching from being an importer to being an exporter. But so long as *xzp* is less than *pvs*, the rest of the world would still gain. The second possibility is that P_2' may be the price in the rest of the world because, in addition to agricultural protection in rich countries which depresses the domestic relative price in the international market, there are policies in place in poorer countries which keep their domestic relative price of food below even the depressed international price. Anderson and Tyers (1991a) show that, in the presence of such anti-agricultural policies in the rest of the world, agricultural liberalization in rich countries can improve the rest of the world's welfare even if the poorer countries remain a net importing group, provided they would be food exporters in the absence of their own policy distortions and they transmit a sufficient proportion of the international price rise to their domestic market (and thereby attract resources away from their protected non-agricultural sectors in which they have a lower comparative advantage). Such welfare gains to the rest of the world would be even greater of course if the poorer countries were to reduce their negative incentives to agriculture at the same time.

8.2.2   *Assuming there are environmental externalities*

It is being ever more widely recognised that agricultural production can degrade the natural environment and impair human health. The use of chemical fertilizers and pesticides pollutes the air, soil and water, concentrations of manure from intensively-produced livestock adds to that pollution, the ploughing of sloped land can lead to soil erosion and silting of downstream dams, irrigation can create salinity problems, and so on (see Eckholm, 1976, and OECD, 1989, for amplification). Any positive externality which agricultural production provides in the form of scenic beauty of the rural landscape (over and above the externality provided by the alternative uses of farmland for golf courses, forests or whatever) is more or less offset by these negative externalities. Even the alternative use of farm labour and capital is likely to be relatively unpolluting in rich countries, as it would tend to be employed in the relatively unpolluting service sector or in industrial activities which already have environmental protection policies in place. Hence in rich countries the social marginal cost curve is probably above the private marginal cost curve for agriculture, say S_1^s in Figure 8.2. In that case there is an additional welfare gain from a reduction in the domestic price from P_1 to P, namely $bgkj$ which is society's valuation of the damage to the environment that is avoided by producing $Q_1^s Q_1$ less units of food (and more units of other goods).

What about in the rest of the world where farm production expands when rich countries liberalize their agricultural protectionist policies (and would expand even more if the rest of the world's policies discriminate against agriculture and those policies also are liberalized)? Such an expansion would result in part from increased use of farm chemicals and irrigation, which have a negative effect on the environment. Some expansion of land area may occur as well, reducing perhaps the world's forest area and hence its wilderness areas, its variety of animal and plant species and its capacity to absorb carbon dioxide emissions. And more labour and capital would be employed in agriculture than would otherwise be the case. However, that labour might otherwise have been employed in ekeing out a subsistence income on marginal hillsides, which could have contributed more environmental damage than when employed in an expanding commercial agricultural sector. Or it might have been employed in the manufacturing sector which, if it had insufficient environmental regulations, could well be more pollutive in these poorer countries than the agricultural sector at the margin. Thus, it is difficult to guess whether the world's marginal social cost curve for agricultural production in the rest of the world is above or below marginal private cost.

If on average the externalities from extra agricultural production in the price range $P_2 P$ in poorer countries are the same as those from the alternative uses to which resources would otherwise be put, then the marginal social and private cost curves coincide and no further modification to Figure 8.2 is required. That is, the social welfare gain to the rest of the world from the price increase $P_2 P$ remains $qrvs$, in which case the global welfare gain from liberalizing agricultural trade is underestimated by $bgkj$ when environmental considerations are ignored. The gains to both country groups and hence to the world would be even greater if the optimal environmental tax also was introduced in the rich countries when their trade was liberalized.

It may be that S_2 overstates the marginal social cost of food production in the rest of the world, in which case its and the world's welfare gain would be even greater. In terms of Figure 8.2 if S_2'' was the social marginal cost curve for the rest of the world, an increase in the price of farm products would raise welfare not only by the shaded area but also by $rr''v''v$.

On the other hand, suppose S_2 understated the world's marginal social cost of farm production in poorer countries, perhaps because deforestation is encouraged in poorer countries by higher prices there for farm products. In that case the welfare gain from liberalization would be lower. It is unlikely to be negative, however, for several reasons. First, from a global viewpoint, if S_2' was the social marginal cost curve in the rest of the world the area $rr'v'v$ would have to be more than the sum of the four dark-shaded triangles plus $bgkj$ in Figure 8.2 for global welfare to fall following liberalization. Even from just the poorer countries' viewpoint, welfare would fall only if $rr'v'v$ exceeded $qrvs$ and if S_2' represented the national social cost curve. Where there are negative international spillovers, however – as is the case with deforestation – the poorer countries' social cost curve is closer to S_2 than is S_2' (the global social cost curve). In that case it is even less likely that the rest of the world would be worse off following agricultural liberalization when, relative to rich countries, those poorer economies have a comparative advantage in and lower prices for farm products (and provided they transmit a sufficient proportion of the international price rise to their domestic markets).

Moreover, it is possible for those economies to *guarantee* their welfare improves by introducing the optimal environmental policy at the time of liberalization, such as a tax on land clearing if the externality results from deforestation. To avoid complicating Figure 8.2, consider Figure 8.3 which reproduces the right-hand part of Figure 8.2 and, for simplicity, assumes these economies are too small to influence the international price of farm products. Suppose it is perceived that these countries' forests would be threatened if farm product prices rose from P_2 to P following liberalization abroad, such that S_2^g represents the global marginal social cost of farm production in these economies. The national social cost curve may coincide with or even be below the private cost curve S_2, but suppose it is above S_2 at S_2^n. Welfare in these poorer economies would decrease when the price rises from P_2 to P if $rvba$ exceeds $qrvs$ in Figure 8.3. But if the optimal environmental policy intervention is introduced to equate the national marginal social cost with the marginal social benefit (P) at the time of liberalization, production would increase only to Q_2^n and so welfare in these economies necessarily would increase, by shaded area $qracs$.

However, global welfare may not have increased if the rich countries place a sufficiently high value on retaining forests in poorer countries. This

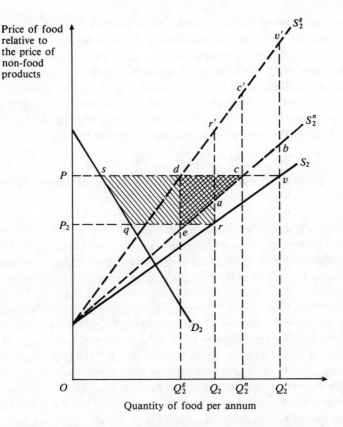

Figure 8.3 Effects of a rise in international food prices on production in poorer countries and on welfare

is because rich countries' welfare is reduced with deforestation in poorer countries, represented by $acc'r'$ in Figure 8.3 if Q_2^n is produced and $abv'r'$ if Q_2' is produced. The globally optimal farm output in these poorer countries in Q_2^g if the international price is P. Should poorer economies be forced to reduce output from Q_2^n to Q_2^g, their welfare would be reduced by the dark-shaded area *cde*. That is, for the poorer countries to be as well off economically, rich countries would need to pay them an amount equivalent to *cde* out of the rich countries' (larger but non-monetary) welfare gain of $cc'de$ arising from the lesser deforestation associated with producing at Q_2^g instead of Q_2^n.

In short, reducing agricultural price and trade distortions is likely to increase welfare in liberalizing countries as well as in the rest of the world even when the effects of liberalization on the natural environment are taken into account. Whether the improvement in the environment in countries removing their agricultural support policies more or less than offsets any new environmental damage caused by expanding farm production in the rest of the world cannot be answered *a priori*. But, even if environmental degradation in poorer countries were to increase, welfare in those poorer economics is still likely to improve – and is certain to improve if the appropriate environmental policy is introduced at the time the international price rises. Furthermore, if rich countries value the retention of forests in poorer countries, they could afford to bribe those economies not to clear as much forest land in response to the increase in international food prices.

8.3 Empirical estimates of the effects of liberalizing food trade[6]

There are numerous empirical models available to estimate the effects on rich and poorer countries of liberalizing agricultural trade. To the author's knowledge, none of these place welfare values on changes to the natural environment associated with the relocation of production. Even so, it is helpful to look at estimates of the production and welfare effects of agricultural liberalization as a beginning to the process of understanding likely effects on the environment of such policy changes. For present purposes, results from work recently summarized by Anderson and Tyers (1991a) and reported in more detail in Tyers and Anderson (1992) will be used. That work makes use of their multi-commodity simulation model of world markets for grains, meats, dairy products and sugar.

The model specifies the extent to which domestic food markets in 30 countries or country groups spanning the world are insulated from fluctuations in international food markets. This is done using estimated price transmission equations which capture both the protection and the stabilization components of food policies. For developing countries, indirect effects of non-food price distortions and overvalued exchange rates on farmers' incentives are also incorporated, drawing on estimates from Krueger *et al.* (1988) among others. Using the long-run, comparative static version of the Tyers model, the reference simulation for 1990 is compared with two other simulations of what food markets could have looked like in 1990; the first with all advanced industrial countries' protectionist food policies removed; the second with the absence of distortions to food prices in both industrial and developing countries (but not in Eastern Europe or the USSR, about which too little was known at the time the simulations were run). In both liberalization scenarios it is assumed that induced technological change occurs in the sense that farm productivity growth responds positively to product price changes.

The key results of relevance to the present chapter are reported in Tables 8.1 and 8.2. When only the advanced industrial economies liberalize, it is estimated that international food prices would be higher by one-quarter on average. However, when both industrial and developing

Table 8.1 Effects on international food prices of liberalizing world food markets, 1990 (per cent)

	Wheat	Coarse grain	Rice	Beef and sheepmeat	Pork and poultry	Dairy products	Sugar	Weighted average[a]
Reform in advanced industrial economies only	15	5	23	48	9	109	24	26
Reform in industrial and developing economies	0	-10	-3	6	-24	84	-15	-1

Note: [a] Weights based on value of each item in world food trade.
Source: Printouts from the Tyers model used by Anderson and Tyers (1991a).

Table 8.2   Effects on net economic welfare (conventionally measured) and on food production of liberalizing world food markets, 1990

	Reform in advanced industrial economies only				Reform in industrial and developing economies			
	Change in annual net economic welfare (1985 US$ billion)	Change in production, 1000 tonnes (&%)			Change in annual net economic welfare (1985 US$ billion)	Change in production, 1000 tonnes (&%)		
		grain	beef and sheepmeat	sugar		grain	beef and sheepmeat	sugar
Australasia	3.0	790 (3)	420 (11)	280 (8)	0.5	-2,140 (-9)	50 (1)	-690(-19)
Japan	23.0	-5,190(-45)	-410(-77)	-770(-72)	40.8	-5,650(-49)	-450(-84)	-840(-79)
North America	5.5	10,050 (3)	1,160 (10)	-860(-14)	7.8	-23,410 (-6)	-1,240(-10)	-1,650(-26)
Western Europe	15.1	-32,980(-20)	-5,190(-50)	-5,060(-28)	24.2	-40,330(-25)	-7,880(-76)	-7,810(-44)
TOTAL, Advanced Industrial Economies	46.6	-27,330 (-5)	-4,020(-15)	-6,410(-23)	73.3	-71,530(-12)	-9,520(-36)	-10,990(-40)
Bangladesh, India, Pakistan	1.4	1,710 (1)	250 (13)	130 (1)	1.6	-2,000 (-1)	230 (11)	930 (4)
China	2.9	7,950 (2)	520 (26)	650 (8)	12.9	8,100 (2)	1,730 (102)	1,230 (15)
Indonesia, Philippines, Thailand	0.9	1,680 (3)	300 (38)	440 (6)	0.6	1,270 (2)	-60 (-7)	-1,630(-21)
South Korea, Taiwan	-1.1	0 (0)	10 (6)	40 (6)	6.9	-1,710(-18)	-80(-58)	-100(-16)
Other Asia	0.5	90 (0)	120 (12)	30 (2)	1.7	660 (1)	240 (23)	80 (4)
SUB-TOTAL, Developing Asia	4.6	11,430 (2)	1,200 (21)	1,290 (3)	23.7	6,320 (1)	2,060 (36)	510 (1)

Argentina	5.4	4,310 (11)	1,420 (37)	0 (0)	5.1	4,180 (11)	3,710 (97)	1,500 (111)
Brazil	2.9	3,750 (8)	560 (19)	2,370 (23)	0.8	6,530 (14)	1,260 (43)	3,470 (34)
Mexico	1.2	2,840 (12)	130 (11)	−220 (−5)	0.9	1,530 (6)	540 (45)	2,960 (69)
Other Latin America	3.2	910 (5)	940 (31)	710 (4)	0.8	3,310 (18)	1,730 (58)	5,090 (28)
SUB-TOTAL, Latin America	12.7	11,810 (9)	3,050 (28)	2,860 (8)	7.6	15,550 (12)	7,240 (66)	13,020 (38)
North Africa and Middle East	−2.6	−210 (−0)	150 (5)	130 (3)	−0.2	−220 (−0)	490 (17)	−20 (−0)
Sub-Saharan Africa	1.9	880 (1)	680 (17)	120 (2)	2.2	5,900 (9)	1,930 (47)	2,970 (42)
SUB-TOTAL, Africa and Middle East	−0.7	670 (0)	830 (12)	250 (2)	2.0	5,680 (4)	2,420 (35)	2,950 (26)
TOTAL, Developing Economies	16.6	23,910 (3)	5,080 (22)	4,400 (5)	33.4	27,550 (4)	11,720 (50)	16,480 (19)
TOTAL, WORLD[a]	62.4	−3,560 (−0.2)	1,600 (2.6)	−2,000 (−1.5)	106.5	−45,950 (−2.8)	2,690 (4.4)	5,450 (4.2)

Note: [a] Includes the (small) effects in Eastern Europe and the USSR.
Source: Printouts from the Tyers model used by Anderson and Tyers (1991a).

economies liberalize, the average level of international food prices is almost the same as forecast in the reference scenario. This comes about because the effect of lowering the protected prices in rich countries is offset by the raising of depressed relative prices of food in poor countries when their distortionary policies against agriculture also are removed. The price effects vary considerably across commodities, although in both scenarios it is the products of cattle (milk and beef) whose prices go up most and grain prices which move the least (Table 8.1).

In examining Table 8.2, it needs to be kept in mind that the two liberalization scenarios assume that complete adjustment to the new long-run equilibrium occurs instantaneously. This is unrealistic, both because in practice full adjustment to complete liberalization would take as much as two decades and because any actual reforms are likely to be partial and gradual.[7] Nonetheless, the extreme results are useful because they give a sense of what the world food economy might have looked like in 1990 if distortions had been absent for a decade or two prior to that year.

8.3.1   Conventionally measured welfare effects of reforms

The first column of Table 8.2 reports the effects of current distortions on net economic welfare conventionally defined (that is, without regard to effects on the natural environment). Not surprisingly, industrial market economies would be substantially better off without their agricultural protection policies. Consumers and taxpayers gain only partly at the expense of producers in those economies, the difference being a net gain of US$47 billion per year in 1985 dollars. More surprisingly, almost all groups of developing economies gain as well. The only exceptions are those with the strongest comparative disadvantages in food production, namely oil-rich countries in the Middle East and the densely populated, newly-industrialized economies of Northeast Asia. Not all of the other become net food exporters, but most would do in this scenario if they did not discriminate indirectly against their farmers via protection to manufacturing and overvalued exchange rates.[8] The overall net gain to developing countries is US$17 billion per year, three-quarters of which would go to the highly indebted countries of Latin America. Global benefits thus amount to $62 billion per annum.

If in addition to industrial countries the developing countries also removed their own distortionary policies affecting their food markets directly or indirectly, as in the second simulation experiment, the global (conventionally measured) welfare gains would be 70 per cent larger at $107 billion per year. By reducing their discrimination against agriculture and thereby depressing international prices, such reforms in developing countries improve the terms of trade for reformed food-importing industrial economies. Hence the latter are made even better off while food-exporting

Australasia is less well off when poorer countries also reform their policies. Developing countries may be better or worse off in this as compared with the earlier scenario depending on whether the gain from their own domestic policy reform is reinforced or more than offset by the international price changes. As a group they are twice as well off when they also liberalize as when only advanced industrial economies liberalize ($33 billion compared with $17 billion per annum).

8.3.2 *Production effects of reforms*

The above measure of economic welfare is incomplete not just because it comes from a partial rather than general equilibrium economic model but also because changes in the natural environment that would result from liberalization are not accounted for. As a beginning step towards understanding what those environmental changes might be, it is useful to examine the model's projected changes to the global volume and international distribution of food production in these simulations. These are reported in Table 8.2 for the most ecologically important products, namely grain, meat from hoofed animals and sugar.

The first striking feature of these results, shown on the final row of Table 8.2, is that total world food production hardly changes as a result of these reforms. If rich economies reduced their agricultural protection the reduction in their food output would, as it happens, be almost equally matched by increased output in developing countries (despite the abandonment of the US acreage set-aside program assumed in the liberalization scenario). And the same is true, but to a larger extent, if the developing economies also were to remove their distortions to food prices.[9]

In both scenarios grain production falls. This occurs in part because by liberalizing trade in beef and sheepmeat and in dairy products, less grain feeding and more grazing of pastures occurs globally. Grain production would fall most in Western Europe, but it would also fall about 6 per cent in North America if developing countries liberalized their policies as well. China and Latin America would be the main regions of expansion, although China's expansion would be small relative to its total production (2 per cent). Sugar production from beet in temperate areas would decline to give way to cane production in the tropics, especially if developing economies raised their low prices for cane as in the second scenario. And beef production would expand from low bases in China and Sub-Saharan Africa and from considerable bases in Latin America. The expansion in beef production that would occur in Australasia and North America if the reform is confined to rich economies would not occur if developing economies also were to liberalize, reflecting the repression of Latin America's livestock sector by the policy discrimination against agriculture in those countries.

8.3.3   Effects of reforms on the environment

How the environment is affected by these production changes depends on how the use of inputs and primary factors of production would alter as a result of such reforms. With respect to variable inputs, it is clear from Tables 8.3 and 8.4 that chemical fertilizer applications are strongly correlated with producer price incentives: in the mid-1980s countries with relatively low producer prices such as Argentina, Australia and Thailand used less than one-twentieth the amounts of chemical fertilizer per hectare than high-priced countries such as Switzerland use, while in Asia's rice areas the range in the latter 1970s was even wider. An econometric study of 11 Asian countries found that the elasticity of demand for chemical fertilizer with respect to the relative price of rice to fertilizer was between 0.4 and 0.7 in the short run and higher still in the long run, and was larger the greater a country's current use of fertilizer per hectare (Barker *et al.*, 1985).[10]

Similarly, there is a very high correlation between producer price incentives and the use of farm pesticides. The Asian experience is again telling.

Table 8.3   Agricultural producer subsidy equivalents and the use of chemical fertilizer per hectare, various market economies, 1980s

	Agricultural producer subsidy equivalent (%), 1979–89	Chemical fertilizer use[b] (kg per ha of arable land and permanent crops), 1985
Argentina[a]	−38	4
Thailand[a]	−4	21
India[a]	−2	50
Australia	11	24
Indonesia[a]	11	94[c]
New Zealand	20	30
Brazil[a]	22	42
United States	30	94
Canada	35	50
Austria	36	255
European Community-10	39	303
Sweden	46	141
South Korea[a]	61	376
Finland	62	210
Japan	68	427
Switzerland	71	437
Norway	73	277

Notes: [a] Producer subsidy equivalent (PSE) for 1982–87 only, from Webb *et al.* (1990). All other PSEs are from OECD (1990b).
[b] Total consumption of nitrogenous, phosphate and potash fertilizers.
[c] The Indonesian government provides nitrogenous fertilizer (produced domestically from local petroleum) at very low cost to farmers.
Sources: OECD (1990b), Webb *et al.* (1990) and the Food and Agriculture Organisation, *Fertiliser Yearbook 1986*, Rome.

Table 8.4 Producer-to-border price of rice and use of chemical fertilizer and pesticides per hectare, various Asian economies, 1970s

	Producer-to-border price of rice, 1976–80	Chemical fertilizer use per ha. of agricultural land, kg per year 1976–79	Pesticide use per ha. of agricultural land, kg per year 1970–78
Burma	0.37	9	0.16
Thailand	0.70	11	0.97
Sri Lanka	0.76	65	0.11
India	0.76	32	0.33
Philippines	0.77	29	1.36
Bangladesh	0.93	11	0.02
Indonesia	0.98	57	0.38
Taiwan	1.68	205	3.48[a]
West Malaysia	1.73	97	1.92
South Korea	1.87	311	10.70
Japan	3.91	340	14.30

Note: [a] Based on cultivated land area only, for 1979–81, from Department of Agriculture and Forestry, *Taiwan Agricultural Yearbook*, Taipei, 1988.
Source: Barker *et al.* (1985, pp. 77, 89 and 237).

For the countries shown in Table 8.4, the price of rice in the latter 1970s varied over a three-fold range from Thailand to South Korea (or a ten-fold range if the extreme outlyers, Burma and Japan, are included). The range of pesticide applications per hectare was highly correlated with the price of rice but was far wider than the price range, again suggesting a very high elasticity of demand for pesticide inputs with respect to the price of farm outputs.

Notwithstanding the fact that yields per hectare are somewhat higher in protected agricultural sectors, these empirical data suggest that an international relocation of cropping production from high-priced to low-priced countries would reduce substantially, and quickly, the use of chemicals in world food production.[11] Furthermore, the relocation of meat and milk production from intensive grain-feeding enterprises in densely populated rich countries to pasture-based enterprises in relatively lightly populated poorer countries also would be associated with lower use of chemicals such as growth hormones and medicines for animals (the latter partly because animals are less valuable in less-protected countries and partly because the risk of diseases spreading is lower with range feeding than in intensively housed conditions). The greater use of these less-intensive production methods would reduce not only air, soil and water contamination by farmers (see OECD, 1986) but also the chemical intake by the world's food consumers on average. Food consumers in densely populated Western Europe and Japan, where price and trade policies and high land prices currently encourage the heaviest use of farm chemicals, would have the most to gain from this effect of such reforms.

While primary factors of production are considerably less responsive to farm product price changes than are variable purchased inputs, they none-theless do respond over the longer term. Labour is particularly responsive to long-term product price increases because the normal out-migration of labour from farm households which necessarily accompanies economic growth can simply slow down (Johnson, 1973). This is especially the case in densely populated countries where more part-time, off-farm work opportunities are available within commuting distance for farm family members. But even in sparsely populated countries the labour force in agriculture is responsive to product price changes. For example, Cavallo (1989) found, using a 70-year time series, that in Argentina labour is almost as responsive as physical capital equipment – although for both factors less than half the full adjustment occurred in the first ten years after a price change (Table 8.5). Needless to say a slowdown in the flow of labour to urban areas would reduce urban environmental problems, especially in developing countries where that labour is more likely to be employed in smokestack industries than is the case in rich countries.

What about land use? A key concern of environmentalists is the extent to which any international relocation of agricultural production would affect natural forests. Their concern is not only with the preservation of animal and plant species and wilderness areas but also with the capacity of remaining forests to absorb the world's ever-larger emissions of carbon dioxide. Certainly large-scale deforestation has taken place in many tropical countries in recent decades. According to one source, the average annual rate of net deforestation in developing countries during the 1980s was 0.6 per cent, or 0.8 per cent if China's reforestation program is excluded (Table 8.6). And much of the forest land that is cleared is subsequently used for agriculture.

However, this does not necessarily mean that increasing agricultural product prices has or would add significantly to deforestation. One cause of deforestation may be high prices for tropical logs. Another may be tax incentives to develop rangeland or coal mines, as in Brazil (Binswanger, 1989b). Moreover, 80 per cent of wood produced in developing countries

Table 8.5 Price elasticity of output supply and primary factor use in Argentine agriculture

Number of years after real agri-cultural product price change	Agricultural output	Labour use	Physical capital use	Land use
1	0.07	0.00	0.05	0.03
3	0.16	0.07	0.18	0.07
5	0.36	0.17	0.38	0.12
10	0.71	0.42	0.90	0.23
15	1.19	0.82	1.39	0.34
20	1.78	1.52	1.80	0.48

Source: Cavallo (1989).

Table 8.6 Forest area and its depletion, developing economies, 1980s

	Forest area, million hectares	Average annual deforestation net of reforestation		Proportion of harvested wood devoted to fuel and charcoal (%)[a]
		million hectares	% of forest area	
Africa	684	3.47	0.5	88
Central America	506	1.04	0.2	81
South America	858	10.42	1.2	70
China	115	−4.55	−4.0	65
Other Asia and M. East	352	3.49	1.0	82
ALL DEVELOPING ECONOMIES:				
-including China	2,515	13.87	0.6	79
-excluding China	2,400	18.42	0.8	81

Note: [a] 1985–87 only.
Source: World Resources Institute (1990, Tables 19.1 and 19.2).

is not for industrial use but simply for fuel, it being the cheapest source of energy for many poor people (see last column of Table 8.6). Once cleared for firewood, marginal land is then often used for food production by squatting, poverty stricken, landless labourers unable to find enough paid work. An increase in agricultural product prices would serve to increase employment on commercial farms. It also would increase wages and incomes in rural areas, thereby making alternative fuels to firewood both more affordable and relatively cheaper (since the labour time involved in collecting firewood would be more highly valued).

According to the modelling results discussed in connection with Table 8.2, liberalizing food trade would boost producer surplus from farming in developing countries by US$32 billion per year (in 1985 dollars) if rich counties removed their agricultural protection policies, or by US$70 billion if both industrial and developing country policies were liberalized (Anderson and Tyers, 1991a). Such employment and income increases are thus likely to do much to reduce the incentive for rural people in tropical countries to engage in the activity of deforestation for its own sake.

But would deforestation occur for the sake of expanding the area for farming in the wake of higher prices that would result in developing countries from agricultural trade liberalization? The answer to that question is to be found in empirical price response studies. The evidence in Table 8.5 suggests that land area is by far the least responsive factor to changes in farm output prices, at least in Argentina: a 20 per cent permanent increase in the real price of agricultural products would cause the area farmed to have increased by less than 10 per cent even after two decades (compared with increases in farm labour and capital equipment use of 30 to 36 per cent, respectively). Similar results were found by Lopes (1977) for Brazil.

According to his estimation (quoted in Lutz, 1990), a 20 per cent across-the-board increase in Brazil's agricultural prices would increase land use by 12 per cent, labour use by 36 per cent and capital equipment use by 54 per cent in the long run. These and related studies,[12] together with the large body of evidence suggesting the price elasticity of aggregate agricultural supply response is generally less than unity even in the very long run (Chhibber, 1988), would lead one to be confident that agricultural trade liberalization *per se* is unlikely to bring forth wholesale destruction of tropical rain forests.

Moreover, any negative impact of such liberalization on tropical forests is likely to be very small compared with the negative impact of inadequate enforcement of forest property rights and of tax incentives which encourage felling for cattle raising and mines (Repetto and Gillis, 1988; Binswanger, 1989b). And in any case any such negative impact would need to be weighed against the positive environmental effects of (a) foregone production in other sectors of developing countries where productive resources would otherwise have been employed (e.g. smokestack industries) and (b) reforestation on former farm land in industrial countries following the reductions in government assistance to farmers there.

8.4 Implications for agricultural policies

Virtually all activities of production and consumption make some use of the natural environment, and food is no exception. Soil and water degradation by farmers has been going on for millennia, perhaps the worst ancient example being the destroying in Old Testament time of the gardens of Babylon (now the marshy wasteland of southern Iraq — see Eckholm, 1976). But farmers continue to learn better ways of looking after the land and water resources they use, and have shown themselves able and ready to respond quickly to changing economic incentives to do so. What the above analysis suggests is that a liberalization of agricultural policies would involve a change in incentive structures that not only raises income substantially in rich and poorer countries but also is likely to reduce both the damage inflicted on the global environment and the chemical residues in the food produced by the world's farmers.

Both the environment and welfare could be enhanced even further if the removal of distortions to the relative price of food products were to be accompanied by the introduction of optimal environmental policy instruments and/or the removal of distortions to farm input prices. Among the former, the final part of Section 8.2 above demonstrates that if a developing country believes the increase in farm product prices following trade liberalization would cause excessive deforestation, a production tax on logging and/or stronger enforcement of forest property rights could overcome that externality and still allow the economy to benefit from the higher food price. Should other, richer countries be concerned that deforestation would be too great even in the presence of the developing country's (nationally) optimal environmental policy on logging, the analysis shows that those richer countries could afford to pay the developing country to increase the disincentive to fell trees and still be better off in terms of their welfare broadly defined. [13] This illustrates the general proposition that, because there are more efficient policy instruments than trade policies for preserving the natural environment, trade liberalization not only need never be put off for environmental reasons but its benefits can be enhanced if appropriate environmental instruments are introduced at the time of liberalization.

The second additional way in which the environment and welfare can be enhanced has to do with coupling output price policy reforms with reforms of policies affecting farm input prices. Many countries subsidize farm inputs as a supplement to or a substitute for output price support policies. The best-known are fertilizer and irrigation subsidies, which contribute to the excessive use of these inputs from both efficiency and ecology viewpoints. If following trade liberalization in food domestic output prices were to increase in developing countries, the perceived need for such input subsidies to boost farm incomes and output would be less. Their elimination at the time of liberalization, and possible replacement by a tax on their use to correct for the negative externality involved, would thereby reduce even further the possibility of such liberalization worsening the environment.

If the use of chemicals in developing country agriculture nonetheless did increase with higher food prices following trade liberalization, should this be of concern to people in those countries (or in rich countries on behalf of those poorer people)? It seems unlikely, because if those developing countries plan to export to rich countries, they will need to meet the relatively strict food safety standards of those rich countries. And if the poorer countries were still concerned, they could always impose even stricter national standards. Again, it is simply a case of solving the problem with an appropriately targeted policy instrument rather than the much blunter and less efficient instrument (for that purpose) of trade policy.

Finally, what would be the impact of also liberalizing food markets in the CPEs of Eastern Europe and the Soviet Union? There the price of food is well below international levels, and yet they are on average about 95 per cent self sufficient in the main staples (Anderson and Tyers, 1991b). The price set domestically is not a market-clearing price, however, so while liberalizing their food markets would cause production to expand, the abandoning of rationing via queuing may result in food consumption expanding as well. Nonetheless, assuming the domestic consumer price is allowed to rise, net food imports by these CPEs would decrease and so food policy reform there would, *ceteris paribus*, simply add somewhat to the effects analysed above of reforms in other developing countries. That is, even more of the world's food production would be located outside Western Europe and Japan.

The gains within Eastern Europe and the Soviet republics of allowing more of the rise in international food prices to be transmitted to their domestic markets could be extremely large, for several reasons. First, producers' incomes would rise, and more so the more rural property rights are transferred to farm operators as part of the reforms. Second, welfare of food consumers could rise: even though they would face higher food prices, the volumes of food available to them would be greater and rationing via queues could disappear. Third, new technologies could be imported as part of the opening up of these economies. And fourth, the greater profitability of agriculture would draw more resources to the sector, thereby ensuring fewer resources are employed in less-productive – and generally much more pollutive – industrial activities. Indeed it could be argued that no other single action by the West could do more for the political and economic development of the countries of Eastern Europe and the Soviet Union, and incidently for their (and hence also Western Europe's) environment, than the inclusion of substantive cuts in agricultural protectionism as part of an Uruguay Round agreement.

Notes

Thanks are due to Rod Tyers for the use of printouts from our earlier joint research and to Carlos Primo Braga and Bernard Hoekman for helpful comments on an early draft.
1. During 1982–87, direct financial producer subsidies for coal producers (from Jolly *et al.*, 1990) were the following percentages of coal import prices (from the International Energy Agency, *Energy Prices and Taxes*, 1990): Belgium, 80 per cent; Germany, F. R., 66 per cent; United Kingdom, 42 per cent; and Japan, 90 per cent. In addition, producers enjoyed protection from import competition which contributed to higher domestic prices than would otherwise be the case. Again using data from Jolly *et al.* (1990, Tables 2 and 3), the combined effect of import protection plus direct producer subsidies was to cause domestic producer prices for coal to be above border prices in 1986 by about 100 per cent in the United Kingdom, 240 per cent in West Germany and 290 per cent in Japan. See also Steenblik and Wigley (1990). The same International Energy Agency publication suggests that, on the assumption that the German import price is an appropriate indicator of the border price for Eastern European countries, then in 1988 the domestic price of steaming coal for electricity was only 17 per cent of the border price in Czechoslovakia, 27 per cent of that price in Poland and 44 per cent in Hungary. Burniaux *et al.* (1991, Table 2) suggest that coal prices in China and the USSR in 1985 were less than 40 per cent of those of Western Europe – possibly very much less when evaluated at equilibrium exchange rates. For more on the USSR's potential as a coal exporter at international prices, see Dobozi (1991) and Radetzki (1991).
2. To the extent that the demand curve is further to the right in the CPEs than illustrated and rationing is practiced at the low domestic price of P_3, then the adoption of free trade by the CPEs would have a smaller negative impact on the international price level and a smaller positive impact on emission

reductions and welfare in the CPEs. On the other hand, since coal is produced in the CPEs by cumbersome state-owned enterprises it is conceivable that, if the reform included the privatization of those enterprises and the importing of lower-cost mining technologies, the domestic supply curve would also shift to the right. Whether this supply shock would more or less than offset any effect of eliminating rationing is a difficult issue to resolve *ex ante*. As well, if there were simultaneous reforms in other sectors, these would shift the CPEs' coal supply and demand curves also.

3. As well, government revenue would increase because the producer subsidy net of import tariff revenue would be replaced by a consumer tax of $P_c P_2'$ per unit consumed. For a detailed exposition of the appropriateness of the consumer/producer surplus approach to measuring social welfare, see Just *et al.* (1982). The methodology used throughout this chapter draws on the more general analysis in the author's Chapter 2 in this volume.

4. Only if CPE reforms were to depress the world price substantially below P_2 in Figure 8.1 is it possible that global emissions from coal consumption could expand, and even then it would occur only if governments in non-protected market economies did not intervene to discourage expanded coal consumption in their countries.

5. It is possible that some countries in the rich-country group, or even the group as a whole, may have set P_1 above the level at which the S_1 and D_1 curves intersect in Figure 8.2, in which case an export subsidy is needed to dispose of the excess supply. In that case the two shaded triangles are larger and overlapping and the tariff revenue rectangle is replaced by a taller export subsidy rectangle, so trade liberalization necessarily generates a welfare gain for the rich countries.

6. This section and the next draw heavily on Anderson (1992). For more general discussions of ways in which agricultural trade and environmental issues interact, see Kozloff and Runge (1991), OECD (1989) and Reichelderfer (1990).

7. A gradual and partial liberalization experiment is reported in another study by Anderson and Tyers (1992) where it is shown that even if there is as much as a halving of agricultural protection rates in advanced industrial economies during 1991–95, food production levels in those protectionist economies would still be greater by the year 2000 than in 1990. This occurs simply because the positive effect on output of the assumed rate of normal productivity growth outweighs the negative effect of reduced price supports. The eventual long-run effect of liberalization is less easy to see from such a dynamic simulation than from the comparative-static simulation reported here, however.

8. The inclusion of these indirect means by which developing country policies reduce farm output distinguishes the above results from other partial equilibrium modelling results (including earlier versions using the Tyers model) which embody only direct policy distortions.

9. The reason international food prices nonetheless rise in the first scenario is that the insulating and (usually) price-depressing components of the food policies of developing economies (and of Eastern Europe and the USSR) are still in place in that scenario, so only a portion of the international price changes are transmitted to the distorted domestic markets of the poorer countries. In the case of Eastern Europe and the USSR the estimated price transmission elasticities used are very low, hence the reforms are projected to have little impact on those former communist economies.

10. Binswanger (1989a), in his review of studies of the responsiveness of agricultural inputs and output to changes in farmer incentives, provides additional evidence from numerous countries of the rapid change in the use of fertilizer

in response to product price changes, both absolutely and relative to the use of primary factors such as land, labour and capital equipment. Particularly striking is the following evidence which he drew from Johnson (1950) for the United States during the Great Depression:

Year	Price of agricultural output	Quantity of agricultural output	Land area planted	Total labour input	Power and machinery input	Quantity of fertilizer used
1929	100	100	100	100	100	100
1930	86	98	101	99	101	103
1931	60	107	103	99	100	79
1932	46	104	104	98	97	55
1933	48	96	103	97	89	61
1934	60	81	93	97	84	70

In that setting the initial increase in land planting and the almost complete absence of labour shedding was because off-farm opportunities to earn income were also very depressed at the time. A more contemporary study of US agriculture by Ball (1988) found 'other purchased inputs' (not including land, labour, farm capital, equipment and energy) to be most responsive of almost all input groups to changes in the prices of various farm products.

11. The use of agricultural chemicals would decline globally even if food producer prices were equalized around the world. This is because part of the explanation for lower applications of agricultural chemicals in countries with low food prices is that the price of labour relative to capital is relatively low in those countries, making labour-intensive tasks such as weeding and the spreading of manure cheaper practices than applying chemicals. Trade liberalization is likely to reduce but not necessarily eliminate the cost differential.

12. From a recent growth-accounting study, Fan (1991) found that for China during the 1965–85 period, none of its farm output growth was attributable to land expansion and only 8 per cent to increased labour use. A quarter of the output growth was attributed to increased fertilizer, a quarter to the introduction of the household responsibility system, one-fifth to greater machinery use and one-sixth to technological change.

13. Environmental groups in rich countries may even consider buying – and indeed some groups already have purchased – tropical forest land in poor countries. In addition to ensuring preservation of the forest, this also provides people in poor countries with financial capital to invest in other sectors.

References

Anderson, K. (1992), 'Agricultural Trade Liberalization and the Environment: a Global Perspective', *The World Economy* 15 (forthcoming March).

Anderson, K. and R. Tyers (1991a), 'More on Welfare Gains to Developing Countries from Liberalizing World Food Trade', mimeo, Australian National University, Canberra, July.

Anderson, K. and R. Tyers (1991b), *Global Effects of Liberalizing Trade in Farm Products*, London: Harvester Wheatsheaf for the Trade Policy Research Centre.

Anderson, K. and R. Tyers (1992), 'Effects of Gradual Food Policy Reforms in the 1990s', *European Review of Agricultural Economics* 19 (forthcoming January).

Ball, V. E. (1988), 'Modelling Supply Response in a Multiproduct Framework', *American Journal of Agricultural Economics* **70**: 813–25.

Barker, R., R. W. Herdt and B. Rose (1985), *The Rice Economy of Asia*, Washington, D. C.: Resources for the Future.

Binswanger, H. (1989a), 'The Policy Response of Agriculture', pp. 231–58 in *Proceedings of the World Bank Annual Conference on Development Economics 1989* (a supplement to Vol. 3 of the *World Bank Economic Review*).

Binswanger, H. (1989b), 'Brazilian Policies that Encourage Deforestation in the Amazon', Environment Department Working Paper No. 16, Washington D.C.: The World Bank.

Burniaux, J-M., J. P. Martin, G. Nicoletti and J. O. Martins (1991), 'The Costs of Policies to Reduce Global Emissions of CO_2: Initial Simulation Results with GREEN', Working Paper No. 103, Department of Economics and Statistics, OECD, Paris, June.

Cavallo, D. (1989), 'Agriculture and Economic Growth: The Experience of Argentina, 1913–84', in *Agriculture and Governments in an Interdependent World*, edited by A. Maunder and A. Valdes, London: Dartmouth for the IAAE.

Chhibber, A. (1988), 'The Aggregate Supply Response in Agriculture: A Survey', in *Structural Adjustment in Agriculture: Theory and Practice*, edited by S. Commander, London: James Curry Publishers.

Dobozi, I. (1991), 'Impact of Market Reforms on USSR Energy Consumption', *Energy Policy* **19**: 303–24.

Eckholm, E. P. (1976), *Losing Ground: Environmental Stress and World Food Prospects*, New York: W. W. Norton.

Fan, S. G. (1991), 'Effects of Technological Change and Institutional Reform on Production Growth in Chinese Agriculture', *American Journal of Agricultural Economics* **73**: 266–75.

Johnson, D. G. (1950), 'The Nature of the Supply Function for Agricultural Products', *American Economic Review* **40**: 539–64.

Johnson, D. G. (1973). *World Agriculture in Disarray*, London: Fontana.

Jolly, L., T. Beck and E. Savage (1990), 'Reform of International Coal Trade: Implications for Australia and World Trade', Discussion Paper 90.1, Canberra: Australian Bureau of Agricultural and Resource Economics.

Just, R. E., D. L. Hueth and A. Schmitz (1982), *Applied Welfare Economics and Public Policy*, Englewood Cliffs: Prentice Hall.

Kozloff, K. and C. F. Runge (1991), 'International Trade in the Food Sector and Environmental Quality, Health and Safety: A Survey of Policy Issues', Staff Paper P91-12, Dept. of Agricultural and Applied Economics, University of Minnesota, St Paul, May.

Krueger, A. O., M. Schiff and A. Valdes (1988), 'Measuring the Impact of Sector-Specific and Economy-Wide Policies on Agricultural Incentives in LDCs', *World Bank Economic Review* **2**: 255–72.

Lopes, M. (1977), 'The Mobilization of Resources from Agriculture: A Policy Analysis for Brazil', Unpublished Ph.D. dissertation, Purdue University, Layfayette.

Lutz, E. (1990), 'Agricultural Trade Liberalization, Price Changes and Environmental Effects', Divisional Working Paper No. 1990–14, Environment Department, The World Bank, Washington, D.C. December.

Newbery, D. M. (1990), 'Acid Rain', *Economic Policy* **5**, (11), 297–346.

OECD (1986), *Water Pollution by Fertilizers and Pesticides*, Paris: OECD.

OECD (1987), *National Policies and Agricultural Trade*, Paris: OECD.

OECD (1989), *Agricultural and Environmental Policies: Opportunities for Integration*, Paris: OECD.

172 Kym Anderson

OECD (1990a), *Modelling the Effects of Agricultural Policies*, OECD Economic Studies No. 13, Paris: OECD.

OECD (1990b), *Monitoring and Outlook of Agricultural Policies, Markets and Trade*, Paris: OECD.

Parikh, K. S., G. Fisher, K. Frohberg and O. Gulbrandsen (1988), *Towards Free Trade in Agriculture*, Dordrecht: Martinus Nijhoff for IIASA.

Radetzki, M. (1991), 'USSR Energy Exports Post-Perestroika: Survey of Prospects and Issues', *Energy Policy* 19: 291–302.

Reichelderfer, K. (1990), 'Environmental Protection and Agricultural Support: Are Trade-offs Necessary?' pp. 201–29 in *Agricultural Policies in a New Decade*, edited by K. Allen, Washington, D.C.: Resources for the Future.

Repetto, R. and M. Gillis (eds.) (1988), *Public Policies and the Misuse of Forest Resources*, Cambridge: Cambridge University Press.

Steenblik, R. P. and K. J. Wigley (1990), 'Coal Policies and Trade Barriers', *Energy Policy* 18: 351–69.

Stoeckel, A. B., D. Vincent and S. Cuthbertson (ed.) (1989), *Macroeconomic Consequences of Farm Support Policies*, Durham: Duke University Press.

Tyers, R. and K. Anderson (1992), *Disarray in World Food Markets*, Cambridge: Cambridge University Press (in press).

UNCTAD (1990), *Agricultural Trade Liberalization in the Uruguay Round: Implications for Developing Countries*, a joint UNCTAD/ UNDP/WIDER(UNU) study, New York: United Nations.

Webb, A. J., M. Lopez and R. Penn (eds.) (1990), *Estimates of Producer and Consumer Subsidy Equivalents: Government Intervention in Agriculture 1982–87*, Statistical Bulletin 803, Washington, D.C.: US Department of Agriculture.

World Resources Institute (1990), *World Resources 1990–91*, New York: Oxford University Press.

Zietz, J. and A. Valdes (1990), 'International Interactions in Food and Agricultural Policies: Effects of Alternative Policies', Ch. 3 in *Agricultural Trade Liberalization: Implications for Developing Countries*, edited by I. Goldin and O. Knudsen, Paris: OECD.

9

International economic integration and the environment: the case of Europe

Michael Rauscher

We are living in a period of increasing international economic interdependence and integration. The former centrally planned economies are increasing their participation in the international division of labour through their adoption of market-economy principles. The creation of the Single Market in Western Europe will have the effect of further integrating the economies of its member states through the free movement of goods and factors and the harmonization of monetary and other policies. Lastly, the growth of East Asia's newly industrializing economies has shown the success of an export-orientated development strategy as opposed to an import-substituting one. Of course, there continue to be tendencies towards protection and bilateralism in the international trading system, but in the long term it is expected – or at least hoped – that these tendencies will be dominated by the aforementioned movements toward regional and global integration.

If it is true that the world's economies are becoming increasingly more integrated and interdependent, what will be the consequences for the environment and hence for environmental policies? In the past environmental policies mostly have been decided on and carried out at a national or sub-national level. Ideally those policies internalize the external effects of pollution by applying either the polluter-pays or the pollutee-pays principle. Pigovian taxes and subsidies are the instruments that have been recommended to re-establish a Pareto-optimal allocation of resources.

The environmental policy of a large open economy, however, may affect the country's terms of trade. By raising the price of environmental factors of production, the government raises the world market prices of goods that use this factor intensively in their production. This terms of trade change will be beneficial to the country if it is an exporter of these goods and harmful if it imports them.

Second, environmental policies may have indirect effects. If a country decides to reduce domestic emissions through an environmental policy, it may induce international movements of mobile factors of production. These will be relocated to places where environmental standards are lower. Should pollution from such places spill over into the home country, it is possible that the increase in pollution from abroad may dominate the reduction of domestic emissions. A restrictive environmental policy in that case may be harmful to a country's environment (Merrifield, 1988; Rauscher, 1991a).

Finally, there is the problem of jurisdictional competition. Many environmentalists fear that the process of economic integration will increase competition among countries for internationally mobile factors of production, particularly capital. An investor will choose the location where the productivity of capital is the highest. Everything else being equal, he/she will invest in a country where pollution abatement requirements and costs are relatively low. If countries wish to attract these mobile factors of production, they have to offer favourable conditions to potential investors. The argument then is that competition among nations for mobile factors of production will lead to an unacceptably low level of environmental regulation.

This chapter attempts to analyse the environmental impact of international economic integration with special emphasis on Europe. It focuses on changes in environmental quality and in environmental policies that are induced by the removal of trade barriers. The question of whether there may be harmful competition in setting environmental standards is discussed. The following section of the chapter sets out the framework for the analysis. Next, the integration effects are investigated – first for the case of given environmental policies and second for a world in which governments adjust their legislation to changes in the economic environment. The latter case is investigated by looking at comparative-static results for a Nash equilibrium of environmental policies.

Two types of model are used in the analysis. In the first, the government maximizes national welfare in the conventional sense while in the second, the government takes into account the possible effect on unemployment of international mobility of factors of production. Unemployment may occur if there are rigidities in the labour market and the government uses its environmental policy as a vehicle to prevent job displacement. The benefits from harmonizing environmental policies are also addressed. The analysis is then applied to the process of economic integration in Europe.

9.1 The economic integration of Europe: some stylized facts

There are two major aspects of European economic integration: the creation of the internal market in Western Europe after 1992 and the integration of the former centrally planned economies of Eastern Europe into the world market for goods and factors. Each of these integration processes is characterized by features which affect the choice of the appropriate framework for analysis.

According to the Cecchini Report (1988), the creation of the single market will raise the output of the European Community (EC) considerably. But what will be the effects on international trade? For many goods, barriers to trade within the EC are already rather low. There are, however, still substantial non-tariff barriers that affect trade in some goods and particularly the international mobility of factors. Differences in product norms and national biases in public procurement are the most important trade barriers (Jacquemin and Sapir, 1988; Winters, 1991). The abolition of these barriers should induce additional trade and factor movements. Other effects that are also of importance, such as increasing returns to scale, will not be taken up here: the analysis will be restricted to perfectly competitive situations in which factors are remunerated according to their marginal productivities.

Another issue of major importance is the setting of external trade barriers that will replace the current national barriers to trade imposed by individual member states. It is assumed that the external barriers to trade remain unaffected by the process of integration, although it should be kept in mind that this is a *ceteris-paribus* qualification, not a forecast. Indeed most commentators expect the wide array of EC discriminatory external trade barriers to increase in the 1990s (Anderson, 1991; Winters, 1991).

Environmental pollution may be created either by production processes (e.g. manufacturing industries) or by consumption of final goods (e.g. household refuse). The following analysis will deal exclusively with the former category. Of course, the internalization of consumption externalities has trade implications too (see Chapter 4 of this volume by Snape). But these regulations affect domestic and foreign producers of a good in the same way. Moreover, the possibility of using product norms for consumption goods as a barrier to trade tends to be eroded by the application of the country-of-origin principle in the EC.[1]

There are some special features that have to be considered when dealing with the integration of the former centrally planned economies. During the 1980s, the share of international trade between these countries and the rest of the world represented a mere 3 per cent of total world trade, meaning that these countries formed a nearly autarkic block within the world economy. Therefore, the main effects of increased openness should occur inside these countries, when they adjust to world market prices. Major effects on the rest of the world, e.g. changes in the terms of trade, may occur only when the volume of external trade of the former centrally-planned economies increases considerably.

A two-country model is the simplest feasible framework for examining the effects that occur inside the integration area. It is useful for modelling both the effects of the 1992 programme in Western Europe and the effects of East European integration into the world market if the repercussions of East European integration on the rest of the world are negligible. However, in order to analyse effects on non-member countries when those affected are not negligible, a three-country model must be used.

Assume there are just two factors of production, sector-specific capital and polluting emissions, which can be substituted to some extent for each other.[2] Capital is internationally mobile, whereas the environmental factor of production is not. Emissions are affected by national environmental laws. Economic integration is modelled as a reduction of barriers to international capital mobility. Trade in final goods would occur if the intersectoral mobility of factors was greater than international factor mobility, but when barriers to the latter are lowered there is no need for trade in goods in this model.[3]

The analysis draws on established literature on environmental policies in open economies (Baumol, 1971; Markusen, 1975; Pethig, 1976; Siebert, 1977; Siebert *et al.*, 1980). This literature is mainly concerned with extending the results of standard trade theory to situations in which environmental pollution is internalized within the production process. In principle, some of the results correspond to earlier models in which the supply of factors of production is variable (Kemp and Jones, 1962). An exception is Markusen's article which explicitly considers transfrontier pollution and the terms-of-trade effects of environmental policies. This aspect has been developed further by Merrifield (1988), Krutilla (1991), and Rauscher (1991a).

9.2 Effects of economic integration with constant emission taxes

The analysis begins with the effects of international economic integration assuming environmental policies are given.[4] In what follows, the country which owns a part of the capital stock employed in the other country will be referred to as the capital-rich country whereas the other country is relatively capital-poor or well endowed with environmental resources.

If the emission levels were fixed by policy in both countries, economic integration would not alter environmental quality. Welfare effects may, however, result from changes in the rate of return on mobile capital. As a consequence of integration, capital moves from the capital-rich to the capital-poor country. The marginal productivity of capital is thereby increased in the capital-rich and reduced in the capital-poor country. Both countries experience welfare gains since the size of the Harberger triangle of efficiency losses is reduced and the resulting increase in income is distributed among the countries.[5]

More interesting results can be derived if emission levels are not constant, that is, if the governments employ emission taxes as the instrument of environmental policy. After increasing the mobility of capital, this factor moves from the capital-rich to the capital-poor country since the rate of return abroad (marginal productivity minus marginal mobility cost) is larger than its marginal productivity at home. If the capital stock is reduced, the marginal productivity of the other factor of production (emissions) is reduced.[6] The value of the output produced by means of the last unit of emissions is smaller than the emission tax that has to be paid for emitting this unit of pollutants. Therefore, there is an incentive for domestic producers to reduce their emissions.

The opposite is true for the foreign, capital-poor country. The productivity of emissions increases and it therefore pays to discharge more pollutants there. The changes in emissions affect the marginal productivities of capital in both countries. The country increasing its emissions experiences an improvement in its capital productivity whereas the productivity of capital is reduced in the other country. This creates an additional incentive to invest in the country which is well-endowed with the environmental factor of production. There will be an impact on emissions again which in turn affects foreign direct investment. Assuming the production function has the appropriate properties, this process is stable and leads to the following conclusion: *if emission taxes are constant in both countries, the capital-rich country will reduce its emissions and the capital-poor country will increase its emissions as a response to economic integration* (Proposition 1).

There are three types of welfare effects. First there are efficiency gains due to improved factor allocation, from which both countries will gain. Second there is an effect caused by changes in domestic emissions. If the emission tax rate is lower than the Pigovian tax, then this effect is positive for the capital-rich country, which reduces its emissions, and negative for the other country. Third, the change in emission levels in one country affects welfare of the other country via transfrontier diffusion of pollutants. According to Proposition 1, the capital-rich country will experience a welfare loss whereas the country relatively well endowed with environmental resources will gain.

For a small economy that opens its borders to capital flows, one obtains similar results. The country will increase (reduce) its emissions if it is capital-poor (capital-rich). The transfrontier pollution effect becomes negligible since the impact on the rest of the world is minuscule in this case.

Matters are more complicated if a non-member country is introduced into the model. In general, the effects of integration are ambiguous. In the special case of a constant-returns-to-scale production function, however, one can show that Proposition 1 still holds for the member countries. The non-member country will not be affected by changes in the allocation of factors of production (Rauscher, 1991c). There may, however, be effects due to changes in transfrontier pollution. If the non-member country is located geographically near the capital-poor member country which increases its emissions, then the former will suffer from a deterioration of its environmental quality. If it is located closer to the capital-rich country, the non-member will profit from integration in terms of its environment.

9.3 A Nash equilibrium model of environmental policies

While it is reasonable to assume as above that in the short to medium term the environmental policies of the government are fixed, in the longer term to be considered in this section laws can and will be adjusted to changes in the environment. The government is assumed to maximize national welfare, which itself is dependent on national income (i.e. the consumption possibilities) and on the quality of the environment. In the small-country case, matters are relatively simple. If a country is capital-poor, it will attract additional capital after the removal of barriers to factor mobility. This will raise the marginal productivity of emissions. The marginal welfare derived from the consumption of the goods that can be produced by means of the last unit of emissions exceeds the disutility due to the reduction of environmental quality caused by this last unit of emissions. Therefore, the optimal policy reaction is to allow for an increase in emissions. The opposite is true if the country is capital-rich. That is, *the optimal policy reaction of a small country to an increase in openness is to increase its emissions if it is capital-poor and to reduce them if it is capital-rich* (Proposition 2).[7]

If the countries are large, matters are more complicated. If there are no negotiations on common environmental policies, the countries will choose their legislation independently of each other. Each country takes the environmental policy of the other country as given. This implies a Nash model of governmental behaviour. In an open economy, the emission tax then serves two purposes: it internalizes the external effects of environmental pollution and it can be used to influence the rate of return of the mobile factor if the country is not small.

Assume as stated before that each country takes the emissions in the other country as given. Then the optimal emission tax will have two components: a tax which internalizes domestic social costs (the Pigovian tax component), and a rate-of-return component as environmental policies affect the rate of return of the mobile factor. A restrictive environmental policy reduces the scarcity of capital and lowers its rate of return. This is beneficial for the capital-poor country and harmful for the capital-rich country. Thus, this tax component is positive for the country relatively well-endowed with the environmental factor of production and negative for the other country. If there were trade instead of factor mobility, there would be a terms-of-trade effect of environmental policy. The tax component corresponds to the optimum tariff in international trade theory (Johnson, 1953/4).[8]

The integration effects can be analysed by looking at the Nash equilibrium of environmental policies. The shapes of the reaction curves can be determined by analysing the effect of a change in the emissions of one country on the optimal emission level chosen by the other country. In order to keep matters simple, no transfrontier pollution is assumed for the first part of the analysis.[9]

If the foreign country increases its emissions, then it will attract capital from the home country. The policy-maker in the capital-rich country must then consider two effects. First, the marginal productivity of emissions is reduced, which implies a reduction in emissions. Second, the other country makes the environmental factor, with which it is well-endowed, less scarce. This increases its income and a part of this income gain could be sacrificed in order to improve the environmental quality.

The first effect is the same for the policy-maker in the capital-poor country. The second effect, however, is the opposite. Since the capital-rich country increases the relative scarcity of capital by increasing its emissions, the income of the capital-poor country is reduced, and this provides an incentive for the policy-maker to relax environmental policy. Thus, two scenarios are possible. In one of them, the reaction curve of the capital-poor country is negatively sloped, in the other one, the slope is positive. This is represented in Figure 9.1 where E and E^* denote emissions and R

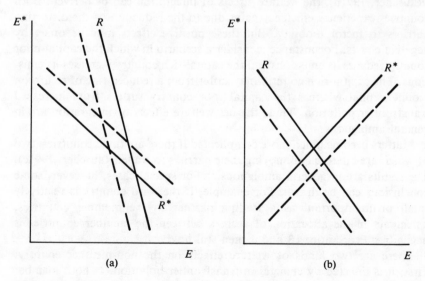

Figure 9.1 Economic integration and the Nash equilibrium of optimal emission policies

and R^* represent reaction curves of the capital-rich and the capital-poor country, respectively.

The impact of increased openness can also be decomposed into a productivity and an income effect. Integration implies efficiency gains and, therefore, causes income increases in both countries. If environmental quality is a superior good, this makes both countries reduce their emissions. The productivity effects differ across countries. Due to the additional capital movement from the capital-rich to the capital-poor country, the productivity of emissions will be reduced in the capital-rich and increased in the capital-poor country. This implies a more restrictive environmental policy in the capital-rich country whereas the optimal reaction in the capital-poor country is to increase the emissions. Thus, *for any given level of emissions in the other country, an increase in factor mobility will make the capital-rich country reduce its emissions, while the reaction of the other country is ambiguous* (Proposition 3).

Combining this with the two scenarios concerning the shapes of the reaction curves (see Figure 9.1) yields the following results. In the first scenario, the capital-rich country reduces its emissions and the capital-poor country increases its emissions. In the second scenario, the capital-poor country reduces its emissions whereas the response of the other country is ambiguous. This leads to the general result that *as a consequence of economic integration, at least one country reduces its emissions* (Proposition 4).

Since this result is maintained when transfrontier pollution is introduced (Rauscher, 1991b), the welfare effects of integration can be derived. Both countries experience efficiency gains due to the reduction of the distorting barriers to factor mobility. But these positive effects may be offset by negative effects. For instance, consider a scenario in which the capital-poor country reduces its emissions and the capital-rich country increases its emissions. The capital-rich country may suffer from a reduced rate of return on mobile capital whereas the capital-poor country suffers from increased transfrontier pollution. Thus, the net welfare effects of integration are in general ambiguous.

Matters become much more complicated if there are three countries, two of which are bilaterally removing their barriers to trade (Rauscher, 1991c). The results are in general ambiguous.[10] For special cases, however, some conclusions can be drawn. For example, if the third country is relatively small or unimportant as a trading partner to the member countries, its impact in the allocation of factors between the member countries is negligible. Propositions 3 and 4 then still hold.

There are two kinds of welfare effects on the non-member country. First, it is affected by changes in transfrontier pollution. If both member countries reduce their emissions, then the third country will benefit. If the country is geographically close to a member country which increases its emissions, however, then it will experience a welfare loss. The second impact is the rate-of-return effect. The productivities of capital in the member countries tend to converge during the adjustment process. If the changes in environmental policies are relatively small, then capital productivity is increased in the capital-rich country and reduced in the capital-poor country. The effect on the third country will depend on whether it is a capital importer or a capital exporter and on its trading partners. A capital-poor developing country, for instance, which has imported capital from the capital-rich country in the past, is likely to lose from integration since the rate of interest it has to pay has increased. Matters are different if there are substantial emission reductions in the member countries. Then the capital productivity is reduced and so is the rate of interest. The impact of integration on the environmental policy of the non-member country is completely indeterminate.

9.4   Increased competition for the mobile factor

The previous section of the chapter is devoted to optimal environmental policies, i.e. measures that maximize national welfare defined as a weighted function of income and the quality of the environment. It was shown that in such a framework the problem of harmful legislative competition among countries does not occur: at least one of the two countries chooses more-restrictive regulation. This approach may not, however, be very realistic. The main objective of a government is not to maximize welfare but to be reelected. And in a representative democracy, the objective of being reelected is not perfectly correlated with the target of welfare maximization. Pressure groups influence the policies of the government.[11]

This section examines a situation in which the government has an incentive to attract more capital than in the welfare-maximization framework. This is possible for instance if there are rigidities in the labour market, for then an outflow of capital increases unemployment at home and reduces it abroad. If the chances of being reelected depend on the employment situation, the capital stock becomes an argument in the policy-maker's welfare function. Favourable conditions will tend to be offered to foreign investors in the form of relaxing environmental regulations.

If the capital stock is an argument in the utility function, there will be an additional component of the optimal emission tax rate which measures the effect of an increase of this tax rate on the policy-maker's utility via the change in the capital stock. Since a high emission tax rate drives mobile capital out of the country, this component is unambiguously negative. The environmental legislation desired by the politician is less restrictive than the socially optimal legislation. By charging too low a price for the use of environmental resources, the government gives hidden subsidies to producers.

Does this mean that economic integration will lead to harmful competition which will result in unacceptably low levels of environmental protection? This question will be addressed by making the extreme assumption that only the capital stock and the quality of the environment occur in the objective function. The Nash equilibrium can be analysed by investigating the properties of the reaction curves. With the conventional assumptions on the shapes of the production and utility functions, none of the countries produces without emissions. If a country increases emissions, it withdraws capital from the other country. The optimal reaction of this country is to employ a less-restrictive environmental policy too, in order to prevent the capital from moving abroad, so that the reaction curves are positively sloped (see Figure 9.2).

If there is an increase in capital mobility, then additional capital will move from the capital-rich country to the country well endowed with the environmental factor of production. The effects of economic integration are as follows. Due to lower costs of mobility, capital is shifted from the capital-rich to the capital-poor country. The marginal utility of capital in the capital-poor country is reduced, while in the capital-rich country it is increased. Therefore, the capital-poor country has an incentive to reduce its emissions, whereas the capital-rich country prefers a less-restrictive environmental policy. Both reaction curves in Figure 9.2 are shifted to the right. It can be seen that there are different possibilities for the location of the new equilibrium, though one case can be excluded: *if there is direct competition for the internationally mobile factor, then a scenario in which*

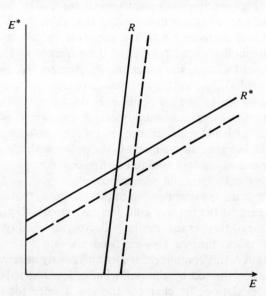

Figure 9.2 Economic integration and legislative competition for mobile capital

the capital-rich country reduces its emissions and the capital-poor country relaxes its environmental regulation does not occur (Proposition 5).

The most likely case is the opposite one: the capital-rich country increases its emissions, and the country relatively well endowed with environmental resources employs a more-restrictive policy. Thus, there will be a tendency towards a convergence of environmental policies.

The welfare effects of integration in this case are ambiguous. If both countries reduce their emissions, they will both profit from reduced transfrontier externalities. This effect may dominate all the other effects that are possible in this model. The opposite scenario, in which both countries experience welfare losses, is also feasible. Consider the most likely situation in which the capital-rich country increases its emissions and the other country chooses a more-restrictive policy. The capital-poor country suffers from increased transfrontier pollution. The capital-rich country will experience welfare losses due to the reduction of the rate of return on capital since the other country has increased the scarcity of its relatively abundant factor. (Of course, it is also possible to construct intermediate scenarios in which one country loses and the other country gains from the process of economic integration.)

In a three-country world, the effects of integration are again ambiguous and some special assumptions have to be made if interpretable results are to be derived. Assume again that the non-member country is small compared to the other countries so the results derived for the member countries from the two-country version of the model continue to hold. If there is a convergence of environmental policies inside the trade union, the marginal productivity of capital is reduced in the capital-poor country and increased in the capital-rich country. If the third country is a capital-poor developing country which has imported capital from the capital-rich member country in the past, it will suffer from a loss of foreign capital. In order to avoid unemployment, the country has to attract additional capital and, therefore, relaxes its environmental standards. Moreover, it may suffer from an increase in the interest rate. As before, these effects are not unambiguous. Without the special assumptions made here, anything can happen.

9.5 Harmonization of environmental policies

Up to this point it has been assumed that national governments unilaterally decide on their environmental policies. Since there is an ongoing discussion on harmonizing national regulations on an EC-wide basis, this issue must be addressed when the impact of economic integration is discussed. In the case of environmental policies, harmonization would imply the introduction of identical standards all over Europe regardless of the assimilative capacity of nature and of social preferences. The effects of harmonizing environmental regulations on the allocation of factors and on the welfare of the member countries are now considered.

Assume that the harmonized regulation is a weighted average of the individual regulations. This implies that environmental resources become scarcer in the capital-poor country and less scarce in the other country, which is well-endowed with capital. The marginal productivity of capital is reduced in the capital-poor country and increased in the capital-rich country. Thus, mobile capital leaves the capital-poor country and moves abroad. If there is an emission tax in both countries, this implies a change in emissions which in turn induces additional capital migration and so on. As before, the process is assumed to be stable, so that *a harmonization of environmental policies reverses the direction of the movement of the mobile factor that would otherwise occur when barriers to international capital flows are lowered* (Proposition 6).

If the environmental policies were optimal in the initial situation, the welfare effects are negative for both countries. Applying restrictive standards to countries well endowed with environmental resources reduces the productivity of other factors of production and results in income losses that are only partly compensated for by improvements in environmental quality. On the other hand, the application of lower standards to countries in which the environment is a scarce resource reduces the environmental quality substantially and causes welfare losses, since the increase in income is not sufficient to compensate people for the deterioration of environmental quality.

There may be some changes in transfrontier pollution spillovers that have positive welfare effects. The capital-rich country benefits from the reduction of emissions in the other country. But, in general, there is no reason to level the playing field by harmonizing environmental regulations. On the contrary, harmonization reduces the potential welfare gains from the international division of labour and is, therefore, not desirable from an economic point of view.

However, given the substantial externalities caused by transfrontier pollution and by the terms-of-trade and rate-of-return effects of national environmental policies, markets may not always function in an optimal manner and some form of international cooperation may be desirable. It is not always clear how the desirable type of cooperation can be achieved in practice (see Mäler, 1990). In particular, the incentives to over-report the costs of pollution and pollution abatement in combination with the national sovereignty of environmental legislation create problems that are difficult to tackle. This area will demand a substantial amount of effort in the future, both in practical policy-making and in theoretical economics.

9.6 European integration and the environment

The basic results derived from the above analysis have been summarized in

Propositions 1 to 6. In a situation in which environmental legalisation is not adjusted, economic integration leads to increased specialization. Capital-rich countries will reduce their emissions and there will be an increase in emissions by capital-poor countries. If there are adjustments of environmental policies as a response to the new economic situation, matters may be quite different. In the case of socially optimal environmental policies, reductions in emissions by all member countries are possible. If there is direct competition for the mobile factor of production, there may be a convergence of environmental policies. Third-country effects are in general ambiguous.

It is not an easy task to apply the results derived from a simple two-by-two model to the real world in which there are many countries and many factors of production, among them a large variety of pollutants.[12] One difficulty is the quantification of environmental scarcity and of the restrictiveness of national environmental policies. Prices are ideal measures of scarcity. However, most countries do not yet price the utilization of environmental resources. Besides that, there is an aggregation problem. Environmental quality is affected by many types of pollutants and, therefore, it appears to be impossible to construct a one-dimensional measure of environmental scarcity as assumed above.

There are also particular problems with the former centrally-planned economies. The above analysis is based on the assumption that firms are competitive and prices reflect scarcities. This is an heroic assumption to make even in the case of market economies, and certainly makes less sense for the former centrally-planned economies of Eastern Europe where state-owned monopolistic firms have dominated the supply side for decades. Another problem is the discrepancy between the actual levels of emissions allowed and the legislated emission standards in these countries which, on paper, are among the most restrictive in the world.[13] Some of the standards allowed have been labelled 'absurdly low' (Hughes, 1991). Due to this discrepancy, one is left with the question of how restrictive the environmental policies actually are and, more important, how restrictive they will be in the future. Will the standards be maintained and enforced or will the regulation of the utilization of environmental resources become less restrictive? As long as this question remains unanswered, it is impossible to decide what the degree of environmental scarcity will be in these countries.

Nevertheless, some speculations on future environmental policies are possible. Certain reflections may be drawn from examining the factors that determine environmental policies. Three factors stand out in this context: physical abundance of environmental resources, level of development, and preferences. Everything else being equal, a country is well endowed with environmental resources if its assimilative capacity is large. One proxy of that capacity is population density, but there are also other variables influencing the assimilative capacity of a country's natural environment. According to these measures, the Scandinavian countries, the Soviet

Union, Turkey, Spain, and Ireland are physically well-endowed with environmental resources.

Secondly, the level of economic development, as proxied by per capita income, is an important variable determining the demand for environmental quality. If income is relatively high, then the marginal utility of consumption is small compared to the marginal utility derived from environmental quality. Thus, high-income countries like Norway, Sweden, Denmark, Germany and Switzerland will, *ceteris paribus*, have a high demand for environmental quality. People in poorer countries such as the former centrally planned economies, Turkey, Greece and Portugal will demand lower levels of environmental quality.[14]

Preferences or emotional variables such as the concern for environmental issues are impossible to measure, but it can be argued that people in Scandinavia, Switzerland, Germany and The Netherlands are particularly concerned about the environment.

If it is true that Southern and Eastern Europe are well endowed with environmental factors of production, then one should expect mobile capital to move into these areas when barriers to trade are removed. Everything else being equal, emissions will be increased in these areas whereas the rest of Europe should reduce its emissions.

The effects of integration on transfrontier pollution are less clear. As far as air pollution is concerned, the results depend on whether Great Britain is well-endowed with environmental resources or not. If it is, then the situation could become worse for Central Europe and Scandinavia since the predominant wind direction in Europe is from west to east. One should also expect increasing transfrontier air pollution problems in the Soviet Union. As far as water pollution is concerned, the problems in the Mediterranean and Baltic seas may be aggravated.

Some caveats are, however, necessary. In the former centrally planned economies, the integration effects will be accompanied by effects of price changes and structural changes caused by the introduction of the market (Hughes, 1991). The removal of subsidies on energy utilization should have effects similar to those of the oil-price shocks on the market economies in the 1970s/early 1980s (an effect not considered in the above analysis). Moreover, increased monitoring and enforcement of environmental legislation can be expected to improve the situation in these countries.

As has been argued in Section 9.2 of this chapter, there will be additional welfare effects if the prevailing laws are not sufficient to internalize all the externalities that are caused by emissions and pollution. In this case, the removal of trade barriers will improve the environmental situation in countries that are poorly endowed with environmental resources. This would imply that there would be welfare gains for Central and Western Europe, while Southern and Eastern Europe would experience welfare losses (with the 'everything-else-being-equal' qualification again in place). Improvements in the enforcement of regulations and the structural changes induced by the introduction of the market economy are likely to dominate the negative effects of integration.

In the longer term, legislation is more flexible and can be adjusted to the economic situation prevailing after the process of integration. In the theoretical part of the chapter, two scenarios have been analysed. The first model, assuming a benevolent government that acts in the interests of the people, is not as realistic as the second approach which assumes governments adjust environmental standards as part of their competition for mobile capital. When barriers to trade and factor mobility are reduced, the capital-poor countries will find it easier to attract the foreign capital they need. Thus the capital-rich countries will be confronted with an increasing outflow of capital. To the extent that they respond by relaxing environmental standards, there will be some convergence of environmental policies in the integrating area.

What does this expected endogenous change to environmental policies imply for Europe? Everything else being equal, emissions will tend to increase in the north, the west and in the centre, whereas in the south and the east they should tend to be reduced by integration with instead of without endogenous environmental policy changes. This will reverse the transfrontier pollution effects discussed earlier. With the west being the predominant wind direction, air pollution problems in Europe are likely to be aggravated while there may be improvements for the Mediterranean countries. As far as the terms-of-trade and rate-of-return effects are concerned, this endogenous policy scenario implies that both groups of countries increase the scarcity of the factors with which they are relatively well endowed. These forces point in opposite directions and the combined effect is, hence, ambiguous. Again, the *ceteris-paribus* qualification plays an important rôle.

It may be, however, what the developments described here will be overridden by a general development towards increasingly restrictive environmental regulations. This would mean that the prices of pollution-intensive goods will rise in all countries. This would be beneficial for countries specializing in the production of these goods, i.e. the capital-poor countries of the periphery.

The implications for non-member countries are difficult to assess. Some non-member countries have already been mentioned (e.g. Norway and Sweden). They will be affected in particular by changes in transfrontier pollution externalities. As far as the global pollution effects of European integration are concerned (for example, carbon and chlorofluorocarbon gases), the results are ambiguous. In most of the scenarios, there are some member countries which will reduce their emissions and others which tend to increase them. Moreover, there are associated rate-of-return and terms-of-trade effects. If the capital-rich countries relax their environmental regulation, their capital-poor, non-member trading partners will tend to experience welfare losses due to the deterioration of their terms of trade or an increase in the rate of interest. But this is not an unambiguous result. Welfare gains by non-member countries are also possible.

9.7   Summary and conclusions

The analysis of interdependence of economic integration and environmental policies has left open several ambiguities and unanswered questions. In the models examined, the welfare effects on member and non-member countries have been shown to be indeterminate.

The findings concerning factor allocation are less ambiguous. In the short- to medium-term when the national environmental regulations are taken as given, the countries relatively well endowed with environmental resources tend to increase their emissions whereas emissions are reduced in other countries. This is due to increased specialization after the removal of trade barriers. In the longer term, regulations are adjusted to the changes in the economic environment, but competition which would lead to unacceptably low levels of environmental regulation is unlikely. This result can be established both for a conventional welfare-maximizing model and for a model in which international competition for mobile capital is allowed. In the first case, it can be shown that at least one country chooses a more-restrictive policy after integration. In the other case, a convergence of environmental policies is likely.

Applying these results to the European situation, if it is true that Eastern Europe and the Mediterranean countries are relatively well-endowed with environmental resources, then these countries are likely to specialize in pollution-intensive goods. Everything else being equal, this may cause additional problems for the Mediterranean and the Baltic Sea. If industries that primarily pollute the air also move to the south and the east, some of the transfrontier pollution problems like acid rain may be mitigated in Western Europe, whereas the Soviet Union will likely bear the burden in the shape of increased acidification. But everything is not equal, and other changes such as a drastic tightening of acceptable domestic pollution standards in the former centrally planned economies may dominate these developments. In the other scenario, in which national environmental policies are more flexible, a convergence of environmental legislation is likely and this may reverse the effects of increased specialization.

The effects on non-member countries have been shown to be ambiguous. Some European countries will be affected predominantly by changes in transfrontier pollution whereas non-European countries will experience welfare gains or losses mainly from changes in the rates of return on capital or in their terms of trade. The impact of European economic integration on global pollution is also indeterminate.

Notes

I wish to thank Kym Anderson, John Black, Richard Blackhurst and Patrick Messerlin for their valuable comments on an earlier version of this paper. The usual disclaimer applies.

1. For a more detailed analysis of the importance of ecologically motivated product norms in the European Community, see Folmer and Howe (1991).
2. This means that there is a capital-intensive pollution abatement technology which is not modelled explicitly.
3. In a model incorporating trade in final goods, the basic results concerning the environmental impact of economic integration would be the same. Only the mechanisms of transmission would change. In such a model, a reduction of barriers to trade affects the world market prices of final goods which leads to an intersectoral relocation of the factors of production inside each country. If there is factor mobility, a reduction of the barriers to (factor) trade affects the remuneration of the mobile factors of production and this causes international factor migration.
4. This part of the paper draws on Rauscher (1991c).
5. In a three-country model, however, in which one of the countries does not participate in the process of integration, there may be welfare losses (see Rauscher, 1991c). Note that the efficiency gain can be redistributed by lump-sum payments in such a way that every country gains.
6. The underlying assumption is that the substitution possibilities between capital and emissions are limited or, more formally, the elasticity of substitution is finite.
7. The same results are obtained if there is trade in final commodities instead of international factor mobility. See Rauscher (1991a).
8. Markusen (1975) has identified two additional components of an optimal emission tax in an open economy. This is due to his assumption that the other country is expected to keep its emission tax instead of its emission level constant. Thus the conjectures as to what kind of policy instrument the other country uses affect the optimality conditions and the location of the Nash equilibrium (Rauscher, 1991a). A similar result has been derived by Wildasin (1988) in a model in which the mobile factor of production is taxed. For the importance of conjectural variations in environmental economics see Cornes and Sandler (1985).
9. The general model with international external effects is discussed in Rauscher (1991b).
10. This ambiguity is a standard property of general-equilibrium models of customs unions. As an example, see Lloyd (1982). Matters are much simpler in a partial-equilibrium framework in which trade creation and trade diversion effects are discussed. The results may, however, be misleading, since the interdependencies between markets are neglected.
11. For a detailed analysis of the impact of lobbying in an open economy, see Chapter 10 of this volume by Hillman and Ursprung.
12. It is known that some results of the simple Heckscher–Ohlin model can be generalised to k-country, n-factor models, but generally these results hold only 'on average' (Ethier, 1984).
13. These deviations of what is from what should be are due to monitoring and enforcement problems (Hughes, 1991).
14. Walter and Ugelow (1979), for instance, show that the restrictiveness of

national environmental policies is positively correlated with a country's state of development and per-capita income. On a household level, 'willingness-to-pay' studies support the hypothesis that the demand for environmental quality has a high positive income elasticity.

References

Anderson, K. (1991), 'Europe 1992 and the Western Pacific Economies', *Economic Journal* **101** (forthcoming November).

Baumol, W. J. (1971), *Environmental Protection, International Spillovers, and Trade*, Stockholm: Almqvist and Wiksell.

Cecchini, P. (1988), *The European Challenge 1992: The Benefits of a Single Market*, Aldershot: Wildwood House.

Cornes, R. and T. Sandler (1985), 'Externalities, Expectations, and Pigouvian Taxes', *Journal of Environmental Economics and Management* **12**: 1–13.

Ethier, W. J. (1984), 'Higher Dimensional Issues in Trade Theory', pp. 131–184 in *Handbook of International Economics*, edited by R. W. Jones and P. B. Kenen, Amsterdam: North-Holland.

Folmer, H., and C. W. Howe (1991), 'Environmental Problems and Policy in the Single European Market', *Environmental and Resource Economics* **1**: 17–41.

Hughes, G. (1991), 'Are the Costs of Cleaning up Eastern Europe Exaggerated?' Discussion Paper No. 482, Centre for Economic Policy Research, London.

Jacquemin, A. and A. Sapir (1988), 'International Trade and Integration of the European Community: An Econometric Analysis', *European Economic Review* **32**: 1439–49.

Johnson, H. G. (1953/4), 'Optimum Tariffs and Retaliation', *Review of Economic Studies* **21**: 142–53.

Kemp, M. C. and R. W. Jones (1962), 'Variable Labor Supply and the Theory of International Trade', *Journal of Political Economy* **70**: 30–36.

Krutilla, K. (1991), 'Environmental Regulation in an Open Economy', *Journal of Environmental Economics and Management* **10**: 127–142.

Lloyd, P. J. (1982), '3 × 3 Theory of Customs Unions', *Journal of International Economics* **12**: 41–63.

Mäler, K.-G. (1990), 'International Environmental Problems', *Oxford Review of Economic Policy* **6**: 80–108.

Markusen, J. R. (1975), 'International Externalities and Optimal Tax Structures', *Journal of International Economics* **5**: 15–29.

Merrifield, J. D. (1988), 'The Impact of Abatement Strategies in Transnational Pollution, the Terms of Trade, and Factor Rewards: A General Equilibrium Approach', *Journal of Environmental Economics and Management* **15**: 259–84.

Pethig, R. (1976), 'Pollution, Welfare and Environmental Policy in the Theory of Comparative Advantage', *Journal of Environmental Economics and Management* **2**:160–69.

Rauscher, M. (1991a), 'Foreign Trade and the Environment', in *Environmental Scarcity: The International Dimension*, edited by H. Siebert, Tübingen: Mohr.

Rauscher, M. (1991b), 'National Environmental Policies and the Effects of Economic Integration', *European Journal of Political Economy* (forthcoming).

Rauscher, M., (1991c), 'Economic Integration and the Environment: Effects on Members and Non-members', *Environmental and Resource Economics* **1** (forthcoming).

Siebert, H. (1977), 'Environmental Quality and the Gains from Trade', *Kyklos* **30**: 657–73.

Siebert, H., J. Eichberger, W. Gronych and R. Pethig (1980), *Trade and the Environment: A Theoretical Inquiry*, Amsterdam: North-Holland.
Walter, I. and J. L. Ugelow (1979), 'Environmental Policies in Developing Countries', *Ambio* **8**: 102–09.
Wildasin, D. A. (1988), 'Nash Equilibria in Fiscal Competition', *Journal of Public Economics* **35**: 229–40.
Winters, L. A. (1991), 'International Trade and '1992': An Overview', *European Economic Review* **35**: 367–77.

PART 4

The political economy of interactions between environmental and trade policies

10

The influence of environmental concerns on the political determination of trade policy

Arye L. Hillman and Heinrich W. Ursprung

The purpose of this chapter is to investigate how environmental interests might influence the determination of international trade policy when production or consumption of an industry's product has an adverse environmental impact. At the onset, we wish to make clear that our analysis is positive, not normative. The theory of international trade (see, for example, the survey by Ethier, 1987) contains both normative and positive propositions. The normative propositions are proscriptive in relating to what 'ought to be', and underlie the recommendations that might be made to governments concerning the desirable conduct of trade policy. The positive propositions, on the other hand, attempt to explain why observed policies are implemented. The positive propositions are the basis for prediction about actual (as opposed to recommended) behaviour. There are no elements of judgement associated with positive propositions; that is, no evaluation is intended regarding whether outcomes are 'good' and 'bad'. If a policy choice is predicted, there is in particular no associated inference that such a policy is desirable and 'should' be adopted. The positive theory proposes that under specified circumstances particular policies will arise. Trade policies are thereby endogenously explained in a political-economy framework as the consequence of particular conjunctions of objectives, incentives, and circumstances. It is within this positive framework for economic analysis that we consider how the emergence of environmental interest groups might influence international trade policy.[1]

As a preliminary question, one may well ask why trade policy should be used as an instrument of intervention to achieve environmental objectives, since it is well-known from the theory of economic externalities that the first-best normatively desirable policy solutions for achieving Pareto-efficiency in the presence of adverse environmental impacts take the form of Pigovian tax-subsidy interventions, or are facilitated by property-rights assignment and Coase-type transactions. Normative questions of policy rankings and issues of first-best policy choice are addressed in Chapters 2 to 4 in this volume by Anderson, Lloyd and Snape; Anderson in particular considers the use of trade policies in conjunction with more efficient instruments directed at environmental problems. Our focus on trade policies as the sole instruments of intervention places policy choice in at least a second-best world.

From our positive perspective, if suffices to observe, as has been noted by Siebert (1974), Blackhurst (1977), and other subsequent authors, that international trade policy has environmental consequences; hence, if environmental interest groups are cognizant of the links between trade and the environment, they will seek to influence international trade policy accordingly. The question that is then raised is: what are the consequences for the determination of trade policy of the exercise of political influence by environmentally-conscious interest groups? Consideration of possible answers requires as a prerequisite a specification of the mechanism that underlies policy choice.

10.1 Institutional mechanisms for policy choice

Two basic institutional mechanisms for policy choice are direct and representative democracy. Under direct democracy, voters directly choose a policy via a specified rule, such as majority voting. If majority voting is used, the median voter then determines the policy outcome. In this direct-democracy setting, governments and politicians exercise no policy discretion, and there is no role for political influence, since voters directly determine without political intermediation the outcome that they want – or, more precisely, the policy chosen is that in accord with the median voter's preferences.[2]

Under conditions of direct democracy, voters would thus directly dictate environmental policy. A whole range of feasible policy instruments, including in particular the instrument yielding the Pareto-efficient first-best outcome, could be presented as the object of voters' choice. With property rights defined and appropriate compensation payments feasible, the implementation of the first-best policy could be assured.

In practice, however, democracies tend to be of the *representative* rather than direct type. That is, voters elect politicians, who then in principle represent the interests of their constituents in taking policy positions. However, in practice, a principal-agent problem arises under representative democracy because the voter may not be able to monitor and control the decisions of his agent, the representative. Indeed, the individual voter may be 'rationally ignorant' regarding the policy positions on various issues taken by representatives or by candidates for political office. Voters' rational ignorance arises because of the low expected benefit of an individual's acquiring information on politicians' policy positions on different issues. Since there are in general many issues and it is permissible in general to vote for but one candidate, the voter is furthermore obliged to choose among candidates on the basis of a 'bundle' of positions. This further diminishes the significance for voters of the position taken by a candidate on any one particular issue, and enhances policy discretion by politicians.

Prominently important under representative democracy are the campaign contributions and endorsements received by a candidate for political office.[3] By accepting political support, a candidate can enhance his 'appeal' to the electorate at large and thereby improve his likelihood of electoral success. We shall consequently portray optimizing candidates for political office as seeking to identify and as adopting policy positions that maximize political support.

Environmental interest groups who seek to influence trade policy positions taken by candidates will confront other interest groups with agendas of their own. Domestic industry interests will be seeking protectionist policies. Opposed to protection will be consumers at large, domestic exporting industries that fear retaliatory protectionist consequences abroad and, depending on whether they gain from the proposed regulation of international trade, also foreign producers who seek to maintain market access for their exports.[4] Environmentalists may have common cause with one interest group or another, depending on whether the environmentalists favor liberal or protectionists trade policies.

Not all interest groups can be expected to be equally politically effective or active, since individual members of different coalitions with an interest in the determination of policy confront different incentives to contribute towards influencing policy positions taken. The incentive to contribute (see Ursprung, 1990, for a detailed analysis) depends on a combination of (i) free-rider effects and (ii) the stakes in the policy outcome of a particular agent. Free-rider considerations enter because of the public-good nature of political contributions: a political contribution made in support of a protectionist (or liberal trade) position benefits all others who gain from such policies. Organizational characteristics also influence 'free-riding' behaviour. It is important to recognize though that, left to themselves to choose their individually optimal private contribution to public-good provision (here the influence on the policy outcome), agents do not necessarily choose to 'free-ride' in the sense of a zero contribution. Whether the Nash-equilibrium (independently chosen) contribution is zero or positive depends on the diversity of individuals' valuations of the public good and/or the stake that an individual has in the policy outcome.

Stakes are of course high for domestic producers who benefit from protection. Among the losers from protection, the stakes in the outcome of the trade-policy determination *with regard to any one industry* are low for individual consumers who spend low budget shares on an industry's output. With many exporting industries, the stakes are also low for exporting firms who stand to lose from foreign protectionist retaliation. A quest to locate the highest individual stakes among supporters of a liberal trade policy for a domestic industry leads to producers abroad in the same industry who lose market access as the consequence of domestic protectionist policies. However, the foreign producers (and their domestic distributional agents) have allies in their support for liberal trade policies in domestic consumers and domestic exporting industries.

With interest groups seeking to influence trade policy, candidates may be expected to respond by choosing policy positions to maximise their probabilities of election. The equilibrium probabilities of election reflect political support that derives from policy positions taken, and determine in turn the probabilities of designated policies being implemented (on the supposition that a candidate if politically successful keeps the campaign promises made to his political contributors). We shall show how the appearance of interest groups with environmental objectives influences the policy equilibrium that emerges from such political competition under representative democracy.

The consequences depend upon environmentalists' objectives. As a summary device for identification of objectives, we distinguish between environmentalists who are 'greens' and those who are 'supergreens'. The term 'greens' will be used to designate environmentalists whose concerns are limited to their own country; 'supergreens' will be used to refer to environmentalists concerned with adverse environmental impacts without regard for geographical location.

The supergreen position may be based on self-interest – the supergreen may be concerned with the effect of his or her welfare of the clearing of foreign rainforests because of the implications for photosynthesisation. Or the supergreen position may be motivated by an aesthetic or altruist (or paternalistic) concern regarding environmental consequences of production and consumption activities abroad. In either case, supergreens are indifferent as to whether an adverse environmental impact occurs in their home country or abroad, while the more narrowly focused greens are concerned only with environmental consequences at home. Clearly, the type of environmental impact dictates whether there is any point to being merely a green; for concerns about global warming and ozone layer depletion, rational environmentalists can but be supergreens.

10.2 Formalization of policy determination

To evaluate how the presence of environmental interest groups ('greens' or 'supergreens') affects the international trade policy adopted towards an industry, we require a formalization of the process of policy determination. The formalization which we adopt, although specified to portray the essential characteristics of political competition under representative democracy, is more generally appropriate in its implications to any circumstances where policy determination is subject to the political influence of gainers an losers from particular policies. Our precise conception of the policy-determination process is that of two opposing candidates for political office, who make trade-policy pronouncements on the issue of protection for an industry with the objective of maximizing their relative shares of campaign contributions received as a consequence of the stands taken. To differentiate themselves, one candidate adopts a liberal trade-policy stance, the other a protectionist position. The former candidate seeks a policy position that maximizes relative political support expressed as $\theta = L^*/(L^* + L)$, and the latter candidate a policy position that maximizes $(1 - \theta) = L/(L^* + L)$, where L^* and L are total campaign contributions that are made in support of liberal and protectionist policies, respectively.

We proceed in two stages to evaluate policy equilibria. In the initial stage, the environmental interest group will be absent. Then we subsequently investigate how the introduction of an environmental interest group, labelled as 'greens' or as 'supergreens', affects the probabilities that different policies emerge.

With environmentalists absent, we restrict ourselves to portrayal of active political participation by those agents with the highest stakes in the policy outcome for a particular industry: the industry interests at home who seek protection and the industry interests abroad who seek free market access for their exports. So only producer interests matter, and domestic and foreign producers are then the respective sources for the political contributions L and L^*. These contributions are composed of individual outlays, made independently by the individual producers.

We do not wish to impose the restrictive characterisation of the industry seeking protection as consisting of perfectly competitive producers. Nor do we wish to impose the restrictive characterization of monopoly. Accordingly, we shall consider an industry which, in each of two countries, is oligopolistic, with individual firms choosing their outputs in a Cournot–Nash manner. The industry in country 1 is composed of n firms, and in country 2 of m firms. These measures of n and m then respectively reflect the competitiveness of the domestic industry in each country: as n and m increase, each industry respectively approaches the competitive outcome.

The numbers of firms, n and m, are two parameters of our formalization of endogenous policy determination. A third and final parameter is the degree of substitutability in consumption between domestically produced and imported goods. In country 1, we posit the following demand functions for domestically produced and imported goods:

$$P = a - bs + \gamma P^* \tag{1}$$

$$P^* = a - bs^* + \gamma P \tag{2}$$

where γ (with values $0 \leqslant \gamma < 1$) is the measure of substitutability in domestic consumption between the goods produced by domestic firms and imported substitutes. P and P^* are the domestic prices of home-produced and imported goods, and s and s^* are respective domestic sales of domestic firms and foreign exporters. The domestic price of imports, P^*, is subject to influence by protectionist policies, which also then via substitutability in consumption affect the price P that domestic firms receive in their home market. The price changes in turn underlie changes in sales of domestically produced and imported goods.

The extent to which protection leads domestic sales to increase at the expense of domestic consumption of imports depends upon the value of the measure of substitutability γ. The extent to which domestically produced goods are substitutes in consumption for imports is evidently of importance in specification of the link between environmental consequences and trade policy. The more closely substitutable in consumption are domestically produced and imported goods, the greater the increase in domestic production due to protection of domestic producers and the lower the decline in domestic consumption.

As a measure of adverse domestic environmental impact, we introduce $Z = z(s + s^*)$ when domestic consumption (composed of sales of domestic output s and imports s^*) is the source of the adverse impact; and $Z \equiv z(s + x)$ when the source of the adverse impact is domestic production (allocated between domestic sales s and exports x).

The above demand functions apply with reverse symmetry to the trading partner, wherein there is an adverse environmental impact Z^*. 'Greens' in countries 1 and 2 are respectively concerned to minimize Z and Z^*, while 'supergreens' in each country are concerned to minimize the combined adverse environmental impacts $(Z + Z^*)$.

With environmentalists not politically active, political contributions derive only from producers, for whom environmental impacts are taken to be of no consequence. Producers confront uncertainty in making political contributions, since the contributions are made to influence candidates' election prospects before the outcome of political competition is known. With one political contest taking place in each of two countries, firms confront four states of the world: in each country, the outcome can be either electoral victory for a protectionist or liberal trade-policy candidate. Only after the trade policy regimes are known are producers obliged to make decisions regarding output and sales. The policies that derive from the political process of course affect sales and output decisions. In particular, trade policy abroad will determine the conditions of foreign market access for exports, if market access is at all available.

Let it be an import duty t that is the potential protectionist instrument. With a constant unit cost of production c, *profits from sales in country 1* are respectively, for domestic producers and foreign exporters,

$$\pi_i = (P - c)s_i - L_i \qquad\qquad i = 1, ..., n \qquad\qquad (3)$$

$$\pi_j^* = (P^* - c - t)s_j^* - L_j^* \qquad\qquad j = 1, ..., m \qquad\qquad (4)$$

where, as we have indicated, political contributions L_i and L_j^* are chosen *ex-ante* (before the outcome of political competition, and hence before policies are known) and sales s_i and s_j^* are chosen *ex-post*.

Establishing Nash equilibrium profit-maximizing values of sales s_i and s_j^* permit firms' profit functions to be re-expressed as

$$\pi_i = [b(1 - \gamma^2)A^2]^{-1}\{[m(1 - \gamma) + 1]B + (1 - \gamma^2)\gamma mt\}^2 \qquad (3')$$

$$\pi_j^* = [b(1 - \gamma^2)A^2]^{-1}\{[n(1 - \gamma) + 1]B - (n + 1)(1 - \gamma^2)t\}^2 \qquad (4')$$

where $A \equiv (n + 1)(m + 1) - mn\gamma^2 > 0$ and $B \equiv (1 + \gamma)[a - c(1 - \gamma)] > 0$.

In the form given by (3') and (4'), profits are revealed to depend upon the level of the import duty that is endogenously determined by political competition for given exogenous values of n and m (respectively reflecting home and foreign competitiveness) and γ (reflecting the degree of substitutability in consumption between domestically produced and imported goods). As depicted in Figure 10.1, firms' profits from sales in country 1's home market are convex functions of the level of the import duty – profits of course increase with protection for domestic firms and decline for foreign exporters (up to the level of import duty t_a, at which imports are altogether excluded from the domestic market; where t_a is the Nash-equilibrium autarkic duty).

Under these circumstances, in a two-candidate contest, the Nash equilibrium outcome is that each candidate announces one of the polar policies in Figure 10.1: the liberal trade-policy candidate maximizes his share of

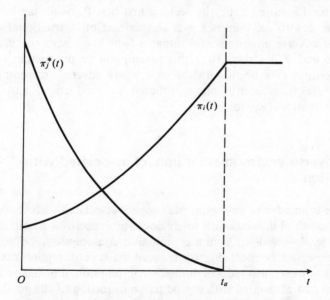

Figure 10.1 Profits of domestic and foreign firms as functions of the level of the home country's import duty

political contributions by announcing free trade and the protectionist candidate maximizes his share of political contributions by announcing complete prohibition of market access (the duty t_a). The equilibrium is thus not a Hotelling-type policy outcome where both candidates occupy the middle (moderate) ground back-to-back, but rather there is maximal divergence of policy positions.[5] It is evident from Figure 10.1 that each candidate's constituency is concentrated at the polar ends of the policy spectrum. The equilibrium policies reflect this concentration. A more formal proof of this result of policy divergence that arises when an import duty is the instrument of trade intervention is provided in our 1988 paper.

The candidates are driven in their policy decisions by the economic benefits which their policies confer on their producer constituencies. Producers choose political contributions to maximize expected profits, given for domestic producers and foreign exporters respectively by

$$E\pi_i = \theta\pi_i(t_o) + (1 - \theta)\pi_i(t_1) - L_i \qquad i = 1 \dots n \qquad (5)$$

$$E\pi_j^* = \theta\pi_j^*(t_o) + (1 - \theta)\pi_j^*(t_1) - L_j^* \qquad j = 1 \dots m. \qquad (6)$$

Equilibrium choice of political contributions yields the condition

$$\theta = (1 + \Delta\pi_i/\Delta\pi_j^*)^{-1} \qquad (7)$$

where $\Delta\pi_i$ and $\Delta\pi_j^*$ are producers' stakes in political success for the candidate with the preferred policy, relative to his opponent.

With this equilibrium as our frame of reference, we now proceed to introduce politically active environmental interests. Environmentalists here do not pursue Pareto-efficiency by seeking first-best Pigovian tax-subsidy policies, but seek to use influence over the conduct of international trade to minimise adverse environmental impacts (which we have specified in terms of Z and Z^*) associated with consumption or production of an industry's output. We begin with the case where adverse environmental impacts derive from consumption, proceed to production, and then consider international spillovers.

10.3   Adverse environmental impact associated with consumption

When there is an adverse environmental impact associated with consumption, environmental interests with solely domestic concerns – by our designation, 'greens' – seek to minimize domestic consumption. Of course, consumption could be most directly reduced via a consumption tax. An import duty however also reduces domestic consumption, albeit at an additional social cost associated with a production distortion (if the good – or a close enough substitute – is domestically produced, as we have taken to be the case).

To establish values for domestic consumption, we observe that sales of home produced goods and imports are respectively

$$s_i = \{[m(1 - \gamma) + 1]B + [\gamma(1 - \gamma^2)m]t\}(bA)^{-1} \tag{8}$$

$$s_j^* = \{[n(1 - \gamma) + 1]B - [(1 - \gamma^2)(n + 1)]t\}(bA)^{-1}. \tag{9}$$

An increase in the protective duty increases total sales of domestically produced output in accord with

$$n \cdot ds_i/dt = n\gamma(1 - \gamma^2)m(bA)^{-1} > 0 \tag{10}$$

and reduce total domestic sales of imports in accord with

$$m \cdot ds_j^*/dt = -m(1 - \gamma^2)(n + 1)(bA)^{-1} < 0 \tag{11}$$

From (10) and (11), the condition for total domestic consumption to decline as the consequence of a marginal increase in protection is $\gamma < (n + 1)/n$. Since γ cannot exceed unity, this latter condition is necessarily satisfied – although the higher is γ, the less domestic consumption declines in response to an increase in the protective duty, reflecting the greater substitutability in domestic consumption between domestically produced goods and imports. The greens would of course wish substitutability to be low, so that domestic consumers discouraged from consumption by the higher price of imports are less inclined to purchase domestically produced goods as substitutes. But, without regard for whether γ is high or low, the greens are here unambivalently protectionist, and would support a candidate espousing a protectionist policy platform.

We shall present two alternative portrayals of the political activity of the greens. In the first, the greens are viewed as having a given sum to allocate to the protectionist candidate; in the second, the greens are viewed as making political allocations to maximize their expected utility, or in effect to minimize expected disutility associated with adverse environmental impacts.

10.3.1 *Fixed political outlays by the greens*

If the greens have a fixed sum L^g, to outlay in quest of political influence, the protectionist candidate's probability of electoral success is amended to $(1 - \theta) = (L + L^g)/(L + L^* + L^g)$. The greens' political expenditure is, from the perspective of domestic producers seeking a protectionist policy, a transfer made in the form of a contribution to provision of a service yielding collective benefit. This benefit is enhancement of the prospects of electoral success of the protectionist candidate. If the greens and domestic producers continue to behave independently (i.e., adopt Nash behaviour) in choice of campaign contributions, the following possibilities arise:

(i) If the political contribution of the greens is less than that originally made individually by domestic producers, the latter reduce their campaign contributions correspondingly, leaving unchanged the total contributions received by the protectionist candidate. However, the greens and domestic producers are now contributing together in support of the same candidate. Since the greens have but replaced a component of preexisting contributions made in support of a protectionist outcome, the political equilibrium remains unchanged. Domestic producers have however benefited from the public-good transfer made by the greens, and domestic producers' profits increase by the amount of the political expenditures made by the greens.

(ii) Should the political contributions of the greens *exceed* the original political contributions of domestic producers, the latter cease to make political contributions; for given the greens' political contribution, the marginal benefit of an additional contribution by a domestic producer is zero. The greens thereby entirely displace domestic producers as the source of political contributions for the protectionist candidate. The probability of electoral success of the protectionist candidate will have increased since the greens are contributing more than domestic producers in aggregate did in their absence. The gain to domestic producers from the greens' political activity is thus two-fold. Profit are increased by the value of previous political outlays, and also expected profits are greater by virtue of the higher probability of electoral success of the protectionist candidate. Insofar as the greens undertake all the pro-protectionist political activity, they can be viewed as having been 'captured' by domestic producer protectionist interests.

(iii) If the greens' political outlay exceeds the stake in the policy outcome of free-trade interests, the latter cease political contributions – as would then also domestic producer interests if they were making positive political outlays – and in that event only the protectionist candidate receives campaign contributions, leaving the free-trade candidate with no source of political support and no motive to take a position.

(iv) If the domestic or foreign industries are sufficiently competitive, the entry of the greens into political activity with a given sum to be allocated to the protectionist candidate must have some effect; for as industries become more competitive, individual firms' stakes in the policy outcome decline, thereby enhancing the effectiveness of any political outlay of given value made by the greens.

These above consequences of greens' political activity are based on Nash (or independent) behaviour by greens and producers. The protectionist bias of the greens' political activity is reinforced if domestic producers adopt non-Nash behaviour, and reduce their political contributions by less than the perceived transfer provided by the greens' political contribution. We have also supposed that political contributions made by the greens have the same effectiveness as contributions made by domestic protectionist interests; however, because of the self-interest connotations of the political outlays made by producers, a dollar (or franc or mark) contributed by the greens may be more politically effective than the same contribution made by domestic producers. In that case, domestic producers have an interest in channelling their campaign contributions through the greens. Who in these circumstances has been captured by whom becomes a matter of interpretation.

10.3.2 *Expected disutility*

Rather than having at their disposal a *fixed* sum to allocate to a protectionist candidate, the greens may be alternatively viewed as choosing a political allocation to minimize the expected disutility associated with an adverse environmental impact. With t_0 and t_1 once more representing the policy pronouncements of the liberal and protectionist candidates, the greens' expected disutility associated with trade-policy outcomes is

$$EU = \theta \lambda z s(t_0) + (1 - \theta) \gamma z s(t_1) - L^g \qquad (12)$$

where λ facilitates expression in disutility terms. The greens' stake in the policy outcome (the difference in disutility associated with the realization of protection and free trade) now determines how environmental concerns influence political competition. If the greens' stake in securing a protectionist outcome is less than that of a domestic producer, the greens refrain from making political contributions; and conversely, with the relative magnitudes of stakes reversed, domestic producers refrain from making political contributions. That is, because of the properties of Nash-equilibrium contributions towards provision of a public good, beneficiaries 'free-ride' if contributions by others surpass the contribution that they would independently have made in the absence of the public-good transfer. 'Capture' implications are as before: if the greens have the higher stake, they undertake the pro-protectionist activity, on behalf of and to the advantage of domestic protectionist interests. And in the event of non-Nash behaviour and superior political effectiveness of greens' contributions, domestic producers again have an interest in contributing to the political campaign funds of the greens rather than directly to protectionist candidates.

The benefits of the political alliance (implicit or otherwise) between the greens and domestic producers are enhanced to the potential advantage of both, the less competitive is the domestic industry (the smaller is n). The benefit to producers from higher concentration is the increased profits when protection eliminates the market access of competitive imports (which depends on the value of γ). Producers also benefit more, the more concentrated is the domestic industry, the greater the decline in domestic consumption due to elimination of import competition, and hence the more favorable the outcome to the greens. Ideally, from the vantage of their objectives, the greens would wish to see production undertaken by a protected monopolist.

10.3.3 Supergreens

Environmentalists with global concerns – 'supergreens' in our terminology – wish to minimize consumption, independently of the geographical location of the consumption activity. This is achieved by eliminating all international trade in the offending good. For imports in each country are then no longer available for domestic consumption, while the elimination of import competition permits domestic producers to exercise their domestic market power.

Supergreens are thus also unambivalently protectionist and would support protectionist candidates.

10.3.4 International consensus

The greens in different national jurisdictions confront no conflict of interest in supporting protectionist policies in each jurisdiction. An international convention of greens – even if not supergreens – would reach consensus on the need to make political contributions to protectionist candidates only in all political contests. We shall see, however, that matters are more complex when the source of the adverse environmental impact is production rather than consumption. For then the greens in different jurisdictions may confront a Prisoners' Dilemma (or coordination problem) in choice of which policy to support, or it may not be possible for greens in different jurisdictions to achieve consensus on preferred trade policies.

10.4 Adverse environmental impact associated with production

We consider now the case where production is the source of the adverse environmental impact. Four levels of domestic production can be distinguished, contingent on the trade policies that can emerge from the political equilibrium at home and abroad. There are thus four associated values of adverse environmental impact in each economy. These values are established as follows.

(i) With free trade at home and protection abroad, the domestic industry is deprived of the opportunity to make foreign sales and confronts import competition in its home market. The adverse environmental impact of production, which is specified as linearly related to output, can then be established to be $\alpha \equiv zn[m(1 - \gamma) + 1]B/bA$ where A and B are as previously defined.

(ii) If the foreign market is now opened up to domestic producers, via a change in foreign trade policy from protectionism to free trade, domestic output – by symmetry – doubles and the adverse environmental impact of production is 2α.

(iii) If foreigners are denied market access by a change in country 1 from free trade to protection, domestic output increases because of the protective effect to yield an adverse environmental impact of $(2\alpha + \beta)$, where β can be explicitly derived as given by $zmn\gamma[n(1 - \gamma) + 1]/(n + 1)bA$. Observe that if $\gamma = 0$, then $\beta = 0$; that is, if there is no substitution in domestic consumption between domestically produced output and imports, the protective effect on domestic output of eliminating import competition is zero.

(iv) Finally, if both economies adopt protectionist policies, the domestic industry loses its foreign sales. So the adverse environmental impact declines by α, to $(\alpha + \beta)$.

When the adverse environmental impact was due to consumption, the greens cared only about minimizing domestic consumption, which was achieved by protection independently of whether foreigners adopted free-trade or protectionist policies. Now, however, as depicted in Table 10.1, the adverse environmental impact associated with production depends upon the combination of trade policies at home and abroad.

10.4.1 *The Nash equilibrium*

Suppose that the greens in each country independently decide which trade policy regime to support. Table 10.1 reveals that the Nash equilibrium is support for free-trade policies by each country's greens. If country 2 chooses free-trade, the adverse environmental impact is minimized in

Table 10.1 Environmental impact of production under alternative trade policy scenarios influenced by 'greens'

		Country 2	
		Free Trade	Protection
Country 1	Free Trade	$2\alpha, 2\alpha^*$	$\alpha, 2\alpha^* + \beta^*$
	Protection	$2\alpha + \beta, \alpha^*$	$\alpha + \beta, \alpha^* + \beta^*$

country 1 by a free-trade outcome (since $2\alpha < 2\alpha + \beta$); and if country 2 alternatively chooses protection, free trade is again the best response for country 1's greens (since $\alpha < (\alpha + b)$).

10.4.2 A Prisoners' Dilemma for the greens?

One is led to ask whether an outcome with mutual protectionist policies might not be superior for both countries' greens to the Nash equilibrium of mutual free trade. Mutual protectionism yields adverse environmental impacts of $(\alpha + \beta)$ and $(\alpha^* + \beta^*)$, which is superior to mutual free trade for country 1 if $(\alpha + \beta) < 2\alpha$, i.e., if $\alpha > \beta$, and is correspondingly superior to mutual free trade for country 2 if $\alpha^* > \beta^*$. If the inequalities $\alpha > \beta$ and $\alpha^* > \beta^*$ obtain, the Nash equilibrium does not yield the mutually preferred outcome, and the greens in the two countries confront a Prisoners' Dilemma in their choice of which trade policy to support in the domestic political competition.

Observe that $\alpha > \beta$ implies that domestic output declines in country 1 (and correspondingly for $\alpha^* > \beta^*$ in country 2) in a move from mutual free trade to mutual protection: α reflects the decline in domestic production due to foreign protectionism, and β reflects the increase in domestic output due to domestic protection. A net decline in domestic output implies a net decline in adverse environmental impact, in accord with the objective of the greens.

To establish whether and under what circumstances a Prisoners' Dilemma might arise to confront greens in the two trading economies, we evaluate

$$\alpha - \beta = z\,[m(1-\gamma) + 1 - \gamma m(n+1)^{-1}(n(1-\gamma)+1)]\,nB/bA$$
$$= F(n,m,\gamma) \tag{13}$$

The expression in the second country for $F^*(n,m,\gamma)$ is symmetric. The functions $F(n,m,\gamma) = 0$ and $F^*(n,m,\gamma) = 0$ are depicted in Figure 10.2 for different values of γ. In Region 2, $\alpha > \beta$ and $\alpha^* > \beta^*$, and accordingly for combinations of n, m and γ in this region, greens confront a Prisoners' Dilemma in the choice of which trade policy to support.

Figure 10.2 demonstrates the roles of substitutability in consumption and market structures in giving rise to the Prisoners' Dilemma. Region 2 is larger, the smaller is γ; and for any value of γ, symmetric market structures (n approximately equal to m) give rise to outcomes in Region 2.

Outside of Region 2, the dominant strategy of one country's greens is support for free trade. In Region 1, country 1's greens can do no better than support free-trade policies, although country 2's greens prefer mutual protectionism. The converse is the case in Region 3.

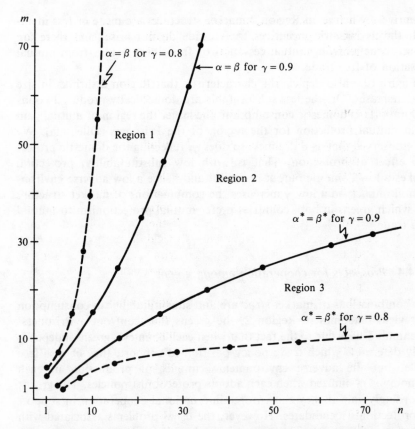

Figure 10.2 Determination of environmentalists' trade policy positions

10.4.3 *The source of the Dilemma: free-riding by greens*

Underlying the Prisoners' Dilemma are incentives for free-riding behaviour by each country's greens. Since domestic production is the source of the adverse environmental impact, greens are pleased to see imports replace domestically produced goods in domestic consumption. Free trade thus permits a country's greens to free-ride on foreign production; but by both supporting free-trade policies, the national greens in each country damage each other via this free-riding behaviour. It can be to the greens' mutual advantage to cease to free-ride on each other's production, and this is the case in Region 2.

In Region 1, country 2's industry is more competitive than that of country 1. Hence, under free trade, country 1's greens confront a more competitive import supply response than do country 2's greens. The asymmetries in market structure therefore give rise to asymmetries in free-riding incentives. When as in Region 2 market structures are more or less identical, the asymmetric incentives to free-ride do not arise, and there are shared benefits from mutual cessation of free-riding – i.e., from mutual cessation of free trade.

Figure 10.2 also depicts the characteristic that Region 2 shrinks in size as γ increases. Or, the less substitutable are domestically produced goods and imports in domestic consumption, the larger the region of mutual gain from mutual protection (or the region of the Prisoners' Dilemma). We have observed that as β declines, so does γ, reflecting the domestic protective effect of protection. That is, with low substitutability, protection evokes a low domestic output response, and hence a low adverse environmental impact; so a low γ increases the combinations of market structure for which greens in both countries prefer mutual protectionism to mutual free trade.

10.4.4   *Prospects for cooperation among greens*

For combinations of market structure and substitutability in consumption that yield outcomes in Region 2, the greens thus confront a Prisoners' Dilemma. This is due to the fact that when each country's greens independently determine which trade policy position to support, they choose free trade, but the adverse environmental impact of production in each economy is minimized when each adopts protectionist policies. The greens accordingly gain if they can enforce international cooperation in support of protectionist candidates. However, the usual problems associated with defection are present. The greens in each country have an incentive to defect from any agreement with their foreign colleagues since, from the perspective of a national group of greens, the best outcome remains that where the foreign country places protectionist barriers in the way of exports of their country's firms but their home firms continue to confront import competition. This most-preferred position of the greens is, of course, in direct conflict with the preferred combination of trade policy outcomes sought by domestic producers in the greens' home economy: the greens wish their domestic producers to be excluded from markets abroad but to be subject to competition at home.

There are particular difficulties which can be anticipated to impede cooperation among greens in different countries to avoid the Prisoners' Dilemma. Political contributions can, by their nature, be difficult to monitor, and the most that an interest group can do is attempt to influence the probabilistic political determination of policy. If subsequent to an international agreement of cooperation among greens to support protectionist candidates, the outcome in a political contest in a jurisdiction were nevertheless victory for the free-trade candidate or party, the greens in that country could still claim that they tried to secure political victory for the protectionists. But given the nature of the Prisoners' Dilemma, these greens would be quite content with the election outcome that resulted in success for the free-trade candidate. Given monitoring problems and imperfections in associating the outcomes of political contests with actions taken to influence the outcome, the greens would be required to be very principled to avoid the Prisoners' Dilemma, in particular if protectionist candidates abroad were to be consistently unsuccessful.

Outside of Region 2, where there is no Prisoners' Dilemma, there is no basis for consensus or cooperation regarding which trade policies to support. As we have observed, for combinations of market structure and substitutability in consumption in Region 1, the greens of country 1 prefer to provide political support in favour of a free-trade candidate, even if their brother (and sister) greens abroad can commit to supporting protectionism in their own country, with the converse the case in Region 3. Asymmetric benefits of 'free-riding' on the foreign industry's exports preclude potential gains from support for mutual protectionist policies.

10.4.5 Supergreens

Supergreens compute and compare global environmental outcomes when formulating a position on which trade policy to support in which country. Thus, they determine which policies to support by locating the minimum value in Table 10.2.

We can readily establish that $\alpha^* - \beta = 1 - \gamma/(n+1) > 0$. Hence α^* exceeds β and similarly α exceeds β^*, where in a change from mutual free trade to mutual protection, α^* represents the withdrawal of the foreign producers from the domestic market and β is as before the increase in production for domestic sales by domestic producers. Protected domestic producers accordingly increase output by less than the output withdrawn from the domestic market as a consequence of denial of market access to foreign producers.[6]

It follows from Table 10.2 that supergreens unambivalently support protectionist candidates in all political contests.

Table 10.2 Environmental impact of production under alternative trade policy scenarios influenced by 'supergreens'

| | | Country 2 | |
		Free Trade	Protection
Country 1	Free Trade	$2\alpha + 2\alpha^*$	$\alpha + 2\alpha^* + \beta^*$
	Protection	$2\alpha + \beta + \alpha^*$	$\alpha + \beta + \alpha^* + \beta^*$

10.4.6 *Political activity*

The analysis of the environmentalists' political activity in the case of adverse environmental impact via production proceeds in a manner similar to the case of adverse impact via consumption, once the environmental interest group has established the trade policy that it wishes to support. Again, political contributions constitute a public good via the collective benefits that are associated with trade-policy outcomes. Depending on whether the Prisoners' Dilemma is resolved, the environmental interest group with national concerns will find itself the ally of domestic protectionist interests, or of liberal trade-policy interests that include predominantly foreign producers. The 'capture' implications are symmetric with those established in the previous section.

10.4.7 *Spillover effects*

We thus far supposed that there are no international spillover effects whereby production or consumption in one country has an adverse environmental impact in the other. Should spillover occur via consumption, greens have reason to seek to restrict exports, but this requires an export tax rather than an import duty. The export tax would of course be resisted by domestic producers. Protectionist policies have no role.

Protectionist policies do on the other hand have a potential role when the adverse environmental impact derives from foreign production. Table 10.2 can be utilized to describe circumstances of production spillover effects, when the adverse environmental impact of production in one country is felt only in the other and the recipient country continues to be adversely impacted by its own production. Values in Table 10.2 then relate to the impacted economy only. Greens in the adversely impacted economy – and supergreens – are clearly protectionist.

However, the *only* source of adverse environmental impact may be foreign production. If this relation is symmetric, with each country adversely affected by production in the other, greens in each country formulate their trade policy positions with the objective of minimising foreign production. Consider then Table 10.1 when each country's greens seek to minimize the *foreign* valuations. The Nash equilibrium is mutual protectionism. There can be no Prisoners' Dilemma, since mutual free trade is inferior for both countries' greens to the mutual protectionist outcome (since $\alpha^* + \beta^* < 2\alpha^*$ and $\alpha + \beta < 2\alpha$). Mutual protectionism is nevertheless not the preferred outcome for any one country's greens. Since $\alpha^* < \alpha^* + \beta^*$ and $\alpha < \alpha + \beta$, each country's greens would, if they could dictate trade policy, impose free trade abroad and protectionism at home, which is also precisely the preferred policy outcome for domestic producers. The policy combination of free trade abroad and protection at home minimizes foreign production and thereby minimizes the adverse environmental spillover effect. But achievement of the preferred policy outcome for both countries' greens is inconsistent, since the greens are in conflict with their foreign counterparts regarding the trade policy that they wish the foreign greens to support. Although the greens prefer free trade abroad, the equilibrium is mutual protectionism.

10.5 Quantitative import restrictions and voluntary export restraint agreements

We have proceeded on the supposition that trade policy positions are formulated with reference to levels of a protective tariff that political candidates offer to implement if elected. Alternatively, trade restrictions can take the form of import quotas. Under conditions of perfect competition, tariffs and quotas are known to yield identical market equilibria and also, if quota rights are competitively auctioned, identical government revenue; but the two instruments of trade intervention are not identical in their effects on prices, quantities, and revenue, once one departs from conditions of perfect competition.

Producers' policy interests remain the same, however, under the two instruments. As with a protective duty, the domestic import-competing producers who benefit from quota protection have an interest in altogether eliminating import competition, and producers who benefit from market access and who are thus beneficiaries of free trade seek to avoid imposition of quota restrictions. Constituencies are thus, as with the tariff, at the polar extremes of quota values. The consequence is a polar outcome of political competition of the type that arises when an import duty is the instrument of trade restriction. The interest of environmental groups in influencing trade policy when import quotas are the instruments of protection, and the effects on the policy outcome of political competition, are also correspondingly similar to the circumstances and outcomes that we have described as arising when an import duty is the instrument of trade restriction.

This similarity between tariffs and quantitative restrictions hinges, however, on the supposition that the rents or revenues from trade restriction do not accrue to gainers or losers from protection, that is, that tariff revenue accrues to the treasury and that quota rents either also accrue to the government (as a consequence of auction of quota rights) or accrue to third-party importers. This latter condition is not satisfied when the recipients of quota rents are the foreign producers of imports, as occurs when quotas take the form of voluntary export restraint agreements (VERs).

When VERs are used as the instruments of trade restriction, the outcome of political competition is indeed the very *opposite* of the polarized equilibrium that arises when tariffs are employed. In contrast with the polar or divergent equilibria of tariffs, VERs yield convergent equilibria of the Hotelling type. That is, as we have formally demonstrated previously (Hillman and Ursprung, 1988) beginning from non-identical policy pronouncements by protectionist and liberal trade-policy candidates, under VERs the candidates converge to a policy equilibrium wherein they both announce the *same* policy.

It is characteristic of VERs that restriction of trade can yield potential mutual gain to both domestic and foreign producers. In effect, the quantity constraint and export-sales allocation imposed by the VER leads foreign exporters to act as if they had formed a perfectly monitored and enforced cartel. Of course, a foreign monopolistic exporter could not gain from a VER, since the exporter in choosing profit-maximizing foreign sales will already have set his most beneficial export restraint. But quite evidently producers in a sufficiently competitive foreign industry can increase profits from export sales via a sufficiently restrictive constraint on allowable exports. The VER thus functions *as if* exporting producers were collusively restricting their foreign sales. Also, a VER of course benefits domestic producers.[7]

The introduction of a politically active environmental interest group can however destroy the conciliatory, mutual profit-enhancing VER equilibrium. The outcome depends upon the intensity of the environmental interest groups's concern regarding the adverse environmental impact. This intensity of concern is formally measured by λZ, where λ it will be recalled transforms the adverse environmental impact Z into disutility terms for the environmental interest group.

Suppose that an environmental interest group supports a liberal trade-policy candidate; that is, either the greens' Prisoners' Dilemma is not resolved, or (as outside of Region 2 in Figure 10.2) support for free trade is the environmental interest group's dominant strategy. By entering into the political-determination arena in support of free trade, the environmental interest group expands the range of feasible policy equilibria. When only producers were sources of political support, candidates' choices of policy pronouncements were from within that range of VERs in which increasing restrictiveness give rise to decreasing profits for foreign producers. However, with the environmental interest group present, there is a constituency for free trade.

So long as environmental concern expressed in λZ is sufficiently small, the convergent VER equilibrium obtained in the absence of political activity by an environmental interest group is maintained. But as λZ increases, the range of VERs that sustains the preexisting stable policy equilibrium diminishes, and for a sufficiently high value of λZ, political candidates reformulate their policy positions such that the original interior common policy pronouncement equilibrium disappears. Indeed, policy positions are then again polarized much the same as when an import duty is the instrument of protection and the protectionist candidate announces prohibitive protectionism while the liberal trade-policy candidate announces free trade as his policy. The environmental interest group will thus have destroyed the policy consensus that in its absence was the political equilibrium. Rather than being conciliatory, trade policy again becomes politically contentious.[8]

The conciliatory political equilibrium that arises in the absence of political activity by the environmental interest group is a reflection of the potential mutual gains from VERs for domestic and foreign producers who are the respective sources of political support for protectionist and liberal trade-policy candidates. It is important to note that the conciliatory policy equilibrium achieved when environmental interests are absent is not established by direct collusion among domestic and foreign producers to mutually increase profits, but is the outcome of political competition with producers independently making political contributions to their preferred candidate. It is inappropriate therefore to declare that the appearance of the environmental interest group destabilizes a collusive producer equilibrium. Yet this is nevertheless the effect, even though not the mechanism. The mechanism is political competition. The destabilizing effect of the presence of an environmental interest group derives from the candidates' incentives to alter their prior policy positions when the environmental interest group becomes politically active. The environmentalists have no interest in supporting regulation of international trade that mutually enhances domestic and foreign producer profits. Political candidates seeking to maximize their political support respond correspondingly, thereby displacing the interior convergent policy equilibrium.[9]

10.6 Summary remarks

We have been concerned with how environmental interest groups affect the balance of political support for and against policies that protect domestic industries from import competition. The mechanism that has been employed as background for the determination of policy outcomes has been political competition in a setting of representative democracy. This setting portrays circumstances where political candidates follow optimizing principles with the intention of maximizing political support, or maximizing their probability of election. Political support has been expressed in terms of the relative share of campaign contributions received on the issue of protection for a domestic industry that is the source of an adverse environmental impact via either consumption or production.

The polarized outcome of political competition when candidates propose protective import duties to maximise political support as expressed by self-interested gainers and losers from industry protection, has been shown to be sustained when an environmental interest group appears to participate in the process of influencing candidates' policy positions. However, the political activity of the environmental interest group changes the probabilities of liberal market access and protectionist policy outcomes.

The pro-environment coalition either captures or is captured by narrower industry interest whose positions on trade policy are determined by the consequences for producers' profits rather than the concerns of the environmentalists. The phenomenon of capture arises because of the public-good nature of the campaign contributions that are the expression of political support. Capture is formally synonymous with free-riding behaviour with respect to policy influence. The environmentalists are 'captured' if they make a sufficiently high predetermined political allocation, or when their stakes in the outcomes of the different trade policies, as reflected in their disutility of associated environmental impacts, likewise lead them to make campaign contributions of sufficient magnitude to displace political outlays made by industry interests seeking the same objective. Another manifestation of capture is that producer interests may find it expedient to channel their political contributions via the environmental interest group.

Which trade-policy position is supported by an environmental interest group has been shown to depend upon whether the source of the adverse environmental impact is in consumption or production and on whether there are interjurisdictional spillovers. Market structures in conjunction with the extent to which domestically produced goods and imports are substitutes in consumption establish whether an environmental interest groups has reason to take a liberal or protectionist trade policy stance for an industry.

Most generally environmental interest groups appear to have common cause with protectionist interests in industry. This is unambivalently so when the adverse environmental impact derives from consumption of an internationally traded good: then national groups concerned only with their home environment as well as environmentalists who adopt a universalist perspective support protectionist candidates, and are potentially captured by domestic protectionist interests. Whether pro-environment coalitions are protectionist when domestic production is the source of an adverse environmental impact, is however subject to considerable qualification. The environmentalists with a global perspective again are unambivalently protectionist. However, we have shown that national environmental groups can confront a Prisoners' Dilemma.

The circumstances giving rise to the Prisoners' Dilemma are low substitutability in consumption between domestically produced goods and imports and similar market structures in two trading partners. When these circumstances arise, environmentalists in different national jurisdictions making independent decisions regarding political support adopt free-trade positions, but would be better off if they could coordinate with environmental interest groups abroad to support mutually protectionist policies. The usual considerations of monitoring and ensuring commitment impede the requisite cooperative behaviour among national environmental interest groups that would avoid the Prisoners' Dilemma.

However, environmentalists with global concerns who seek to minimize adverse environmental impacts of production independently of geographical location have been shown to confront no such dilemma, and unambivalently to support political candidates who espouse protectionist policies.

If substitutability between domestically produced goods and imports is on the other hand high or industry structures are asymmetric, there is also no Prisoners' Dilemma confronting environmentalists with narrow national concerns. Such environmentalists in the different policy jurisdictions are in conflict regarding the desirability of the mutual protectionist policies which, from a global perspective, minimize the adverse environmental impact. We have indicated how the conflict arises because of asymmetric incentives for free-riding by national environmentalists, via free trade, on foreign production. Coordination under these circumstances requires that one country's environmentalists be compensated by those in another for supporting a protectionist policy rather than free trade in their home country. The transfers to provide such compensation could in principle be made. However, monitoring and defection problems remain, since the preferred independent outcome for the national environmentalists confronting the more competitive foreign export supply response remains free trade in their own economy.

Where the Prisoners' Dilemma arises, no such transfers are required, since mutual protection is mutually beneficial. But even though considerations of minimizing globally adverse environmental impacts imply support for mutual protectionist policies, there are no mutual gains from cooperation in support of such policies when market structures in two trading economies are asymmetric. It is then not the failure of achievement of a credible mechanism for cooperation that leads the environmentalists to depart from support for protectionist policies, but a basic conflict of interest regarding national environmental consequences of trade policies.

We have demonstrated that conflicts regarding support for trade policy positions also arise when there are interjurisdictional spillovers – not when the adverse environmental impact is due to consumption, in which case environmentalists are again unambivalently protectionist – but when production is the source of the adverse impact. When the spillovers occur reciprocally, nationally focused environmentalists independently choosing which trade policy position to support are protectionist. However each national environmental interest group would prefer to have the other support free trade policies in its own country, since import competition would decrease the foreign production which is the source of the adverse domestic environmental impact.

We have also considered how environmental interest groups can be

218 Arye L. Hillman and Heinrich W. Ursprung

expected to influence the determination of international trade policy when quantity rather than price instruments are used as protectionist devices. In the case of voluntary export restraints, where the quota rents then accrue to the foreign exporters, an environmental interest group has been shown to be capable of affecting both the nature of the policy equilibrium and the probabilities that particular policies will be implemented – whereas when tariffs are protectionist instruments, the political activity of the environmental interest group affects only the latter probabilities of policy implementation and leaves unchanged the polar nature of politically optimal policy pronouncements.

The considerations to which we have directed attention in establishing whether environmental interest groups can be expected to support liberal or protectionist policies apply independently of the means of protection. Thus, for example, if a Prisoners' Dilemma arises when a protective tariff is the means of protection, the Dilemma will also arise if a voluntary export restraint agreement is proposed to restrict imports. The substantive difference between the two is the potential for displacement of the policy equilibrium in the case of VERs that would have arisen from political competition, when environmental interest groups do not exercise political influence.

From the perspective of producers, the distinguishing feature of VERs is that, unlike with protective tariffs, there can be mutual gains for both the protected industry and foreign exporters. Since the environmental interest group can disrupt and polarize the policy equilibrium that yielded mutual producer gain, the environmentalists are no longer in the position of necessarily having (implicit or explicit) producer allies. If the environmentalists are protectionist, then they do have common cause with producers – those in their own domestic industry producing import-competing output. But, if the environmentalists support free trade policies via elimination of standing VERs, their political involvement in policy determination is contrary to the interests of both domestic producers who have benefited from protection, and foreign exporters benefiting from the regulation of international trade. Environmentalists seeking to influence trade policy can then expect to find themselves confronting the opposition of both domestic and foreign producers. The possibilities of capture of environmentalists by producer interests associated with tariff protection then cannot arise.

Trade policy will have been an issue before the environmentalists appeared, with domestic producers seeking a prohibitive restriction of imports and foreign exporters optimally seeking a VER set at the foreign collusive profit-maximizing quantity of exports. The political equilibrium is in general such as to satisfy neither producer interest with respect to the preferred policy. Nevertheless domestic and foreign profits can increase relative to free trade – and the restricted equilibrium position is conciliatory for politicians, who are led to make common policy pronouncements.

The appearance of environmentalist interest groups, however, makes trade policy contentious. Rather than the issue being how to redistribute the gains from the regulation of international trade, the polar equilibrium policy pronouncements of free trade and prohibitive protection introduce producer gainers and losers. That is, the environmentalists have changed a contest from one which offers mutual producer gain, to one whose outcome offers profits to one group of producers but at the expense of the other. From the producers' or industry perspective, trade policy has become politically divisive, as it was under the import duty. The source of the divisiveness is the presence of the environmental interest group.

The chapter emphasizes that a fundamental issue in identifying how environmental interest groups can be expected to influence the political determination of trade policy is whether environmentalists' objectives are those which we have attributed to 'greens' or 'supergreens'; that is, whether the environmental interest group is concerned with environmental consequences in its own country only, or has a broader global perspective. The presence of industrial pollution suggests a greens' perspective, while concerns such as global warming and the ozone layer suggest a supergreens' perspective. Supergreens' objectives have been seen to lead to unambivalent support for protectionist policies, but not so the greens' objectives. Indeed, the greens' objectives lead them to involvement in strategic decisions and to encounter problems of coordination and ensuring commitment in determining support for trade policy positions for particular industries. The greens also confront information problems in establishing the environmental consequences of different trade policy decisions taken. They must know elasticities of substitution in domestic consumption as between domestically produced goods and imported substitutes, and between supply elasticities of domestic producers and the foreign producers who are the sources of competitive import supply.

Notes

1. Similarly, Chapter 11 of this volume by Hoekman and Leidy also adopts a positive perspective. For a survey of the more-general literature on the political economy of trade policy, see Hillman (1989).
2. For a review of this and other approaches to incorporating the political process into analysis of policy determination, see Ursprung (1991).
3. For associated observations, see Magee *et al.* (1989).
4. See Hillman (1990) on the various means whereby producers whose exports are the objects of trade restriction can gain from the regulation of international trade.
5. See Hotelling (1929).
6. This confirms, as we noted in the previous section, that domestic consumption is minimized by a unilateral protectionist policy.

7. See Hillman and Ursprung (1988) for the derivation of the condition under which a VER yields mutual producer gain. A broader perspective on VERs that encompasses welfare consequences and different government motives is provided by Ethier (1991).
8. For a formal proof, see Hillman and Ursprung (1991).
9. Provided, as we have noted, that environmental interest groups exert sufficient political influence, or provide sufficient political support.

References

Blackhurst, R. (1977), 'International Trade and Domestic Environmental Policies in a Growing World Economy', pp. 341–64 in *International Relations in a Changing World*, by R. Blackhurst *et al.*, Geneva: Sijthoff-Leiden.

Ethier, W. J. (1987), 'The Theory of International Trade', pp. 1–57 in *International Economics*, edited by L. H. Officer, Boston and Dordrecht: Kluwer.

Ethier, W. J. (1991), 'The Economics and Political Economy of Managed Trade', pp. 283–306 in *Markets and Politicians: Politicized Economic Choice*, edited by A. L. Hillman, Boston and Dordrecht: Kluwer.

Hillman, A. L. (1989), *The Political Economy of Protection*, London and New York: Harwood.

Hillman, A. L. (1990), 'Protectionist Policies as the Regulation of International Industry', *Public Choice* 67: 101–10.

Hillman, A. L. and H. W. Ursprung (1988), 'Domestic Politics, Foreign Interests, and International Trade Policy', *American Economic Review* 78: 729–745.

Hillman, A. L. and H. W. Ursprung (1991), 'Greens, Supergreens, and International Trade Policy: Environmental Concerns and Protectionism', mimeo, Institute for Economic Research, Bar-Ilan University, June.

Hotelling, H. (1929), 'Stability in Competition', *Economic Journal* 39: 41–57.

Magee, S. P., W. A. Brock and L. Young (1989), *Black Hole Tariffs and Endogenous Policy Theory: Political Economy in General Equilibrium*, Cambridge and New York: Cambridge University Press.

Siebert, H. (1974), 'Trade and Environment', pp. 108–21 in *The International Division of Labor: Problems and Perspectives*, edited by H. Giersch, Tubingen: J. C. B. Mohr.

Ursprung, W. H. (1990), 'Public Goods, Rent Dissipation, and Candidate Competition', *Economics and Politics*, 2, 115–32.

Ursprung, W. H. (1991), 'Economic Policies and Political Competition', pp. 1–25 in *Markets and Politicians: Politicized Economic Choice*, edited by A. L. Hillman, Boston and Dordrecht: Kluwer.

11

Environmental policy formation in a trading economy: a public choice perspective

Bernard Hoekman and Michael Leidy

Environmental externalities are often embodied in specific products or generated by production processes. And governments generally have a variety of instruments at their disposal to mitigate the environmental impact of product- and process-based pollution. These include taxes on production or consumption, tradeable pollution permits, limiting production through quotas on output, restrictions on the use of specific inputs or production technologies, and product standards. Yet despite the fact that there exists a large body of economic theory indicating that market- or price-based instruments such as taxes or tradeable permits will often be the efficient (i.e., least-cost) option, in practice environmental policies tend to be of the 'command-and-control' variety, taking the form of quantity regulation or specific technical product/process standards. At times, of course, this is because price-based instruments may be entirely inappropriate. An example pertains to instances where there is a need to ban or sharply limit the use of specific substances embodied in products (e.g., cancer-causing pesticides or radioactive inputs). Frequently, however, inefficient quantity- or standards-based instruments are used because the political support for such measures proves overwhelming. In a similar vein, even if a product or process standard is necessary to deal with an environmental externality, the type of standard imposed will not, in general, achieve the environmental objective for the least cost.

Building on seminal work by Olson (1965), Tullock (1967), and Stigler (1971), a substantial literature has developed that analyses the political economy of policy choice. Contributions in this area focus on *how* public policy is determined, taking it as given what public policy *should* be implemented. That is, the analysis is positive, not normative, the main goal being to identify some of the obstacles that may block the adoption of socially desirable policies. This chapter explores the political-economy dimension of the social choice of domestic environmental policy instruments in an open economy setting.[1] The basic premise is that environmental policies do not arise in a passive and benevolent fashion to correct an acknowledged market failure. Instead, environmental policies, like any other area of regulation and social choice, take shape through an engagement between interest groups, mediated by existing political institutions. Coalitions form as points of convergence become clear, countervailing forces draw lines in the sand, concessions are made, weaknesses are identified and exploited, politicians put fingers to the wind and ultimately a policy emerges.

This policy will have two elements: (a) the *level* of the desired environmental improvement, that is, which pollution externalities need to be reduced and by how much; and (b) *how* the desired level of environmental improvement should be achieved. As a rule, there is no reason whatsoever to expect the policy to be efficient, let alone optimal.[2] Even if the optimal policy could be identified in principle, political economy considerations will invariably lead to over- or undershooting of the socially desirable abatement level. And, adding insult to injury, the amount of pollution abatement that is achieved will tend to come at a social cost that is unnecessarily high. Because the efficient policy leaves little or nothing on the table for the industry, there is a strong incentive for all interest groups to agree on a mutually acceptable inefficient approach.

The existing environmental economics literature tends to neglect the nature and extent of possible trade policy and environmental policy linkages.[3] The possible trade-distorting effects of alternative environmental instruments, as well as the trade policy pressures that may result from an active environmental policy are a central element of this chapter. In practice, of course, it is not always straightforward to distinguish environmental policies from trade policies, as the former can easily have trade effects, while the latter may be environmentally motivated. A central theme of this essay is that a given domestic environmental objective may easily lead to a policy response that generates an unnecessary or unintended increase in trade barriers.

While the focus of this chapter is on the practical difficulties that constrain the adoption of efficient environmental policies, this is not to say, of course, that environmental concerns should not be pursued. Indeed, the underlying premise is that there *is* an environmental problem and that policies need to be put in place to ameliorate matters. Ideally, such policies would be 'optimal', in the sense of accurately balancing social costs and benefits and attaining the environmental objective for a minimum social cost. However, forces will usually exist that make it quite difficult to achieve this, and in practice the best that can be achieved is to implement efficient policies that attain a given abatement objective at least cost. To increase the likelihood that efficient environmental policies are put in place, such forces need to be identified, understood, and then neutralised.

The chapter is organised as follows. In the first section a number of examples are offered that illustrate how industry and environmental groups may both seek to have the government implement excessively costly environmental policy instruments. These examples pertain to instruments that are frequently encountered in the environmental setting: quantity restrictions on output, production process regulations (e.g., restrictions on input use), and product standards. The next section turns to the trade-distorting and trade-policy-altering effects of environmental policies. While some environmental policies will have a trade-inhibiting effect, others may initially stimulate imports, providing import-competing industries with additional leverage to gain protection under existing administrative rules and practices such as antidumping laws and voluntary export restraint agreements (VERs). The existence of environmental lobbies may increase both the probability that such protection is granted and the likelihood that an inefficient instrument is employed to restrict imports. Again, the focus will be on quantity regulation, production technology requirements, and product standards. Section 3 turns to the potential role of various foreign interests in influencing the choice of environmental policy instrument and briefly addresses the relevance of political economy insights in cases where environmental externalities (spillovers) are international in nature. Section 4 discusses some of the implications of the analysis for policy and further research, followed by concluding remarks.

11.1 The political economy of environmental policies

Governments usually have a number of alternative instruments at their disposal to deal with environmental externalities. This section explores why regulations tend to dominate price-based instruments, by analysing the incentives facing major interest groups to prefer non-price instruments − such as quantity-based regulation requiring a reduction in production, process standards (production technology requirements or input use restrictions) and product standards. The discussion makes no claim for comprehensiveness or generality. The aim is simply to illustrate that once political economy considerations are introduced, in many circumstances one cannot assume that the optimal level of pollution abatement will be chosen, or that, once an objective is chosen, the efficient (least cost) policy will be adopted to achieve that goal. International trade effects and commercial policy implications of domestic environmental policy are introduced in the next section.

11.1.1 *Quantity regulation*[4]

In many instances a straightforward way to diminish pollution is to reduce production of the firm(s) that generate the externality. In what follows it is assumed that given existing technologies each unit of production generates a fixed amount of environmental pollution. Each unit of domestic production, therefore, yields a corresponding unit of a 'public bad' for which no social compensation is paid. The polluting industry is assumed to be perfectly competitive and to be located in a small country that cannot affect its terms of trade. It therefore competes with imports that are supplied at a fixed (world) price.[5] Furthermore, it is assumed that the authorities can accurately measure and monitor these emissions and that they have determined the amount by which they wish to reduce them.[6]

For purposes of comparison, consider first the imposition of a penalty tax per unit of production. The tax is imposed only on domestic firms since the pollution is embodied in production, not in the product itself.[7] This has the initial effect of increasing both average and marginal costs in the domestic industry by the amount of the tax. The domestic market supply curve shifts upward, and given the constant world price for output, domestic firms experience transitional losses. In response, exit occurs and total domestic production begins to decline. Imports rise to fill the demand gap at the stable world price, factor prices fall and cost curves shift downward. Equilibrium is restored when the factor-price effect has fully offset the effect of the tax on long-run average cost. Firms remaining in the industry will once again be achieving normal profits and producing at the minimum efficient scale. In this sense the pollution abatement is achieved efficiently.

As an alternative to the penalty tax, policy makers could simply impose production restraints on existing domestic firms. The restricted level of domestic output could be achieved by assigning equal production quotas to each firm in the domestic industry. Although such a policy achieves the pollution-abatement objective, it does so inefficiently in the sense that each firm is assigned a quota below its minimum efficient scale. In addition, inefficiency implies that for a given set of factor prices the regulated industry will require a greater quantity of all factors than under the tax-based scheme.[8] Thus, to produce the restricted level of output under the regulatory solution requires a smaller decline in factor demand, and so in factor prices, than under the penalty tax. The social cost of pollution abatement under output regulation, therefore, exceeds that under the tax.[9]

There is another sense in which the penalty tax is socially superior to regulated output.[10] Equilibrium in the case of regulated output, like any cartel equilibrium, requires enforcement to maintain it. Each firm has an incentive to cheat on its quota allotment, other things equal, since the world price exceeds marginal cost at the restricted level of output. Hence some monitoring and enforcement expenses must accompany the regulated solution. However, while each firm has an individual incentive to break its quota in the absence of effective enforcement, each also has an incentive to support an effective enforcement mechanism as part of the regulatory package. In addition, regulators must deter entry in order to achieve and maintain the pollution-control objective. Neither entry deterrence nor an enforcement mechanism is required in the case of a penalty tax since normal profitability prevails in the post-tax equilibrium.

Like the penalty tax, output regulation creates a demand gap that is filled by imports. Total imports rise – the domestic industry's market share declines – by exactly the same amount as under the tax. The demand for sector-specific factors – and therefore factor prices – falls by somewhat less than in the tax-based case since aggregate output is produced inefficiently. The distribution of layoffs differs from the penalty tax. Layoffs are distributed evenly under the quantity regulation whereas all-or-nothing layoffs occur under the tax. There is no industry exit,[11] but the market share of each firm is necessarily less than that of those firms that remain in the industry after a tax is imposed. In addition, as mentioned above, each firm now has excess capacity which was not the case under the tax.

The differences between the effects of a tax and quantity-based regulation are crucial in determining the preferences of the principal interest groups. In this section, we consider only domestic interest groups. The preferences of environmentalists, the polluting industry, and a sector-specific factor are examined. Consumers perceive no direct interest since the price of the good is unaffected in the small-country setting.[12]

For simplicity of exposition sector-specific factors are treated collectively as a composite of nontradeable sector-specific labour. Because total industry output is produced inefficiently under the quantity regulation, industry-wide factor demand falls by less than under the penalty tax. This suggests that while sector-specific factors may oppose environmental protection in the first place (since factor prices and employment decline), once the decision to intervene has been made, the penalty tax poses a greater threat to employment and wages than does output regulation. Furthermore, under regulated output layoffs are distributed evenly across existing firms, while under the penalty tax a firm either becomes a casualty of restructuring or it weathers transitional losses ultimately to survive at its original scale of operation.

If labour and politically aligned groups perceive evenly distributed layoffs to be more equitable (in a self-interested sense) than the all-or-nothing purges of a tax, the strict preference for the regulated approach to pollution control is strengthened.[13] In addition, the burden of the proportional layoffs under regulation will most likely affect employees with the least seniority. To the extent that the interests of workers with greater seniority are protected over those of more recent vintage, the threat of evenly distributed layoffs appears the more attractive alternative. Finally, the rents accruing to domestic firms under output regulation offer a potential carrot to labour. The prospect of capturing any share of these rents should render the quantity restraint the preferred approach. Under the penalty tax no rents accrue to the penalised industry.

Environmentalists can be expected to value both current and expected future environmental quality, largely to the exclusion of all else. Given such focused preferences, how will they evaluate a penalty tax versus the quantity regulation? Both achieve the same pollution objective. The penalty-tax approach is attractive since there is no incentive for firms to deviate from the new equilibrium, other things equal. At the same time, firms are not *required* to reduce output and pollution. An exogenous decline in factor prices or the introduction of cost-saving technologies that are equally polluting will induce firms to step up production, and so emissions.[14] Thus, the penalty tax may not provide sufficient assurance of ongoing pollution abatement to satisfy environmentalists. In practice, market-based approaches to pollution control have indeed been viewed with disdain by environmentalists as granting firms a 'licence to pollute.'

The regulatory alternative carries with it the potential problem that it is not self-enforcing. However, when packaged with a credible enforcement component and effective barriers to entry, the regulatory approach is likely to dominate the tax-based abatement scheme from the environmentalist's perspective. It has two principal advantages. First, the level of pollution cannot rise in this sector because production is controlled directly by government regulators, and violations are penalised severely.[15] Second, environmentalists may be concerned with the cleanup of past environmental degradation. Under the penalty tax scenario some firms are forced to exit the industry and those that remain earn zero economic profits. Under the quantity regulations no firms exit and each earns supranormal profits. The presence of ongoing supranormal profits provides assurance that these firms will have the wherewithal to correct past abuses. While governments can impose barriers to exit if certain cleanup criteria have not been met, firms still require resources to engage in any cleanup activity. Just as labour might see the rents associated with the regulatory approach as being potentially captured at a later date, so environmentalists may view these rents as assuring latent resources for expected future cleanup. In this sense the excess profits of the regulatory solution are attractive to both environmentalists and industry-specific labour.

As emphasised by Buchanan and Tullock (1975), the interests of the polluting firms lie firmly in the regulatory approach, since cartel-like profits are potentially available.[16] Indeed, as long as the proposed quantity restraint does not overshoot by too much the underlying cartel solution, domestic polluting firms will support precisely the same regulatory approach preferred by environmentalists, viz., production quotas with strict enforcement measures and binding barriers to entry. In practice the barriers to entry selected by governments tend, not surprisingly, to appease both firms and environmentalists. Frequently, any prospective new entrants must meet more stringent pollution control standards than those imposed on existing firms, so that the right to emit more pollution per unit of output tends to be grandfathered for existing firms.[17] Potential entrants are thereby placed at a substantial cost disadvantage making entry all but impossible. The environmental objective offers polluting firms a socially attractive pretext for cartelising their industry, with the government covering enforcement costs and establishing the required barriers to entry.

Up to this point, the focus of discussion has been on the political economy of the public choice of an environmental instrument, taking the desired *level* of pollution abatement as given. Usually the environmental objective will itself be the outcome of a political process in which interest groups play a prominent role. The two groups that are likely to be the most affected and thus involved in the determination of the abatement target are environmentalists and the polluting industry. Experience suggests the former will tend to insist on the complete elimination of any adverse environmental consequences of production, whereas the industry can be expected to oppose such extreme environmental objectives. Unfortunately, there is no reason to expect this confrontation to produce the socially optimal policy. The industry will press for the cartel solution which may over- or undershoot the socially optimal level of pollution abatement. As environmentalists will want to overshoot, for there to be any reasonable probability that the political process will produce a level of abatement close to what is optimal it is necessary that the cartel solution undershoots the social optimum. In general the level of abatement may be higher or lower than the 'optimal' level, depending on the relative strength of the groups involved.

11.1.2 *Process standards*

Environmental policies frequently take the form of restrictions on the use of certain inputs (such as air or water) or requirements that specific production technologies be employed by an industry. Such policies will be called process standards in what follows. The effect of a process standard is similar to that of a pollution tax in that firms will be confronted with an increase in the shadow price of pollution. Thus, firms will be induced to substitute away from the affected 'environmental' input. Such regulation will tend to be less efficient than a pollution tax, however, as the standards that are imposed are unlikely to be those that achieve the desired reduction in pollution at least cost.[18]

As was the case with quantity regulation, in part the reason why one observes extensive recourse to process standards is that, when properly conceived, they can advance the interest of directly affected groups. In the setting of a perfectly competitive industry consisting of identical firms, the three groups discussed above can be expected to prefer process standards over pollution taxes for many of the same reasons they would prefer a quantity restriction on output. Maloney and McCormick (1982) showed that a cost-increasing process standard can increase profits in an otherwise competitive industry as long as the industry demand curve is downward sloping[19] and entry barriers are granted as part of the regulatory package. In this context entry barriers are commonly achieved by imposing more stringent pollution-control standards on new firms. In the new equilibrium, the market price can rise by more than average costs, while the standards-based barriers to entry help to secure any profits that may arise. Thus, existing firms have an incentive to seek process standards that satisfy this profit-enhancing profile. Sector-specific factors may favour such an approach since these secured rents provide a potential carrot, some of which might later be captured. And environmentalists have no reason to oppose the standards as long as they achieve a favourable environmental outcome.

In many instances the firms making up an industry are unlikely to be homogenous. For example, frequently firms may employ somewhat different production technologies. Any given process standard will then have a differential impact on firms, so that they will not have the same preferences over the set of all possible standards. Thus, at times there may be *strategic sub-groups* within an industry that will vie for the standard which they find most advantageous. Maloney and McCormick (1982) and Oster (1982) have argued that such sub-groups will invest resources to influence regulatory outcomes to advance their competitiveness. This is because such regulation results in implicit intraindustry transfers as well as entry barriers.[20]

Such effects may also arise if the industry is not perfectly competitive. For example, Salop and Scheffman (1983) consider an industry characterised by a low-cost dominant firm that engages in price leadership and a competitive fringe of small firms that follows the price set by the dominant firm. The good produced by the industry is assumed to be homogenous. It may then be in the dominant firm's interest to seek a regulation that raises the unit costs of its rivals by more than its own unit costs, thereby reducing sales and profits of the competitive fringe. This strategy will augment the dominant firm's profits if increased demand for its output outweighs the resulting increase in average costs. The dominant firm's strategy need not reduce fringe firm profits, however. Although their costs will rise, so will prices, which may compensate for the cost increase. Thus, under certain conditions the cost-raising strategy may result in increased profits for all firms in the industry.[21]

If there are subgroups in the industry, those having cleaner technologies will be less affected by either an emissions tax or a process standard. Indeed, both a tax and a standard may result in relatively 'dirty' firms exiting the industry while not greatly affecting the 'greener' firms. Even so it is likely that process standards will continue to be preferred to taxes. The reasons are similar to those offered in the preceding subsection. Standards will tend to imply greater rents for those firms remaining in the industry, especially if combined with grandfathering: imposing more stringent standards on prospective entrants. They also may allow the industry to exert more control over the costs of pollution abatement, as the standard can be written in a manner that minimises additional costs for the firms remaining in the industry (the 'green' group hereafter).

What about the less efficient ('dirty') firms? To the extent that a tax per unit of emissions is less costly than the additional cost implied by retooling to meet the standard pursued by the 'green' subgroup, the 'dirty' subgroup will push for a tax.[22] However, the 'green' group may be able to dominate this opposition by aligning themselves with environmentalists. After all, a tax may allow some of the 'dirty' firms to remain in business where the process standard might induce them to exit. Indeed, in addition to the arguments mentioned earlier, this is likely to be another reason to expect environmentalists to prefer a regulatory approach. Finally, factors of production specific to the industry will prefer a standard if this results in a smaller decline in net employment and/or wages. Under both a tax and a standard, layoffs will be distributed asymmetrically, with those of the 'dirty' group exceeding those of the 'green' group. Moreover, layoffs of 'dirty' firms are likely to be relatively greater under a standard than under a tax, and vice versa for 'green' firms. Thus, specific factors will also be split into two groups. Which group will have greater political influence will depend on factors such as relative size, the technologies employed by the two groups of firms (factor intensity), and geographic location. However, one conclusion that can again be drawn is that a standard is likely to be preferred insofar as it provides specific factors with the perspective that some of the resulting rents accrue to them.

As in the case of output regulation, in most instances it is not clear whether the public choice regarding the *level* of abatement will be too high or too low. This depends on the relative strength of the affected groups, the degree to which technologies differ across firms in the industry, and so forth. To the extent that a 'green' subgroup exists that is able to propose a strict standard that would end up giving it substantial market power, lobbying by environmmentalists may result in the imposition of pollution abatement targets that exceed what is socially optimal. Again, the less the objective of environmentalists conflicts with the cartel outcome, the greater the probability that 'overshooting' will occur.

11.1.3 *Product standards*

Product standards, technical regulations and certification systems are essential to the functioning of modern economies. Both standards and regulations are technical specifications for a particular product. A product standard differs from a regulation in that the former is voluntary, usually being defined by an industry or by a nongovernmental standardization body.[23] Technical regulations are mandatory (legally binding), and are often imposed in order to safeguard public or animal health, or the external environment. Not surprisingly, in most industrialized economies the number of product standards far exceeds the number of technical regulations. Certification systems comprise the procedures that must be followed by producers in establishing that their products or production processes conform to the relevant product standard/regulation. Environmentally-related product standards are used to address externalities that are not production-based. Instead, the environmental externality derives from consumption activities, with the negative impact falling on the consumer and/or on third parties. Unless stated otherwise, in what follows it is assumed that standards are mandatory, as this is usually the case in the environmental context.

Most of the economic literature on standards focuses on industry product standards. One strand of that literature focuses on the possibility that product standardization may increase the technical efficiency of the economy by reducing transaction costs – e.g., allowing greater substitution across products – thus fostering competition and allowing economies of scale to be attained. This is of little relevance in the environmental context. Another strand that is of greater significance focuses on the impact of product standardization under imperfect or asymmetric information.

A distinction has been made between *search, experience* and *credence* goods (e.g., Tirole, 1988). For the first category a consumer can establish the quality (characteristics) of a good before purchase. In contrast, the quality of an experience good can only be determined after purchase, while that of a credence good can only be determined once a significant amount of time has elapsed, and may never be determined at all. Because potential consumers cannot determine quality *ex ante*, producers of experience and credence goods may have an incentive to offer lower quality products than otherwise. Examples of experience goods are plastic products that are supposed to be biodegradable, or recycled paper that is claimed to be as durable as new paper. Examples of credence goods are foods claimed to be 'additive free', purportedly 'ozone-friendly' sprays, 'turtle-friendly' shrimp (see the next section), or catalytic converters that are supposed to eliminate nitrogen oxide emissions. In the absence of credible testing (certification) by independent agencies, the consumer simply has to believe the claims of the producer concerning the quality of credence goods. Product standards with associated certification and verification procedures are screening devices intended to keep out 'low quality' products or producers.

In what follows the term 'quality' is used as shorthand for the set of specific environmental characteristics embodied in a product. The environmental 'quality' of a product can frequently be considered as just another of its defining characteristics. Thus, the biodegradability or ozone-friendliness of a good may determine its quality as perceived by (potential) consumers. Environmental quality is often a continuous variable, in that different types of products will be more or less harmful to the environment and/or the consumer. In many, if not most, instances the environmental quality of a product may never be directly discernible to the consumer so that we are dealing with credence goods. In contrast to regulation of output or production processes, product standards will at times be the optimal instrument to deal with an environmental externality. In many cases market-based instruments such as taxes will simply not be feasible. In other cases where they are feasible in principle – e.g., emission taxes for cars – they may be too costly to implement so that emission standards are preferable. Product standards therefore offer a good opportunity to analyse the possible determinants of the public choice concerning the *level* of environmental externality abatement as opposed to the *type* of instrument to be used. For purposes of discussion, in what follows it is assumed that products standards are the optimal instrument to deal with an environmental externality.

While product standards may help mitigate an environmental externality, they may easily create other distortions. As with previously discussed instruments, the intent to adopt a product standard motivated by environmental concerns may enable incumbent firms to increase their market power by raising rivals' costs, possibly inducing exit, and/or by inhibiting new entry. Whenever the reduction in aggregate supply due to the imposition of the standard leads to higher profits, it is likely that the standards are too restrictive. To the extent that this occurs, the standard has created rents and the standards-setting activity helps to produce a collusive outcome. The product standards that are imposed or proposed are endogenous, the precise wording depending upon the preferences and strength of the environmental lobby and on factors such as the number and relative size of the firms in the industry, their production technologies, research and development capability, and the type of good involved.

Numerous examples can be constructed to illustrate the possible divergences of interests *within* an industry regarding the choice of a product standard. Much depends here on the ease of entry into the industry. For example, Leland (1979) has analysed the case where potential buyers have less information on quality than suppliers, no entry is possible, and suppliers cannot differentiate themselves from one another. In this case higher quality firms have an incentive to persue excessively strict standards, thereby forcing lower quality firms to exit. Shapiro (1983) relaxed the no entry and no differentiation assumptions and showed that this was likely to lead to opposite conclusions. If buyers can differentiate across suppliers and are likely to engage in repeat purchases, this gives firms an incentive to build a reputation for producing products of a certain quality. The higher the quality of the product, the greater the incentive to invest in reputation-building. In this case, although a standard may raise costs disproportionately for low quality firms, those lower quality firms that remain or decide to enter the market are compensated by lower costs of establishing a reputation and by a higher demand for their output. High quality firms lose from a minimum quality standard as they experience a capital loss – the asset value of their investment in reputation declines – and suffer the loss of those customers that shift to other suppliers (whose quality is now known). A third model that illustrates the scope for differences in firm preferences concerning the imposition of a standard is that of Salop and Scheffman (1983) noted earlier.

As with other regulatory instruments, environmentalists are likely to support (a sub-set of) the industry in favouring socially sub-optimal standards. Environmentalists will usually prefer to see standards adopted that totally eliminate the environmental externality. As a result, while some product standard is the 'optimal' instrument by assumption, pressure by environmental groups for stringent standards might aid a strategic industry sub-group to hijack the standards-setting process. That is, it might allow the industry to use public concern about an environmental problem to its advantage. In general, the standard that will emerge may overshoot or undershoot the social optimum.[24]

11.2 Trade policy consequences of environmental policies

The possible relationships between environmental policies and international trade are twofold. First, environmental policies of any kind may affect trade flows. They may do this by directly restricting imports of a product, or indirectly by inducing consumers to either substitute away from or towards imports. Second, environmental policies may lead to an endogenous trade policy response. That is, given that an environmental policy is under consideration, interest groups may be induced to concurrently or subsequently petition the government to limit imports for reasons connected to the environmental policy change. These two possibilities are related, of course, as a necessary condition for the latter is that the environmental policy can be argued to discriminate 'unfairly' against domestically produced goods.

The extent to which trade patterns are altered by environmental policy will depend on the nature of any endogenous trade policy response. The pressure for protection may be direct or may emerge through increased invocation of existing administered forms of protection such as antidumping procedures. In general, because of the anticipated profits associated with restricting imports, the greater prospect of protection is likely to make the regulatory approach to pollution control (as opposed to a market-based approach) additionally appealing to the industry concerned.

11.2.1 *Quantity regulation*

It was noted earlier that quantity regulation will lead to an increase in imports. And it can be shown that corresponding to the increase in imports, import-competing firms in the regulated industry will experience 'injury' in several dimensions.[25] As a result, the likelihood that unfair trade laws or voluntary export restraint agreements (VERs) will be pursued increases following the institution of a quantity-based approach to production-based environmental pollution. Four factors will contribute to this.

First, declining domestic sales, market share, production, and employment offer evidence of the injury that is required under current rules, and these occur while the level and share of imports rise. Because satisfying the injury criterion is the principal constraint in gaining protection in this area, the prospect of protection rises, other things equal.[26]

Second, the regulatory regime established to enforce production quotas provides a formal institutional setting for cooperative behaviour that reinforces the ability of firms to pursue other (non-pollution abatement) areas of mutual interest, including efforts to petition for protection. Empirical studies have shown that on average it pays to present a united front in petitions for protection.[27] Internalising industry-wide incentives, including the incentive to petition for protection, is part of the attractiveness of the regulatory approach.

Third, the regulatory regime establishes a precedent for market sharing that may pave the way to cover foreign firms as well.[28] Domestic firms might be able to use the market-sharing arrangement imposed for environmental reasons to argue for its extension to foreign firms. That is, should protection be granted it may be marginally more likely that a negotiated voluntary restraint agreement will be the chosen instrument. Other things equal, such quantity-based protection offers greater scope for the consolidation of market power and thus greater profits.

Fourth, because of the barriers to domestic entry established under the regulatory pollution-abatement scheme, the prospective profits of protection will not be dissipated by competition over time.[29] This means that the regulatory scheme serves to increase the expected present value of the profits of protection, thereby increasing its appeal.

As a result of these four conditions the pressure for protection and the likelihood that it is granted under the regulatory scheme is enhanced, since the domestic industry experiences injury in several dimensions, this injury coincides with a surge in imports, regulatory barriers to entry increase the expected capitalised value of protection, and the cooperative behaviour enforced by the regulations furthers the industry's ability to speak with one voice.

It should be noted that the endogenous contingent trade policy response leading to increased trade barriers might also appear through a more direct path. Adoption of an environmental policy may cause new pressure for protection in any event, as the domestic industry can now claim that this creates a 'nonlevel playing field'. While injury criteria play no formal role in implementing newly legislated trade barriers, the fact that domestic industries *can* claim to be injured by increased imports subsequent to the imposition of the environmental policy is likely to facilitate the adoption of such measures if they are pursued.

11.2.2 Process standards

As in the case of quantity regulation, if domestic environmental policy takes the form of process standards applied to domestic producers, imports will increase. If the domestic industry is homogenous, arguments similar to those made above will apply equally to process standards-based regulation. Domestic firms are injured, imports are rising, and so forth. The existence of import competition and contingent trade policy instruments may increase the preference of domestic interest groups for process standards. For example, suppose that environmentalists are concerned with excessive killing of turtles by shrimp fishermen and have managed to impose a standard that domestic fishermen must use nets that incorporate effective turtle exclusion devices. The domestic industry may then argue that as a result of this policy they face unfair competition from foreign sources not subject to this regulation. Moreover, environmental groups can be expected to insist that foreign imports of shrimp meet the same standards, not because of any concern for the plight of domestic fishermen, but because of their concern for turtles.

In contrast to the quantity regulation case, a tariff or a quota on imports is unlikely to be acceptable to either group. Instead, they are likely to demand a ban on imports.[30] Although there might be a stated willingness on the part of environmentalists to exempt those foreign sources that can prove they do not kill turtles, in practice this will be very difficult to establish. It involves not only allowing inspection of trawlers, but also providing assurance that no mixing of sources occurs. Even if this can be done by foreign suppliers, it will take time, time during which they are likely to be subjected to import barriers or to a consumer boycott. Furthermore, establishing the 'turtle-friendliness' of their products is costly, so that the environmental policy will make it more attractive to shift to third markets.[31] Domestic fishermen will push for restrictions on all sources, even from waters without turtles, as they can argue that: (a) the standard forces them to compete on unfair terms with foreigners; and (b) they are being injured by increased imports. In conclusion, it is clear that uniform application of the process standard will both have significant trade-distorting effects and is very likely to increase the level of protection.

What if there are strategic sub-groups in the domestic import-competing industry that have different preferences concerning the level of abatement and/or type of environmental policy instrument? This may have implications for the probability of success in petitioning for protection. In particular, the prospect of protection may again facilitate the adoption of a process standard. To the extent that the adoption of the standard implies a significant reduction in imports – as would be the case if all imports that do not meet the standard are prohibited – the 'green' group may be willing to offer the 'dirty' firms some compensation, so that their resistance may be reduced. Such compensation may take the form of adoption of a standard that is somewhat less antagonistic to the interests of the 'dirty' group. The negative impact of such compensation on profits of the 'green' group will be partially offset by the restrictions imposed on imports. Of course, the likelihood of this occurring depends largely on the credibility of a threat by the 'dirty' group to oppose petitions for protection, which in turn will be a function of the institutional requirements that have to be met in order to obtain protection.[32]

11.2.3 *Product standards*

Product standards provide an example where environmental regulation in itself may have direct effects on international trade. Because they are usually applied to all products, irrespective of origin, they will inhibit imports in all cases where: (a) the product standards differ from those (if any) applying in the exporters' home and other markets; and (b) this difference implies an increase in unit costs of production and/or transportation. To the extent that either occurs one speaks of standards forming a technical barrier to trade. Clearly, import-competing firms have an incentive to adopt unique standards and to ensure that they are strictly enforced at the border. Even if identical standards are applied to domestic and foreign goods, a tariff-like effect may result because the standard differs from those applied in other markets. Any standard, even if applied on a national treatment and nondiscriminatory basis, may inhibit trade if the standard differs in a significant manner from those used in other markets.

In general, if standards or regulations differ across countries this will segment markets, even if the same standards are applied by each country to domestic and foreign goods. Prices for similar goods of comparable environmental quality need not be equal across countries, as the different standards will inhibit arbitrage. An example comes from Italy, where pasta 'purity' laws require that pasta be made of duram wheat, a high quality, high priced wheat produced in the south of the country. This increases the cost of pasta in comparison with other European community (EC) countries, where pasta tends to consist of a mix of wheat qualities. Related examples include a German law requiring that only 28 per cent of all beer and softdrinks containers can be disposable and attempts in the US to forbid any quantity of lead in wine (French wine bottles contain traces of lead due to wrapping the cork in lead) even though imports meet international standards.

The interests of import-competing firms concerning the specification of a standard depend on the type of product involved, whether there are information asymmetries or externalities, and so forth. It is usually assumed that standards will have a protective effect, as they frequently tend to impose relatively higher costs on foreign producers. Thus, import-competing firms benefit at the expense of consumers and foreign exporters. However, this is not necessarily the case. Donnenfeld *et al.* (1985) investigated the effect of standards in a setting where a domestic industry has market power because consumers are uncertain as to the (environmental) quality of foreign goods, but have perfect knowledge concerning the quality of domestically produced goods. This imperfect information inhibits foreign competition, as it acts to differentiate domestic from foreign goods. Without the information asymmetry the industry would lose its market power. The imposition of a minimum quality standard in this setting raises average quality of imports, inducing some consumers to shift to foreign goods. In order to differentiate its product from imports, the domestic industry responds by increasing the quality of its goods. As a result profits fall, both because this is costly and because market share declines. Instead of acting to protect the domestic industry, a standard in this case will injure it.[33] Of course, public choice considerations suggest that if this is the case it will be quite unlikely that such a standard is ever adopted.

Once the trade-distorting effects of product standards are taken into account, it becomes more probable that interest group pressures will result in the 'public' choice of a sub-optimal standard. In contrast to environmentally-motivated quantity regulation or process standards, in the case of product standards, domestic import-competing firms frequently will not have to worry about a reduction in their competitiveness vis-à-vis foreign producers. On the contrary, if the domestic industry can control the process of standard setting, the standard will tend to be tailored to the existing capabilities of domestic firms and will thereby inhibit imports. Foreign producers will not only have to meet the standard, they will have to bear the recurring testing and certification costs associated with establishing that the standard has indeed been met. In practice, purportedly uniform standards will have a greater negative impact on foreign producers because of larger per unit costs of testing and certification.[34]

The preference of environmental groups for maximum pollution abatement is likely to lead them to pursue stringent product standards, irrespective of product origin. It may then be in the interest of the domestic industry to pursue a somewhat more stringent standard if the detrimental impact of this on exporters more than offsets any additional costs. Thus, the presence of import competition may well lead to a more restrictive standard being chosen than otherwise. And the opportunity to sell such a standard to the public as environmentally friendly may facilitate its adoption. Finally, in the unlikely event that environmentalists manage to get the government to adopt an environmental regulation that benefits foreign producers to the detriment of the domestic industry, the resulting increase in imports and the corresponding injury will increase the domestic industry's access to contingent trade policy instruments.

11.3 Foreign interest groups and international spillovers

Environmental policies undertaken by an importing country tend to have an impact not only on foreign exporters, but also on other interested groups such as foreign environmentalists. Anticipated foreign responses may affect the actions of domestic interest groups. For example, foreign environmental groups, if any, may perceive a beggar-thy-neighbour dimension to the environmental policy if it stimulates local polluting activity. Foreign exporting firms experiencing transitional supranormal profits as a result of output restrictions or process standards imposed on their competitors in the importing country can be expected to resist the erosion of these rents. Assuming that the preferences of such foreign interest groups have some influence on domestic policy formation, do such groups strengthen or weaken pressures to adopt relatively inefficient environmental policies?

Domestic environmentalists may be concerned with foreign as well as local pollution. It should be noted that such concerns do not require there to be physical spillovers. All that is required is that domestic environmentalists care about what happens abroad. For example, they may feel that their efforts are being thwarted if foreign production rises as a result of domestic environmental policy. Thus, another issue that arises is what effect such 'spillovers' (psychological or physical) have on the preferences of environmental groups.

Examples can readily be constructed where foreign interest groups have an incentive to support the pursuit of the inefficient environmental policy favoured by domestic groups. For example, take the case of quantity regulation for a perfectly competitive industry facing import competition. Imports rise equally under both an (efficient) penalty tax and the regulatory approach, suggesting foreign suppliers might be indifferent between the two regimes. However, the structural upheaval in the domestic market is likely to increase the probability that trade restrictions will be imposed (see the previous section), and exporters will not be indifferent as to the type of trade barrier that is used. Unlike tariffs or quantitative restrictions where the quota rights are auctioned, VERs may confer rents on both foreign exporters and domestic firms. Because the market-sharing (quantity regulation) approach to pollution abatement increases the likelihood of a mutually advantageous VER being negotiated, exporting firms should express a strict preference for the regulatory approach.[35]

The prospect of a VER also means that the expected level of additional environmental degradation abroad under the regulatory approach will be less than that under a tax-based approach. Indeed, the expected restraint agreement may be sufficiently restrictive as to imply reduced production/pollution abroad. The enhanced prospect of restraining foreign production/pollution through trade policy should make the regulatory approach attractive to *foreign* as well as domestic environmental interests. In this sense, the linkage between a nonmarket-based approach to environmental control and the prospects for a cartelising VER is part of the attractiveness of regulation to both firms and environmentalists, at home and abroad.

This congruence of interests may not emerge in the case of process standards. Foreign producers will be negatively affected by the associated ban on imports of goods produced via methods that do not meet the standard. Thus, they can be expected to oppose the standard, and push for a pollution tax with an associated import tariff equivalent. Foreign environmental groups in the exporting country are likely to prefer that the importing country impose a standard with extraterritorial application, however, as this results in a greater reduction in local production and thus pollution than a pollution tax/tariff would. Furthermore, the preference of environmentalists in the importing country for process standards will be strengthened for the same reason.

In the case of product standards, similar conclusions emerge. Foreign producers are likely to oppose the product standard,[36] while foreign environmental groups will support it because it increases the probability that local industry will adopt similar standards, thereby improving the local environment. Indeed, it can be argued that the industry will have to adopt equivalent standards if it wants to continue to export. The adoption of a relatively stringent standard in the importing country may enable foreign environmentalists to obtain standards at home that they otherwise would not be able to get enacted. Of course, to the extent that this is the case, and assuming that there are 'spillovers', the preference of environmentalists in the importing country for a relatively stringent standard will be strengthened further.

11.4   Implications for policy

The general conclusion that emerges is that there often will be powerful political obstacles blocking the path to efficient environmental policies. Because such policies tend to neglect the interests of the groups most concerned, they are likely to be more costly and trade-distorting than they need to be to accomplish a given objective. What might be done by policymakers to alter the incentives facing interest groups so that such obstacles might be swept aside?

Since inefficiency implies foregone income, an important element in any effort to 'tame' rent-seekers who block efficient policies will be to inform the general public of that loss. While the benefits to pressure groups under an existing inefficient system are concentrated and the social costs dispersed, there can be no hope of overcoming the free-rider problem unless the costs to consumers and/or the direct benefits to special interests are made well known.[37] More information is also a necessary condition to reduce the social costs of environmental product standards and regulations. The effect of such requirements are rarely obvious to consumers, as they tend to be highly technical. Different standards may have equivalent environmental effects. In such instances the trade-inhibiting effects of standards and regulations could be diminished by either harmonising them or pursuing a policy of mutual recognition. Space constraints prohibit a discussion of these options.[38]

Insofar as quantity regulation and process standards are concerned, another possibility is to credibly precommit to the distribution of the revenues associated with (more efficient) pollution taxes or permits to one or more of the interested parties. In this way government might shift the balance of lobbying power toward the efficient policy. Generally, the potential profits available to firms under a regulatory regime (without considering international cartelisation) will fall short of total tax revenues.[39] In principle, it might appear therefore that the revenue generated by the tax is sufficient to 'buy' the support of the polluting industry. But this is not the case. If the government imposes a penalty tax and commits to redistributing the revenue in lump sums independent of production (as it must be to maintain efficiency) to polluting firms, free entry will still drive industry profits net-of-tax and net-of-tax revenue to zero. In order to enlist the industry's support for a tax, the expected net benefit must be at least as great as under the regulatory approach. This cannot be achieved by any possible redistribution of tax revenues without also granting special privileges to existing firms, e.g., grandfathering the rights to the tax revenues.

Environmentalists, however, may be persuaded to support a tax given a credible plan to divert a share of tax revenues to the environment. Recall that the original source of environmentalist's support for a regulatory approach was the perceived greater certainty of a favourable environmental outcome, including the possibility that the restraint is more likely to be extended to foreign producers via a commercial policy response. The tax-based approach leaves it to firms to decide how much to cut back. If a share of total tax revenues were set aside for environmental causes, any autonomous increase in output will generate revenues for environmentalists while it also increases pollution. What was perceived as a fault before is now at worst a mixed blessing. Hence such an approach may undermine the primary source of environmentalist opposition to a penalty tax scheme. Even if this is the case, there is of course still no guarantee that the interests of domestic import-competing firms will be blocked. In fact, the expected economic profit under the regulatory approach provides firms with resources that may be used to induce environmentalists to support their preferred policy in the same way that government might use tax revenue to that end. So the proposal that a share of any environmentally-based tax revenues be committed to environmental causes is probably necessary but not necessarily sufficient to render a tax-based policy politically feasible.

Although 'command-and-control' approaches to environmental problems continue to be the prevalent form of intervention to deal with both domestic and international spillovers,[40] an encouraging trend can be discerned in a number of countries to implement market-based environmental policies, largely spearheaded by the United States. More often than not, these are based on a regulatory approach but exploit the fact that firms within an industry will face different costs per unit of pollution abatement. Firms are allocated pollution permits and allowed to exchange these among themselves. Such an approach is in some respects equivalent to an efficient tax, an important difference being that all the associated revenues accrue to the polluting firms. Thus, it reflects a 'status quo bias', in that the initial distribution of implicit property rights is formalised, and existing firms are given pollution 'rights' free of charge. The 1990 amendments to the US Clean Air Act are a representative example, allowing for marketable pollution permits. Initially these permits will be allocated to existing firms free of charge. While the government might have auctioned the pollution permits (implying perhaps a more equitable distribution of property rights to the environmental resource), political considerations such as those outlined in this chapter probably blocked that alternative. Indeed, commenting on the recent amendments, Hahn and Noll (1990) have argued that a necessary component in *any* tradeable-permits scheme is that firms be allowed to keep the profits from trading permits.[41] Although this implies that pollution abatement will be achieved efficiently, potentially troubling equity considerations remain.

11.5 Concluding remarks

There will often be a confluence of concentrated interests pushing for the adoption of inefficient policy instruments to achieve a given pollution abatement target. The reason is that such instruments may create rents that can be captured by these groups. The efficient policy generally leaves nothing on the table for the polluting industry, and thus it has a strong incentive to find an inefficient policy on which it and other groups can agree. In practice governments are beginning to use market-based instruments to pursue environmental objectives. The message of this chapter is not that such instruments will never be used, but that there will be strong incentives for interest groups to push for inefficient instruments. And, practical experience demonstrates that more often than not such pressures prove overwhelming.

Furthermore, trade matters. In an autarkic setting taxes and regulatory instruments tend to raise the costs of affected industries, even though the impact on subgroups of firms within industries may differ. Once trade is allowed for, regulatory instruments no longer have broadly similar effects. Product standards may directly restrict imports, while process standards or output restrictions imposed on domestic firms may foster imports. Thus, environmental policies may reduce the competitiveness of domestic firms vis-à-vis foreign exporters.[42] As a result the direct pressures for protection can be expected to increase. Moreover, because such firms may be in a better position to demonstrate injury, they may have ready access to existing instruments of administered protection. Even if governments and environmental groups have no intention to increase trade barriers through environmental policy, existing rules make such an increase likely. Indeed, because such instruments are administrative, not political, governments may find it difficult to oppose such protection.

The problem suggested for the world trading system by a public-choice approach to the environmental policy formation process is that there may be direct and indirect opportunities to create new barriers to trade. Existing rules for contingent protection, particularly antidumping, and grey area measures like voluntary restraint agreements provide an institutional setting in which environmental policy efforts might set off unintentional increases in administered protection. Alternatively, calls for new environmentally-motivated product or production-process standards may stimulate import-competing interests to pursue measures that impose disproportionate costs on their foreign competitors. The theory of public choice, experience with policies in the areas of anti-dumping, countervailing duties, and VERs, and some current proposals for revising trade policies to take into account environmental concerns[43] all point strongly to the likelihood that the manipulation of environmental objectives for protectionist purposes, as well as the appearance of unintended protectionist consequences of environmental policies, are and will continue to be serious problems.

By calling attention to the deformities of the policy formation process we are presented with the opportunity to design laws and institutions that will properly constrain interest group behaviour or harness it to the public interest. As observed by Adam Smith over two hundred years ago, individuals acting in their own self interest through voluntary exchange in markets, though it is not their intent, can indirectly advance the public interest. But it is well known that Smith's observation requires a guarantee of property rights, laws against fraud and misrepresentation, and the like. By analogy, in principle an institutional setting can be designed that will channel the energies of pressure groups acting in their own self interest to indirectly advance the public interest. Only by first opening the clenched fist of special interest politics can we hope to pursue that end. Unless there is some attempt by policymakers to constrain the efforts of interest groups, or to harness these to the public interest, the environmental policy/protectionism nexus will likely continue to threaten ongoing trade liberalization efforts.

Notes

The views expressed in this essay are those of the authors and should not be attributed to the GATT Secretariat or GATT Contracting Parties. We are grateful to Kym Anderson, Richard Blackhurst and Patrick Messerlin for helpful comments and discussions.

1. The political economy of environmental policy formation appears to be a rather neglected topic. Whereas most recent textbooks on international trade tend to contain a chapter focusing on the political determinants of trade policy, this is rarely the case for environmental/natural resource economics textbooks. A literature search revealed only a handful of contributions dealing with this issue, none of which allow for international trade. These include Buchanan and Tullock (1975), Dewees (1983), Hahn (1989), Maloney and McCormick (1982), Oster (1982), Yandle (1989), and Zeckhauser (1981).

2. An optimal policy consists of the socially desirable level of pollution abatement (that which equates the marginal social benefit with the marginal social cost), in conjunction with an efficient instrument to attain the objective (one which is least cost). In general, instances in which governments are able to determine the optimal level of pollution abatement will be quite rare, as this requires the authorities to have detailed knowledge of the preferences of every citizen. In practice, it will usually be impossible to obtain this information.

3. Recent exceptions include Runge (1990) and Whalley (1991).

4. Those interested in a more detailed and formal analysis of the issues explored in the sub-section, including commercial policy linkages, are referred to Leidy and Hoekman (1991), on which much of the discussion is based.

5. The focus is on a perfectly competitive industry because this provides the clearest indication of the incentives for firms to prefer an inefficient environmental policy.

6. We do not assume that the abatement target is 'optimal' in the sense of equating marginal social benefits and costs. The public choice concerning the level of pollution abatement is discussed below. What we do assume is that the industry, as an important interest group, had a say in determining the selected level. It is assumed that the level supported by the industry is the cartel solution and that the government's choice does not depart so far from the cartel solution as to eliminate the potential for some excess profits.

7. In what follows it is assumed that any potential revenues generated from a penalty tax flow to the treasury and are not earmarked for any special purpose.

8. Assuming there are no inferior factors.

9. See Leidy and Hoekman (1991) for a full description of the equilibration process under a quantity-based approach.

10. These comments follow Buchanan and Tullock (1975).

11. That there is no exit, of course, hinges on our assumption that the level of pollution abatement was selected in part to accommodate industry interests. Thus there are positive profits associated with the selected quantity and each firm shares in these identically.

12. Even when the price is affected, consumer's interests are not sufficiently concentrated for them to be mobilised.

13. Also, since such all-or-nothing layoffs are likely to have regional implications, and since regional trade union officials are likely to want to avoid the prospect of their demise, it seems likely that a preference for the evenly-distributed layoffs associated with the regulatory approach will emerge over the all-or-nothing option tied to the penalty tax.

14. Of course, in terms of optimal policy this is precisely what *should* occur. This is part of the value of a market-based approach to pollution control. But environmentalists are not by assumption interested in aggregate social welfare. They care about pollution alone.

15. And, if they are not, environmentalists can sue the regulators and/or the industry.

16. Had the analysis considered a domestic industry that is already highly concentrated and exercising substantial market power, neither form of pollution control might have appeared attractive. If, however, a monopolised sector saw sufficient value in shifting the ongoing expense of deterring entry to government regulators, the regulatory approach might then be supported in order to capture that prize.

17. Such process standards are discussed in the next subsection.

18. There is an extensive literature focusing on the relative inefficiency of process standards, e.g., Baumol and Oates (1988).

19. In the case of an internationally traded good the small-country case is ruled out.

20. This may also occur in the quantity regulation case discussed earlier. For example, if firms are subject to different returns to scale, a given percentage reduction in output will effect each firm differently.

21. This will always be the case if all firms in the industry have identical costs. See D'Aspremont *et al.* (1983).

22. This comparison must take into account tax and subsidy effects. There may be subsidies such as investment credits that lower the real cost of retooling. Tax rules pertaining to depreciation will also play a role.

23. Examples include the American National Standards Institute (ANSI), the British Standards Institution (BSI), the Deutsches Institut für Normung (DIN), and the Association Française de Normalisation (AFNOR).

24. Experience indicates that overshooting is not uncommon. The requirement of the US 1972 Clean Water Act that the discharge of pollutants into navigable waters be eliminated by 1985 is an example of overshooting. The same can usually be said of agreements to ban the use of chlorofluorocarbons, hardwoods, etc.

25. The sense in which injury is experienced under a tax-based approach versus a quantity-based regulatory approach is analysed in Leidy and Hoekman (1991). The fact that industry profits tend to rise under quantity regulation need not be an obstacle to showing injury.

26. The injury criteria established under existing legislation offer substantial discretion in evaluating the health of an industry. See Finger and Murray (1990) or Kaplan (1991). The main value of injury for voluntary export restraint (VER) protection is that it helps to mobilise the political resources needed to induce export-restraint negotiations.

27. See, for example, Herander and Pupp (1991).

28. The interests of foreign firms are discussed in Section 3.

29. Observe that no such barriers exist under the penalty tax. Protection from foreign competition would at best offer transitory profits under that regime.

30. To the extent that this may violate GATT obligations, an alternative is a consumer boycott organized by environmental and domestic producer groups. A recent example where this occurred was a boycott of Korean consumers of imported apples thought to be treated with alar.

31. Such diversion is likely to be a general result of any domestic environmental policy.

32. Although a common front will generally maximise the probability of success, this is not necessary. In practice, all that is required is that a significant share of the domestic industry is on board.

33. Profits decline independent of what happens to price. The welfare effects of the standard are ambiguous. Welfare may rise if the increase in quality of products offered by domestic industry more than outweighs any increase in price.

34. Both in an absolute sense – i.e., costs are higher because of language problems, having fewer certified testing agencies, or not being allowed to self-certify – and in a relative sense, as the volume of exports to the affected market as a percentage of total output is likely to be less than for domestic firms.

35. Hillman and Ursprung (1988) argue that because VERs are a conciliatory trade policy, whereas tariffs come at the expense of foreign exporters, VERs tend to be chosen over tariffs whenever that policy choice is available. In the current model the political support for a VER is strengthened.

36. Except, of course, if the standard is in their interest. As discussed earlier, this may occur if there are informational externalities. Alternatively, it may arise because the standard is already met (i.e., is not binding).

37. See Finger (1982) and Koford and Colander (1984) for a menu of additional possibilities.

38. See Abraham (1991) for a discussion of the EC approach to technical harmonisation and standardisation.

39. This is shown in Leidy and Hoekman (1991).

40. Thus, recent multilateral initiatives such as the Montreal Protocol to phase out the use of chlorofluorocarbons, the 1989 ban on ivory trade and the inclusion in the Lomé convention of a two-way ban on trade in toxic waste between the EC and the Africa-Caribbean-Pacific (ACP) countries do not employ a market-based approach.

41. See also Hahn (1989) for a survey of the experience in the US with market-based environmental policies. Yandle (1989) provides a very illuminating account of the gradual move towards formalising property rights to environmental resources. Without such a move, it is extremely unlikely that relatively efficient environmental policies will emerge from the political process.

42. For example, the Australian chemical industry has blamed environmental regulations for the fact that imports more than doubled during 1989–90. In a recent report it has warned that the emphasis on environmental issues 'has reached unhealthy levels and may result in the substantial de-industrialisation of Australia' (*Journal of Commerce*, February 4, 1991).

43. For example, recently a bill was introduced in the US Senate that would impose countervailing duties on imports produced under less-strict environmental standards than those in the United States (S 984, introduced on April 25, 1991 by Sen. David Boren). Another resolution introduced by Rep. Al Swift calls on the US to negotiate mechanisms that would level the 'comparative disadvantages' between countries that do not impose environmental regulations on their industries and the United States (*International Trade Reporter*, June 20, 1990).

References

Abraham, F. (1991), 'Building Blocks of the Single Market: The Case of Mutual Recognition, Home Country Control and Essential Requirements', mimeo, University of Leuven.

D'Aspremont, C., A. Jacquemin, J. Gabszewicz and J. Weymark (1983), 'On the Stability of Collusive Price Leadership', *Canadian Journal of Economics* **16**: 17–25.

Baumol, W. and W. Oates (1988), *The Theory Environmental Policy*, Cambridge: Cambridge University Press.

Buchanan, J. and G. Tullock (1975), 'Polluters' Profits and Political Response: Direct Controls versus Taxes', *American Economic Review* **65**: 139–47.

Dewees, D. (1983), 'Instrument Choice in Environmental Policy', *Economic Inquiry* **21**: 53–71.

Donnenfeld, S., S. Weber and U. Ben-Zion (1985), 'Import Controls Under Imperfect Information', *Journal of International Economics* **19**: 341–54.

Finger, J. M. (1982), 'Incorporating the Gains from Trade into Policy', *World Economy* **5**: 367–77.

Finger, J. M. and T. Murray (1990), 'Policing Unfair Imports: The United States Example', *Journal of World Trade* **24**: 39–55.

Hahn, R. (1989), 'Economic Prescriptions for Environmental Problems: How the Patient Followed the Doctor's Orders', *Journal of Economic Perspectives* **3**: 95–114.

Hahn, R. and R. Noll (1990), 'Environmental Markets in the Year 2000', Discussion Paper No. 205, Centre for Economic Policy Research, forthcoming in *Journal of Risk and Uncertainty*.

Herander, M. and R. Pupp (1991), 'Firm Participation in Steel Industry Lobbying', *Economic Inquiry* **29**: 134–47.

Hillman, A. L. and H. W. Ursprung (1988), 'Domestic Politics, Foreign Interests, and International Trade Policy', *American Economic Review* **78**: 729–45.

Kaplan, Seth (1991), 'Injury and causation in USITC Antidumping Determinations: Five Recent Views', *Policy Implications of Antidumping Measures*, edited by M. Tharakan, Amsterdam: North Holland.

Koford, K. and D. Colander (1984), 'Taming the Rent-Seeker', *Neoclassical Political Economy: The Analysis of Rent Seeking and DUP Activities*, edited by D. Colander, Cambridge, MA: Ballinger.

Leidy, M. and B. Hoekman (1991), '"Cleaning Up" While Cleaning Up: Pollution Abatement, Interest Groups, and Contingent Trade Policies', mimeo, GATT Secretariat, Geneva, April.

Leland, H. (1979), 'Quacks, Lemons and Licensing: A Theory of Minimum Quality Standards', *Journal of Political Economy* **87**: 1328–46.

Maloney, M. and R. McCormick (1982), 'A Positive Theory of Environmental Quality Regulation', *Journal of Law and Economics* **25**: 99–123.

Olson, M. (1965), *The Logic of Collective Action*, Cambridge: Harvard University Press.

Oster, S. (1982), 'The Strategic Use of Regulatory Investment by Industry Subgroups', *Economic Inquiry* **20**: 604–18.

Runge, C. F. (1990), 'Trade Protectionism and Environmental Regulations: The New Nontariff Barriers', *Northwestern Journal of International Law and Business* **11**: 47–61.

Salop, S. and D. Scheffman (1983), 'Raising Rivals' Costs', *American Economic Review* **73**: 267–71.

246 *Bernard Hoekman and Michael Leidy*

Shapiro, C. (1983), 'Premiums for High Quality Products as Returns to Reputations', *Quarterly Journal of Economics* **48**: 659–79.

Stigler, G. (1971), 'The Theory of Economic Regulation', *Bell Journal of Economics and Management Science* **2**: 3–21.

Tirole, J. (1988), *The Theory of Industrial Organization*, Cambridge: MIT Press.

Tullock, G. (1967), 'The Welfare Costs of Tariffs, Monopolies and Theft', *Western Economic Journal* **5**: 224–32.

Whalley, J. (1991), 'The Interface Between Environmental and Trade Policies', *Economic Journal* **101**: 180–89.

Yandle, B. (1989), *The Political Limits of Environmental Regulation*. New York: Quorum Books.

Zeckhauser, R. (1981), 'Preferred Policies When There is a Concern for Probability of Adoption', *Journal of Environmental Economics and Management* **8**: 215–37.

12

Promoting multilateral cooperation on the environment

Richard Blackhurst and Arvind Subramanian

When analysing policy options for dealing with environmental problems, it is useful to distinguish between problems according to the nature of the effects on other countries. In one category are those environmental problems in which (a) the environmental effects are limited to the country in which the environmentally harmful activity is taking place, but (b) the government's policy response, or lack of response, to those adverse environmental effects has an impact on other countries via its impact on trade and capital flows. In such a situation, the country's behaviour does not create an environmental problem for other countries. The concerns of other countries are commercial, not environmental. The principal challenge to the international community when the environmental externalities are exclusively domestic is to agree on a set of rules that will minimize commercial friction between countries.[1]

The second broad category groups those environmental problems which involve transnational externalities – either physical spillovers between countries or what may be called 'psychological' spillovers. Physical spillovers are primarily pollution problems of a regional or global nature, such as acid rain in Western Europe or the emission of chlorofluorocarbon (CFC) gases worldwide. Psychological spillovers generally involve either a threat to something whose continued existence is important to significant numbers of people worldwide, such as a particular species of animal or plant, or allegations of cruelty to animals, such as dolphins, baby seals or battery hens. In contrast to the domestic externalities in the first category, physical or psychological spillovers create environmental problems for residents of other countries (subsequent policy reactions could produce trade and capital flow effects as well).[2]

When physical or psychological spillovers are involved, countries will want to influence directly the behaviour of other countries – that is, of the countries from which the spillovers are originating – for environmental rather than commercial reasons. This introduces new and difficult elements into countries' relations with one another, including the need to agree on regional or global norms and standards for shared resources, and on the distribution between countries of the costs of environmental improvement and protection. These difficulties, in turn, add considerably to the challenge of finding ways to convince the necessary number of sovereign countries to participate in regional or global cooperative agreements.

This chapter focuses on the second rather than first category of problems: on achieving and sustaining multilateral cooperation to deal with environmental problems involving physical or psychological spillovers between countries. The cooperation in question is the kind that involves non-trivial costs for countries. That is, it extends beyond simple exchanges of views and information to include commitments concerning national behaviour and national policies.[3]

Following a brief look at the pressures for, and obstacles to, multilateral cooperation on environmental issues, the second section examines the contribution which game theory has made to the topic of multilateral cooperation. The third section first reviews the obstacles to cooperation in more detail, and then takes up the question of creating incentives for countries to participate in multilateral efforts to deal with environmental problems. As is evident from the discussion in the third section, the relevance of this topic for trade policy stems from the fact that certain trade policy actions may (a) be intended to alter the behaviour of other countries, either directly or through encouraging their participation in a multilateral agreement, or (b) be designed to prevent actions which would undermine such an agreement.[4]

12.1 The challenge of multilateral cooperation

Awareness of the fact that environmental problems often fail to respect national boundaries is not new. What is new – relative to the period surrounding the first United Nations conference on the environment in 1972 – is the perception that an increasing number of environmental problems are regional or global in nature. It is now generally accepted that the use of chlorofluorocarbons (CFCs) and halons contributes to the depletion of the ozone layer, generating adverse consequences for all countries. While there is a wider range of opinion on the threat posed by the burning of carbon-based fuels, and the resulting release of carbon dioxide and other gases, the possibility of a rise in mean global temperatures and of other unforeseeable climatic changes is very widely discussed. These are examples of spillovers affecting environmental 'common property' resources owned by no one country or individual. But spillovers can also occur when a resource is, in a conventional legal sense, the property of a particular country or group of countries. The indiscriminate killing of elephants for ivory, possibly threatening their extinction, has a spillover effect because people in other countries value the continued existence of elephants. The felling of forests within national boundaries can generate international spillovers in terms of the potential loss of genetic biodiversity, the services which the trees provide as absorbers of harmful carbon-related gases, and the amenity value of a wilderness area.

No single factor explains this emergence of regional and global environmental problems. Hahn and Richards (1989) identify four forces which they believe are driving what they refer to as the internationalization of environmental issues: improved scientific understanding, which has helped to define the scope of problems and to promote international solutions; heightened public awareness and concern regarding environmental risks; increased political interest and activity on the part of national and international environmental groups, public officials and politicians; and economic factors, including the added strain on environmental resources from continuing economic growth, and the impact of higher per capita incomes on the demand for environmental amenities. A degree of progress in several industrial countries in dealing with purely domestic, pollution-related environmental problems may also be a factor behind the increased attention to regional and global problems. Finally, the ongoing economic integration of the world economy and a sense that people are 'living closer together' is probably also playing a role.

Experience since the early 1970s makes it clear that agreement *within* countries on environmental norms, standards and the distribution of costs is often difficult. At the regional or global level, agreement and enforcement is often much more difficult for a variety of reasons (four of which are examined in Section 3 below). Some of those obstacles to cooperation are underscored by the experience with international cooperation in an area not far removed from the environment area, namely public health.

Puzzled by the great difficulty which the major industrial countries have in cooperating to frame and manage their monetary, fiscal and exchange rate policies, despite the obvious interdependence of their respective policies, Cooper (1989) examined the history of international cooperation in public health to see if it could shed light on problems of cooperation in the area of macroeconomic policy. The answers he found are, if anything, even more relevant to current efforts to promote international cooperation on environmental matters than to efforts at cooperation in the macroeconomic area.

Although there exists today an institutionalized system for monitoring outbreaks of contagious diseases and for taking concerted multilateral actions to control their spread – effective enough to have eradicated smallpox in 1977 – any notion that international cooperation in controlling contagious disease was easy to achieve is quickly refuted by the intriguing story Cooper relates. The twelve International Sanitary Conferences held between 1851 and 1912 were mostly characterised by sharp disagreements and lack of results, despite the widely shared objective of limiting the spread of virulent and often fatal disease. More generally, Cooper notes that

> It took over seventy years from the first call for international cooperation in the containment of the spread of contagious disease in 1834 to 1907, when an international organisation was first put in place to deal with the problem – and even that represented only the beginning. Why did it take so long to achieve international cooperation despite the widely shared objective of preventing the spread of virulent disease? It is now evident that it was due to conflicting views over how best to tackle the problem, over means-ends relationships. The ends were shared: to stop the spread of epidemic disease. But there were sharp disagreements over how best to do this. The means were costly, and their costs would have been borne unevenly by different countries. Each party understandably wanted to pay the lowest possible costs.
>
> Costs were related to remedies, and remedies in turn were related to the causes of the diseases, about which disagreement continued for much of the century. (pp. 236 – 37)
>
> So long as costs are positive and benefits are uncertain, countries are not likely to cooperate systematically with one another; and so long as sharply differing views are held on the relationship between actions and outcomes, at least some parties will question the benefits alleged to flow from any particular proposed course of action. (p. 181).

Even a brief review of the current literature is sufficient to document the existence of similar disagreements over the interpretation of scientific evidence on leading environmental issues. In one important sense, the range of disagreement on environmental issues is even greater than it was with public health. No one doubted the existence of contagious disease, nor that it was important to try to eliminate it, or at least limit its spread. In the case of contemporary environmental problems of a regional or global nature, in contrast, not only are there fierce debates over causes and cures of problems, but also examples both of continuing debate over whether a problem actually exists (for example, global warming) and of wide difference over the importance of avoiding certain activities (for example, the accidental killing of dolphins or activities that could lead to the disappearance of certain animal or plant species).[5]

12.2   Game theory and multilateral cooperation

Formal approaches to analysing the conflict between the pursuit of self-interest and the collective interest have become a major field of study in several disciplines. To a large extent game theory provides the rigourous underpinnings for many important aspects of the work in this area. For the problem at hand – multilateral cooperation to deal with environmental problems involving physical or psychological spillovers between countries – analysts frequently choose to work with one particular type of game, namely the Prisoners' Dilemma (PD):

> The PD is the standard representation of externalities (including public goods) where in the pursuit of their own private gains actors impose costs on each other *independently of each other's action*; that is, in the pursuit of its national interest State A makes State B worse off regardless of what the latter does, and vice versa (Snidal 1985, pp. 926 – 27, emphasis in the original).

Consider the structure of payoffs in Table 12.1 (adapted from Snidal). C and NC represent the cooperative and non-cooperative strategies for the two countries, which are assumed to be symmetrical (identical) players. It is useful to think of C as a 'high' level of pollution abatement and NC as 'low' level of abatement action. The pairs of payoffs, to A and B respectively, measure the net gain to each after the cost of pollution abatement has been deducted from the gross gain due to the cleaner environment. Country A will select the NC strategy, hoping to get a payoff of 4 (rather than the 3 available from pursuing the C strategy). That is, since A bears all of its own abatement costs, but must share the gains from a cleaner environment with B, it will select the low abatement option. In effect, it 'underinvests' in pollution abatement because it cannot capture all the gains. For exactly the same reasons, country B also selects NC, hoping to get a payoff of 4. The result is that each gets a payoff of 2, whereas if each had selected strategy C, both would have received a payoff of 3. It is clear that (a) both countries are better off if they enter an agreement to cooperate, and (b) even if they reach a cooperative agreement, there will be a continuing incentive for each to defect from the agreement since if one country stays with C, the other country gains by shifting to a NC strategy.[6]

Because there is no supra-national authority to enforce the cooperative solution, countries A and B will be stuck more or less permanently in the lower right-hand quadrant (2,2 payoff) of Table 12.1. However, if the restrictive assumptions implicit in this very simple model are relaxed, the likelihood of cooperation generally increases. Specifically, the following analysis considers, in turn, the effects of game repetition, of having

Table 12.1 Prisoners' dilemma*

| | | Country B | |
		C_B	NC_B
Country A	C_A	3, 3	1, 4
	NC_A	4, 1	2, 2

Note: *The first in each pair of numbers is the payoff to country A, while the second is the payoff to country B, given the strategies adopted by the two countries.

several non-identical players, of reciprocity, and of allowing for the general equilibrium effects of interventions.

12.2.1 Repetition increases the likelihood of cooperation

It has been shown that if the single-play game is repeated over time, the prospects of cooperation can be increased through a wide variety of strategies. These includes a tit-for-tat strategy whereby each player cooperates if the other player has cooperated in the previous period, and threatens to retaliate by not cooperating if the other has not cooperated in the previous period.[7] Another example is provided by Dasgupta (1990) who shows that there are alternative strategies, involving social norms or codes of conduct, which could lead to cooperation in repeated games. One such strategy or norm is the adoption of cooperative behaviour by one player if the other does so and of non-cooperative behaviour for the rest of the 'game' if the other cheats. Many variations on this unforgiving strategy can also be shown to sustain a cooperative equilibrium. Yet another example due to Kreps and Wilson (1982) and Kreps *et al.* (1982) is a finitely repeated PD game in which uncertainty about payoffs can produce cooperative as well as other equilibria. Because of this, it might be in the interest of each player to signal an intention to cooperate hoping that other will reciprocate. This is an example of reputation or trust-building strategies facilitating cooperation.

Strategies based on enhanced reputations and ongoing cooperation are important not just in single issue areas, but also in situations involving multiple issues. The availability of PD 'games' in several different subject areas could increase the incentive to cooperate by more than the option of repeated plays of a single game, as countries would fear that non-cooperation in any one area would spread to the other areas:

> Indeed, this is a much more important aspect of issue-linkage than the more often discussed exchange form of linkage based on the linking of issues in a bargaining context. It is directly related to broader questions about the emergence of an international society with multiple overlapping interests and concerns. To the extent that such a society is emerging, the individual PD situation becomes embedded in a broader social context, and cooperation is increasingly possible with less formal centralised enforcement (Snidal, 1985, p. 939).

This passage calls attention to two closely related considerations. The first is that the environment area is just one of many areas in which the effects of the ongoing integration of the world's countries – globalization – are being felt. Second, it is likely that the prospects for success in dealing with regional or global issues in one area (such as the environment) will be influenced to a greater or lesser extent by progress in other areas.

12.2.2 *Allowing for many countries and asymmetry*

Expanding the PD from two countries to many countries and dropping the assumption of symmetric players may increase or decrease the prospects for cooperation. When public goods are involved, as is the case with most environmental problems, an increase in the number of countries reduces the prospects for cooperation, in part because the free-riding problem is exacerbated. However, if the assumption that all countries are identical is also relaxed (allowing countries to differ with respect to preferences and costs of emission reduction), the prospects for cooperation are generally enhanced. This is because the more asymmetric the distribution of benefits, the smaller is the number of countries required to achieve a given level of pollution reduction. In a very asymmetric situation, the key countries can reach an agreement that solves most of the problem (subject, of course, to strategic considerations operating among themselves), provided they are prepared to tolerate free riding by the non-key countries. (Olson, 1971). This is good news since many regional and global environmental problems are primarily the result of the activities of a relatively small number of countries (see, for example, MacNeill, *et al*, 1991).

12.2.3 *Reciprocity also increases the likelihood of cooperation*

Drawing partly on the results of Axelrod's (1984) work on the effectiveness of the tit-for-tat strategy in inducing cooperation in the repeated Prisoners' Dilemma game, and partly on theories of social exchange, Keohane (1986) argues that reciprocity has an important role to play in contemporary international relations: 'Reciprocity [in this case] refers to exchanges of roughly equivalent values in which the actions of each party are contingent on the prior actions of others in such a way that good is returned for good, and bad for bad (p. 8).'

One form of reciprocity he labels *specific reciprocity*, defined as situations in which specified partners engaging in a specific transaction exchange items of equivalent value. While specific reciprocity is an attractive strategy in certain situations, free-riding makes its application problematic when large numbers of countries and public goods are involved. By definition, free-riders cannot be excluded from consuming public goods, and with large number of countries involved, individual countries have less incentive to police the agreement by retaliating against defectors since they risk being criticized by other nations for 'aggressive' actions, while at the same time they capture only a small share of the benefits of enforcing the agreement. It follows that reliance on sanctions against free-riders (the negative side of reciprocity) is not likely to be effective in enforcing a cooperative environmental agreement when the agreement requires the participation of a large number of countries.

The second form of reciprocity is *diffuse reciprocity*. It is a broader concept, in the sense that equivalence of behaviour, identity of the other players and the range of events over which the equivalence of behaviour takes place are all defined less precisely than in the case of specific reciprocity. There is a sense of obligation among countries, and they are expected to conform to generally accepted standards of behaviour (Keohane, 1986). This notion of diffuse reciprocity is also captured in Sugden's (1984, 1986) approach under which the action of agents is guided or constrained by moral considerations of fairness or reciprocity, namely that, 'if others are contributing to the provision of a public good, so must I'. Closely related to Kant's categorial imperative, this approach is cited by Kindleberger (1988) as an alternative, if unlikely, solution to the public good problem. Under this approach it has been shown that the free-rider problem can be overcome even in a single-period game.

Within families and small communities, diffuse reciprocity is common. As the relevant political unit gets larger, diffuse reciprocity becomes more difficult, but certainly not impossible. (Sugden cites the examples of voluntary contributions to the lifeboat service in the United Kingdom and to the Wilderness Society in the United States, and Keohane describes unconditional most-favoured-nation treatment in trade as an example of diffuse reciprocity.) That such considerations play a role especially in the environment area is seen for example in Norway's offer to set up an international fund on global climatic change to the extent of 0.01 per cent of GDP if others also did so, and in debates in the United Kingdom where contributions to environmental problems have been urged on grounds of fairness (Barrett, 1990a).

Two aspects of diffuse reciprocity are of particular interest to efforts to promote international cooperation on environmental issues. One is evidence that the successful pursuit of specific reciprocity – either over time on the same issue, or across issues – can create the confidence between countries that is necessary for diffuse reciprocity. Second, as has been noted, diffuse reciprocity is possible only when there is a widespread sense of obligation. This will not be easy in the environment area as long as there are important differences between countries on such fundamentals as the adequacy of scientific evidence, the ranking of environmental issues on the national agenda, and the appropriate international distribution of costs. But neither should these obstacles be exaggerated. Few things impact so universally on mankind as the hospitality of the earth's physical environment. It follows that the possibilities for a change in preferences favouring cooperation – that is, for developing a sense of shared commitment among countries in dealing with regional and global environmental problems – should be commensurately large.

12.2.4 General equilibrium effects of environmental actions

The discussion to this point has been vague about the precise nature of the structure of incentives facing individual countries. The numbers in the above pay-off matrix reflect the net gain after the cost of pollution abatement has been deducted from the gross gain from reduced pollution. This purely quantitative approach was subsequently expanded to allow for the impact on incentives of such things as concerns about reputation, a desire to carry a 'fair share', and the need to cooperate through time in the area in question or in other areas which would benefit from international cooperation.

As is readily apparent from several papers in this volume, there can be important additional economic effects which are not captured by a simple comparison of pollution control costs and environmental benefits, nor by the inclusion of the more qualitative factors. For example, a unilateral reduction in production of a particular product by one country or a sub-group of countries would raise producer prices in other countries and thus stimulate output. Alternatively, if they reduced consumption of the product in question, consumer prices would decline and thus stimulate consumption in other countries. The impact of likely changes in the terms of trade on national welfare would also have to be taken into account by each country in assessing the overall costs and benefits of its environmental actions.

The preceding examination of international cooperation has highlighted a number of forces that work both against and in favour of cooperation. It confirms the lessons of experience, namely that while some cooperation occurs more or less spontaneously, achieving the necessary level of international cooperation can be a formidable challenge when participation involves substantial economic costs.

12.3 Promoting and maintaining multilateral cooperation on environmental issues

Since it is likely that there will be instances in which the necessary degree of international cooperation in dealing with physical and psychological environmental spillovers will not be forthcoming automatically, it is necessary to consider the options available to promote international cooperation. This section begins with a review of four important obstacles to cooperation, and then turns to an examination of options available to overcome those obstacles. The issue has important implications for trade policies because, as was noted above, it is evident from existing and proposed agreements, as well as from recent bilateral developments, that governments and environmental interest groups see a role for trade policy in the promotion and enforcement of international cooperation on environmental issues.

12.3.1 *Why a country may not be willing to cooperate*

As was noted above in Section 1, there are at least four reasons why a country might decline, at least initially, an invitation to join one or more other countries in a cooperative effort to solve an environmental problem. First, in the case of a physical spillover, the country may find the scientific evidence unconvincing, and therefore either does not accept that there is a problem, or believes that the risks are exaggerated or that the proposed remedies will be ineffective. These differences result from the fact that in some instances the scientific evidence concerning an environmental problem is mixed and circumstantial, while at the same time the cost of underestimating the seriousness of the problem could be very high (for example, global warming and tolerable levels of carcinogenic residues in food and beverages). In the case of a psychological spillover, there may also be a disagreement over scientific evidence (for example, regarding the claim that a particular animal or plant is close to extinction).[8]

Second, the country may accept that a particular environmental problem exists, but attach a lower priority to solving it than do the countries backing the proposed international agreement. This disagreement may also take the form of a dispute over the relationship between benefits and costs. Levels of concern about environmental issues can differ among countries due to differences in preferences, per capita income,[9] environmental endowments, expectations about the pace of future technological innovations, the degree of concern for future generations, and socio-cultural traditions. The existence of specific problems, such as a high level of foreign indebtedness, can also influence a country's priorities.

Third, the country may disagree with the proposed inter-country allocation of responsibility for dealing with regional and global environmental problem. Responsibility can include modifying behaviour (for example, consuming less hydrocarbons), paying for cleaning-up existing problems, income transfers to compensate individual countries for taking care of global environmental assets, and assistance to low-income countries in obtaining environmentally friendly technology.

The allocation of responsibility on environmental issues is linked to the question of property rights. At the national level a number of countries have chosen to follow the 'polluter pays principle' (PPP), in part for its efficiency advantages (if administered correctly, it creates incentives for polluters to search for less polluting ways to carry out their activities) and in part out of the public's sense of fairness (the view being that if a private entity is polluting a public environmental resource, the private entity should bear the cost of reducing or ceasing that activity). The alternative is the 'victim pays principle' (VPP), in which polluters receive government subsidies in order to cover part or all of the costs of reducing the amount of pollution discharged. PPP amounts to assigning environmental resource property rights to the public of the country in question, whereas VPP amounts to assigning the property rights to those who are emitting the pollution.

At the multilateral level, the PPP/VPP distinction is much more problematic.[10] In regard to global resources such as the ozone layer, the atmosphere and most marine resources, which transcend national boundaries, the fundamental question is how to allocate rights between countries to the scarce capacity of these common property resources to absorb waste. Ultimately, the answer probably hinges on moral or ethical considerations.[11] In the context of the possible institution of a system of internationally tradeable permits for carbon emissions, for example, it has been suggested that such permits be allocated on a per capita basis. Another approach advocated by some countries is that the allocation of future property rights in the context of the global warming problem should be inversely related to a country's cumulative contribution to the stock of greenhouse gases over the last hundred or more years. The argument in this case is that there should be some intertemporal equity in the right to emit sustainable amounts of waste into the atmosphere and hence in the right to future growth opportunities. A third option would be for each country to reduce current carbon emissions by an equal percentage – a proposal which implicitly allocates rights to discharge carbon into the atmosphere on a first come, first served basis. The income distributional implications of these various proposals – between different groups within a country, as well as between countries – are sizeable and thus could be expected to have a major impact on the willingness of particular countries to participate in an agreement to reduce the emission of greenhouse gases.[12]

As regards flows of services from certain environmental resources located within national boundaries, there are differences of opinion about the obligations of the rest of the world to pay for those services. A good example is the Amazon forest, which Brazil views as a national resource rendering environmental services to the rest of the world in the form of carbon absorption and species variety. Accordingly, Brazil could ask to be paid by the rest of the world for these international flows of services (or, in what amounts to the same thing, it could ask for compensation for the preservation of the forest). The other view is that these services of the Amazon forest are a universal resource. On this view, the world has a right to the forest's preservation and conversely its destruction should result in the rest of the world being compensated by Brazil. Most psychological spillovers are likely to fall into this category (with exception of the treatment of animal life in the high seas).

Fourth, the country may be trying to free-ride on the efforts of other countries to solve the problem.[13] Public goods, it will be recalled, satisfy two criteria: first, 'that if any person in a group ... consumes it, it cannot feasibly be withheld from others in that group'; and second, that there is jointness of supply, in the sense that 'making it available to one individual means that it can be easily or freely supplied to others as well' (Olson, 1971, p. 14). It is clear, therefore, that most environmental services are public goods. The dominant economic characteristic of public goods is the likelihood that a sub-optimal amount will be supplied if private markets are the sole suppliers. This follows from the fact that since all citizens can benefit from the public good regardless of who pays for it, they have (so it is argued) little or no incentive to contribute voluntarily to the cost of the good. This phenomenon has variously been termed the 'free-rider' problem and the 'tragedy of the commons' among economists and ecologists.

At the domestic level, the provision of public goods is, in principle if not in practice, relatively straightforward. They are provided by the government. The free-rider problem is solved by coercing citizens into paying (through the tax system) for such public goods as national defence and police and fire protection, or by coercing (through the judicial system) private agents into contributing their share of the reduction of pollution or other externality-generating behaviour. Put in these terms, it is immediately apparent why the provision of international public goods – such as those which are the subject of this chapter – presents such a challenge. With no world government, the only option is voluntary cooperation among sovereign nations.

Free-riding at the international level can occur anytime the 'production' of a public good does not require the participation of all countries. (By definition, a country whose participation is essential to the production of the public good cannot free-ride.) That is, in a world in which everyone accepted the existence of a problem, gave the same priority to solving it, and considered the allocation costs equitable, there could still be countries which held back from cooperating on the assumption that a group of other countries will deal with the problem and that they will be able to enjoy the benefits – for example, of a stable ozone layer – without having to contribute to the costs of solving the problem. It is important to note that the characterization of 'free-riding' presupposes a view about the appropriate allocation of property rights. Differences of views about the latter could lead to a country's actions being viewed as free-riding by some, but as a legitimate exercise of its property rights by the country itself.

In many situations involving cooperation problems, two or more of the four reasons will be interacting to influence a country's attitude toward participation. For example, relatively weak scientific evidence for the existence of a problem could influence the priority which a country attaches to solving it. Furthermore, any of the first three reasons could reduce a country's willingness to engage in the diffuse reciprocity described by Keohane, and thus reinforce the temptation to try to free-ride.

It is useful to recall in this context a point made earlier in the chapter, namely that most – perhaps all – environmental agreements do not require that all countries participate in order for the agreement to deal effectively with the environmental problem in question. Many countries' activities make only a marginal contribution to a particular problem (which means they can make only a marginal contribution to solving it), in which case a decision on their part to free-ride would not threaten the agreement. On the other hand, it is also evident that where to draw the line can be subjective and thus a source of potential friction between participants and non-participants. The fact that only a small number of countries are participating can also raise political problems related to reciprocity and fairness. [14]

12.3.2 Cooperation with leaders

Game theory offers a number of alternatives to the Prisoners' Dilemma game, including some which are based on more explicit forms of cooperation (but which do not necessarily exclude the non-cooperative approaches outlined earlier). These approaches share one or both of two features – the existence of leadership and reliance on side-payments and side-sanctions. Barrett's work (1990b, 1991), which is the basis for the following brief discussion, incorporates both features. In his model two types of countries are postulated. The first type, which could be called leaders, are willing to behave cooperatively in their choice of abatement action, that is, they are willing to take into account the effects of their actions on other leaders. Leaders behave like members of a club maximizing their joint net benefits. Although the model does not deal explicitly with the issue of how the leaders emerge and reach agreement among themselves, the preceding analysis of the case in which the benefits of a cleaner environment are distributed asymmetrically offers one explanation for the emergence of a sub-group of countries with the incentive to take the initiative in establishing an agreement.

The other group – followers – behave non-cooperatively. [15] The followers can include countries whose participation is essential to the agreement (in which case the leaders have yet to put together the critical mass of countries) but which are reluctant to participate for one or more of the first three reasons listed above, and actual free-riders.

If the participation of one or more of the followers is essential for an agreement, or if the leaders are not willing to let all of the followers free-ride, the problem of securing cooperation turns on how to provide the appropriate incentives to the followers to join in a possible agreement. There are two principal options – offering side-payments or threatening sanctions. These two possibilities can be illustrated in terms of the payoff

Table 12.2   Pay-off matrix with leaders committed to cooperation*

		Leaders	
		Compensation C	Sanctions S
Followers	C	5, 6	3, 6
	NC	4, 1	2, 1

Note: *The first in each pair of numbers is the payoff to country A, while the second is the payoff to country B, given the strategies adopted by the two countries.

matrix shown in Table 12.2, which is similar to the one used to describe the PD game.

Assuming the leaders are committed to the cooperative strategy (and known to be so), the use of promises of compensation and threats of sanctions ensures that cooperation is the dominant strategy for the followers. In the first column of Table 12.2 the cooperative strategy of followers is rewarded and in the second column the non-cooperative strategy is penalized, both of which render cooperation as the equilibrium.[16] Note, however, that the two equilibria involve different payoffs for the follower (5 versus 3). Thus the resources accruing to countries which are reluctant to cooperate on environmental issues will depend crucially on whether compensation or sanctions is used to secure cooperation (a question which has obvious parallels with the issue of polluter pays versus victim pays). From a game-theory perspective, the credibility of this approach, namely of altering the payoffs to followers, would depend on whether in any given situation the offer of a side payment or the threat of sanctions is in the broader interests of leaders. That is, side payments or sanctions would have repercussions not only on the followers, but also on the leaders themselves – repercussions which on net could be either positive or negative from the individual leaders' points of view.

12.3.3   *Options for promoting cooperation*

There are two basic strategies for promoting cooperation. One is to identify which of the four reasons listed above are behind the decision to not participate, and then to try to 'eliminate' them (without recourse to side-payments or sanctions). With the first three reasons, this would require eliminating the difference(s) between countries – through better scientific evidence, persuasion to change rankings, or new proposals for allocating costs. If a country were inclined to free-ride, an attempt could be made to get it to participate by stressing the advantages of diffuse reciprocity, either in the environmental area alone or in its more general relations with other countries. A willingness to engage in diffuse reciprocity could also help overcome remaining differences between countries on the first three points.

The second basic strategy for promoting cooperation is for those countries which are taking the initiative in organizing the agreement to create incentives for participation by other countries – incentives that are strong enough to overcome one or more of the four reasons why the countries have initially opted for non-participation. The incentives, in turn can be divided into negative incentives, which would worsen the situation of non-participants relative to the non-cooperative situation, and positive incentives which would improve the situation of a participant relative to the non-cooperative option.

12.3.3.1 Sanctions as negative incentives

The term 'negative incentive' brings to mind immediately the threatened use of a sanction as a way of getting a country to participate in a multilateral environmental agreement. Sanctions can take various forms, such as suspension of scientific and cultural cooperation, restrictions on financial transactions with the country in question, or discriminatory trade measures (typically increased import restrictions) on products which are unrelated to the environmental problem at hand. Some sanctions can be privately organised, the most obvious example being a consumer boycott against goods or services from a country which is refusing to join a particular environmental agreement.

One revealing finding from the literature on international cooperation is the prevalence of the view that the use of sanctions is not, in general, a desirable or effective way of promoting international cooperation. The formal game theory models are understandably neutral on the issue of negative versus positive incentives. But the other authors either fail to mention negative incentives (sanctions) when they discuss ways of encouraging participation in agreements (Sand, 1991; MacNiell, 1991), or explicitly caution against the use of such measures. Chayes and Chayes (1991, p. 289), for example, argue that 'The structural realities of international life preclude "enforcement" by means of sanctions except in very special circumstances.' This view is supported by Stern (forthcoming):

> There is also reason to doubt that even draconian trade policies such as embargoes can ever be very effective in changing the behaviour of foreign governments and their constituencies. Trade can have powerful effects. But when used as a weapon, it seems more likely to generate resistance, rather than fear, in the hearts of its victims. ... On the other hand, it is conceivable that trade policy might be more successful in influencing policies abroad if it were oriented toward providing positive rather than negative incentives in the political sphere. This is certainly worth exploring further.

Mohr (1990) has called attention to parallels between efforts to deal with the international debt problem and the challenge of designing an international greenhouse convention. In the course of discussing the issue of carrots versus sticks, he observes:

> Theory and evidence of international debt relations suggest, however, that sanctions pose only a very moderate threat in international relations. ... From this experience one is bound to conclude that the main burden of stabilising international greenhouse agreements rests on the carrot of payments to opportunistic countries. In general a 'carrot-only' approach can be able to stabilise a contract. (pp. 24–25)

These sentiments no doubt explain in part why none of the existing multilateral environmental agreements contain provisions for trade sanctions – that is, for measures to be taken against unrelated products in the case of non-participation or defection. Another part of the explanation may be countries' awareness that if the threat of a trade sanction is not sufficient to induce participation, and they have to increase trade barriers, their own economy will be harmed.[17]

12.3.3.2 *Trade provisions as positive/negative incentives*

A minority of current multilateral environmental agreements contain trade provisions that are applicable to products directly related to the environmental problem which the agreement is intended to address. Perhaps the best-known example is the trade provisions in the Montreal Protocol on CFCs (see Chapter 7 by Enders and Porges in this volume). Many agreements covering flora and fauna also contain trade provisions.[18]

Generally speaking, the primary purpose of such trade provisions is to prevent developments in the trade of non-participants from undermining the effectiveness of the agreement. But in most instances, the trade provisions have the incidental effect of treating participants more favourably than non-participants. From one point of view, therefore, the trade provisions create a positive incentive to join the agreement. But is is also the case that non-participants can find themselves worse off relative to the cooperative situation (*and* relative to their situation prior to the agreement coming into force). Thus the trade provisions may also be viewed as creating a negative incentive to join, even though the agreement contains no explicit sanctions. What distinguishes this from the sanction situation is that the product(s) affected by the trade provisions are directly related to the environmental problem in question, whereas trade sanctions – as that term is used in this chapter – are applied to unrelated products.

Trade provisions which are not essential to prevent the undermining of the agreement would be, of course, de facto sanctions. Also worth noting is the point that as long as participation in an environmental agreement is not universal, trade provisions will be, like trade sanctions, discriminatory.

12.3.3.3 Compensation and side payments as positive incentives

As has been noted, most analysts with practical experience in promoting international cooperation have a clear preference for relying on positive incentives rather than sanctions whenever the necessary level of cooperation is not voluntarily forthcoming. The views of Chayes and Chayes (1991) have already been noted. On the basis of his assessment of experience with a broad range of multilateral environmental agreements, Sand (1991) calls attention to four selective incentives that can help make ambitious agreements attractive to a wider range of countries: access to funding for work directly related to the agreement; access to natural resources being protected by the agreement (for example, marine fish and seals); access to markets for the products covered by the agreement (for example, wildlife and wildlife products); and access to environmental technology.[19] (Note that the second and third selective incentives involve trade provisions which, as was noted above, can be viewed as creating positive or negative incentives.) He also discusses the option of having an asymmetric regime, with treaty obligations differentiated according to the special circumstances of each party.

The positive incentives just described are incentives which can be provided within the context of the agreement under consideration. It is also possible to provide incentives from outside the context of a particular agreement. This could include linkages with other environmental issues, or linkages with issues that have little or no relation with the environment. MacNeill, *et al.* (1991) observe that

> In any really big deals, financial arrangements would also have to involve the multilateral banks and the trade and bilateral agencies of the developed countries concerned. Trade policies, aid policies, and debt policies will be essential components of many of these bargains, certainly the large ones involving nations in Africa and Latin America (pp. 85–86).

They do not indicate what they have in mind for 'trade policies', but it is reasonably clear from the context that they are referring to increased market access for exports of *unrelated* goods and services.

12.3.3.4 Maintaining the agreement

Much of what has been said up to this point applies more or less equally to what are, in fact, two overlapping but distinct issues – getting a sufficient number of countries to join an environmental agreement, and ensuring that countries comply with their obligations once they have joined (that is, avoiding de facto or explicit defection). This distinction can be important, however, since there are positive incentives – mostly of an institutional nature – which are relevant primarily to the issue of compliance and which can be used in conjunction with the more generally applicable types of positive incentives.

The inability to force countries to comply with the provisions of international agreements has led to the development of non-coercive procedures for promoting compliance (Chayes and Chayes, 1990). Central to these procedures are accountability, transparency and provisions for conciliation and dispute settlement. The result is a reliance on peer pressure, and countries' willingness to pursue diffuse reciprocity, to play the key roles in ensuring countries' compliance with their obligations.[20]

Commenting on the question of relying on state responsibility for environmental damage to encourage compliance, Sand (1991, p. 269) observes that ' ... most transnational environmental regimes have learned to avoid the adversarial state-liability approach, and instead have used or developed different methods of ensuring compliance with treaty obligations'. These include reliance on local legal remedies, provision of formal nonjudicial complaint procedures, the granting of 'custodial' responsibilities to a particular institution, and environmental audits. The use of sanctions is not on Sand's list of alternatives to litigation as a means of enforcing environmental agreements.

12.3.4 *The domestic politics of side payments and sanctions*

Even though analysts with practical experience have a pronounced preference for side payments over sanctions, there is no guarantee that countries will follow this route in the future. What has been left out of the analysis in this chapter thus far are the political factors, considered in the papers in this volume by Hillman and Ursprung, and Hoekman and Leidy (Chapters 10 and 11, respectively). To get an insight into what the future may hold, it would be necessary not only to examine the individual environmental problems in detail, but also to introduce into the detailed analysis the push and pull of domestic interest-group politics. The reality of such activity in the area of trade and environment is vividly illustrated by the domestic debate in the United States in April and May 1991 over the administration's request for an extension of the fast-track authority for negotiating a free trade agreement with Mexico (the principal focus of the debate) and for the Uruguay Round.

Space limitations rule out any attempt to deal rigorously in this chapter with the issue of the domestic politics of side payments and sanctions. One point is worth noting, however. It concerns the very real risk that traditional protectionist groups will 'capture' environmental concerns and manipulate those concerns to their own ends. In the case at hand, this would take the form of biasing political decision making in the direction of a reliance on trade sanctions (including de facto sanctions through the inclusion of unnecessary trade provisions in environmental agreements), as against such alternatives as side payments or financial sanctions. To the extent that their activities result in an increase in protection which in turn reduces economic growth, there is likely to be a reduction in the amount of resources the public is willing to devote to improving and protecting the environment. It is even possible that protectionist groups would manipulate the design or implementation of environmental measures to such a degree that the net effect would be an *increase* in environmental degradation.

Notes

The authors would like to thank Kym Anderson, Alice Enders and Sherry Stephenson for comments on an earlier draft.

1. Commercial frictions could arise from perceptions that environmental standards are too low and thus confer an 'unfair' commercial advantage, or that they are too high and thus result in the creation of non-tariff barriers to trade. Or there could be different views about the appropriateness of a government granting subsidies or increasing trade barriers to industries for environmental purposes. Multilateral rule-making to deal with such issues often is not easy. But it is essentially no different from rule-making designed to minimize commercial disputes stemming from countries' pursuit of a variety of other goals, including attempts to protect employment in certain sectors or to promote certain industries. Past experience is both a guide and a source of encouragement regarding the feasibility of such multilateral rule-making.

2. There are individuals for whom the purely domestic pollution in the first category creates disutility even though they live in another country and are never directly (physically) affected. For such individuals, the first category of environmental problems does not exist. That is, for them *all* environmental problems involve physical or psychological spillovers.

3. Cooper (1989, p. 241) identifies six 'levels' of international cooperation: 'There can be exchange of information; agreement on common concepts and standards; exchange of views on prospective national policy actions; agreement on rules that set boundaries to national behaviour, but leave decisions at the national level; formally coordinated national policy actions; and joint action under common direction and (if appropriate) shared expenditure.' The latter three are the ones of primary interest to this paper.

4. The issue of using trade policies as a means of persuading countries to participate in multilateral agreements is distinct from the issue of whether a trade policy measure is the best policy, from a narrow economic efficiency standpoint, for dealing with a particular physical or psychological spillover. See Chapters 2 (Anderson), 3 (Lloyd) and 4 (Snape) in this volume for analyses of the latter issue.

5. For a concise presentation of a sceptical viewpoint on ozone depletion and global warming, see Lal (1990) and the references cited therein; see also Ray (1990). A relaxed view on species extinction is available in an article by Wilfred Beckerman in the 30 January 1991 edition of *The Times* (London).

6. This feature distinguishes the environment/prisoners' dilemma game from the assurance game (see Sen 1967). In the latter, once a cooperative outcome is reached through 'assurance' or some other form of coordination, there are no incentives to defect. Thus cooperation in this game is easier to achieve.

7. It has been argued, for example by Kindleberger (1988) and Keohane (1986), that tit-for-tat strategies are potentially dangerous when adopted by governments as they could lead to wars or deadlocks.

8. It is also possible to accept the scientific evidence and still deny that a problem

exists because the predicted change is considered to be unimportant – or even positive – rather than negative. It has been argued, for example, that some geographic regions might benefit from moderate global warming (see, for example, Lal, 1990), while some individuals would no doubt take the view that the world would be a nicer place in which to live if certain species of animals or plants became extinct.

9. There is considerable empirical evidence that the demand for environmental amenities is positively correlated with per capita income. See, for example, Baumol and Oates (1979, pp. 176–80; 1988, Chapter 15), Thompson (1973, p. 73) and Tucker (1982, Chapter 1).

10. See Mäler (1990) for evidence of the prevalence of VPP at the multilateral level.

11. As Coase (1960) points out, at an appropriate level of abstraction the allocation of property rights as between two parties does not affect the efficiency of the outcome, but does affect the distribution of income between the two parties.

12. See Chapters 3 (Lloyd), 4 (Snape), 5 (Winters) and 11 (Hoekman and Leidy) in this volume regarding the effects of alternative environmental policies on the distribution of income. There are some important parallels between the challenge of agreeing on a basis for allocating rights to discharge carbon into the atmosphere, and the problems encountered – in the context of the Law of the Sea negotiations – on the issue of exploiting mineral resources in the deep seabed.

13. The free-rider problem is considered in Chapters 6 (Piggott, Whalley and Wigle) and 7 (Enders and Porges) in this volume.

14. See, for example, MacNeill *et al*, (1991); nevertheless, they are cautiously optimistic about such agreements, 'Provided the financial and other conditions are right, the potential for a large number of small bargains is significant' (p. 86). Hahn and Richards (1989) also mention both a 'perception of fairness' as an important element in reaching agreements on environmental issues, and the negative impact of a larger number of countries on the likelihood of getting an agreement.

15. In technical terms each follower equates his marginal costs with his own marginal benefits while each leader equates his marginal cost with the marginal benefits accruing to all leaders.

16. It can be shown that when there is more than one follower, the magnitude of the incentives to be provided or the sanctions to be threatened is considerably increased because a free-rider problem is set up in the side-payments game. Essentially each follower is reluctant to take up the offer of side-payments, because he is better off if another follower takes it up while he remains a non-signatory.

17. Recent experience suggests that one should not be too sanguine about the use of trade sanctions. In a 1991 dispute with Japan over Japan's imports of the shells of hawksbill see turtles (which are on the endangered species list), for example, the United States threatened to ban imports from Japan of all animal products, including more than $300 million in fish, plus pearls. According to press reports, the domestic basis for this action was a United States law that requires the President to take 'appropriate action' against countries trading in endangered species (20 June 1991 edition of the *Asian Wall Street Journal*). Japan responded by agreeing to ban importation of the shells by the end of 1992.

    Moreover, it is not clear to what extent there is full transparency concerning the threatened use of trade sanctions for environmental purposes, particularly when there is no multilateral agreement in force. On a more general level, numerous analysts have noted an increased tendency in recent years for certain countries to use threats of trade sanctions in order to get other countries to reduce barriers to trade in goods and services. See, for example, Bhagwati and Patrick (1990).

18. There have been instances of countries threatening or taking trade actions (outside the context of multilateral agreements) which resemble the trade provisions of agreements, in that they apply to products directly related to the issue at hand. One recent example involves a decision by the European Communities to ban the importation of ermine, sable, lynx and other furs from countries that allow the use of leghold traps. Animal-rights groups have condemned such traps as cruel. The import ban will take effect in 1995, at the same time as a ban on the use of leghold traps inside the EC takes effect. See the 15–16 June 1991 issue of *The International Herald Tribune*.

19. MacNeill *et al.* (1991 p. 85) also mention financial arrangements and the transfer of technologies and know-how, as likely elements in most agreements, adding that 'The potential for innovative bargaining in both areas is considerable'.

20. The role of peer pressure is discussed in Blackhurst (1988), but not – as it should have been – the role of diffuse reciprocity.

References

Axelrod, R. (1984), *The Evolution of Cooperation*, New York: Basic Books.

Baumol, W. and Oates, W. (1979), *Economics, Environmental Policy, and the Quality of Life*, Englewood Cliffs, NJ: Prentice-Hall.

Baumol, W. and Oates, W. (1988), *The Theory of Environmental Policy*, Cambridge: Cambridge University Press.

Barrett, S. (1990a), 'The Problem of Global Environmental Protection', *Oxford Review of Economic Policy* 6: 68–79.

Barrett, S. (1990b), 'Economic Analysis of International Environmental Agreements: Lessons for a Global Warming Treaty', mimeo, London Business School, November.

Barrett, S. (1991), 'The Paradox of International Environmental Agreements', mimeo, London Business School, January.

Bhagwati, J. N. and H. T. Patrick, editors (1990), *Aggressive Unilateralism: America's 301 Trade Policy and the World Trading System*, London: Harvester Wheatsheaf.

Blackhurst, R. (1988), 'Strengthening GATT Surveillance of Trade-Related Policies', in *The New GATT Round of Multilateral Trade Negotiations: Legal and Economic Aspects*, edited M. Hilf and E.-U. Petersmann, Deventer: Kluwer.

Chayes, A. and A. H. Chayes (1991), 'Adjustment and Compliance Processes in International Regulatory Regimes', in *Preserving the Global Environment*, edited by J. T. Mathews, New York and London: W. W. Norton.

Coase, R. H. (1960), 'The Problem of Social Cost', *Journal of Law and Economics* 3: 1–44.

Cooper, R. (1989), 'International Cooperation in Public Health as a Prologue to Macroeconomic Cooperation', in *Can Nations Agree? Issues in International Economic Cooperation*, by R. Cooper *et al.*, Washington, D. C.: The Brookings Institution.

Dasgupta, P. S. (1990), 'The Environment as a Commodity', *Oxford Review of Economic Policy* 6; 51–67.

Hahn, R. W. and K. R. Richards, (1989), 'The Internationalisation of Environmental Regulation', *Harvard International Law Journal* **30**: 421–46.

Keohane, R. O. (1986), 'Reciprocity in International Relations', *International Organisation* **40**: 1–27.

Kindleberger, C. P. (1986), 'International Public Goods Without International Government', *The American Economic Review* **76**: 1–13.

Kindleberger, C. P. (1988), *The International Economic Order: Essays on Financial Crisis and International Public Goods*, London: Harvester Wheatsheaf.

Kreps, D. M., P. Milgrom, J. Roberts and R. Wilson (1982), 'Rational Cooperation in The Finitely Repeated Prisoner's Dilemma', *Journal of Economic Theory* **27**: 245–52.

Kreps, D. M. and R. Wilson (1982), 'Reputation and Imperfect Information', *Journal of Economic Theory* **27**: 253–79.

Lal, D. (1990), *The Limits of International Cooperation*, Twentieth Wincott Memorial Lecture, London: Institute of Economic Affairs for the Wincott Foundation.

MacNeill, J., P. Winsemius and T. Yakushiji (1991), *Beyond Interdependence: The Meshing of the World's Economy and the Earth's Ecology*, New York: Oxford University Press.

Mäler, K-G. (1990), 'International Environmental Problems', *Oxford Review of Economic Policy* **6**: 80–108.

Mohr, E. 1990, 'Global Warming: Economic Policy in the Face of Positive and Negative Spillovers', paper presented at the conference on Environmental Scarcity: the International Dimension, at the Kiel Institute of World Economics, 5–6 July.

Olson, M. (1971), *The Logic of Collective Action*, Cambridge: Harvard University Press.

Ray, D. L. (1990), *Trashing the Planet*, Washington, D.C., Regnery Gateway.

Sand, P. H. (1991), 'International Cooperation: The Environmental Experience', in *Preserving the Global Environment*, edited by J. T. Mathews; New York and London: W. W. Norton.

Sen, A. K. (1967), 'Isolation, Assurance and The Social Rate of Discount', *Quarterly Journal of Economics* **81**: 112–24.

Snidal, D. (1985), 'Coordination versus Prisoners' Dilemma: Implications for International Cooperation and Regimes', *The American Political Science Review* **79**: 923–42.

Stern, R. M. (forthcoming), 'Conflict and Cooperation in International Economic Relations', in *New Approaches to International Conflict*, edited by H. Jacobson and W. Gimmerman.

Sugden, R. (1984), 'Reciprocity: The Supply of Public Goods Through Voluntary Contributions,' *Economic Journal* **94**: 772–87.

Sugden, R. (1986), *The Economics of Rights, Cooperation and Welfare*, Oxford: Basil Blackwell.

Thompson, D. N. (1973), *The Economics of Environmental Protection*, Cambridge: Winthrop.

Tucker, W. (1982), *Progress and Privilege: America in the Age of Environmentalism*, Garden City, NJ: Anchor Press/Doubleday.

Index